Institutional Issues
in
Public Accounting

ACCOUNTING PUBLICATIONS OF SCHOLARS BOOK CO.

INSTITUTIONAL ISSUES IN PUBLIC ACCOUNTING

Papers and Responses from Accounting Colloquium III

cosponsored by

The University of Kansas School of Business
and
The Arthur Young Foundation

Edited by Robert R. Sterling

Scholars Book Co.
P.O. Box 3344
Lawrence, Kansas 66044

Manufactured in the United States of America

Contents

Preface

The purpose of Accounting Colloquium III was to examine the socio-economic and politico-legal environment of the public accounting profession. In contrast to past colloquia, at which problems in accounting theory have been examined, this Colloquium was to focus on the problems presented by the environment in which accounting operates. The impetus of the examination was my belief that the structure of this environment is equally as much a deterrent to progress in accounting as are the unresolved problems in accounting theory.

In considering the profession's role in the establishment and enforcement of accounting principles some of us have tended to conceive of the performance of this role as exclusively a problem in accounting theory. That is, when faced with a problem, accountants would (1) gather and interpret the evidence in light of accounting theory and (2) reach a decision based upon those theoretical considerations. The only thing left to do, according to this view, was for the APB to issue an Opinion or the CPA to express an opinion, depending upon the context. It has become painfully obvious that this is a naive view of the way in which accounting principles are established and enforced.

In the establishment of principles, the APB met considerable resistance. Since the APB did not have the power to overcome this resistance, APB Opinions appeared to be influenced equally as much by political feasibility as by theoretical validity. In enforcing the principles, the CPA met considerable resistance. Since the CPA did not have the power to overcome this resistance (he could qualify his opinion and be replaced or he could resign and be replaced), auditors' opinions appeared to be unduly influenced by factors other than auditors' convictions. As a result of these kinds of considerations, I came to believe that the acquisition of power—governmental or organizational—is a prerequisite to progress in accounting.

The above thoughts were communicated to each of the invited authors. They were asked to prepare papers on institutional problems, as opposed to problems in accounting theory. Beyond that, no restrictions were placed on the subject matter. The authors were free to examine any aspect that they wished; they were free to defend or criticize the thoughts expressed by me or to ignore them and take a different tack. The papers, responses and discussions in this volume are in the order in which they were presented at the Colloquium.

The Colloquia Series and the Professorship is made possible by a grant from Arthur Young & Company personnel who are alumni of the University of Kansas. I am solely responsible for the selection of topics, participants and arrangements of the Colloquia as well as for the ideas that I express. Arthur Young & Company has meticulously avoided infringing on my academic freedom. Despite my economic dependence, I am completely independent in all other respects. (The astute reader will recognize that my situation is a contradiction of the argument that the CPA is not independent of management because he is economically dependent on management. Undoubtedly, Arthur Young has also noted the contradiction but they have been kind enough to refrain from pointing it out.) I am most grateful for both the funds and the freedom.

R.R.S.

Lawrence, Kansas
1973

Accounting Colloquium III

Participants

Robert D. Arnett
Haskins & Sells, Kansas City

Donald F. Arnold
State University of New York, Albany

William F. Bentz
University of Kansas

Arthur H. Bowen
Arthur Young & Company, Kansas City

John W. Buckley
University of California, Los Angeles

Thomas J. Burns
Ohio State University

John C. Burton
SEC

Douglas R. Carmichael
AICPA

Donald H. Chapin
Arthur Young & Company, New York

W. B. Coutts
University of Toronto

Joe J. Cramer, Jr.
Pennsylvania State University

John D. Crouch
Touche Ross & Co., Kansas City

Philip L. Defliese
Coopers & Lybrand, New York

J. B. Dunlop
Price Waterhouse & Co., Toronto

Thomas R. Dyckman
Cornell University

R. A. Edwards
University of Kansas

John H. Evers
Arthur Young & Company, Kansas City

William L. Felix, Jr.
University of Washington

Ted J. Fiflis
University of Colorado

John H. Fisher
University of Kansas

Richard E. Flaherty
Oklahoma State University

Werner G. Frank
University of Wisconsin

Laurence A. Friedman
University of Kansas

Norman E. Fuller
Coopers & Lybrand, Kansas City

Dale L. Gerboth
AICPA

Larry F. Glennemeier
Coopers & Lybrand, Kansas City

Robert L. Gray
New York State Society of CPAs

Wallace F. Grundeman
Ernst & Ernst, Dallas

Gary L. Holstrum
University of Texas

Charles T. Horngren
Stanford University

Wilmer E. Huffman
University of Kansas

Jerry B. Jackson
Touche Ross & Co., Kansas City

Gordon M. Johns
Haskins & Sells, New York

Glenn L. Johnson
University of Kansas

Vernon Kam
California State University,
   Hayward

Harvey E. Kapnick, Jr.
Arthur Anderson & Co., Chicago

John N. Kissinger
University of Kansas

Charles W. Lamden
Peat, Marwick, Mitchell & Co., New
   York

Stephen Landekich
National Association of Accountants

Carl D. Liggio
Arthur Young & Company, New
   York

David F. Linowes
Laventhol Kreckstein Horwath
   and Horwath, New York

Robert A. Long
Arthur Andersen & Co., Kansas
   City

Andrew D. Luzi
University of Kansas

Robert K. Mautz
Ernst & Ernst, Cleveland

Dennis J. McCarthy
Arthur Young & Company, Kansas
   City

Herbert E. Miller
Arthur Andersen & Co., Chicago

Paul D. Montagna
Brooklyn College

Maurice Moonitz
University of California, Berkeley

Shane R. Moriarity
University of Kansas

Robert S. Mueller
Arthur Young & Company, Kansas City

Gertrude Mulcahy
Canadian Institute of Chartered Accountants

Melvin C. O'Connor
Michigan State University

Ronald J. Patten
Financial Accounting Standards Board

Joseph A. Pichler
University of Kansas

Delmas D. Ray
University of Florida

Lawrence Revsine
Northwestern University

Howard Ross
McGill University

Robert J. Sack
Touche Ross & Co., New York

Roland F. Salmonson
Michigan State University

Leonard M. Savoie
Clark Equipment Company

Stephen J. Schroff
University of Kansas

William D. Schulte
Peat, Marwick, Mitchell & Co., Kansas City

John K. Simmons
University of Minnesota

Ross M. Skinner
Clarkson Gordon & Co.

Earl A. Spiller, Jr.
Washington University

Robert R. Sterling
University of Kansas

Howard F. Stettler
University of Kansas

Chester B. Vanatta
Arthur Young & Company, Chicago

Lawrence L. Vance
University of California, Berkeley

Turgut Var
University of Kansas

James H. Weimer
Price Waterhouse & Co., Dallas

Donald E. Wilke
University of Kansas

John J. Willingham
University of Houston

Floyd W. Windal
University of Georgia

Stephen A. Zeff
Tulane University

Charles T. Zlatkovich
University of Texas

PART I
THE SETTING

CHAPTER 1

Public Accounting: The Dynamics of Occupational Change

PAUL D. MONTAGNA*

During the past several years a debate has intensified in the world of finance and accounting over the issue of accounting principles. Many people, both in and out of the public accounting profession, feel that the present generally accepted accounting principles must be strengthened by specifying a general framework of concepts or postulates. It is believed that this framework will permit CPAs to limit the ability of managements of corporations to manipulate their financial statements and thereby will result in the presentation of fair and accurate information to the investor or potential investor. Although most feel that these concepts are needed, there are many disagreements as to what these concepts should cover, who should construct them, and who should have authority in enforcing them and in what manner.

Reading through the accounting literature, one senses that the future success of the profession depends on the outcome of these questions, and that public accounting will stand or fall depending on its role in formulating and administering these rules. It is the attempt of this paper to examine this accounting principles debate as only one of several areas of conflict in the profession. I wish to provide a theoretical framework for the analysis of development and change in public accounting and thus place in perspective the import of accounting principles and other significant professional events. The theory is one

*B.S. 1958, American International College; M.B.A. 1960, Syracuse University; Ph.D. 1967, New York University. Associate Professor of Sociology, Brooklyn College. Author, *Certified Public Accounting: A Sociological View of a Profession in Change* (forthcoming); (with E. Smigel) *Occupations and Society* (forthcoming). Contributor to sociology periodicals.

The author would like to thank Douglas Carmichael and his staff at the American Institute of CPAs for their help in locating accounting sources.

3

of conflict among groups at three levels: (1) between groups within the profession, (2) between groups in the profession and outside groups, and (3) between professions. For each level, the findings of organizational theory are utilized.

In this analysis I depend heavily on published reports and papers of CPA practitioners and academicians. It is a distinct disadvantage not to have the benefit of day-to-day conversations on developing issues and of informal information channels in the profession. Therefore, I have quoted more extensively than usual so that the reader may determine whether he feels the sources selected have led to any inordinately biased views.

1. RESPONSIBILITY IN PUBLIC ACCOUNTING

The responsibility of the certified public accountant (hereafter referred to as "accountant" unless otherwise specified) is a heavy one. Accounting is unique among professions in that the accountant has a clear and definite responsibility not only to his clients (management— the people who pay his fee), but also to stockholders, credit grantors, governmental agencies, and potential investors—the so-called third parties. The accountant is responsible to all these for maintaining an independent position in his analysis of corporate finances and systems of internal control. Generally accepted accounting principles serve as guidelines for this independence.

Many accountants have emphasized that the public as third party is really their most important client (Bevis, 1965: 19; Savoie, 1968; AIA, 1934). This, however, presents a dilemma. On the one hand, the accountant naturally has advocacy sentiments for his clients. As the director of management advisory services for Lybrand, Ross Bros. & Montgomery argues, when reasonable, the accountant should practice forensic accounting because if not, he *prevents* independence. He would purposely narrow his vision so much as to fault the client in needed "perception, discrimination, or moral judgment" (Kaufman, 1967: 719). On the other hand, there is the question of "perceived independence" by third parties. Merely the appearance of the lack of independence may be almost as damaging as the reality. Even the potentiality of loss of independence may, in certain instances, be enough to threaten professional standing (Carey and Doherty, 1963: 20; Carmichael and Swieringa, 1968).

So, maintaining responsibility is somewhat of a balancing act between clients and third parties. Primary responsibility must be shared among these groups. However, even though accounting principles may be able to clarify the nature and degree of this responsibility, they will not be able to specify a comprehensive set of rules for every possible situation. This is based on the assumption that "Risk is an essential element of responsibility, that is, assuming responsibilities entails making decisions whose outcome is uncertain" (Blau, 1964: 219). Without risk there is no responsibility. Specified rules take the place of responsibility; there is little room for decision-making. The situation becomes rationalized—organized according to the canons of logic and efficiency. Furthermore, the power of a group—in this case the public accounting profession—is reduced when its source of uncertainty, the ability to make judgments, has been rationalized (Crozier, 1964).

It is precisely this problem that many accountants are now speaking to. Some feel that if broad general principles are not developed, detailed rules will be the only way of preventing "accounting anarchy." As Sprouse (1972) indicates, there is an increasing trend to solve financial accounting issues by setting up detailed rules that, in effect, remove professional judgment. APB Opinion No. 15 is given as an example. He concludes that, instead, we need basic concepts of accounting; otherwise we will be like tax advisors with the Internal Revenue Code in hand, having no pretense of independence, but just following the rules. It will be straight advocacy for the client. Others feel that general concepts should be developed, but that the best way to develop them is through inductive reasoning, through the past experience of business practice, and through "substantial authoritative support." (This point will be elaborated on below.)

Thus, it is a question of *power* to which we are addressing ourselves in this issue. This is to be distinguished from the concept of *authority*. It is appropriate at this point to describe and define these concepts as they relate to recent organizational theory and to a more general analysis of the public accounting profession.

2. UNCERTAINTY AND POWER IN ORGANIZATIONS[1]

The process of rationality in organizations results in a high degree of predictability of the system of action within its direct sphere of influence. Yet, no matter how rationalized[2] the organization, there remain areas of uncertainty unnoticed or too difficult for rationality. Control over the source of uncertainty means control over positions affected by this uncertainty. This is power, a form of influence which produces intended and successful control of others (Wrong, 1968: 673).

As related to uncertainty in organizations, "people have power over other people insofar as the latter's behavior is narrowly limited by rules whereas their own behavior is not." As already mentioned, the power of a group is reduced when its source of uncertainty has been rationalized, especially with regard to the amount, specificity, and extent of rules and procedures. In time this previously private knowledge becomes part of the public (or organizational) domain. In order to gain new power to replace that lost, a group will seek a new source of uncertainty. This is accomplished in part by risk-taking. Groups are reciprocally dependent on power relations, power being ever-present in the organization because of the impossibility of eliminating uncertainty (Crozier, 1964: 158–86). Thus, the mobilization of power is central to the organization. It is exercised through decision-making.

3. JUDGMENT

Judgment, a type of decision-making, is choosing from among alternatives to action when there is only a small amount of knowledge of the alternatives available. The gaps in knowledge are filled by making assumptions concerning past, present, and future events, based on value standards. Control over the body of knowledge in which judgments are made is jealously guarded by those who have the responsibility and right to make them. It is the man whose value standards fit with his group (or client) and who applies those standards to bring wealth, prestige, and power to the group, who is considered to have good judgment, or wisdom.

The making of judgments can be viewed on a continuum of uncertainty, from least certain to most certain. It is implicit in the work of early writers on organization theory. Chester Barnard (1938: 309–320) categorized classes of material with which the mind works, going from "precise information," to "hybrid material," to "speculative material," and corresponding to the occupations of appellate lawyer, accountant, and politician, respectively. Peter Drucker (1950: 52–59) related it specifically to cost accounting, running in four stages starting from the most certain: replacement, obsolescence, risk proper, uncertainty. Most recently, in accounting, the continuum has been utilized to analyze how unusual uncertainties in auditing should be handled as related to degree of qualification of the auditor's opinion (Carmichael, 1972: 69–71). As Carmichael notes: "The auditor's evaluation of uncertainty is a formulation of judgment on the degree of rational belief and not a conclusion concerning numeric probability."

4. AUTHORITY

Authority is legitimated power. The grounds of obedience are the belief of the follower in his obligation to obey and the belief of the leader in his obligation to command and to expect the follower to obey his commands. Power may be legalized. (In sociological terms it is formalized, regularized, and established—in other words, institutionalized.) But only authority is legitimated (Buckley, 1967: 196–97). Authority is itself a source of power because those in positions of authority assign responsibility that may or may not be legitimated. For example, the Securities and Exchange Commission may assign responsibility to the accounting profession to develop a set of regulations on accounting for investment credits, but unless the SEC fully backs the profession in its implementation of these rules, management will consider this nothing more than a power play on the part of accountants. Thus, what is perceived as a system of authority by one group (accountants) is seen as a system of power by another (management).

5. THE DYNAMICS OF ORGANIZATIONAL CHANGE

The common tendency of organizations is to rationalize their operations, for in so doing, they increase efficiency and thereby increase profits. In a great many cases, experts help by lending their special talents to the organization. However, in the rationalization process there is a paradox. The extreme rationality results in the loss of power of the very same groups that aided in the rationalization. As Crozier points out, as soon as an expert's field is well covered, as soon as its innovations can be translated into rules and programs, his power disappears. Such groups as production specialists and budget analysts find their power decreasing as soon as scientific management or economic stabilization has made difficulties liable to rational prediction (Crozier, 1964: 164). The organization absorbs this power for its own uses. If a group of professionals within the organization wishes to survive intact, it must seek out new areas of uncertainty in order to maintain its power position relative to competing groups. However, care must be taken that neither too much nor too little uncertainty is generated, for the former can lead to organizational disruption and instability, and the latter to stagnation.

One study of a manufacturing company (White, 1961) explained how R&D managers increased uncertainty in investment and time by introducing new products. A great deal of risk was involved in developing new knowledge for these new products. The managers also contributed to certainty of the organization by obtaining a high profit rate when introducing the new product on the market. However, conflict developed when other groups in the company saw a threat to their control over their own areas of uncertainty. Production and staff managers, responsible for the control of costs and accounts, opposed uncertain experimentation and new product development. They saw it as a threat to their autonomy. However, they also realized that outside opinion of customers who wanted sizable R&D programs in the firms from whom they bought was an important factor. The production managers had to adjust their opinion and accept more uncertainty. Thus, a group reacts to uncertainty partly on the basis of its sensitivity to outside opinion and on the basis of its tactical position in intraorganizational conflicts.

6. THE DYNAMICS OF OCCUPATIONAL CHANGE

William Goode is one of the very few researchers who has utilized principles of organization to analyze structure and processes of occupations as units. In his study of librarians he saw not only individuals in organizations competing with one another in their efforts to achieve in the class system but also occupations engaged in the same competition. They may, he states, "move up or down in power, prestige, or income."

> Both systems may be viewed as zero-sum games. The income which one individual [occupation] receives cannot be claimed by another. If an occupation rises in income level or in prestige ranking, necessarily the other will lose. . . . An expanding economy may yield more real income for nearly all occupations; but at any given time there is only so much income to be distributed, each occupation has a higher or lower average income than others, and those which have risen have done so at the expense of others. (Goode, 1961)

Thus, if librarians wish to professionalize (and thereby receive the power, prestige, and income that goes with autonomy), they must be willing to engage in risk-taking behavior, some of which may impinge on the expertise of other professions. They also must develop scientific principles to serve as guidelines for their work. For example, they could apply communications theory to routing and sorting of knowledge entering the library in all forms. They would accept the task of making judgmental decisions in areas of values, e.g., book selection for public or specialist reading.

We can conclude that there are at least three levels of conflict of power over areas of uncertainty:

1. *in organizations:* between groups internal to the organization (between departments)
   in occupations: between groups within the occupation (between partnerships and sole practitioners)
2. *in organizations:* between internal groups and external groups (between management and the community)
   in occupations: between internal groups and external groups (between a professional association and clients or a governmental agency)
3. *in organizations:* between the organization as a whole and other organizations (between a manufacturing company and other manufacturing companies for their share of the market)
   in occupations: between an occupation and other occupations (between one profession and others for exclusive or controlling rights over a body of knowledge)[3]

What is true for organizational conflict and change at each of the three levels is also true of occupations. If we look at accounting, there are some parallels to be made in several areas. For the sake of clarity they will be examined in the following order: (1) accounting principles, (2) accounting art and accounting science, (3) computerization in auditing and management advisory services, (4) social measurement.

Accounting Principles

It was not too long ago that the accounting profession took an official stand that alternative methods of accounting should not be tampered with just for the sake of uniformity (AICPA, 1950) However, a growing number of dissenters argued that if more uniformity was not in the offing, it would drastically affect the stature of the profession, even to the point of forfeiting the attest function to the federal government or some other group (Wise, 1960; Anthony, 1963; Storey, 1964; Spacek, 1965). The Accounting Research Studies of the 1960s attempted to clarify in writing the basic assumptions of accounting (ARS No. 1), the principles stemming from these assumptions (ARS No. 3), and in some cases the specific procedures for applying these rules (ARS No. 7).

The Accounting Principles Board was formed to interpret and develop these and earlier professional rules. However, as Moonitz (1972: 124) notes, the AICPA, "working by itself, cannot agree upon a set of generally accepted accounting principles." The APB just does not have the power to enforce its opinions on the clients of independent auditors. It needs an ally to do so, and there are two possibilities, says Moonitz. One ally, if the profession stays strictly in the private sector, is the New York Stock Exchange. Following up on ARS No. 3 on cash flow analysis, the APB issued Opinion No. 3, "The statement of source and application of funds." With cooperation from the NYSE, by 1970 most American-listed companies were presenting this statement as part of their annual report. In March, 1971, the APB made it formal with Opinion No. 19, "Reporting changes in financial position." Moonitz believes that if this setup with the NYSE had been a formal one, this and other rulings would have been instituted much more quickly.

The other ally, which would involve parts of the public sector, is the SEC. The present strong informal cooperation between the AICPA and the SEC should be made formal so that the two could agree beforehand on major policy statements, such as those issued by the APB. Perhaps then the SEC would be willing to delegate some of its authority to the APB (or its successor) if relations were formalized. Moonitz concludes that the accounting profession, through the AICPA, would supply the technical expertise to form generally accepted accounting principles. The NYSE and/or SEC would act as representative of the public and as enforcer of the agreed-upon rules.

However, recent events would not seem to support the latter alliance. When the SEC reversed its statement on the investment credit issue, thus undermining the APB position, it made for a situation in which the clients (management), through organized lobbying, were in effect measuring their own performance. As Horngren (1972) has said, it's like having the baseball batter calling the balls and the strikes. He adds that management cannot circumvent the APB too often because then it will destroy this handy buffer between the SEC and itself. He agrees with Moonitz that the SEC and the AICPA should work together in developing principles.

The SEC is the logical ally for the accounting profession. It holds the authority (the "ultimate power"—Sprouse, 1972: 11; Horngren, 1972: 38) in financial reporting. As a representative of the state it could act in a quasi-judicial fashion, as it occasionally has in the past. However, to be truly professional, the accountant should be able to advocate for his client just as the lawyer does. For the primary function of professionals is to serve their clients, regardless of their stated purpose or ideal of service to the public. The service ideal of selflessness in serving "society," "the public," the "public good," or the "public interest," as the most important basis of a profession has been espoused by students of the professions (Laski, 1935; Greenwood, 1957; Deskins, 1965; Carey, 1965), but is not considered to be of primary importance by the practitioners themselves in at least two professions—management consulting (Lynch, 1959) and accounting (Montagna, forthcoming). As the average practitioner[4] sees it, you don't bite the hand that feeds you—unless the difference between what the client wants and what the auditor sees becomes material. This area of nonmateriality is where the accountant maintains his independence; this is his area of responsibility, which manifests itself in the audit opinion. By working within these limits set by the SEC (Rule 2-01, Regulation S-X) and ratified and elaborated in its code of ethics by the AIA and AICPA, the accountant receives his own authority as the sole party examining the financial records of publicly traded companies.

The fact that accountants are presently in the position of trying to gain power over their clients (Mautz, 1972; Sterling, 1973) instead of advocating for them from a position of independence, is a clear indication of the need of the SEC and the profession to construct a solid base of underlying objectives and general principles for accounting. If such concepts could be developed, they would in the long run increase the power of the accountant. Judgment potential will increase with these guidelines because they will establish the accountant's *authority* to remain within limits of materiality.[5] The client would not be so eager to jump from one accountant to another if he knew the accountant was working in his best interests, within the limits of independence specified by the guidelines. The accountant would be less likely to bow to the wishes of the "tough-guy" client. This is more than the power of persuasion; it is authority based on expertise—authority based on the accountant's own body of knowledge as supported by the state.

If the CPA is considered to have a responsibility to his client, then his authority is limited to his expertise in audit and related procedures. He is independent to the extent that a lawyer is independent; he is not, however, a judge. Judges are not professionals in that they do not hire themselves out to a client for a fee. The judiciary is a special arm of the state, representing the public interest. If the accounting profession is to possess authority to match its responsibility to the public, then it must be given at least some of the rights and powers of a judge. In *Yale Express,* the court stated that the accountant has as much responsibility to the public interest as to his client. He "must report fairly on the facts as he finds them whether favorable or unfavorable to his client." "Fairly" presumably means within the limits of materiality as set by concepts and principles. However, in *Continental Vending,* the question of materiality was decided not by members of the profession but by the public (the jury), who in effect considered the GAAP inadequate. This is like having the baseball fan calling the balls and strikes.

To improve on this situation, the profession must obtain judicial legitimacy in the economic sector. Independence here for the judging group would necessarily exclude the accepting of fees and selection to the judiciary by political appointment or public election. In this sense, an accounting court would seem to be a logical step. One accountant (Kam, 1973) has suggested that the Financial Accounting Standards Board be mandated to be the judging body. Adoption of the scientific approach to accounting theory and principles would be likely to give such a body the necessary legitimacy in the eyes of the public—an important step toward stronger professionalization.

The conflicts between the profession and external groups over this issue of general principles (an example of conflict at the second level of occupational organization) are central to the future of the accounting profession and greatly influence other areas of conflict, especially the argument of art versus science in accounting.

Accounting Art and Accounting Science

Members of the profession have generally taken divergent views of the body of knowledge in public accounting, which follows the division of strain found in all professions—that between the practical and the theoretical (Hughes, 1963: 661). This is a good example of conflict at the first level—between groups within the occupation. The ideological boundaries are clearly set and well recognized by accountants. Generally, the practitioner is the more conservative in viewpoint, less willing to accept rapid change and more inclined to construct his judgments on the basis of the inductive logic of experience. For him, accounting is an art. The theorist, on the other hand, is desirous of further developing an intellectual discipline by utilizing the deductive method of science on accounting events, inducing abrupt change into accounting practice. As Spiller (1964) has described it, in accounting theory business transactions and events are dealt with by abstraction, in terms of assumptions which are the basis for deduction, which leads to conclusions, whereas in accounting practice they are dealt with in problems, in terms of procedures, which are the basis for induction, which leads to generalizations. As might be expected, very few populate the extremes of these two positions. In their own formulations most combine ideas representative of both sides, with leanings to one or the other position.

But the ideologies are there. They extend to the professional associations: the AICPA, representing the practitioner; the American Accounting Association, representing the theoretically oriented (Mautz, 1965; Summers and Hermance, 1969). They therefore can be expected to influence the type of literature emanating from these and other sources. In the first edition of *Auditing Theory and Practice,* Robert Montgomery called accounting a science, ". . . and it should be possible to present its underlying principles so that they may be comprehensible to the average mind" (Montgomery, 1912: 7). Those who view it as an art emphasize the element of creative judgment—that is, where, at best, only rough probability estimates can be made concerning the events in question. A high degree of uncertainty is present.

The practitioner is the practical realist like his client, the American businessman. He sees accounting as an art and himself as the artist shaping the financial picture. As one large-firm manager put it, "Decisions are made with a knowledge of firing-line business conditions, not with a pure or academic knowledge." The theorist, on the other hand, tends to stress deduction, which gives more significance to ideas (e.g., Burke, 1964; Buckley, Kircher, and Mathews, 1968). However, as the philosopher of science, Karl Popper, points out, in deduction, in which the analysis of classes of events takes place, it is only through attempted refutation that the empirical value of an idea can be verified. The deduction, the idea, necessarily interacts with induction, which builds up to and leads from that idea. The necessity for a balance of deduction and induction has been stressed by some in the profession (Littleton, 1948; Vatter, 1963; Imke, 1966; Ross, 1967; McDonald, 1967; Kam, 1973).

There have been a few attempts by accountants to integrate social science theory and concepts to accounting thought (Aoyagi, 1958; Willingham, 1964), which have been met with heavy criticism from practitioners. A partner of one medium-sized firm commented on the approach taken by accounting theoreticians: "The problem is, 'What is the problem?' It's not the answers given so easily in *The Accounting Review*. They think it's easy to define the problem, but it's not. Most of the time they don't define it correctly and are miles from it." However, the practitioner is just as guilty of misunderstanding the purpose of the scientific method as the theorist is in dealing with concrete problems. The May, 1966, editorial in the *Journal of Accountancy* equates the empirical verity of science with the a priori truth of formal logic alone. Then it takes issue with "social science jargon," as used by accountants, for writing about what "is so obvious, that, if put in plain English, it wouldn't be worth saying." This criticism has so many times been answered by analyses proving the "obvious" to be incorrect.[6] Also, some jargon is necessary in science because one of the principles of science is parsimony, an economy of concepts to promote precision and even to suggest new research problems (Lazarsfeld and Merton, 1964).

There are several problems attached to this "conservative" anti-scientific point of view. One is that the present GAAP are constricting to the profession. The concept of "acceptance" or "general acceptance" is directly in opposition to innovation. Accepted accounting principles are those principles having "substantial authoritative support." Evidence of this support is found in opinions of committees of the AICPA, the SEC, other regulatory commissions, to the extent that "their rulings are not in conflict with accepted accounting principles from other sources, textbooks of recognized standing, experienced and competent CPAs and in the practices commonly followed by business entities" (Grady, 1965: 16). An accounting innovation, by definition, would lack this acceptability, as Richard Leo Smith interprets his analysis of the AICPA rejection of a U.S. Steel innovation (Smith, 1955: 283–86). Moreover, wide variations in alternative methods allow clients to make presentations that are in accordance solely with their interests. As Spacek has commented:

> To illustrate the absurdity of allowing control to rest in the sterile hand of the so-called "acceptance" of accounting variations, one needs only to imagine what the government policy would be if acceptance also controlled decisions in civil rights cases, regardless of the merits of the issue (Spacek, 1965).

A scientific analysis of accounting events would supply empirical evidence for the truth-value of a principle. Application of the principle would have the weight of the integrity received from the methodology of science. That is, the public will more likely permit collective self-control if it *believes* there is a developed body of abstract knowledge, of general scientific concepts in which complex intellectual activities take place. In his study of librarians, Goode has warned, "The failure to define adequately the nature of the intellectual problem means that practitioners themselves often fail to see the challenge of developing the field." As a discipline that deals directly with the public, accounting needs strong grounds for legitimation, more than what would be supplied by the precept that accountancy is limited to summarizing past and present events, to the exclusion of the future, and more than a compendium of generally accepted practices.

However, as shown by the movement into innovative fields, especially into management advisory services and related areas of uncertainty, there is a great deal of danger in going too far in the opposite direction. Those who stress that the profession must move into such new areas are concerned about the increasing automation rationality of auditing and consequent loss of judgment. These include those who advocate a scientific approach, both practitioners and theorists, as well as those who do not. Many practitioners commented on how the annual audit has become the "annual nuisance." As one Big Eight audit manager said, "The auditor is like a dentist—you go to him only if you have to." But the big danger, many feel, is the one created by conflict of interest. As Harvey Kapnick of Arthur Andersen suggests, the field of financial planning and computer control systems may be taken away by court action because of this (*Business Week*, 1972: 58).

Computerization in Auditing and Management Advisory Services

As with most areas of development in accounting, computerization in auditing has supporters on both sides of the issue. One side feels that the new services of automated systems analysis will someday find the CPAs without a job unless they move into these services (McRae, 1962; Davidson, 1963; Carey, 1965; Adams and Williams, 1966). One accountant asks: "The computer doesn't need your traditional fiscal tide tables. As managers gradually become aware of this, will you have new oracles ready for them?" (Whisler, 1965: 32). For a good many, the answer is yes, and the oracle is MAS. The response of a large-firm MAS supervisor is representative of the feeling of many practitioners on this matter: "The trend in auditing is to reduce the amount of work performed and to make what remains more regulated and therefore automatic. Growth in value and stature of the profession can occur only in tax advice and MAS." "MAS is one of the few areas where there is creative work, rather than just looking over someone's shoulder to check," says an auditing manager of another firm.

Thus it is that the profession has become deeply involved in management consulting, engaging in direct heavy competition with the management consulting profession (conflict at the third level of occupational organization) for the large areas of uncertainty where power is inherent (*Forbes*, 1966; Kaufman, 1967). Analyses on mergers, reorganizations, factory location, issuing of stocks or bonds, executive recruitment, and the like are not rationalized processes easily adapted to computerization.

However, the other side argues quite convincingly that auditing is not a "cookbook process" which can be programmed step by step and utilized on successive occasions without any modifications. The fear that auditing is becoming obsolete is unwarranted (Grady, 1965; Fremgen, 1967; Kaufman, 1971). They cite the new and changing definitions of profit, assets, companies involved in exploratory ventures and leaseback arrangements. The leeway an auditor has here in questions of materiality is very wide. Others (Hartley and Ross, 1972) warn that the conflict of interest that develops from stepping outside the traditional accounting role is a severe one and jeopardizes the accountant's independence. How, for example, can an auditor be critical of a company that he recommended the client purchase the year before?

Nevertheless, the profession has embarked on a course of expansion into MAS and related areas. This move is buttressed by the expanded definition given by accountants that theirs is the natural profession to be in charge of planning, measuring, attesting and communicating the total information services of an economic nature—the operational audit. Increasingly, all professions which advise large-scale organizations are involved in a struggle, (whether they are partially unaware of it or not) for the status and prestige which results from it. Therefore, accountants compete (or soon will) with management consulting, law, banking, actuary, and to a limited degree, administrative science and sociology. The sociologist, Paul Lazarsfeld (1964), writing for the AICPA a decade ago, viewed this conflict from an organization focus (at the first level):

> The computer is invading all divisions of business and this raises the issue of who should control the computer. A power fight could develop between accountants and other groups, for the division which controls the computer also controls the investments of the company. The stakes are high in this conflict or collaboration issue, for the status and prestige of the various professions will be dependent upon the outcome.

This prediction is limited to corporation accountants. But we can "modernize" it by giving it an occupational focus (at the third level), which emphasizes the role of *public* accounting:

> The computer has invaded all types of economic organizations. This raises the issue of which profession can best utilize the computer to provide a total information service for the administrative groups of society. A power fight has developed between accountants and other professions. The stakes are high in this conflict or collaboration issue, for the status and prestige of the various professions involved will be dependent upon the outcome.

Viewing these two perspectives on how the profession as a whole should move into the future, one has the feeling that movement to either extreme would severely weaken it. If a conservative stance is taken that things should stay the way they are, that no principles should be specified, that the emphasis should remain on auditing alone and thus keep the knowledge unknown and esoteric, the profession may find itself outflanked by other groups willing to enter the arena. On the other hand, if it strives for too much uncertainty, it may find itself compromising its independence by developing disproportionate power and overstepping its bounds. This last remark would be made with tongue in cheek if one listened to the opinions of certain stock-brokers, management consultants and other financial people who presently see the CPA as a weak sister, merely rubber-stamping management's desires. But the profession is in a good position to clarify its goals and strengthen its position. That its leaders intend to do so and to maintain and improve its stature is evident in many of its current actions and concerns. One among these is the examination of the accountant's role in the increasingly important field of social measurement.

Social Measurement

With the explosion in the number of human services agencies, both governmental and private, and the continued growth in size and complexity of modern organizations has come the need for evaluation of social policy. With the aid of systems analysis, the social sciences have begun to develop indicators that attempt to measure quantitatively the social causes and results of political and economic actions and events. Because of their interest and abilities in examining the total information system of organizations, accountants are naturally interested in developments in this field of social measurement and have given it the name "socio-economic accounting." Last year, the AICPA sponsored a seminar in which leading representatives from business, accounting, and the social sciences discussed the meaning and implications of social measurement, the contents of which are summarized in *Social Measurement* (AICPA, 1972).

Accountants have already been engaged in measurement of social indicators. Probably the most publicized case has been the Detroit war on poverty operation, in which a team from Touche Ross & Co. worked with the Mayor's Committee for Human Resource Development. A major criticism of this project, which is a general criticism of the social indicators field as a whole, is that the more subjective elements affecting the programs being investigated are not taken into consideration (Montagna, 1971: 486–87; Linowes, 1973). Accountants who take this point of view feel that one must learn how to measure changes in values and norms of a group as well as net worth (Capon, 1972: 30; Eisner, in AICPA, 1972). This group, which we might label the "humanists," feels that indicators do not determine our value choices but rather that value choices determine how we look at indicators. For example, a recent study of the happiness level of the U.S. population shows that the lower the income the less happy people are. (The question: "Taken together, how would you say things are these days? Are you very happy, happy, not so happy, etc.") Another national survey asked: "All things considered, how satisfied are you with life in the United States? Very satisfied, satisfied, etc." It was found that, generally, the lower the income the more satisfied people are. Thus, an estimate of the chances for pressures for social change from below, if based (value-judged) on happiness studies, would be seen as more likely than if based on satisfaction studies.

The more humanist-oriented accountants view accounting as probabilistic in nature (Trueblood, 1966; Roy and MacNeill, 1967; Woodfield, 1967; Larson, 1969). Accounting should assume a normative stance, that it be responsible for determining what should be rather than what the client has requested (Bedford, 1967). The "rationalists," on the other hand, tend to stick with systems theory when dealing with macro-accounting phenomena (Jasper, 1966; Moravec, 1966; Gynther, 1967; Dickhaut, 1969; Beyer, 1969). There is a tendency for this group to view the nature of accounting as consensual and not conflictual, as concerned with the maintenance of the status-quo entity and not with "subcoalitions." There is a tendency for a value-free system to be constructed. Affective elements are consciously eliminated from any model of system operation. The free-floating intellectual and his total ideology, his vision of the present, past, and future, is being replaced by the scholar-expert who does not accept value-laden schemes. In the words of one severe critic, Noam Chomsky (1967), he becomes an intellectual mandarin. The language of systems theory today reflects the "machine metaphor" (social engineering, equilibrium) and not the "organic metaphor" (open systems, adaptation, development). In the process, man becomes dehumanized, there is "action without deliberation" (Wolin, 1969).

Will the narrow theory of systems analysis completely envelope accounting to become the ideological whip of an Orwellian future? Some have voiced the fear that it might unless those who define, measure, and interpret socio-economic functions and structures begin to examine their own set of values. The results of such an examination in accounting would be, according to Toan (1971), the equivalent of the famous Hawthorne Studies, which disclosed the importance of the social factors in management-employee relations. The study of the effect of accountants' behavior and values on their clients and vice-versa has yet to be done. This study would want to utilize a new method of sociology called "ethnomethodology," the study of procedures (methodology) used by everyday man—in this case, the accountant—to cope with the world.

Along with the leaders of the business world, accountants are coming in for heavier criticism from from various segments of society. They are seen as supporters and participants in exploitative financial ventures throughout the world. As one example, the editors of *Monthly Review* (December, 1972) point to the partner and director of the international business practice of Arthur Andersen, a member of the Committee on Balance of Payments of the International Economic Policy Association, as a prime example of "what the most powerful section of the U.S. ruling class thinks, and indirectly what it intends to do." Accountants must be able to anticipate the major value changes in society that create these criticisms and be prepared to apply new techniques and judgments as they become necessary.

As supporters of the systems theory perspective, accountants must consider the serious social limitations of this view in carrying out social measurements. This is especially true in light of the great amount of attention being paid to the thesis of the Harvard philosopher, John Rawls (1971). In *A Theory of Justice,* considered by many to be one of the most important books of the twentieth century, he states:

> The total scheme of institutions no longer emphasizes social efficiency and technocratic values. We [must] . . . regard the distribution of natural talents as a common asset and . . . share in the benefits of this distribution whatever it turns out to be. Those who have been favored by nature, whoever they are, may gain from their good fortune only on terms that improve the situation of those who have lost out.

He emphasizes that the inequalities of birth and natural endowment must be compensated for by giving more attention to those who are not as well endowed. One such program might be to spend more time and money on the education of the less intelligent than on that of the more intelligent, at least during the earlier years of school.

If this political philosophy and similar debates on inequality do, in fact, do much to shape the programs of the last part of this century, accountants will have to adapt to and innovate on this principle in order to collaborate in and possibly lead the social measurement process. The speculative accountant, DR Scott, writing early in the century, clearly saw the nature of social change in the accounting profession as an endless series of reorganizations of value-systems. Thus what is radical and subversive in one era (e.g., systems theory) becomes the conservative dogma of the following era.

7. SUMMARY

In this analysis the accounting profession is viewed as an occupation in conflict, as are all others: for occupations, as kinds of organizations, are inherently conflictful. The attempt of the profession to assert its dominance in areas of uncertainty (in which power is intrinsic) is manifested primarily in the development of management advisory services, an outgrowth of societal advances in technology and large-scale organization. It seems however that either too rapid a change (e.g., management auditing, actuarial work) or too little change (unwillingness to develop MAS, averting any significant changes in accounting theory or principles) will endanger the status of the profession. This suggests that there may be an optimal route for professional practice—neither too vague nor too precise, too broad nor too narrow—along which the profession must steer a careful course into the future.

Conflict is not limited to that which takes place between professions but also includes contests between external groups and groups within the profession (CPAs versus clients and the public) and between segments within the profession itself (the art versus science debate). In many cases, these conflicts are interrelated in their focus on one issue—e.g., accounting principles. This study has been separated into the three analytical levels in order to better perceive these conflicts.

For this profession, then, as for all professions, there will never be a "solution" to the power question. There will always be continual conflict and accommodation, something that accountants, because of their background of training and experience, may find hard to accept. One area that looks increasingly promising for collaboration (and possibly conflict) is social measurement. The profession's success in this venture will depend much on its ability to understand and interpret emerging political, social, and economic value systems in the measurement of human organizations.

NOTES

1. Parts of this section are summarized from Montagna (forthcoming, Chapter 6).

2. In much of organizational theory the term "bureaucracy" is used instead of rationality. This follows Max Weber's definition of bureaucracy as the maximization of organizational efficiency by means of a division of labor permitting specialization, a hierarchy of authority and responsibility, a system of abstract rules and procedures, and formality of roles (Gerth and Mills, 1946: 196–244).

3. I must agree with Ross (1967) that a profession is not a group in the ordinary sense of the definition. However, its organized association of leaders acts in the name of the profession on certain legal and moral matters. In such cases the profession can be viewed as a concrete category acting as a unit without the danger of reification.

4. The opinions were elicited in interviews with a stratified random sample of personnel (N=51) of five of the Big Eight firms and four medium-sized firms (Montagna, forthcoming).

5. Standards for the limits of materiality are not being called for here (e.g., Holmes, 1972), only general principles of accounting.

6. The four classic volumes, *The American Soldier: Studies in the Social Psychology of World War II* (Princeton University Press, 1949), show how certain common-sense assumptions are often proven false by social science, as was the case of the following:

Better educated men show more psychoneurotic symptoms in the armed forces than those with less education. (Intellectuals are much more prone to mental instability than the ordinary man in the street.)

Men from rural backgrounds usually take Army life in better spirit than men from city backgrounds. (Farm boys are more accustomed to hardships.)

Southern soldiers are better able than Northern ones to stand the climate in the hot South Sea Islands. (Southerners are more acclimated to hot weather.)

White privates are more eager to become non-commissioned officers than Negroes. (Negroes lack ambition.)

While the fighting continued during World War II, men were more eager to return to the States than they were after the German surrender. (One really can't blame a guy for not wanting to get killed.)

REFERENCES

Adams, Sexton and Doyle Z. Williams (1966) "Information Technology and the Accounting Organization." *Management Services* 3 (September–October): 15–23.

American Institute of Accountants (1934) *Audits of Corporate Accounts.* New York.

American Institute of Certified Public Accountants (1950) *Audits by Certified Public Accountants.* New York.

American Institute of Certified Public Accountants (1972) *Social Measurement.* New York.

Anthony, Robert N. (1963) "Showdown on Accounting Principles." *Harvard Business Review* 41 (May–June): 99–106.

Aoyagi, Bunji (1958) "Sociological Accounting." *Journal of Accountancy.* 106 (July): 51–55.

Barnard, Chester (1938) *The Functions of the Executive.* Cambridge, Mass.: Harvard University Press.

Bedford, Norton M. (1967) "The Nature of Future Accounting Theory." *Accounting Review* 42 (January): 82–85.

Bevis, Herman W. (1965) *Corporate Financial Reporting in a Competitive Economy.* New York: Macmillan.

Beyer, Robert (1969) "The Modern Management Approach to a Program of Social Improvement." *Journal of Accountancy* 127 (March): 37–46.

Blau, Peter M. (1964) *Exchange and Power in Social Life.* New York: John Wiley.

Buckley, John W.; Paul Kircher; and Russell L. Mathews (1968) "Methodology in Accounting Theory." *Accounting Review* 43 (April): 274–83.

Buckley, Walter (1967) *Sociology and Modern Systems Theory.* Englewood Cliffs, New Jersey: Prentice-Hall.

Burke, Edward J. (1964) "Objectivity and Accounting." *Accounting Review* 34 (October): 837–49.

Business Week (1972) "Accounting: A Crisis over Fuller Disclosure." (April 22): 55–60.

Capon, Frank S. (1972) "The Totality of Accounting for the Future." *Financial Executive* 40 (July): 28–34.

Carey, John L. (1965) *The CPA Plans for the Future.* New York: American Institite of Certified Public Accountants.

Carey, John L. and William P. Doherty (1963) *Ethical Standards of the Accounting Profession.* New York: American Institute of Certified Public Accountants.

Carmichael, Douglas R. (1972) *The Auditor's Reporting Obligation: The Meaning and Implementation of the Fourth Standard of Reporting.* Auditing Research

Monograph No. 1. New York: American Institute of Certified Public Accountants.

Carmichael, Douglas R. and R. J. Swieringa (1968) "The Compatibility of Auditing Independence and Management Services—an Identification of the Issues." *Accounting Review* 43 (October): 697–705.

Chomsky, Noam (1967) "The Responsibility of Intellectuals." *New York Review of Books* (February 23).

Crozier, Michel (1964) *The Bureaucratic Phenomenon.* Chicago: University of Chicago Press.

Davidson, Sidney (1963) "The Day of Reckoning—Managerial Analysis and Accounting Theory." *Journal of Accounting Research* 1 (Autumn): 117–26.

Deskins, James Wesley (1965) "On the Nature of the Public Interest." *Accounting Review* 40 (January): 76–81.

Dickhaut, John W. (1969) "Accounting Information in Decision-Making." *Management Services* 4 (January–February): 49–55.

Drucker, Peter (1950) *The New Society.* New York: Harper & Row.

Forbes (1966) "Are CPA Firms Taking Over Management Consulting?" 98 (October 1): 57–61.

Fremgen, James M. (1967) "Utility and Accounting Principles." *Accounting Review* 42 (July): 457–67.

Gerth, Hans H. and C. Wright Mills (eds.) (1946) *From Max Weber: Essays in Sociology.* New York: Oxford University Press.

Goode, William J. (1961) "The Librarian: From Occupation to Profession?" *Library Quarterly* 31 (October): 306–18.

Grady, Paul (1965) "The Independent Auditing and Reporting Function of the CPA." *Journal of Accountancy* 120 (November): 65–71.

Greenwood, Ernest (1957) "Attributes of a Profession." *Social Work* 2 (July): 45–55.

Gynther, Reginald S. (1967) "Accounting Concepts and Behavioral Hypotheses." *Accounting Review* 42 (April): 274–90.

Hartley, Ronald V. and Timothy L. Ross (1972) "MAS and Audit Independence: An Image Problem." *Journal of Accountancy* 134 (November): 42–51.

Holmes, William (1972) "Materiality—Through the Looking Glass." *Journal of Accountancy* 133 (February): 44–49.

Horngren, Charles T. (1972) "Accounting Principles: Private or Public Sector?" *Journal of Accountancy* 133 (May): 37–41.

Hughes, Everett C. (1963) "Professions." *Daedalus* 92 (Fall): 655–68.

Imke, Frank J. (1966) "Relationships in Accounting Theory." *Accounting Review* 41 (April): 318–22.

Jasper, Harold W. (1966) "Future Role of the Accountant." *Management Services* 3 (January–February): 51–56.

Kam, Vernon (1973) "Judgment and the Scientific Trend in Accounting." *Journal of Accountancy* 135 (February): 52–57.

Kaufman, Felix (1967) "Professional Consulting by CPAs." *Accounting Review* 42 (October): 713–20.

Kaufman, Felix (1971) "The Computer, the Accountant and the Next Decade." *Journal of Accountancy* 132 (August): 33–39.

Larson, Kermit D. (1969) "Implications of Measurement Theory on Accounting Concept Formulation." *Accounting Review* 44 (January): 38–47.

Laski, Harold J. (1935) "The Decline of the Professions." *Harper's* 171 (November): 676–85.

Lazarsfeld, Paul F. (1964) Counsel as basis for report of the Long-Range

Objectives Committee of the American Institute of Certified Public Accountants, prepared by Norton M. Bedford: *Profile of the Profession, 1975, from the Viewpoint of a Sociologist.*

Lazarsfeld, Paul F. and Robert K. Merton (1964) "Friendship as Social Process: A Substantive and Methodological Analysis," pp. 18–66 in Monroe Berger, Theodore Abel, and Charles H. Page (eds.) *Freedom and Control in Modern Society.* New York: Octagon Books.

Linowes, David F. (1973) "The Accountant's Enlarged Professional Responsibilities." *Journal of Accountancy* 135 (February): 47–51.

Littleton, A. C. (1948) "Fixed Assets and Accounting Theory." *Illinois Certified Public Accountant* 10 (March): 11–18.

Lynch, Richard M. (1959) "Professional Standards for Management Consulting in the United States." Ph.D. dissertation. Graduate School of Business Administration: Harvard University.

Mautz, Robert K. (1965) "The Practitioner and the Professor." *Journal of Accountancy* 120 (October): 64–66.

Mautz, Robert K. (1972) "Toward a Philosophy of Auditing." Paper presented at the University of Kansas Symposium on Auditing Problems (May 11–12).

McDonald, Daniel L. (1967) "Feasibility Criteria for Accounting Measures." *Accounting Review* 42 (October): 622–29.

McRae, Thomas W. (1962) "Looking Backward—The Decline and Fall of the Accounting Profession." *The Quarterly* of Touche Ross & Co. 8 (June): 27–30.

Montagna, Paul D. (forthcoming) *Certified Public Accounting: A Sociological View of a Profession in Change.* Lawrence, Kansas: Scholars Book Co.

Montagna, Paul D. (1971) "The Public Accounting Profession: Organization, Ideology, and Social Power." *American Behavioral Scientist* 14 (March–April): 475–91.

Montgomery, Robert H. (1912) *Auditing Theory and Practice.* New York: Ronald Press.

Moonitz, Maurice (1972) ". . . To Advance the Written Expression of What Constitutes Generally Accepted Accounting Principles . . .," pp. 121–34 in Alfred Rappaport and Lawrence Revsine (eds.) *Corporate Financial Reporting.* Chicago: Commerce Clearing House.

Moravec, Adolph F. (1966) "Using Simulation to Design a Management Information System." *Management Services* 3 (May–June): 50–58.

Popper, Karl (1957) *The Poverty of Historicism.* London: Routledge & Kegan Paul.

Rawls, John (1971) *A Theory of Justice.* Cambridge, Mass.: Harvard University Press.

Ross, Howard I. (1967) "The Current Crisis in Financial Reporting." *Journal of Accountancy* 124 (August): 65–69. Reprinted from *Canadian Chartered Accountant* (May, 1967).

Roy, Robert H. and James H. MacNeill (1967) *Horizons for a Profession.* New York: American Institute of Certified Public Accountants.

Savoie, Leonard M. (1968) Comments from a speech before the Twentieth National Credit Conference of the American Bankers Association. Reported in *Journal of Accountancy* 125 (March): 8–10.

Scott, DR (1931) *The Cultural Significance of Accounts.* New York: Henry Holt.

Smith, Richard Leo (1955) "A Case Analysis of External Accounting Influence over Managerial Decisions." Ph.D. Dissertation. Graduate School of Business Administration: Harvard University.

Spacek, Leonard (1965) Speech given at The Graduate School of Business

Administration (February 18): New York University.

Spiller, Earl A., Jr. (1964) "Theory and Practice in the Development of Accounting." *Accounting Review* 34 (October): 850–59.

Sprouse, Robert T. (1972) "The Future of the Accounting Profession: Rule or Reason?" *World,* Journal of Peat, Marwick, Mitchell & Co. (Summer): 6–11.

Sterling, Robert R. (1973) "Accounting Power." *Journal of Accountancy* 135 (January): 61–67.

Storey, Reed K. (1964) *The Search for Accounting Principles: Today's Problems in Perspective.* New York: American Institute of Certified Public Accountants.

Summers, Edward L. and Robert M. Hermance (1969) "Professors and Practitioners." *Journal of Accountancy* 128 (August): 85–88.

Toan, Arthur B. (1971) "Does Accountancy's View of Human Behavior Meet Today's Needs?" *Price Waterhouse Review* (Summer–Autumn): 12–19.

Trueblood, Robert M. (1966) Speech given at the 50th Annual Meeting of the American Accounting Association. As quoted in *Journal of Accountancy* 122 (October): 12.

Vatter, William J. (1963) "Postulates and Principles." *Journal of Accounting Research* 1 (Autumn): 179–97.

Whisler, Thomas J. (1965) "The Manager and the Computer." *Journal of Accountancy* 111 (January): 27–32.

White, Harrison (1961) "Management Conflict and Sociometric Structure." *American Journal of Sociology* 67 (September): 185–99.

Willingham, John J. (1964) "The Accounting Entity: A Conceptual Model." *Accounting Review* 49 (July): 543–52.

Wise, T. A. (1960) "The Auditors Have Arrived—Part 1." *Fortune* 62 (November): 151–57.

Wolin, Sheldon S. (1969) "A Critique of Organizational Theories," pp. 133–49 in Amitai Etzioni (ed.) *A Sociological Reader on Complex Organizations.* New York: Holt, Rinehart & Winston, 2nd Edition.

Woodfield, Leon W. (1967) "Lessening the Dangers of Uncertainty." *Management Services* 4 (January–February): 51–55.

Wrong, Dennis H. (1968) "Some Problems in Defining Social Power." *American Journal of Sociology* 73 (May): 673–81.

Public Accounting: The Dynamics of Occupational Change—A Response

I was delighted to be asked to discuss Professor Montagna's paper on occupational change in accounting. The pleasure stems from my prior exposure to Montagna's work, particularly his piece on the accounting profession which appeared in a recent issue of the *American Behavioral Scientist* (Montagna, 1971). We seem to share a common interest in the sociology of the profession, though we have arrived there by thoroughly different paths. We also hold a number of other beliefs in common, including the aspiration—if not expectation—that a macro-profession in the information and administrative sciences is *in fetu,* with accountants being highly instrumental in its delivery and development if they choose to be so.[1]

"Montagna on accounting" to date has been largely descriptive, moderately normative, and negligibly critical—all, no doubt, in deference to his felt status as a guest. As he comes to know us better, I look for him to become considerably more incisive in his analysis and definitive in his recommendations.

In this paper, Montagna examines the convulsions in accounting from the viewpoint of conflict theory. His treatment evokes the classical behavior of tribal systems portrayed so vividly by socio-anthropologists. (See Moore, 1967 and Etzioni, 1968: 550.) The reading conjured images of mockingbirds, Uganda kob, and lepilemurs, all fiercely defending their own territories while unscrupulously invading the property of others. A statement by Ardrey came forcibly to mind:

> If, as I believe, man's innumerable territorial expressions are human reponses to an imperative lying with equal force on mockingbirds and men, then human self-estimate is due for radical revision. We acknowledge a few

*B.A. 1961, Walla Walla College; M.B.A. 1962, Ph.D. 1964, University of Washington. Professor of Accounting and Information Systems, and Acting Associate Dean, Graduate School of Management, UCLA. Author, *Contemporary Accounting and Its Environment* (1968); *In Search of Identity* (1972); *Income Tax Allocation: An Inquiry into Problems of Methodology and Estimation* (1972); and *Accounting: An Information Systems Approach* (1973). Contributor to accounting periodicals.

25

such almighty forces, but very few: the will to survive, the sexual impulse, the tie, perhaps, between mother and infant. . . . It may come to us as the strangest of thoughts that the bond between a man and the soil he walks on should be more powerful than his bond with the woman he sleeps with. Even so, in a rough, preliminary way we may test the supposition with a single question: How many men have you known of, in your lifetime, who died for their country? And how many for a woman?

Any force which may command us to act in opposition to the will to survive is a force to be inspected . . . (Ardrey, 1966:6, italics supplied).

It is from this last statement that my dialectic with Montagna ensues, for in line with that methodology I have chosen not to dismember his paper but rather to propose a *counterplan*.[2] I accede to his statement of the problem as it ranges across principles, professional boundaries, the juxtaposition of power and uncertainty, the perennial science-versus-art dialogue, computer impact, and management consulting services.

In areas of agreement, I have no difficulty in recognizing that these are pivotal issues to the future of the accounting profession, as the record testifies (Buckley, 1972: 46 and Buckley, 1973). And I applaud his view that accountants should sustain a vigorous interface with the social environment which surrounds them.

In parenthesis, I noted with humor the casual if not quixotic fashion in which he resolves—in his own mind at least—problems over which we have been haggling for years. Here is standing proof of the benefits of infusion! For issues which have carried over decades, spawned books and articles ad nauseam, prompted eloquent speeches and rebuttals, and brought us at times to the verge of internecine conflict—he disposes of quite deftly in a few cryptic sentences.

Observe his major admonitions [Sec. 6], that: (1) the AICPA, and FASB we must presume, should be linked formally with the SEC; (2) auditors should have an advocacy relationship with their clients similar to that of lawyers; (3) the laborious but futile efforts of Leonard Spacek to engender interest in an "accounting court" should now quicken our earnest consideration and support; (4) adoption of the scientific approach will increase the legitimacy of the profession in the public eye; and (5) increased management advisory services are the key to greater uncertainty and therefore power.

While agreeing basically on diagnosis, our course is tangent in the area of prescription. His summary [Sec. 7] implies that conflict is natural to accounting as with all professions, and we should simply learn to accept it. He counsels us to avoid too rapid change (management auditing) and too little action (no further development of MAS and accounting theory), lulling us into complacency with the ode "neither too vague nor too precise, too broad nor too narrow—the profession must steer a careful course into the future."

Fi donc! This is no time for catalepsy! For while change is constant the need for change is cumulative, reaching—if unattended—an epic where great deeds are needed or all is lost.

We return to Ardrey and recall his pointed observation that defense of territory may well subdue the primitive instinct for survival. This occurs, of course, when exogenous stimulation yields to introversion—a societal state which ethologist Jean-Jacques Petter (1962) refers to as "noyau." (It brings to mind the hypochondriac who became so obsessed with whether his bowels worked that he completely neglected to eat.)

1. WHO CARES?

Parks (1972) has tallied the critical items in the accounting and financial literature and concluded that, by and large, the accountant is his own prosecutor, jury, judge, and victim—but who cares?

Who cares if the profession convulses from its own cannibalism? The same barren acres of accounting thought are plowed with repeated, maniacal zeal, and little effect—but who cares? Who cares if we quibble endlessly over the dots and tittles in financial statements?

Analysts are more interested in the color composition of annual reports, product growth, share of market and industry averages than in the verifiable, objective information we provide (*Wall Street Journal,* 1970: 1). On the other hand, if we are focused on "the average investor," the perennial argument as to whether we communicate with him or not can be resolved through a simple test. Take any annual report onto any street and, after ascertaining that the passersby are indeed investors, ask them to read and interpret it.

The toilsome hours I spent in company with thousands of students differentiating among the numerous depreciation and inventory methods have been brought to naught by Beaver *et alia,* who have bothered to find out that our percipient users normalize the diversive data we provide (Beaver, 1968a and 1968b; Archibald, 1972; Kaplan and Roll, 1972; Beaver and Dukes, in press). Even more alarming to the purist must be the emergence of betas and alphas as the talismans of Wall Street in that they circumvent the published financial statements altogether.[3]

Having rowed in that stream, the wisdom of experience reveals to me the rapids and whirlpools which beset our search for accounting principles. The rhetoric in this area, you will observe, avoids unclothing the reasons for the search for other than semiotic reasons.[4] But of what virtue are principles secured to a vacuous theoretical edifice?

FIGURE 1
A MORPHOLOGY OF ACCOUNTING PRINCIPLES

Parameters	1	2	3	4	5
A. Principal beneficiary	govern ment/ public sector	investors/ analysts	capital/ credit markets	manage ment	accountants
B. Climate	laissez-faire	uniformity	circum-stantial variables	—	—
C. Rationale	inductive theoretic (empirical)	deductive theoretic	pragmatic	authori-tarian	plebiscite (poll)
D. Where authority vests	private-accounting profession	private-consortium	public (govern ment)	quasi-public	—
E. Primary objective	conformity	curb abuses	power	authority	abstract-theoretic
F. Sociological rationale	public protection	public service	private rights	profession's welfare	—
G. Impetus	internal	regulatory	societal	—	—

Possible schema for accounting principles = $5^3 \times 3^2 \times 4^2 = 18,000$

Nor, to date, have we even set parameters to the search. Using Zwicky's morphological technique, I can conceive of at least 18,000 schema for accounting principles (Figure 1) and 230,400 for financial reporting (Figure 2). (See Zwicky, 1962; Ayres, 1969; Gordon, 1961.) With this latitude and the current state of progress our *genius loci* should be engaged busily in "the search" for the next several thousand years! But who cares?

Who cares if we ignore the lesson that tighter rules lead to greater leniency? ("Thou shalt not steal by entering through the bedroom window" makes it difficult to prosecute entrance through the kitchen door.) On this subject, a recent editorial on equity funding predicts an outcry for tougher regulation and goes swiftly to the observation that the alleged deeds have been unlawful "since the promulgation of the Eighth Commandment. The scandal underscores the need not for new laws but for a little common sense and alertness." (*Business Week*, April 14, 1973: 108)

We may well ask if the search for principles and power has not made us insensitive to the real needs of the profession. Could it be that we are defending territory at the cost of survival—and is the price right?

FIGURE 2
A Morphology for Financial Reporting

Parameter	1	2	3	4	5
A. Principal beneficiary (user)	govern ment/ public sector	investors/ analysts	capital/ credit markets	manage ment	accountants
B. Proprietorship .	issuer	attestor	regulator	—	—
C. Scope (cumulative) . . .	tangible economic	intangible economic	non-economic	societal	global
D. Value basis . . .	money	real	current	psychic	—
E. Primary time frame	past	present	future	—	—
F. Communication level	novice	working knowledge	expert	—	—
G. Timing	periodic	continuous	impromptu	when accessed	—
H. Medium	formal-hard copy	formal-soft	informal	on-line	—
I. Validity	surveyed	reviewed	confirmed	guaranteed	—
J. Payee	investors/ analysts	govern ment	client	client association	—

Possible schema for financial reporting $5^2 \times 3^3 \times 4^5 = 230,400$.

Who cares if we demand more "clout" (as suggested by Professor Moonitz in his paper to this Colloquium), less litigation, and less malignity? What do we offer in return—more rules, greater insularity from liability, or custodianship of the last vestige of private rights? In all frankness I see no basis for exchange.

2. BASIS FOR CHANGE

The impetus for great deeds at this time comes from the need to understand and respond to the complex environment which surrounds us as a profession. The basis for change lies in adopting an exteroceptive posture which gives life to the precept of relevance. The tautologous and perfidious search for principles must give way to inquiries which address the significant *needs of others.* Since we are appurtenant to society and the organizations we serve, realism decrees that more often than not our problems will be defined for us.

This leads me to observe that in this period in the history of the profession, real progress hails not from academe or our societies and institutes, but from a small subset in practice who are breaking ground against the overwhelming forces of convention. They are willing to accept risk, develop and test new ideas, press the boundaries of independence and walk the tightrope of liability. Some in this category are not accountants by classical definition, yet they succor and advance a profession which has declined them membership. From the crucible of their efforts comes innovation and the new technology of accounting, long before it takes hold in our literature or becomes incorporated into our curricula.[5] Their motto is *facta non verba*, and those with intellectual bent would do well to study and extend their efforts.

Every trip I make to the arena of practice adds to the cumulative impression that there is where the action is. For given the general perquisites of intelligence, personality and communicative skills, there are—as always—two fundaments to professionalism: *competence* and *integrity*.[6] Competence is exhibited through the effective solution of real problems, and integrity through adherence to moral principle in advance of profit.

3. REAL PROBLEMS

Many real problems urgently await our attention. Over the years I have heard many appeals to the intelligentsia to trade their inutile projects for ones of significance, but response continues to fall far behind need.[7]

Grappling with real problems of significance will elevate our horizons,

FIGURE 3
A SURVEY OF METHODOLOGIES USED IN FUTURES RESEARCH

Scenarios	45	Objectives trees	2
Delphi techniques	41	Operations research	2
Simulation techniques	29	Survey research	2
Trend extrapolation	19	Casual models	1
Dynamic modelling	7	Decision matrices	1
Gross impact analysis	5	Growth curves	1
Correlation plotting	4	Interviewing	1
Expert position papers	3	Operational gaming	1
Relevance trees	3	PERT adaptations	1
Analogy	2	Role play gaming	1
Economic projection	2	Speculation (formal)	1
Morphological approach	2	Values Analysis	1

Source: John McHale, "A Survey of Futures Research in the United States," *The Futurist*, Vol. 4, No. 5 (December, 1970), p.201. The numbers above are the reported frequency in the use of techniques as surveyed by McHale.

improve our competence, and cure the malaise which besets us. Sketched below are some illustrative areas to which we can turn our attention:

Futures Research

Capon (1972: 30) observes correctly that "the future is the only important decision area for humanity," and proceeds to build a convincing case for why more formal planning models are needed in view of rapidly accelerating change.

A whole body of methodology (Figure 3), a growing literature, and application to highly diverse issues (Figure 4), attest to the importance of futurology. This development has largely bypassed accountants, even though it is germane to our future. This is true particularly in education, where we seek to train students for the world of tomorrow.

FIGURE 4
A SURVEY OF SOME APPLICATIONS OF FUTURES RESEARCH

Technological forecasting	41	Long-range planning	2
Socio-economic forecasting	21	Population growth	2
Economic projections	21	Problem-solving	2
Market analysis	15	Product development	2
Corporate planning studies	10	Public affairs forecasting	2
Organizational studies	7	Resources planning	2
Educational planning	7	Socio-technical integration	2
Corporate journal publication	6	Auto-industry projections	1
Policy research	6	Biotechnical forecasting	1
Environmental control	5	Family psychotherapy	1
Research & development	5	General systems analysis	1
Urban planning	5	Technological change	1
Holistic futures	5	Leisure, future of	1
Business forecasting	4	Life extension	1
Individual/society	4	Life styles	1
Political forecasting	4	Medical care systems	1
Manpower utilization	3	Personnel research	1
Social problem-solving	3	Psychiatry futures	1
Society, alternative futures	3	Race relations/ethnicity	1
Urban design	3	Regional development	1
Aero system planning	2	Sex education	1
Conference organization	2	Social systems analysis	1
Educational forecasting	2	Social systems forecasting	1
Educational programs	2	State planning	1
Geopolitical forecasting	2	Threat projection	1
Health planning	2		

Source: John McHale, "A Survey of Futures Research in the United States," *The Futurist*, Vol. 4, No. 5 (December, 1970). The numbers are the reported frequency of application in the survey.

Computer Technology and Systems Analysis

There is no need to reiterate the long-standing pleas that we envelop the computer as a principal tool of accounting. Equity Funding should drive the point home. For the message is clear that we will become increasingly vulnerable to charges of incompetence if, by and large (and especially through formal education), we are not as skilled in the use of computers as those experts who operate (or manipulate) them.

A close link is needed with the burgeoning field of systems analysis. Here is an area that subsumes many of the traditional functions of accounting, i.e., systems design, data processing, and distribution of reports. Systems analysis has been projected as the most rapidly expanding job market through 1980.[8]

Boehm has depicted in graphic terms the major change in emphasis from hardware to software (Figure 5), while a *Wall Street Journal* survey foresees a dramatic extension of computing applications from accounting to other control areas over the next few years (Figure 6). Recognizing

<h3 style="text-align:center">FIGURE 5
Software vs. Hardware Development</h3>

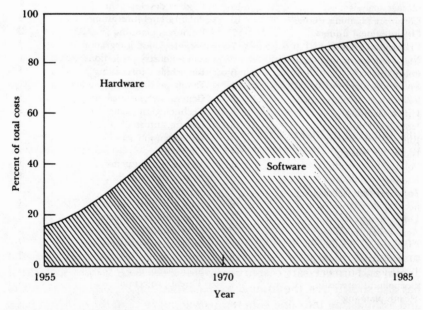

Source: B. W. Boehm, "Software and Its Impact: A Quantitative Assessment," *AIS Working Paper 73–27* (UCLA: Accounting-Information Systems Research Program, April 1973), p. 8

FIGURE 6
NEW APPLICATIONS IN COMPUTING

Computer Applications	Use Now	Anticipated Within:			TOTAL**
		Next 2 Years	Next 5 Years	Do Not Use or Anticipate Within Next 5 Years	
	%	%	%	%	%
Accounting/ Bookkeeping	75.6	10.2	17.7	6.8	100.0
Sales Analysis	45.1	14.0	18.0	36.9	100.0
Inventory control	43.0	18.8	25.2	31.7	100.0
Production control	33.4	15.0	21.8	44.8	100.0
Engineering, scientific problems	31.7	6.3	13.2	55.1	100.0
Materials management	26.6	13.6	18.0	55.4	100.0
Research and development	24.0	9.0	19.2	56.8	100.0
Market research	19.3	16.4	26.0	54.7	100.0
Decision models	15.8	10.2	23.2	61.1	100.0
Miscellaneous other uses	7.7	3.0	4.1	88.2	100.0

*Includes next 2 years.
**Respondents with EDP procurement responsibilities (Base = 634).
NOTE: Among all respondents, the proportion reporting that their companies now use computers *exclusively* for accounting/bookkeeping is 13.7%.
Source: Management and the Computer (New York: Dow Jones & Company, Inc., 1969), p.25.

that integration makes these applications inextricable should spur us to much deeper involvement with the whole field of systems analysis.

Information Economics

We have long regarded ourselves as information experts. As such, what have we done at the practical level to cope with the mounting problem of information overload whose consequences extend beyond apathy and unnecessary cost to involve psychosomatic factors?[9] Research has also shown that the human mind is simply incapable of processing and assimilating into one coherent whole more than six or seven basic items of information. (See Miller, 1956; Hunter and Sigler, 1940; and Zipf, 1949.)

Computing firms cannot be expected to address this issue, but can we rise to the occasion? In my Weldon Powell address I suggested that a beginning should be made in our own back yard (Buckley, 1973). For in recent years we have added several earnings per share figures (resulting in the suggestion that the measure be done away with by Stern, 1973: 69–70), data with respect to accounting methods, the statement of changes in financial position, and many other disclosure requirements. More is anticipated as we look toward forecast, price level, and current value data.

While new and better information is critical to the vitality of the profession, the process should not be cumulative if we are serious about information economics. Perhaps the time has come to delete an existing datum each time a new one is added. If only we knew which data to delete. This causes us to inquire also into decision processes.

Decision Processes

That our information drives the decision-making function is now well established. But what do we know about decision or, for that matter, other abstract processes? Very little.

The prevalent decision model in management and accounting stems from archaic economic theory. It denotes a decision-maker as one who, upon learning of a problem, assiduously calculates and weighs alternatives, and chooses as optimally as an ill-defined state of nature permits.

Social scientists have successfully challenged this concept of "instrumental rationality." Bruner, Goodnow, and Austen (1956) present a convincing argument as to why decision-makers cannot operate in this classic mode, and should not try to do so. Etzioni (1968: 265) states bluntly that "societal decision-makers do not have the basic capacities for making rational decision." And even computers, programmed at exorbitant levels of cost, have been shown to be incapable of solving problems posed in the framework of the rational model (Dreyfuss, 1964).

Surely we have here a critical area for empirical research. Exploration of the "mixed scanning" approach suggested by Etzioni (1968) represents one of the many possible alternatives.

Process Analysis

My own research is taking me into process analysis.[10] I have defined it as *the science which deals with functional relationships and activities.* Its major elements comprise functional definitions, analysis of relationships, evaluation, and transfer.

Observation tells us that processes are widely differentiated. At the one end of the scale are simple, mechanical ones such as time-keeping, canning fruit or pumping gasoline. At the other extreme are highly complex natural, sociological or neural-physiological ones such as continental drift, political revolutions and the thinking process, respectively.

All processes conform to the basic construct of input-output. A rudimentary classification should distinguish at least among simple-mechanical, complex-mechanical, simple-abstract, and complex-abstract for each of the variables of input, transformation and output—yielding the matrix below:

A CLASSIFICATION OF PROCESSES

Dependent Variables	Independent Variables			
	Mechanical		Abstract	
	Simple	Complex	Simple	Complex
A. Input	AI	AII	AIII	AIV
B. Transformation	BI	BII	BIII	BIV
C. Output	CI	CII	CIII	CIV

Mechanical processes are specific and often quantifiable. *Abstract* processes are non-specific and are beyond the scope of current measurement. *Simple* processes are uniramous and hence void of interdependencies, while *complex* processes are interactive.

Some examples of these basic configurations are given below, where a solid line represents a mechanical process and a broken line an abstract one. Transformation is depicted by a rectangle.

Some Process Configurations

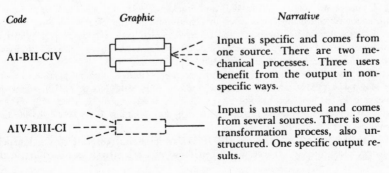

Code	Graphic	Narrative
AI-BII-CIV		Input is specific and comes from one source. There are two mechanical processes. Three users benefit from the output in non-specific ways.
AIV-BIII-CI		Input is unstructured and comes from several sources. There is one transformation process, also unstructured. One specific output results.

The second illustration is typical of committee deliberations where input is likely to come from any member in a non-specified way, is processed non-specifically by the committee as a whole, and exits in the more tangible form of minutes or resolutions.

The matrix supports 64 different configurations, of which very few have been analyzed and made amenable to measurement at present. Further work in this area may shed light on such fundamental processes as learning and decision-making.

4. CONCLUSION

My counterplan to Montagna's is to plot a course tangential to the status quo. I propose that responsible activism replace passivism, and concern for others the current concern for self. This is not a time to "steer a careful course," but rather for bold and imaginative leadership. Our success or failure will be measured by our ability to solve real problems effectively in consort with the highest standards of integrity.

I have touched briefly on some illustrative problem areas. Obviously, there are many others, including a thoroughly different audit focus, social measurement, and studies in ethics and professionalism. As these matters are surfacing, I decided to illuminate less obvious but highly meaningful needs in terms of the future progress of the profession.

We still have the chance to eject the effete intellectual concerns of the past two decades, which in sum have hindered progress, and grasp instead the truth that we are the servants of society, and that we can make a difference in the quality of life for those who come within our orbit of influence.

NOTES

1. Compare Montagna (1971: 488) and Buckley (1972: 42, 65–74). The notion of a profession of "allied information sciences" is also discussed in Sherif and Sherif (1969).

2. Dialectical analysis consists of a forum in which two fully-developed points of view—the plan and counterplan—are articulated and finally compromised. For a discussion of this technique, see van den Berghe (1963) and Mason (1969).

3. This line of analysis is an outgrowth of the definitive work in portfolio theory. See Markowitz (1959), Sharpe (1970), Hamada (1969), and Jensen (1972). Items are appearing in the popular literature; see *Business Week* (April 22, 1972: 72). Several major brokerage firms, including Merrill Lynch, and Oliphant & Co., now provide beta consulting services for their clients.

4. This led Joseph A. Sciarrino (1971: 51), as Technical Director of the Financial Executives Institute, to observe that "even those who are actively participating in the

controversy are hard pressed to explain the 'what' or even 'why' of the debate over accounting principles."

5. Computerized, operational and systems-based auditing are key examples.

6. David F. Linowes (1973: 47) comments on the absence of "ethics" in the traditional curriculum. Buckley (1972: 39–40) distinguishes between *efferent* and *afferent* ethics, and urges greater attention to the latter.

7. An articulate plea was made by Marvin L. Stone (1968) as President of the American Institute of Certified Public Accountants. Suggested topics include auditing, effective communication of data, and information and decision systems.

8. The ten fields in which the greatest expansion in employment is forecast between 1968 and 1980 are:

	1968 Actual	1980 Projected	Rate Per Annum
1. Systems analysts	150,000	425,000	9.1%
2. Programmers	175,000	400,000	7.1
3. Computer operators	175,000	400,000	7.1
4. Pilots and copilots	52,000	114,000	6.7
5. Dental hygienists	16,000	33,500	6.4
6. Computer servicemen	115,000	225,000	5.8
7. Medical laboratory technicians	100,000	190,000	5.5
8. Hospital attendants	800,000	1,500,000	5.4
9. Licensed practical nurses	320,000	600,000	5.4
10. Oceanographers	5,200	9,700	5.3

Source: U.S. Department of Labor, *The U.S. Economy in 1980,* Bulletin 1673, (Washington, D.C.: U.S. Government Printing Office, 1970).

9. Neural transmission rates are discussed by Mason Haire (1964: 375) and by Robert C. Ettinger (1964: 107). For limitations on information processing capacity in humans, see George Miller (1967). The information glut is discussed by James Miller (1963 and 1964). For the relationship between information overload and mental illness, see Association for Research in Nervous and Mental Disease (1964: 98–99), also Usdansky and Chapman (1960: 143–46), and Broadbent (1965: 460). For modes of organizational response to information overload, refer to Meier (1965: 233–273), and Churchill (1965). Finally, violence as an adaptive response is cited in Gilula and Daniels (1969: 404).

10. Processes are distinguished from systems in this line of inquiry. See Anthony (1965: 5) and Buckley and Lightner (1973: 4–26).

REFERENCES

Anthony, Robert N. (1965) *Planning and Control Systems: A Framework for Analysis.* Cambridge, Mass.: Harvard University Press.

Archibald, T. R. (1972) "Stock Market Reaction to Depreciation Switch-Back." *Accounting Review* (January): 22–30.

Ardrey, Robert (1966) *The Territorial Imperative.* New York: Dell.

Association for Research in Nervous and Mental Disease (1964) *Disorders of Communication*.

Ayres, Robert U. (1969) *Technological Forecasting and Long-Range Planning*. New York: McGraw-Hill.

Beaver, William H. (1968a) "Alternative Accounting Measures as Predictors of Failure." *Accounting Review* (January): 113–22.

Beaver, William H. (1968b) "The Information Content of Annual Earnings Announcements." *Empirical Research in Accounting: Selected Studies, 1968,* Supplement to *Journal of Accounting Research* 6: 67–92.

Beaver, William H. and Roland E. Dukes (in press) "Interperiod Tax Allocation and Depreciation Methods: Some Analytical and Empirical Results." *Accounting Review*.

Broadbent, D. E. (1965) "Information Processing in the Nervous System." *Science* (October 22).

Bruner, Jerome; Jacqueline J. Goodnow; and George Austin (1956) *A Study of Thinking*. New York: John Wiley & Sons.

Buckley, John W. (1972) *In Search of Identity: An Inquiry into Identity Issues in Accounting*. Palo Alto: California Certified Public Accountants Foundation for Education and Research.

Buckley, John W. (1973) "Accounting Priorities for the Seventies." Paper prepared for the Weldon Powell Memorial Lecture at the University of Illinois (April 26) UCLA: Accounting-Information Systems Research Program.

Buckley, John W. and Kevin M. Lightner (1973) *Accounting: An Information Systems Approach*. Belmont, California: Dickenson.

Capon, Frank S. (1972) "The Totality of Accounting for the Future." *Financial Executive* (July).

Churchill, Lindsey (1965) "Some Sociological Aspects of Message Load," pp. 274–84, in Fred Masserik and Philborn Ratoosh (eds.) *Mathematical Explorations in Behavioral Science*. Homewood, Illinois: Richard D. Irwin and Dorsey Press.

Dreyfuss, Herbert L. (1964) "Alchemy and Artificial Intelligence." Santa Monica: Rand Corporation, mimeo (August).

Ettinger, Robert C. W. (1964) *The Prospect of Immortality*. New York: Doubleday.

Etzioni, Amitai (1968) *The Active Society*. New York: Free Press.

Gilula, Marshall F. and David N. Daniels (1969) "Violence and Man's Struggle to Adapt." *Science* (April 25).

Gordon, W. J. J. (1961) *Synectics: The Development of Creative Capacity*. New York: Harper and Row.

Haire, Mason (1964) "Biological Models and Empirical Histories of the Growth of Organizations," in Amitai and Eva Etzioni (eds.) *Social Change*. New York: Basic Books.

Hamada, R. S. (1969) "Portfolio Analysis, Market Equilibrium, and Corporation Finance." *Journal of Finance* (March).

Hunter, W. S. and M. Sigler (1940) "The Span of Visual Discrimination as a Function of Time and Intensity of Stimulation." *Journal of Experimental Psychology* 26: 160–79.

Jensen, Michael C. (1972) *Studies in the Theory of Capital Markets*. New York: Praeger.

Kaplan, Robert and Richard Roll (1972) "Investor Evaluation of Accounting Information: Some Empirical Evidence." *Journal of Business* (April): 225–57.

Linowes, David F. (1973) "The Accountant's Enlarged Professional Responsibilities." *Journal of Accountancy* (February).

Markowitz, Harry (1959) *Portfolio Selection: Efficient Diversification of Investments.* New York: John Wiley & Sons.

Mason, Richard O. (1969) "A Dialectic Approach to Strategic Planning." *Management Science* 15 (April).

Meier, Richard L. (1965) *Developmental Planning.* New York: McGraw-Hill.

Miller, G. A. (1956) "The Magical Number Seven, Plus-or-Minus Two, or Some Limits on our Capacity for Processing Information." *Psychological Review* 63: 81–97.

Miller, George A. (1967) *The Psychology of Communications.* New York: Basic Books.

Miller, James G. (1963) "Coping with Administrators' Informational Overload." Ann Arbor, Michigan: Mental Health Research Institute, University of Michigan (October).

Miller, James G. (1964) "A Theoretical Review of Individual and Group Psychological Reactions to Stress," in George Grosser, Henry Weschler and Milton Greenblatt (eds.) *Impending Disaster.* Cambridge, Mass.: MIT Press.

Montagna, Paul (1971) "The Public Accounting Profession." *American Behavioral Scientist* 14 (March–April): 475–91.

Moore, Barrington, Jr. (1967) *Social Origins of Dictatorship and Democracy.* Boston: Beacon Press.

Parks, Thomas (1972) "Who's Crying Wolf?" UCLA: Accounting-Information Systems Research Program, mimeo (Spring).

Petter, Jean-Jacques (1962) *L'Écologie et L'Éthologie des Lémuriens Malgaches.* Paris: Mémoires du Museum National d'Histoire Naturelle, Tome XXVII Fascicule 1.

Sciarino, Joseph A. (1971) "The Thirty Years' War—An Accounting Principles Parody." *Financial Executive* (October).

Sharpe, William F. (1970) *Portfolio Theory and Capital Markets.* New York: McGraw-Hill.

Sherif, Carolyn W. and Muzafes (eds.) (1969) pp. 328–48 in *Interdisciplinary Relationships in the Social Sciences.* Chicago: Aldine.

Stern, Joel M. (1973) "Let's Abandon Earnings Per Share." *Canadian Chartered Accountant* (February): 69–70.

Stone, Marvin L. (1968) "Problems in Search of Solutions Through Research," pp. 59–66 in *Empirical Research in Accounting: Selected Studies, 1968.* Supplement to Vol. 6 of *Journal of Accounting Research.*

Usdansky, G. and L. J. Chapman (1960) "Schizophrenic-like Responses in Normal Subjects Under Time Pressure." *Journal of Abnormal and Social Psychology.* 60: 143–46.

van den Berghe, Pierre L. (1963) "Dialectic and Functionalism: Toward a Theoretical Synthesis." *American Sociological Review* 28: 695–705.

Wall Street Journal (1970) "Annual Reports: A Survey Shows What Financial Analysts Look For." (February 19).

Zipf, George K. (1949) *The Principle of Least Effort.* Reading, Mass.: Addison-Wesley.

Zwicky, Fritz (1962) *Morphology for Propulsive Power.* Pasadena: Society for Morphological Research.

Discussion

Sterling. Since no one else seems to have a question ready, let me present a prepared question to Paul. You make the case that uncertainty is the source of power for a profession and that all professions naturally gravitate into areas of uncertainty in order to maintain or increase their power. You state [Sec. 3] that the making of judgments ". . . is jealously guarded by those who have the responsibility and right to make them." You then go on to state that in order for a profession to maintain or obtain power it ". . . must be willing to engage in risk-taking behavior." [Sec. 6].

It has been my experience that accountants try to avoid risk-taking behavior. They do *not* jealously guard their right to make professional judgments. They do not expand into new areas of uncertainty. On the contrary, it seems to me that they often try to contract their area of uncertainty instead of expanding it. Instead of broadening the definition of accounting and thereby perhaps encroaching on another profession's territory they try to narrow it. I call it a "reverse jurisdictional dispute." For example, I have been arguing for years that we ought to adopt a market value system and abandon historical costs. Most of the opposition to this argument was that we are not valuers (i.e., that we are unwilling to expand our area of uncertainty and encroach on the appraiser's territory) and that values are too subjective (i.e., we are not willing to engage in the risk-taking behavior of determining values).

I have expressed similar views about more traditional topics as follows:

[The argument that the financial statements are the responsibility of the management instead of the auditor] in effect, permits management to make the significant decisions and reduces auditing to a concern with trifles. The most disturbing thing I found was that the partners were not resisting this erosion of their function. Instead they were embracing it and justifying their actions on the basis of the management's statement proposition. This attitude is limiting accounting's function instead of expanding it. I would like to see the trend reversed and the accountant take more and more responsibility for the determination of quantities and the selection of appropriate accounting methods. (*The Accountant's Magazine*, November, 1968: 594)

To let management or the taxing authority make the determinations is a good way to avoid responsibility. However, if we continue to define the accounting process so as to make it safe and so as to avoid responsibility, we may define it so narrowly that it withers and dies. (*Abacus*, September, 1969: 47)

Of course, accountants have expanded in the management services area and other places, but in the financial area I continue to observe "reverse jurisdictional disputes." My question is twofold: First, do you agree with my perceptions? Second, if the answer to the first is affirmative, then do you think that this behavior is desirable?

Montagna. I can't answer your first question because I am not familiar with the field of financial accounting, but if the attitude here is to close up rather than to expand, I think that is the wrong kind of attitude to take. I think that the more expansion the better, within limits.

I think that expansion can take place in terms of the development of objectives and concepts which will help to clarify the methodology of accounting and auditing and the theory of accounting and auditing. I am not sure exactly how this would be done. I am not that familiar with the field of accounting. I am only familiar with the ideas of how other professions work. The way that they work is to develop a very strong set of principles, or guidelines, or objectives, and then attempt to apply them. They may not even develop them, but at least they have the ideology which says that they are developed and this is strong enough to carry them through and to keep that profession strong. This gives them a strong mandate in terms of the licensing of that particular occupation.

Willingham. It seems to me that Buckley doesn't agree with Montagna on where we are on the continuum. Is that the basis of the disagreement?

Buckley. I may agree as to where we are. It is a question of where we should go. What I'm recommending basically is that we abandon the search for principles. I know of no other profession that preoccupies itself with building a glass house of theory. I don't see the physicians worrying about this, or the attorneys, or any other group. Montagna represents the sociologists. Perhaps we ought to worry about this for academic reasons, but it is clear that sociologists are not offering their services to the public for a fee. What might be an appropriate course of action for an academic profession may be quite inappropriate to an applied profession.

Montagna. With regard to the applied professions, it is not true that they are not concerned with a search for principles. For example, in the medical profession there are particular theoretical bases which the medical profession follows. These are general scientific principles and the application of the scientific method. In terms of methodology the scientific method is very important to medical practice, and if you were to look for the basis for medical practice, it is here that you would find it. Physicians, whether they be surgeons or pathologists or whatever, have a particularly strong basis in science which supports their work. I don't find this to be true in accounting—there is no strong basis here. Some people say that the basis is economics, but I don't see economic theory tied in to accounting in a very clear manner. It may be clear to you, but it is certainly not clear to me. I do have some academic training in economics, and I teach economics students courses in industrial sociology. Despite this, the message still doesn't come across. I talk to economists almost daily about sociology and economics, and sometimes about accounting, and I still don't find this firm grounding of accounting in economics. I think such a grounding would strengthen the profession of accounting. I am not sure that there are any real differences between principles and concepts and all of the other terms that have been given to this problem as it has been talked about over the past twenty years in accounting, but I think there is a necessity in accounting to develop a firm basis of the profession in terms of its objectives and concepts.

Jackson. Paul, in Section 2 you state that the power of a group is reduced when its source of uncertainty has been rationalized. Then, in order to replace that power, a group will seek a new source of uncertainty. Do you feel that in accounting this is now being done, or are you recommending that it be done in accounting?

Montagna. Eight years ago, when I had the opportunity to speak to partners, juniors, seniors, and managers of the big eight and five medium-sized firms throughout the country, I posed that question. I asked accountants whether or not they were expanding into new areas of uncertainty. Of course, I didn't ask it in those words, but that was the thrust of my questioning. The general opinion was that accountants are moving into new areas of uncertainty. For example, into management services, the area of social measurements, work in the actuarial field, the management audit, and operational auditing as it was being discussed several years ago. I think the profession is searching for these new areas. There may well be new areas in auditing too, although I don't think there has been the emphasis on developments in auditing that perhaps there should be.

Moonitz. I want to ask a question of John Buckley. This is very subtle, John, so follow me carefully. In your written remarks, when you were summarizing what Paul Montagna said, you say "Adoption of the scientific approach will increase the legitimacy of the profession in the public eye." In your oral remarks you added a critical comment saying, "just at the time that the public is turning away from science." Would you care to reconcile those two? In your mind, is "scientific approach" and "science" synonymous?

Buckley. I can readily distinguish between the scientific approach and science, but I am not sure that laymen can make that distinction.

Moonitz. Who cares? Who cares whether or not the layman can make that distinction?

Buckley. We should care, because if we build our edifice on a scientific solution to accounting problems, it may not lead to the expected good result envisioned by Paul Montagna.

Moonitz. That is not what Paul says. He says, "Let us use a scientific *approach*." That is not the same thing as a scientific solution. Are you advocating a non-scientific approach to the solution of whatever it is that you think we are trying to solve?

Buckley. No. In this connection I agree with Paul. To the extent that medicine and other professions use the scientific approach they are rationalizing their behavior. I would distinguish between that and creating principles. As you know, principles of medicine come from physics and chemistry which are *basic* disciplines. What they do is apply these principles in the context of medicine. In doing so, in order to convince others of the validity of their actions, they use a scientific approach. I don't think that they play it up to the extent that we do, for the very simple reason that there is public disenchantment with science and where it is heading.

Moonitz. I want to ask what you are advocating, not what the public may think about science or the scientific approach.

Buckley. I am advocating that we apply principles developed in the basic disciplines and that we do so in a scientific way.

Sterling. If I understand you correctly, you have changed. The last time we discussed this I thought you were advocating a moral or an ethical approach.

Buckley. Part of the basic disciplines are those of the humanities where ethics are extremely important.

Sterling. Yes, ethics are most important, but they are in the humanities, not in science. Most scientists and philosophers of science would say that ethical questions cannot be approached scientifically.

Buckley. I might just add, Maurice, that I am suggesting a *clinical* approach.

Moonitz. I approve of that. You use the analogy of the medical profession. One thing that they do in surgery is that every surgical operation is subject to a review by other surgeons. We have nothing like that in accounting. I would suggest that we adopt something like that in accounting. It would seem to me that this is scientific approach. Whether it is science or not doesn't bother me. The approach is one of subjecting your hypotheses or procedures to review by others who are competent to judge what it is that you have done. There is interchange among peers and continual testing of the procedures utilized.

Arnold. I have a question on this idea of uncertainty and certainty. If the profession is moving into uncertain areas because of a desire to continue the development of the profession, why is it, on the other hand, that we are becoming more certain in regard to the things that we have traditionally been doing? The kind of thing that I am thinking about are some of the APB Opinions that are becoming very specific in attempting to cover every situation that one can think of. For example, the Opinion on earnings per share. Why on the one hand is the profession expanding its area of uncertainty and, on the other hand, becoming much more certain, or at least more specific, in other areas?

Montagna. I think this is a natural process of the dialectic of the development of organizations and/or occupations. This expansion into areas of uncertainty, while at the same time increasing certainty in other areas, occurs naturally. The natural process is toward increasing certainty. This is the opposite of the second law of thermodynamics, which says that there is a natural tendency toward entropy. In contrast to the physical law, there seems to be a sociological law which says that in human organizations there is a tendency toward rationalizing human behavior and the structures created by human interaction. In these processes, there is a tendency for organizations to search for new areas of uncertainty. There are political and moral overtones which are going to change and influence these tendencies one way or another, but nevertheless, this is the basic process that occurs. I think you could look at almost any human organization and find these two tendencies—these two dialectical tendencies—operating. I would base this primarily on the work of John Dewey in his book *The Quest for Certainty*. Also, the work of social scientists in their broader analyses extending all the way back to the work of Karl Marx and Herbert Spencer. I think you will find these principles written implicitly in their works, even when they are not actually specified.

Defliese. I want to make certain that I have Paul's thesis clearly in mind. Is it your view that there is a causal relationship between the professions branching into other services and the tendency to become more specific in the more traditional areas?

Montagna. Yes, I see that as a causal relation.

CHAPTER 2

An Economic Analysis of Accounting Power

JOSEPH A. PICHLER *

1. INTRODUCTION

The accounting practitioner is enmeshed in a complex web of legal, economic, and professional relationships which both augment and constrain his power. He is at once spider and fly. Although this metamorphic quality is not unique to the accounting profession, few occupational species have codified and camouflaged the predator's role so completely. Few have worked so diligently to win the respect of their prey. These characteristics render the profession a worthy subject for probing and observation.

The introductory paragraph notwithstanding, this paper treats accounting power from an economic rather than an entomologic viewpoint. The second section discusses the general concept of power and uses a simple model to express the conditions that determine the strength of parties engaged in a social exchange. The third, and major, section considers the power of combined practitioners versus clients with respect to the supply and price of accounting services. The historical behavior of the AICPA is analyzed to test the hypothesis that the profession has engaged and continues to engage in activities that limit the supply and raise the price of accounting services. This proposition is tested against the alternative that the sole function of organized market activities

* B.B.A. 1961, Notre Dame; M.B.A. 1963 and Ph.D. 1966, University of Chicago. Professor and Acting Dean, School of Business, University of Kansas. Author (with J. W. McGuire), *Inequality: The Poor and the Rich in America* (1969). Contributor to business periodicals.

The author wishes to express sincere thanks to Professor Howard Stettler for his generous assistance in recommending source material and in discussing the nature of the public accounting profession. The viewpoint and interpretations are solely those of the author.

has been to protect potential clients and the public against unscrupulous practitioners. The fourth section analyzes the power of individual practitioners versus individual clients with respect to the attest function. It is argued that the practitioner's power is enhanced by the absence of standardized accounting principles, and that his economic self-interest would not be served by greater uniformity. The final section of the paper briefly considers the dilemma posed by the preceding sections and makes policy recommendations for its resolution.

2. SOCIAL POWER AND ITS DETERMINANTS

Power may be defined as "individual or collective ability to affect the thoughts, emotions, or actions of one or more other persons" (Pichler, 1973: 2). Unlike other definitions which have been posed, this formulation does not require that the power-wielder intend to affect behavior in a given way or that the affected party offer resistance. Rather, it simply states that power is exercised whenever the actions of one party in a given stimulus situation differ in accordance with the perceived presence or absence of the second party.

The myriad processes by which power may be exercised are divisible into non-interactive and interactive categories. Non-interactive processes involve one-way communications from the power figure; the affected party offers no reciprocal communication. Indeed, the communicator may be completely unaware of the recipient's existence. Such non-reciprocal channels include television and radio broadcasts, motion pictures, and printed material. The ability to send one-way communications is not sufficient to invest power in a party. The sender must also possess some real or fancied characteristic that has value for the affected party sufficient to induce a behavioral change. Some characteristics—such as beauty or fame—generate non-interactive power because others desire to be associated with those who possess them. Power generated by such a desire for association has been termed "referrent power" (French & Raven, 1959). In other cases, non-interactive power is based upon the affected party's belief that the communicator possesses special knowledge and competence in a given area which renders his information or advice worthy of consideration. The accounting practitioner offers an example of non-interactive power based upon presumed expertise. The rendering of an opinion offers public notice that the client's financial statements have been reviewed by a skilled professional who attests that they have been prepared in accordance with generally accepted accounting principles. The opinion is a non-interactive channel because it may be noted by thousands of potential investors who will never communicate with the CPA. The practitioner exercises expert power insofar as the presence of the opinion affects the credibility of the reports upon which at least some parties base their investment decisions.

Interactive power processes are characterized by reciprocal communication between two or more parties who enter a relationship in order to achieve need satisfaction. The term "social exchange" is used to denote such an interaction because all parties are expected to provide rewards as well as to receive them (Blau, 1964). Obviously, a party cannot reward others unless he controls some characteristic that has need satisfaction value. Such valued properties or "resources" include personal traits, physical objects, and access to social networks.[1] It is impossible to enumerate an exhaustive list of resources for any party because the designation of any characteristic as a resource—and its valuation—are made by potential exchange partners rather than by the resource owner or by an objective observer. This does not imply that the controller of any set of characteristics is ignorant of their value. Since others are in search of resources to satisfy their own needs, their valuation of some resource controlled by the first party will be quickly communicated to him in the form of a bid to engage in an exchange. The highest bid received is the correct valuation of any resource. If that bid is sufficient to induce the first party to allocate his own resources in the manner desired by the bidder, then an exchange will occur. In concluding the exchange, the first party's behavior has been affected in a manner desired by the bidder, i.e., the latter has exercised power. Thus, interactive power consists of the ability to induce others to enter into a social exchange of resources. Elsewhere, I have expressed these ideas in a slightly different manner:

> The sum of the resources commanded by a party may be thought of as a capital stock which can be invested or consumed to yield a rate of return. Investment alternatives consist of the various social exchanges which might be entered, and the returns to capital are the rewards obtained through these transactions. Each party attempts to satisfy his needs by inducing others to allocate their resources in a certain way. The inducement takes the form of a reciprocal allocative offer . . . . Interactive power is exercised whenever one party successfully induces another to allocate resources in a manner which rewards the first party. (Pichler, 1973:5)

It is important to recall that the term "resources" is broadly defined and not limited to properties that have monetary value. Thus, the analysis presented above can be generalized beyond financial exchanges. The selection of friends, jilting of suitors, and cultivation of superiors all involve implicit resource valuations, bids, and attempts to exercise power.

Resource control is not a sufficient condition for the existence of interactive power. One party's ability to affect the behavior of another also depends upon the rewards which are available to the second party through alternative exchanges with other resource owners. Thus, power over an exchange partner is constrained by the allocative offers which other resource owners make to that partner. The relationship of power to resource values and alternative offers may be presented in a formula that I have adapted from Chamberlain's collective bargaining model (Chamberlain, 1958: 97–108; Pichler, 1973: 4–9). The power of Party X over Party Y may be expressed as:

$$P_{X/Y} = \frac{\text{Y's Net Cost of Disagreement with X}}{\text{Y's Cost of Agreement with X}} \tag{1}$$

The formula states that X's power over Y increases as Y finds it more costly to disagree with X's terms or as Y finds it less costly to agree with X's terms. But how are these costs to be calculated? Assume that X approaches Y with an offer to engage in a business or social relationship which, by definition, involves the exchange of some type of resources. If Y refuses to enter the relationship, what does he lose? Obviously, Y loses the resources that X would have allocated for his satisfaction. But the refusal to enter an exchange with X leaves Y free to conclude a transaction with alternative partners A,B,C, etc. Thus, Y's *net* cost of disagreement equals the difference between the satisfaction value of X's offer and that available from the most satisfying alternative exchange. On the other hand, if X's offer is accepted, then Y is unable to enter into one of the competing exchanges with A,B,C, etc. The resources that Y could have obtained from the most satisfying of these alternative transactions equals the cost of agreement. Formula (1) may be revised to specify these cost calculations explicitly:

$$P_{X/Y} = \frac{(\text{X's Offer}) - (\text{The Best Alternative Offer Available to Y})}{\text{The Best Alternative Offer Available to Y}} \tag{2}$$

An example may help to clarify the formula's meaning. Assume that Y is a CPA and that Clients X and Z both request that their financial statements be audited on a given day. Client X offers to pay $2 for the service; Client Z offers to pay $1. If we can make the simplifying assumptions that Practitioner Y has no alternative engagements on that date, that Y prefers to spend April 1 auditing books rather than pursuing leisure activities, and that these competing offers are identical in all respects other than the fees to be paid, then Y will accept the engagement with X and forego the exchange with Z.[2] Client X exercises power over Practitioner Y by inducing Y to allocate auditing resources for X's benefit on the specified date. Client Z possesses no power over

Y because he is unable to affect Y's behavior. In terms of Formula (2):

$$P_{X/Y} = \frac{\$2 - \$1}{\$1} = 1; P_{Z/Y} = \frac{\$1 - \$2}{\$2} = -1/2$$

Client X's power over Y is indicated by the positive value of $P_{X/Y}$; the absence of Z's power is indicated by the negative value of $P_{Z/Y}$. The values of $P_{X/Y}$ may range from minus one (indicating that X possesses no resources valued by Y) to plus infinity (indicating that X is the only exchange partner available to Y). A value of zero indicates that the resources offered by X have satisfaction value equal to the resources available to X from the best alternative exchange or from consumption. Party X will be indifferent between such "multiple maximum" offers and will make a random choice.

Clearly, any party's power is limited by the alternatives that are available to the exchange partner. If X and Y individually control resources that are equally satisfying to Z, and if they independently offer Z identical terms of trade, then $P_{X/Z}$ and $P_{Y/Z}$ both equal zero and neither X nor Y can exercise power over Z. Thus the existence of even one equal alternative is sufficient to remove power and prevent "coercion." This has long been recognized as a primary justification for the preservation of competition in economic exchange (Friedman, 1962: 15).

Readers who are acquainted with micro-economics recognize that Net Cost of Disagreement and Cost of Agreement are simply variants of the opportunity cost concept. Others may have noted that the Cost of Agreement is the appropriate market valuation of the resource in question and that Formula (2) is actually a rate of return calculation that measures the net return Party Y receives from investing a resource in an exchange with Party X rather than with the best alternative. As Y's rate of return from the X-Y transaction increases, Y becomes more willing to allocate resources in the manner desired by X. Thus it is not at all paradoxical that the party earning the higher potential return is also the less powerful exchange participant.[3]

The model's value lies in its parsimonious expression of the relationship among factors that determine interactive power. It indicates that a party may increase power by increasing the perceived value of his offer as compared with the partner's best alternative or by reducing the partner's alternatives. Similarly, a party may limit a partner's power by expanding his own options. The following paragraphs briefly discuss common strategies for achieving these alterations in a power relationship.

Party X may increase the perceived value of his bid by offering

Party Y a greater quantity or quality of resources. Alternatively, X may provide Y with additional information, e.g., through advertising, that causes Y to raise the valuation of X's resources or to devalue the best offer made by alternative partners A, B, and C. Either course of action requires an increase in X's resource expenditure. Assuming economic rationality, the choice between investing additional resources in the exchange itself or in informational activities will be made in favor of the option which offers X the highest marginal return.

The reduction of an exchange partner's alternatives generally involves agreement among competing owners to withhold a given resource or to make it available only on jointly specified terms. Often, such an agreement may be augmented by protective legislation. The effect is to confront potential partners with an invariant exchange rate (so that the choice among alternative transactions will be random) or to force them to deal with one specific resource owner. In financial relationships, such collusive arrangements often take the form of price-fixing agreements, market division, "no-raid" pacts for employee recruitment, and mutual prohibition of bidding. Cartel formation is itself a social exchange that requires some degree of resource utilization, and a party would enter such an agreement only if the expected return exceeds the cost of maintaining the coalition.

If there is any dispersion in the terms of trade available in the market, a party's power position may be improved by a search for alternative owners of the desired resource. The investment of time and other resources in such activities produces a positive return if it results in the identification of alternative partners willing to make an exchange on terms more favorable than those known before the search. As the quantity of search increases, the dispersion of offers and the potential return from the search decreases. The activity becomes unprofitable when all dispersion has been removed or the cost of an additional search exceeds its expected return (Stigler, 1961). Search activity as a means for increasing power differs significantly from the others discussed above in that it operates on the power equation which is calculated *against the party* in question rather than upon the equation which the party calculates *against a partner*. Just as Party X calculates $P_{X/Y}$, so Party Y calculates $P_{Y/X}$. The calculation of $P_{X/Y}$ and $P_{Y/X}$ are independent of each other and the total power relationship in exchange is expressed as their algebraic difference. The discussion of such "differential power" is beyond the scope of this paper.[4]

The following section examines the accounting profession in terms of the exchange power processes. Particular attention is devoted to activities that reduce the client's alternative sources of supply and increase his cost of search.

3.   POWER OF PRACTITIONERS AS A COMBINATION

Public accounting constitutes an industry whose product line includes bookkeeping activities, data processing, management consulting, tax services, and the rendering of opinions on financial statements. Individuals, enterprises, and government agencies exchange monetary rewards in return for the expertise, time, and other resources expended by the practitioner in providing those services. The attest function is of particular importance because it notifies the investing public that a firm's statements present fairly its financial position and operating results in conformity with generally accepted accounting principles. This independent stamp of approval provides some assurance to the investor that the numbers contained in the statements have not been invented by management. Thus, the attest reduces one source of investment uncertainty. If the underlying accounting principles parallel economic theory, then the allocation of capital is improved because investors are enabled to choose among firms in terms of resource rates of return.

The desire for objective financial information has resulted in federal, state, and professional regulations regarding disclosure statements and those who render opinions on them. Practitioners took the first step with the founding of the first national society of accountants in 1887 to meet financiers' needs for "a well organized body of professional and public accountants, whose ability, character, and strict business conduct could be relied upon." (Quoted in Carey, 1969: 39) This tradition of technical and ethical self-regulation has been maintained by the AICPA, whose membership includes over two-thirds of all practitioners. The New York State CPA law of 1896 provided the first statutory recognition that accountants are clothed with a public interest. Today, all states have laws governing the issuance of CPA certificates. Federal controls were added in 1933 with the Securities Act, which required that a balance sheet and profit-and-loss statement "certified by an independent public or certified accountant," be filed with a firm's registration statement (Securities Act, 1933: Section 7). The first formal regulation adopted under this act went directly to the matter of objectivity by defining "independent" in terms that imposed an absolute arm's-length relationship between practitioner and client. The following year, the Securities Exchange Act created the SEC and charged it with the administration of both acts. Included in this charge was the power to specify uniform accounting procedures—a power which the Commission declined to exercise in favor of allowing the profession to propose appropriate accounting principles (Carey, 1969: 194–95).

The statutes regulating public accounting and the AICPA's code of professional conduct are of particular interest to the analysis of accounting power. As in the case of other regulated occupations, the statutory restrictions placed upon CPAs have been formally justified on a public interest basis (AICPA Legislative Policy, Item 1). It is argued that public accountancy belongs to that class of occupations whose performance substantially affects such a large group outside the immediate client relationship and whose technical requirements are so far beyond the judgment of laymen, that the transmission of adequate pre-engagement information regarding practitioner qualifications cannot be entrusted to the market system (AICPA, 1972). In terms of the first portion of this paper, the argument states that the resources possessed by certain types of exchange partners are subject to such serious misevaluation that some form of governmental regulation is necessary to reduce the risk, i.e., the dispersion of returns, available from potential exchange partners.

Friedman has analyzed the economic implications of three regulatory policies for filling this void—registration, certification, and licensure (Friedman, 1962: 157–60). The first two place no limits upon entry into the occupation. Registration requires only that those who practice an occupation list their names publicly. Certification, on the other hand, provides notice that a practitioner possesses some specified level of skill; all others remain free to practice the occupation as long as they do not claim to be certified. Certification is itself a resource that increases the practitioner's non-interactive (expert) and exchange power because it communicates expertise at no cost to prospective clients. Price/quality competition strictly delimits such power because clients remain free to purchase services from the uncertified sector; and at some price differential, they surely will do so (Friedman, 1962: 149). The third form of restriction, licensure, goes beyond certification and forbids the uncertified to engage in at least some portions of the occupation. Whereas certification protects consumers by providing them the information necessary to choose a desired level of practitioner competence, licensure protects by stamping out those who are judged to be incompetent. By imposing barriers to entry, licensure limits the client's exchange alternatives and increases the value of the resources possessed by licensees. The restriction of competition grants incumbents a significantly greater amount of exchange power than does certification and this power may be used for economic advantage as well as for public protection. This surely accounts for the extension of licensure to many occupations which have little impact upon the public interest:

One may not be surprised to learn that pharmacists, accountants, and dentists have been reached by state laws, as have sanitarians and psychologists, assayers, and architects, veterinarians, and librarians. But with what joy of discovery does one learn about the licensing of threshing machine operators and dealers in scrap tobacco? What of egg graders and guide-dog trainers, pest controllers and yacht salesmen, tree surgeons and well diggers, tile layers and potato growers? And what of the hypertrichologists who are licensed in Connecticut, where they remove excessive and unsightly hairs with the solemnity appropriate to their high-sounding title? (Gellhorn, 1956: 106)

Although we may share Gellhorn's lack of surprise that accounting is included among regulated occupations, it is instructive to examine the nature of the regulations, their relationship to the Institute, and the latter's Code of Ethics in order to determine whether the public or the profession has achieved the greater protection.

Nature of State Regulations

Economists have long observed that occupational regulations frequently exhibit four common characteristics. First, pressure for their adoption is usually generated by practitioners rather than by clients. Second, they entrust to practitioners the establishment and monitoring of standards for receipt of the certificate or license. Third, the standards tend to rise over time but with specific exemptions for incumbents in the trade. Fourth, regulations that require certification generally evolve into licensure proper.[5] When all of these characteristics are present, the occupational regulation is likely to be more restrictive than is necessary for the public's well-being. If there is a genuine need to protect the public, why aren't clients the primary advocates for restrictions? Shouldn't public representatives determine the minimum level of competence or maximum level of incompetence that can be safely permitted? If increased standards are truly necessary, isn't it dangerous for incumbents to continue practice without meeting the new requirements? Doesn't certification generally provide consumers with all of the information necessary to make informed price/quality decisions?

The regulatory history of public accounting exhibits all four of the characteristics discussed above. The New York law of 1896 was passed after a committee composed of various public and private accounting associations ". . . rallied all interested accountants in support of identical permissive bills in the Senate and Assembly." (Carey 1969: 44) Representatives of the American Association of Public Accountants testified in favor of this certification bill, which restricted the use of the CPA title to those who had passed an examination. A "grandfather clause" exempted incumbents from the examination requirement.[6] The establishment of CPA legislation within every state soon became a major goal of the Association:

> As a sponsor of the first CPA law, the Association was naturally dedicated
> to the enactment of similar legislation throughout the nation. . . . Inevitably
> it was the Association's official policy to encourage and assist state societies
> in bringing about enactment of sound CPA legislation. To this end, its
> committee on state legislation drafted a model CPA law. (Carey, 1969: 102)

The drive for enactment of state legislation was successful. When the
Association was reorganized as the Institute in 1916, legislation had
been adopted by thirty-nine states. Within the next five years all of
the forty-eight states had passed CPA statutes.[7]

There is considerable variation among these laws, but most stipulate
that candidates must meet some combination of age, education, experience, citizenship, and residence requirements (U.S. Army Audit Agency,
1972). However, there is one dimension on which the laws are consistent:
since 1952, all have required CPA candidates to pass a uniform
examination that is constructed, administered, and graded by the
AICPA.[8] Thus, even though the certificate is awarded by the individual
state boards, the minimum standard for entry is established and
monitored by a professional organization largely composed of practitioners. The Institute played an active role in encouraging states to
adopt this uniform standard (Carey, 1969: 272). It was said to be desirable
in view of the growth of interstate practice and the desire of candidates
to qualify simultaneously for certification and for membership in the
AICPA.

The grant of standard-setting authority to practitioners raises public
interest considerations because it may be used to restrict entry and
reduce competition in addition to weeding out incompetents. In the
case of accountancy, this danger is enhanced by the fact that most
states have adopted the Institute's definition of a passing score (AICPA
1961: 11). Although it is difficult to determine the precise extent to
which the uniform examination has limited the number of CPAs, there
is evidence to suggest that its effect has been substantial. In 1945,
Friedman (Friedman and Kuznets, 1945: 41) found that the failure
rate on the CPA examination greatly exceeded that for examinations
to certify doctors, lawyers, and dentists. At the present time, the Institute
does not publish national data on the fraction of applicants who pass
the examination nor will it release such information without the
permission of each state board of accountancy.[9] However, Institute
sources have stated that about 10 percent of those who take the four
parts of the examination pass them all on the first attempt and that
each individual part of the examination is passed by only 30 percent
of those who take it.[10] The apparent constancy of the latter figure
across all portions of the examination suggests that the passing criterion
is based on a "curve" rather than on some absolute standard. This

impression is strengthened by description of the grading system (AICPA, 1961: 24). If, indeed, the standard is a relative one then there is an implicit quota on admission. Moreover, in view of the dramatic increase in the educational background of applicants over the past twenty years, the passage of a constant fraction means that the absolute standard of acceptable performance has increased. The fraction of candidates with at least an undergraduate degree was 47 percent in 1946, 77 percent in 1960, and 95 percent by 1970; the fraction with graduate degrees rose from 4 percent to 10 percent during the same period (Sanders, 1972: 86).

Economic theory predicts that restrictions on entry will raise practitioner salaries above competitive levels, prevent the market from clearing, and create a lengthy queue of unsuccessful candidates. If admission standards rise, the queue will also increase (Rottenburg, 1962: 7–10). Table 1 provides evidence of significant and increasing restriction in

TABLE 1
NUMBER OF CPAS AND EXAMINEES

	1952	1962	1972
Number of CPAs	40,000	75,000	115,000–136,000
Number of Examinees	13,905	26,340	57,928
Number of Examinees per CPA	.35	.35	.50–.43

Source Number of CPAs from Carey (1969: 1) except the 136,000 estimate, which was provided in a letter from Gertrude Darby, AICPA, March 22, 1973.

Number of Examinees provided in letter from Gertrude Darby, AICPA, March 15, 1973.

the accounting profession. When the Uniform Examination was adopted in 1952, there was one candidate for every three practitioners. That is, the length of the waiting line equalled 35 percent of the list of incumbent CPAs. This situation had not changed through 1962. However, by 1972 the queue had grown to 43–50 percent of the list of incumbents. There was one examinee for every 2 to 2.5 practitioners. If our earlier speculation that the pass rate on the examination has remained relatively constant, say at 30 percent, then the absolute number of unsuccessful candidates has grown from 9,700 in 1952 to 16,500 in 1962 to about 40,000 in 1972. The admission of even 10 percent of these unsuccessful candidates would surely have a marked impact upon the price of practitioner services. It may well be true that any welfare loss from admitting these (presumably) less qualified individuals into the profession would be more than offset by the resulting service price decline. Indeed, the marked rise in the average candidate's educational achievement since 1952 suggests that the quality loss from a reduced passing score would be minimal.

Of course, these observations are suggestive rather than definitive evidence that the examination has been used as a device to restrict entry to an unreasonable degree. A complete analysis would require data regarding the increase in demand for professional services in the past 20 years (the increase in gross fees for service would be a suitable proxy), full information regarding the examination failure rate, comparisons of the increases in CPA income relative to that of unlicensed professional groups, and an external validation of the Uniform Examination. Unfortunately, such data are not available.

There is stronger evidence to support the profession's conformity with the general proposition that minimum admission standards will rise and that incumbents will be exempted from the new requirements. Before 1936, no state required that CPA candidates be educated beyond high school (Carey, 1969: 269). In that year, the Institute's committee on education recommended that four years of college be made the minimum requirement for practitioners and that states be encouraged to embody this higher educational standard in their CPA laws. Success in achieving the latter goal was apparently limited. In 1949, the chairman of the Institute's Board of Examiners expressed concern over the high failure rate on the Uniform Examination and again called for improved educational preparation as a means of rectifying this situation. The Institute created an independent Commission on Standards of Education and Experience for Certified Public Accountants, whose membership consisted of practitioners, business professors, and an educational administrator. This committee stated its findings in 1956. The institute responded with the Bailey Report, which called for the bachelor's degree as the immediate minimum certification requirement and recommended that this be raised as quickly as possible to one year of post-graduate study in business and accountancy. This proposed increase in educational standards was made even more specific in 1969 when the Council accepted the Beamer Committee's recommendations that states adopt the five-year requirement by 1975 and waive the experience requirement for those who met this standard (Carey, 1970: 283–84) The Committee also recommended that a transitional standard of an undergraduate degree plus one year's experience be set until 1975.

The drive for increased educational standards has had a notable effect in the past ten years. Table 2 presents the minimum educational requirements for the CPA in 1961, 1972, and 1976. The 1972 data actually understate current requirements because jurisdictions are in-

TABLE 2
MINIMUM FORMAL EDUCATIONAL REQUIREMENTS FOR 53 JURISDICTIONS

	1961	1972	1976
High School only	38	26	22
College—some	1		
2 years	7	7	4
4 years	7	20	27
Graduate Study	0	0	0
	53	53	53

Source: 1961 data from Heimbucher (1961).
1972 and 1976 data from U.S. Army Audit Agency (1972).

cluded in the "two or four years of college" categories only if the requirements are not waivable by virtue of "equivalent education" or experience. Five jurisdictions listed as "high school only" require the equivalent of a baccalaureate degree; three others require the equivalent of two years of college; and four others require formal accounting education beyond high school. The remaining fourteen generally allow a certain number of years of experience—fifteen in the case of New York—to substitute for college work. The 1976 data are constructed in the same way except that they show the future impact of legislation that has *already* been passed but will not become effective until a specified future date. Four states will move from "high school only" to "four years college" and three will increase their college requirement from two years to four years before the close of 1976. Although jurisdictions generally reduce the pre-certification experience requirement for candidates who have gone beyond high school, forty-eight jurisdictions require at least one year of experience even for college graduates. This experience requirement adds an independent hurdle to certification since it has been clearly shown that no relationship exists between success on the Uniform Examination and experience (Sanders, 1972: 87–88).

Despite the steady increase in educational requirements since 1961, present standards are probably less restrictive than the CPA examination itself. As noted earlier, the population of examinees has become increasingly confined to college graduates, a fact which suggests that this preparation is needed to pass the examination. Moreover the increase in statutory requirements continues to lag behind the educational level needed to pass the examination. In 1969 the Institute's Board of Examiners adopted a proposal to raise the examination standards by 1975 to a level of competence which requires at least five years of college study (Hendrickson, 1971: 61–62).

Two significant points should be noted regarding this historical rise in educational standards. First, it was triggered by the AICPA and by others with a vested interest in raising educational requirements, e.g., business school professors, rather than by clients, the public, or the SEC. How did these parties determine that the increase was necessary for the public good? Were their decisions based upon solid evidence of shoddy work from practitioners educated below the graduate level? What consideration was given to the service-price consequences of these additional restrictions? Surely the high failure rate on the Union Examination is not compelling proof that a higher standard was necessary, for—even if one were to assume some relationship between performance on the examination and practitioner skill—those who fail never have the opportunity to mulct the public. We may all agree that more quality is better than less quality, but education is subject to diminishing returns and at some point the costs of increased standards exceed the benefits.[11] These costs are borne directly by clients who must pay higher fees because there are fewer individuals who are able to enter public accounting. Thus, clients and the public body charged to protect the potential client or investor (the SEC) should make a substantial contribution to the process by which minimum standards are determined.

The second point to notice is that none of these recommendations or their implementation in state laws required incumbent practitioners to meet the new standards. Rather, those already certified were implicitly blanketed in by grandfather clauses. If one were to grant the argument that clients are adequately protected only if practitioners possess undergraduate or (after 1975) advanced degrees, then, in the interests of public safety, the certificate should be retrieved from those who continue to practice without having met this standard. Potential conflicts between such a policy and the Fourteenth Amendment could certainly be met if the courts were provided strong evidence of public need and if incumbents were given a reasonable period to meet the new standards. Given the rapid rise in standards combined with widespread use of the grandfather clause, suspicion is cast upon the argument that increased educational and examination standards were necessary for the public interest. Indeed, the same set of events is a common indicator of practitioner self-interest:

> Since only incumbents earn quasi-rents from checking entry by imposing new costs of entry, it is to be expected that there will be successive demands for making entry costs higher. Each generation of entrants will seek to make entry more costly for succeeding generations. That process was noted above: legislatures are not only continuously confronted by requests of unlicensed trades that they be licensed but also by requests of licensed tradesmen that qualifying standards for their trades be raised. Usually, legislatures are offered

a package which includes blanket exemption from the new costs of those already practicing the trade. (Rottenberg, 1962: 11)

Significant quasi-rents cannot be earned unless practitioners are able to restrict entry via laws that require licensure as well as certification. Practitioner control over requirements, continual increases in standards, and the existence of grandfather clauses would bestow only minimal economic power were they not accompanied by licensure. If everyone is free to practice a trade, then the certified practitioner's power is sharply limited by competition from the uncertified sector. Thus, in order to validate the hypothesis that the Institute and state societies have sought legislation to increase practitioners' economic power and protect their interests, it must be shown that these organizations have pursued licensure statutes.

The New York statute of 1896 and the thirty-eight other CPA laws passed before 1917 were "permissive" rather than "restrictive". That is, they set certification standards and limited the use of the CPA title to those who had met those requirements. Other persons remained free to perform every accounting function as long as they did not hold themselves out to be certified. As in the case of other licensed occupations, pressure for the passage of "restrictive," i.e., licensure, laws soon developed. Significantly, this pressure arose from the ranks of practitioners rather than from fleeced clients:

> However, not many years went by before some of those who had obtained the CPA certificate felt the need for protection against the competition of unregulated practitioners who assumed the free title of "public accountant"— not readily distinguishable from "certified public accountant."
>
> In 1917, Oklahoma enacted a restrictive law, which seven years later was held unconstitutional on the ground that it deprived non-certified accountants of their right to earn a living, that it infringed the right of private contract, and that it tended to create a monopoly for CPAs which was not justified by the public welfare. (Carey, 1970: 322)

The Oklahoma law ran afoul of the Fourteenth Amendment because it included a very broad definition of accounting, forbade its practice by non-CPAs, and made no provision for continued practice by uncertified incumbents. These defects were avoided in later laws that narrowed the scope of restricted acts and included grandfather clauses. Apparently, state societies were a consistent force behind such legislation (Carey, 1970: 323).[12] By 1934, ten states had adopted restrictive legislation and the Institute decided to take a position on such laws. Surprisingly, it departed from most state societies and resolved that these statutes were inimical to the profession. Had this position been reached on the grounds that licensure restricted competition or entry, and had this position been maintained, the Institute would stand as a major exception among professional organizations. Unfortunately, the objections appear to have been based on grounds that were more pragmatic than philosophical: such laws were found to be of doubtful constitutionality, to impede interstate commerce, and to "dilute the prestige of the CPA certificate" by granting licenses to uncertified incumbents (Carey, 1970: 323). Within the next twenty-two years, the Institute's position on restrictive legislation swung from opposition to neutrality (1940), to advocacy (1945), back to neutrality (1947), and—inexorably—settled on advocacy (1956). [13] The Institute's current position is clear-cut: "Ultimately all professional accounting services should be performed by certified public accountants who have satisfied education and experience requirements and have demonstrated competence by passage of an examination." (AICPA, 1971: Item 2) To achieve this goal, the Institute favors a law which (among other things):

1. Grants licenses only to those who acquire the CPA certificate and to persons already in practice as public accountants. Continuing licensure of non-CPA's is to be forbidden "since the public would be confused by the perpetual licensing of two classes of professional accountants under similar titles but with different standards."
2. Forbids an unlicensed individual from expressing an opinion on financial statements or other information if that opinion includes any wording indicating that he has expert knowledge of accounting or auditing.
3. Permits such unlicensed individuals to perform other accounting work.

In 1945, Friedman noted that the failure rate on the CPA examination was well above that on examinations for other professions, but found little cause for concern because uncertified accountants were still free to practice. However, his analysis sounded a prophetic note:

Interestingly enough, while there seems to be no deliberate restriction of entry, the institutional arrangements governing the certification of public accountants are so developing as to be peculiarly well adapted to restriction. (Friedman and Kuznets, 1945: 41)

Friedman was particularly concerned that about one-half of the accountants came from states that used the Uniform Examination. In the twenty-seven years since his warning, the Uniform Examination has been universally adopted and the number of jurisdictions that forbid the uncertified to practice has grown from seventeen to forty-three. In these jurisdictions failure of the examination now precludes performance of the attest function. [14] These combined developments have markedly increased the AICPA's power to control the supply of practitioners and affect the price of services. In ostensibly seeking to protect the public interest, the Institute and the state societies have succeeded in obtaining state laws that are more restrictive than the federal act, which stipulates that the attest be performed by an independent practitioner but does not require licensure or even certification. This grant of restrictive power to the profession is particularly questionable in view of its stated ethical code, a subject to which we now turn.

The Professional Code of Ethics

The preceding section dealt with the power of CPAs in terms of legislation that has increased the profession's control over entry and reduced the alternative sources of accounting services available to clients. The present section discusses the implications of the profession's ethical code for this power relationship.

The development and enforcement of a code of behavior is a hallmark of professions (Blau and Scott, 1962: 62–63). Accountancy is no exception. Within six years of its foundation, the American Association had passed its first resolution governing the professional conduct of its members (Carey, 1969: 46–47). By 1907, five behavioral rules had been adopted and the Association combined these for the first time into a "Professional Ethics" section of its bylaws. The AICPA has continued to set standards of membership behavior through its Code of Professional Ethics, which "emphasizes the profession's responsibility to the public." The contents of this Code are relevant to a discussion of power because 65 percent of all CPAs—and a higher fraction of *practicing* CPAs—are Institute members. Moreover, some portions of the Code have been adapted for inclusion in various state CPA laws. Thus, the Code exerts an influence upon a substantial portion of all practitioner/client relationships. Of particular interest for the present discussion are the past and present Institute strictures regarding employee recruitment, advertising, and competitive bidding.

Raiding. In 1919, the Council adopted a rule forbidding members to offer jobs to employees of other Institute members without first informing those members (Carey, 1969: 234). Rule 402 of the present Code has a similar proviso, expanded to forbid such an offer on behalf of a client. Employees remain free to apply for work at other member firms and to respond to public advertisements of such competing firms. Member firms may use classified employment ads, but may not have the firm's name set in type that distinguishes it from the body of the advertisement, or use "display" advertisements that contain the firm's name.

It is difficult to argue that such labor market constraints serve the public interest. Indeed, these limitations on the flow of information damage the public welfare because they reduce the market's ability to allocate human resources in the most efficient manner. From the client's point of view this decline in market efficiency means that the quantity of accounting services will fall and/or the price will rise. From the employee's point of view, it reduces knowledge of alternative employment relationships and increases the firm's exchange power in the employment transaction. This result was clearly foreseen when the provision was adopted. Carey comments that the 1919 rule passed the Institute's Council with "little discussion" and adds:

> Since all members of Council were employers it may be assumed that they welcomed this much protection against raids on their staffs.
> The rule has been criticized by staff assistants, however, as an obstacle to their efforts to secure better positions. (Carey, 1969: 234)

Advertising. The matter of practitioner advertisements for clients entailed a substantially greater amount of debate within the profession. The Association's first resolution on professional conduct forbade members to advertise "in any shape or manner" other than by the insertion in regular journals and newspapers of a card indicating the member's name, profession, address, etc. (Carey, 1969: 47). This prohibition was apparently not enforced, and by 1911 "undignified and unprofessional advertising and soliciting" was the ethical subject of most concern to the profession (Carey, 1969: 33). Widespread use of advertising created strong opposition to a formal rule against public solicitation, and the matter was still being debated when the Institute was formed. In 1922, the Council adopted a rule forbidding all advertising other than by a card of specified size containing the same information as specified in the Association's 1897 ruling. This rule has been embellished during the past fifty years: regular publication of cards was forbidden in 1945; "canned" newsletters to clients and acquaintances on tax advice were stricken in 1953; and public notification of a practitioner's change of address was prohibited in 1958 (Carey, 1970: 460–61). These and other strictures on advertising were codified in the 1962 Opinion No. 11.

Rule 502, the current version of the Code of Professional Ethics, contains a simple statement on solicitation and advertising: "A member shall not seek to obtain clients by solicitation. Advertising is a form of solicitation and is prohibited." (AICPA, 1972: 24–25, references omitted). However, a review of its attached Interpretations shows that the operational restrictions are a baroque delight: firm names may be shown in office building lobby directories if they are of modest size, in good taste, and do not indicate a specialty; telephone listings may not appear in more than one place in the classified section; educational seminars may not be sponsored if they will be attended by non-clients; press releases regarding firm mergers or address changes are forbidden. Many states have written such general prohibitions against advertising into their legal code binding *all* practitioners even if they are not Institute members (Heimbucher, 1961: 44).

Carey's account suggests that the campaign against advertising was motivated in part by the desire to place accountancy on an ethical par with doctors, lawyers, and other professions (Carey, 1969: 231–35; 1970: Chapter 17). References to some advertisements as "crude and vulgar" and "repugnant to any sense of good taste and notions of decency" indicate that practitioners were sincerely offended by the content of published advertisements. Nevertheless, it is highly debatable whether professional self-regulation should wander into the area of esthetics when the proscriptions are likely to exert a restrictive economic impact. The analysis is identical to that already discussed regarding the "no raid" rule. Limitations on advertising reduce knowledge in the market place, reduce client awareness of alternative exchange partners, and increase the economic power of established practitioners over their clients. It is particularly difficult under such circumstances for clients to learn of new practitioners or of those who have expertise in a specialty within the profession. This tends to reduce competition, misallocate resources, and produce higher prices than would otherwise prevail for accounting services.[15]

Bidding. The practice of competitive bidding was viewed negatively from the earliest days of the profession. As in the case of advertising, the submission of a bid was seen as unprofessional and degrading:

> There are some things that cannot properly, or profitably, be placed upon the competitive basis . . . . To ask a competitive bid from a professional man is asking him to admit that his services are worth less than the fee ordinarily commanded by his profession. (Letter from editor of *Journal of Accountancy;* quoted without reference in Carey, 1969: 88)

In addition to sullying the professional image of accountancy, it was argued that bidding operated to the detriment of the client by encouraging practitioners to cut corners and by driving business into the hands of incompetents. This social version of Gresham's law, a favorite in the repertoire of every profession, discredits both client and practioner. It suggests that the former is incapable of making rational price/quality trade-offs and that the latter must be paid to apply professional standards of performance or honesty. Such arguments against bidding acquired considerable force during the Great Depression when ". . . the economic pinch made bidding more and more prevalent." In 1934, the Council adopted a resolution urging members to end the practice because of its detrimental effect upon *clients* and the *public* (Carey, 1969: 244). The timing of this resolution conforms to Friedman's observation that restrictive practices tend to be rationalized ". . . only at times like the Great Depression when there is much unemployment and relatively low incomes." (Friedman, 1962: 153) The policy was given greater force in 1951 when the Institute adopted a formal rule against competitive bidding for public accounting services.

The restrictive economic impact of this rule is obvious and requires no analysis. Even before its adoption, Institute lawyers were aware that it constituted a potential violation of the anti-trust laws. This danger became more apparent when the regulation was challenged by the California attorney general as a violation of that state's monopoly statutes. By 1966 the Council had become convinced that the rule posed a legal danger and recommended that it be deleted. This proposal was put to a membership vote, but failed to achieve the necessary two-thirds majority.[16] The following year, the Justice Department began a preliminary investigation of the rule and the Institute inserted a footnote in the code indicating that it would refrain from disciplining violators until a change in legal circumstances occurred. On June 1, 1972, the Justice Department filed a civil suit against the Institute under the anti-trust laws and five weeks later the AICPA signed a consent decree. The final judgment enjoined the Institute from any course of action prohibiting members from submitting price quotations. The Code's rule against competitive bidding was declared null and void. However, as the Institute was careful to explain to its members, the decree does not prevent parties from seeking enforcement of any state laws relating to competitive bidding. Despite the doctrine of federal pre-emption, the salutary competitive effect of the District Court's ruling may be retarded if no-bid provisions are common among state legal codes.

Summary

This section has discussed the economic implications of state regulations and the ethical code that binds a substantial fraction of accounting practitioners. It was shown that state laws have become increasingly restrictive as licensure has replaced certification and as control over entry has shifted to the AICPA through the universal adoption of the Uniform Examination. It was also shown that there has been an explicit increase in the minimum acceptable examination performance.[17] The active encouragement of these trends by the Institute and by state societies was documented and their restrictive economic effects were found to support the hypothesis that CPAs have increased their economic power through legislation justified as protecting the public interest.

This hypothesis received further validation through a selective examination of the Institute's ethical code. It was argued that provisions against advertising and employee raiding cannot be justified on public interest grounds and that their existence is evidence of an attempt to reduce inter-practitioner competition. The recent District Court ruling nullifying the Institute's rule against competitive bidding was summarized as additional evidence of restrictive practices. The potential competitive impact of these past and present sections of the Code was judged to be large in view of the substantial fraction of practicing CPAs who are Institute members and the inclusion of some portions of the Code in state CPA legislation.

This evidence that the Institute has supported legislation and ethical standards which restrict competition does not constitute proof that such effects have been *intended*. As noted earlier, support for many of these constraints appears to have been based on a genuine desire to raise accountancy to the professional status enjoyed by doctors and lawyers. In most cases, public rather than professional interest was cited as the primary reason for their imposition. The latter justification would have more force were it not for the Institute's procrastination in adopting firm policy regarding certain issues on which public and professional interests were clearly at odds. The most important of these concerned the keystone of public accounting—independence. During the first sixteen years of its existence, the Institute made no attempt to include a definition of independence in the Code of Professional Ethics. In 1932, the ethics committee proposed a rule forbidding members to serve as officers or directors of corporations for which they provided an independent audit.[18] This prohibition of a rather clear conflict of interest was defeated by the Council because of "a lack of enthusiasm for too many restraints on the members' freedom of action." Within a year of that vote, the Securities Act was passed and the first regulation issued under its provisions stated that the Federal Trade Commission would not consider a person to be independent with respect to any registrant for whom he served as officer, agent, employee, director, etc. or in which he held *any* direct or indirect financial interest (Carey, 1969: 198). After the passage of the 1934 Act, the SEC modified this regulation by forbidding the holding of any substantial interest in a registered client. Goaded by the SEC's action (and by the trial of several members who had invested in a client company), the Institute adopted a resolution in 1934 forbidding "substantial" ownership in a public client firm. This no-ownership proviso was not stated as a rule in the Institute's Code of Ethics until 1941. In 1950, the SEC again revised its regulations and forbade practitioners to hold any financial interest in a client firm. During the next decade, the Institute made no similar adjustment in its Code. Even more serious was the continued absence of a rule forbidding "independent" auditors from serving as employees or directors of client firms. Finally, in 1960 the ethics committee proposed amendments to bring the Institute's regulations into conformity with the SEC on both issues. The motion was hotly debated and ultimately rejected at the membership meeting. The following year it was resubmitted and passed with ease.

This synopsis of the profession's "war of independence" raises serious questions about the Institute's ability to safeguard the public interest when it conflicts with practitioner interests. Why was legislation necessary to impose discipline regarding the keystone of public accounting upon a professional group which has long proclaimed its capacity for self-governance? How could an organization write "public interest" regulations so detailed as to specify the permissible size of an advertising card and yet fail for three decades to formally prohibit relationships which pose an obvious threat to independence? In the light of this experience, can the public rely upon the Institute's judgment that legal and professional barriers to competition are necessary for safeguarding the common good?

4. POWER OF THE INDIVIDUAL PRACTITIONER

Previous sections have analyzed the impact of legislative and ethical constraints upon the power relationship between CPAs, considered as a class, and their clients. It was shown that the organized profession has achieved economic power through its virtual elimination of non-CPA sources of public accounting services, acquisition of control over entry, and enforcement of an ethical code that dampens inter-practitioner competition. Despite these market restrictions, the individual practitioner seldom enjoys absolute power in any engagement because the client usually has access to at least one alternative CPA firm. The general exchange model showed that the power of any single practitioner becomes zero if the client is able to find one other CPA who will supply the attest function on equally favorably terms.

Since the terms of trade include the fee for service, its quality, the practitioner's reputation, and the nature of the resulting opinion, it is possible for CPAs to compete for business on a number of dimensions. Institutional restraints on advertising and encroachment suggest that this competition will be passive in form, i.e., that clients themselves must take the initiative in order to become aware of alternative terms of trade available from various practitioners. However, in view of the search costs and the inertia generally associated with professional relationships, clients are unlikely to seek out and engage a new CPA unless they become dissatisfied with the terms of trade obtained from a previously engaged practitioner. Such a change may have implications for the public interest if the source of dissatisfaction is the nature of the opinion rendered by the original CPA. A newly engaged practitioner's willingness to render an opinion preferred by the client may indicate that competition has occurred along the quality dimension and that present and potential investors may not be provided with completely objective financial information. Thus, there may be a serious "neighborhood cost" for investors even though the original practitioner abides by professional principle and refuses to revise an opinion.

Of course, competition on standards need not result in a change of practitioners. The threat of such a change may be sufficient to induce the presently engaged CPA to "swallow his convictions" and revise his opinion (Spacek, 1958). Such a result is likely to occur when the CPA's cost of disagreement is substantial because no equally rewarding alternative engagements are available. The public interest implications of an opinion revision may be even greater than those of a broken engagement, since the latter provides a visible signal to the market that the content of the financial statements may be in dispute.[19]

Spacek (1958), Moonitz (1968), and Sterling (1973) indicate that competition on the quality dimension is *precipitated* by the opposing interests of practitioners versus managers/shareholders and *permitted* by the absence of enforceable operationalized rules for selecting among alternative accounting principles. The practitioner's professional interest—indeed his legal duty in the case of registered firms—is to ensure that financial statements are presented fairly, regardless of their potential market impact. Managers and shareholders are interested in presenting favorable financial statements to ensure a positive market impact:

> In reporting to the shareholders, corporate managements generally feel that they must present the financial position of their companies in the most favorable light. In fact, they have no alternative in our competitive system. Shareholders want the facts about their investment, but they also want these facts presented in the best light in comparison with other companies so that a favorable effect on market value will result. This is natural because they want the best price possible for their investments if they desire or are required to sell, or even if they have no intention of selling. (Spacek, 1958: 368)

This competitive drive for favorable reported results would pose no public interest problem if the choice among alternative accounting principles were constrained by operational criteria. Enforcement would be provided by practitioners bound to divulge any departure from mandated principle. Were such operational criteria in existence, there would be little dispersion among practitioner opinions and the client could achieve no economic benefit (with respect to the content of reports) by engaging a new CPA. In terms of the exchange model, standardization of criteria would remove the client's effective alternatives regarding the statement of results, thereby removing his power over the individual practitioner.

At the present time, such standardized criteria do not exist, and clients are able to whipsaw practitioners in order to present financial statements in the most favorable terms. As noted earlier, the SEC was empowered to establish detailed accounting rules, but chose to await their evolution within the profession. Moonitz has documented the profession's failure to establish such principles and has predicted that this situation is not likely to change in the near future because managers wish to retain reporting flexibility, while practitioners wish to avoid the legal liabilities that might be incurred if they exercised primary responsibility over the financial statements (Moonitz, 1968: 629). He argues that management's responsibility for financial results need not imply a concomitant right to dictate the principles underlying financial statements and calls for practitioners to establish control over the latter.

The public interest would be greatly served by consistent (and economically correct) accounting principles because they would increase comparability among statements, permit investors to choose among firms according to marginal rates of return, and improve the allocation of capital within the economy. However, I believe that the organized profession is unlikely to develop operational principles because their establishment would be contrary to practitioner economic self-interest. This conclusion is based upon two primary considerations. First, narrow standards would substantially increase public accountants' legal jeopardy even if it were well established that management retained primary responsibility for the financial statements. The promulgation of operational standards for selecting the accounting principle appropriate to a given economic circumstance would make deviations quite visible to a jury concerned with determining whether a practitioner had erred in attesting that a statement was prepared in accordance with generally accepted accounting principles.[20] The relationship of legal liability and technical standards has been recognized by the profession:

> The technical pronouncements of the Institute, and its Code of Ethics, therefore, may thus serve as a defense for accountants who comply with them—but may also be used as a weapon against those who have not.
> Thus, as the legal liabilities of professional accountants in the United States have seemed to be extended by court decisions and legislation, the Institute has become increasingly aware that pronouncements or rules which encourage higher standards of performance might be used against its members unfairly in the courts. The natural impulse to assume greater responsibility is met by warnings to hold back. (Carey, 1969: 248)

Second, practitioners would suffer a loss in prestige and power if the range of principles were narrowed because there would be a corresponding reduction in the area within which judgment can be exercised. Public accountancy would lose a major claim to professional status and be shifted toward the category of technician. This loss of mystique would have economic as well as social status consequences. If the application of accounting principles became a programmed activity, it would be difficult for any practitioner to obtain a fee differential on the basis of presumed expertise regarding the attest function. Legislatures might be less willing to impose continually rising minimum standards of education upon candidates since the body of necessary knowledge would become more specific. Licensure statutes would be jeopardized because clients could make informed price/quality trade-offs and would be amply protected by certification alone. The justification for a restrictive code of ethics would be eliminated because a set of operational standards would make practitioner errors more visible and permit injured parties to obtain adequate redress through the judicial system. In view of these legal, social status, and economic consequences, it is presumptive to expect that the private sector will fulfill this public need.

5. POLICY IMPLICATIONS

If it is agreed that the public interest would be best served by the provision of accounting services at the lowest cost consistent with some stipulated minimum level of quality, then certain policy implications flow from the two accounting power relationships that have been discussed. Practitioners acting as a combination have augmented their economic power vis-à-vis clients through legislative and ethical provisions that decrease the supply of CPAs and restrict competition among them. Both effects operate to reduce the quantity and raise the price of accounting services as compared to the levels that would obtain under a free market system. The salutary price and quantity effects of competition could be achieved if the following policies were adopted:

1. All restrictive state CPA laws should be replaced by permissive statutes. That is, licensure should be abandoned in favor of certification. Individual states would be free to set whatever certification requirements were thought desirable. In order to retain the benefits of reciprocity, all states might find it advantageous to require passage of the Uniform Examination as a minimum certification standard. However, unlicensed individuals would be free to perform all public accounting functions in every state.
2. The AICPA should remove all provisions in the Code of Professional

Ethics that in any way restrict employee recruitment, advertising, and encroachment.

3. State CPA laws should be revised to remove any restrictions on competitive bidding in addition to those on recruitment, advertising, and encroachment.

Implementation of these changes would do much to reduce the economic power of CPAs acting as a combination, but would enhance the power of the individual client versus the individual practitioner with respect to the quality of the attest function. That is, these policy changes standing alone might increase the tendency of practitioners to compete along the service quality dimension to the detriment of investors and the public. This danger would be markedly reduced if operational rules were developed to match the appropriate accounting principle to a given economic circumstance. Deviations from these operational rules would be easily identified and form a solid basis for litigation. This increased legal liability would be a powerful deterrent to accountants who might otherwise choose to sacrifice principle for a fee.

The preceding section argued that the development of operational rules would not serve practitioner self-interest. For this reason, it is unlikely that the AICPA will ever succeed in developing such standards or inducing members to accept them. There is some possibility that the newly appointed Financial Accounting Standards Board will be sufficiently independent of practitioner and client power to achieve some success. However, in view of the private sector's history of failure, it may be time for the SEC to exercise its legislative authority and mandate such rules—preferably with active consultation by professional accounting organizations. This need does not imply that all firms would be required to use identical accounting principles. The same principles would be required only when economic circumstances, as defined by operational rules, were identical. If the SEC were to impose this constraint upon client power, the public would obtain the windfall gain of increased comparability among financial statements as well as the price/quantity benefits that would accrue from quality-constrained competition.

NOTES

1. Personal traits are inseparable from an individual, e.g., beauty, expertise, strength.

2. These assumptions are made to simplify the calculations; the model is sufficiently general to permit their relaxation. (See Pichler, 1973: 6–16.)

3. For non-monetary properties such as beauty, wisdom, and strength, the valuation may not be expressable in dollar terms. Nevertheless, parties do make selections among potential seat-mates, friends, and spouses on such dimensions—an observation which strongly suggests that calculations of expected satisfaction from such non-monetary traits

are made at least implicitly. The formulas simply make explicit what is already implicit and are as functional for the calculation of power based upon expected utility estimates as they are for power based upon expected dollar estimates.

4. Interested readers should see Pichler (1973: 9–14).

5. These propositions may be found in Rottenberg (1962: 4, 11), Gellhorn (1956: 109, 115), and Friedman (1962: 144).

6. It is interesting to note that in 1894 the Association chose to support a "certification bill" rather than a "licensure bill." Had this policy been maintained, the accounting profession would represent a departure from the fourth characteristic cited in the last paragraph.

7. Hawaii was added to the list in 1923 and Alaska in 1937. CPA statutes have also been passed in the District of Columbia, Puerto Rico, Guam, and the Virgin Islands.

8. All states did not use the grading service until 1962 (Hendrickson, 1971: 60).

9. Letter from Gertrude Darby, Assistant to Dr. Guy Trump, Vice-President—Education, March 15, 1973. Variation in state statutes, concern for the privacy of candidates from each state, and difficulties of interpreting the data are the stated reasons for this policy. None of these seems compelling in view of the widespread adoption of the Institute's passing grade, the fact that 57,928 applicants sat for the examination in 1972, and the availability of the Institute's research facilities to supply interpretive comment.

10. *Ibid.*

11. Rottenberg (1962: 18) has provided a rather clear example of this point. Illinois law restricts the practice of barbering to those who (among other things) have reached age 19.5, completed 9 months or 1,872 hours of study in a recognized barber school, and passed two examinations over subject areas that include anatomy, physiology, barber history and law, pharmacology, electricity and light, ethics, professional courtesy, ultraviolet radiation, and the use of various preparations in conjunction with galvanic, faradic, and high frequency electricity. (Paraphrase)

12. Carey notes that not everyone welcomed such revised laws. In 1923, Governor Smith of New York vetoed such a law because ". . . many young people would be deprived of an opportunity to render useful accounting services by the ultimate restriction of practice to CPAs."

13. Space considerations prevent an analysis of these oscillations here. However, Carey provides a full discussion of these policy changes. A careful reading will show that the policy revisions were precipitated largely by considerations of professional rather than public interest.

14. *State Public Accounting Laws,* AICPA. Ten states are less restrictive than the AICPA's recommended legislation because they permit continuing registration.

15. For recent evidence regarding the price impact of advertising restrictions within licensed occupations, see Benham (1972).

16. Fifty-two percent of the voters chose repeal.

17. The Littler Report, as previously noted, called for an explicit rise in examination standards to a level generally attained from five years of college study.

18. Unless otherwise noted, all of the material regarding independence is drawn from Carey (1969: 240–42; 1970: Chapter 8).

19. This signal has been strengthened recently by the SEC's reporting rule that the Commission be notified of any change in independent accountants and of any disagreements with the former accountant regarding accounting principles and practices.

20. This point is related to the liability argument made by Moonitz (1968). However the Moonitz article stresses the legal liability associated with responsibility for the financial statements rather than the point that departures from principles would be more easily proved if the latter were standardized.

REFERENCES

American Institute of Certified Public Accountants (1961) *Report of the CPA Examination Appraisal Committee.*
American Institute of Certified Public Accountants (1971) "Legislative Policy," in *Form of Regulatory Public Accountancy Bill.* New York: (January).
American Institute of Certified Public Accountants (1972) *Restatement of the Code of Professional Ethics.* New York.
Anderson, J. H. (1970) "Some University Investment and Accounting Concepts." *Journal of Accountancy* (June): 41–48.
Beamer, Elmer G. (1972) "Continuing Education—A Professional Requirement." *Journal of Accountancy* (January): 33–39.
Beaver, William H. (1971) "Reporting Rules for Marketable Equity Securities." *Journal of Accountancy* (October): 57–61.
Benham, Lee (1972) "The Effect of Advertising on the Price of Eyeglasses." *Journal of Law Economics* 15 (October): 327–52.
Blau, Peter M. (1964) *Exchange and Power in Social Life.* New York: Wiley.
Blau, Peter and W. Richard Scott (1962) *Formal Organizations: A Comparative Approach.* San Francisco: Chandler.
Breener, Vincent C. and Robert H. Strawser (1972) "CPAs Views on Required Continued Education." *Journal of Accountancy* (January): 36–39.
Burton, John C. (1971) "An Educator Views the Public Accounting Profession." *Journal of Accountancy* (September): 47–53.
Carey, John L. (1969) *The Rise of the Accounting Profession From Technical to Professional, 1896–1936.* New York: American Institute of Certified Public Accountants.
Carey, John L. (1970) *The Rise of the Accounting Profession to Responsibility and Authority, 1937–1969.* New York: American Institute of Certified Public Accountants.
Casey, William J. (1972a) "SEC Chairman Casey Suggests New Goals for Profession." *Journal of Accountancy* (November): 10–20.
Casey, William J. (1972b) "Toward Common Accounting Standards." *Journal of Accountancy* (October): 70–73.
Chamberlain, Neil W. (1958) *Labor.* New York: McGraw-Hill.
French, John R. P., Jr. and Berthram Raven (1959) "The Bases of Social Power." *Studies in Social Power.* Ann Arbor: University of Michigan (April): 150–67.
Friedman, Milton (1962) *Capitalism and Freedom.* Chicago: University of Chicago Press.
Friedman, Milton and Simon Kuznets (1945) *Income from Independent Professional Practice.* New York: National Bureau of Economic Research.
Gellhorn, Walter (1956) *Individual Freedom and Governmental Restraints.* Baton Rouge: Louisiana State University Press.
Heimbucher, Clifford V. (1961) "Fifty-three Jurisdictions." *Journal of Accountancy* (November): 42–49.
Hendrickson, H. S. (1971) "The Changing Content of the CPA Examination." *Journal of Accountancy* (July): 60–67.
Horngren, Charles T. (1972) "Accounting Principles: Private or Public Sector?" *Journal of Accountancy* (May): 37–41.
Ijiri, Yuji (1971) "Critique of the APB Fundaments Statement." *Journal of Accountancy* (November): 43–50.

Journal of Accountancy (1972) "Securities and Exchange Commission Adopts 'Substantive' Changes in Regulations S-X." (August): 7–8.

Lamden, Charles W. (1971) "Depreciation—A Reliability Gap." Report is reprinted with permission from *World*, Journal of Peat, Marwick, Mitchell & Co. (Autumn).

Moonitz, Maurice (1968) "Why is it so Difficult to Agree upon a Set of Accounting Principles?" *Australian Accountant* (November): 621–31.

Pichler, Joseph A. (1973) "Power, Influence, and Authority," in Joseph W. McGuire (ed.) *Contemporary Management: Issues and Viewpoints.* Princeton, New Jersey: Prentice-Hall.

Rottenberg, Simon (1962) "The Economics of Occupational Licensing," in *National Bureau of Economic Research, Aspects of Labor Economics.* Princeton, New Jersey: Prentice-Hall.

Sanders, Howard P. (1972) "Factors in Achieving Success on the CPA Examination." *Journal of Accountancy* (December) 85–88.

Spacek, Leonard (1958) "The Need for an Accounting Court." *Accounting Review* (July): 368–70.

Sterling, Robert R. (1973) "Accounting Power." *Journal of Accountancy* 135 (January): 61–67.

Stigler, George J. (1961) "The Economics of Information." *Journal of Political Economy* 69: 213–25.

Stone, Marvin (1972) "The Arguments for Requiring Continuing Education by Legislation." *Journal of Accountancy* (January): 56–60.

U.S. Army Audit Agency (1972) *Provisions in CPA Laws and Regulations.* U.S. Government Printing Office: (July).

Accounting Power: An Alternative to the Economic Analysis

LAWRENCE REVSINE*
AND
HERVEY A. JURIS†

In an interesting first attempt to consider the application of the price theory literature on restraint of competition to the accounting profession—or rather to that segment of it pertaining to the attest function—Professor Pichler argues that the net effect of AICPA efforts in favor of licensure and the AICPA Code of Professional Ethics has been to restrict entry and presumably raise the price of accounting services to consumers, *ceteris paribus.* He also argues that "the organized profession is unlikely to develop [narrowly defined] operational principles because their establishment would be contrary to practitioner economic self-interest." [Sec. 4] We believe that Pichler has opened a very fertile area of investigation, but that by framing his hypotheses solely in terms of economic criteria, he has failed to properly formulate the research question. We will propose an alternative formulation and suggest research opportunities which arise from these propositions.

After a short introduction and a discussion of the concept of power, which is not particularly central to his argument in subsequent sections, Pichler considers three main topics: the economic power of the accounting combine, the power of individual practitioners versus clients, and policy implications of his analysis.

First, with regard to the economic power of the accounting combine, Pichler postulates a model in which:

*B.S. 1963, M.B.A. 1965, Ph.D. 1968, Northwestern University. Associate Professor of Accounting and Information Systems, Graduate School of Management, Northwestern University, CPA, Illinois. Author, *Replacement Cost Accounting* (1973). Contributor to accounting periodicals.

† A.B. 1960, Princeton University; M.B.A. 1962, Ph.D. 1967, University of Chicago. Associate Professor of Industrial Relations and Urban Affairs, Graduate School of Management, Northwestern University. Author (with P. Feuille), *Police Unionism: Power and Impact in Public Sector Bargaining* (1973). Contributor to industrial and labor relations periodicals.

practitioners acting as a combination have augmented their economic power vis-à-vis clients through legislative and ethical provisions that decrease the supply of CPAs and restrict competition among them. Both effects operate to reduce the quantity and raise the price of accounting services as compared to the levels that would obtain under a free market system. [Sec. 5]

Specifically, he tests two hypotheses:

the hypothesis that the profession has engaged and continues to engage in activities that limit the supply and raise the price of accounting services . . . [and] the alternative that the sole function of organized market activities has been to protect potential clients and the public against unscrupulous practitioners. [Sec., 1]

A careful reading of his paper will show that while he never explicitly states it, his methodology is to disprove the second hypothesis and thus accept the first by default. We would propose an alternative interpretation of the data presented in the paper: that the AICPA has acted to protect potential clients and the public against unqualified practitioners and that a concurrent side effect may have been to restrict quantity and raise price relative to what might have prevailed in a free market situation. In other words, Pichler ought not to have rejected the second hypothesis since it can be shown that the behavior of the AICPA is totally consistent with the role of a professional organization in striving to protect the public interest. This is an important distinction, for it suggests that Pichler's public policy recommendations are premature.

Second, in considering the power of individual practitioners versus clients, Pichler argues "that the practitioner's power is enhanced by the absence of standardized accounting principles and that his economic self-interest would not be served by greater uniformity." [Sec. 1] In contrast we will suggest that uniformity is in the economic and professional self-interest of accountants and that the existing absence of uniformity cannot be used to support arguments regarding practitioner self-interest.

Finally, Pichler derives certain policy recommendations which are designed to increase supply and lower price. We will briefly evaluate these recommendations in light of our differences of opinion on the earlier points and suggest further research which is required before any supportable policy recommendations can be forthcoming.

1. THE ECONOMIC POWER OF THE AICPA

While Pichler uses several definitions of the accounting function,[1] he does ultimately agree that it is the attest function which makes the CPA distinctive and that it is the attest function in which the investing public has the greatest interest. Since it is only with regard to the attest function that Pichler suggests possible self-serving restriction of quantity, it remains only for us to establish that licensure of the attest function is a legitimate concern of a professional organization interested in protecting its various publics from substandard practices.

Licensure

To disprove the argument that the profession sought licensure solely in the interest of protecting the public, Pichler cites four common characteristics that economists have found in occupational regulations:

> First, pressure for their adoption is usually generated by practitioners rather than by clients. Second, they entrust to practitioners the establishment and monitoring of standards for receipt of the certificate or license. Third, the standards tend to rise over time but with specific exemptions for incumbents in the trade. Fourth, regulations that require certification generally evolve into licensure proper. When all of these characteristics are present, the occupational regulation is *likely* to be more restrictive than is necessary for the public's well-being. [Sec. 3, italics supplied]

Pichler then asks four questions paralleling each of these four characteristics:

> [1] If there is a general need to protect the public, why aren't clients the primary advocates for restrictions? [2] Shouldn't public representatives determine the minimum level of competence or maximum level of incompetence that can be safely permitted? [3] If increased standards are truly neccessary, isn't it dangerous for incumbents to continue practice without meeting the new requirements? [4] Doesn't certification generally provide consumers with all of the information necessary to make informed price/quality decisions? [Sec. 3]

He then argues that practitioners rather than clients were the primary advocates for restrictions, that the profession rather than the public determines minimum levels of competence, that when the standards are changed, incumbent practitioners are not required to meet these new standards, and that while certification would suffice, the profession has pushed for licensure. While we do not believe that Pichler actually proves any of his assertions (rather he suggests and implies), we are willing to accede on all points and propose an alternative interpretation of the same data set.

Professions and Occupations

We will argue that the behavior Pichler describes would amount to restriction of trade if it were practiced by an occupation in which standards are set arbitrarily high in order to restrict entry to newcomers. However, we would also argue that in a profession where there is a service provided which requires a great deal of formal preparation and specialized knowledge, such behavior may be not only acceptable but necessary to protect potential clients. To do this it will be necessary for us to distinguish between a profession and an occupation, to suggest that accounting is a profession rather than an occupation, and to show that the behavior of the AICPA with regard to the criteria established by Pichler is appropriate to a professional organization and consistent with public interests.

An occupation is the role set a person fulfills in his work.[2] Thus bricklaying, teaching and medicine are all occupations—ways in which individuals earn their livings. At least one of these is generally considered the archetype of a profession—medicine, unfortunately, rather than teaching. However, beyond agreeing that the practice of medicine is a profession, those who study occupations and professions have a great deal of difficulty deciding how to distinguish a profession from an occupation. To get around this many have agreed to view a profession as the ideal model of occupational organization that would result if an occupation became fully professionalized. While this ideal cannot be fully described, there is some agreement that the following characteristics (at a minimum) must be present: intellectual training, specialized knowledge, altruism, practicality, and self-organization.[3] Rather than speak of "profession" as an ideal state, however, it is more appropriate to discuss professionalization—the process of achieving the professional ideal. (See Vollmer and Mills, 1966.) When professionalization is fairly well advanced, it is appropriate to speak of an occupation as a profession. This has two important consequences: professional authority—the profession is supposed to know more about what is good for the client than either the client or the public, and the extension of professional authority—since the profession knows more about its area than the laity, it should be the sole arbiter of criteria for professional training (and by extension, certification). (See Greenwood, 1957.) In short, as in medicine and dentistry, professional authority and control over certification, curriculum, and training are proffered to an occupation by the public because that occupation has met the criteria for becoming a profession. With respect to the attest function we believe that it is not necessary to convince this audience that the public has accorded professional authority to accountants. Against this background, then, let us examine the four characteristics of occupational regulation discussed by Pichler.

Pressure for Regulation Emanates from Practitioners Themselves

It is consistent with public practice for occupations recognized by the public as professions to be allowed to set standards on the basis of their professional authority. Nevertheless, Pichler asks why it is that the clients did not insist on higher standards themselves if higher standards, in fact, were desired. Two reasons are immediately obvious. First, it is the hallmark of a profession that it undertakes to protect the public from misfeasance and malfeasance by *itself* establishing standards, internal sanctions and an ethical code.[4] Second, those familiar with the literature of interest group politics are aware of the distinction between interest groups and potential interest groups. The latter are those with common expectations with respect to a given issue who, because of their multiple interest group memberships (church, family, occupation, geographic region, etc.), become mobilized only in a crisis situation and unlike permanent interest groups (AMA, ABA, ADA, AICPA) tend to disperse after the short run goal is achieved.[5] It would be counter to theory and past practice if client groups were to maintain a permanent aroused interest group.

Practitioners Themselves Establish and Monitor Standards

Pichler introduces the possibility that the CPA examination may be used more to restrict entry and reduce competition than to weed out incompetents. On the basis of correspondence with an AICPA employee, he determined that "each individual part of the examination is passed by only 30 percent of those who take it." [Sec. 3] Because of the apparent cross-sectional constancy of this figure, Pichler suggests that the passing standard is relative and that "there is an implicit quota on admission." To argue his point, he infers that this passage figure may have remained constant over the past twenty years despite a "dramatic increase in the educational background of applicants." Notice that in using this argument Pichler necessarily transforms the fragmentary 1972 cross-sectional data available to him into a sweeping time-series statement encompassing the entire 1952–72 period. Unfortunately, he provides us with no defensible basis for this inference. Obviously, it is quite possible that the passage rate may have actually increased over this period.

Notwithstanding its lack of empirical foundation, let us grant Pichler his hypothesis and see whether—even under these favorable circumstances—his argument regarding admission quotas is valid. He contends that "in view of the dramatic increase in the educational background of applicants over the past twenty years the passage of a constant fraction means that the absolute standard of acceptable performance has increased." [Sec. 3] This is probably true, but it is also irrelevant. That is, one would certainly expect, even demand, that the absolute level of knowledge required in a 1972 medical certification examination would exceed that required in 1952. After all, enormous medical progress occurred over this period. But if we observe this increase in absolute examination knowledge requirements, it does not automatically follow that entry standards into the medical profession have increased. Entry standards increase only if the ratio of examination requirements to knowledge levels in the discipline has also increased.

Thus, even if we assume a constant passage rate on the CPA examination, Pichler's point regarding a rising entry standard would be valid only if the complexity of professional accounting practice was constant over the twenty-year period or rose at a slower rate than did the increase in educational level. In fact, however, the complexity of accounting practice increased by staggering proportions during this twenty-year period. Two related examples should suffice to demonstrate the point. First, the advent of computer data processing capabilities enormously increased the sophistication and complexity of information systems. This, in turn, has necessitated great changes in the review and evaluation of internal control systems and dramatically increased the talents required to design effective means for auditing such systems. Second, geometrically increasing data flows have made greater reliance on defensible statistical sampling techniques imperative in the auditing process. Indeed the professional environment has changed so much that some seriously question the adequacy of standard accounting curricula in meeting demands.

Rising Standards with Exemptions for Incumbents

Pichler suggests that if standards are so important, it is inconsistent for incumbent practitioners to be exempt from meeting new standards as they are set. Actually, this issue is artificial. In all democratic groups, whether they are unions or professional associations in which the leadership governs by consent of the governed, the leadership is required to negotiate with power groups within the organization so that when it enters inter-organizational bargaining it can be reasonably sure of group support for its goals. Where the issue at stake within the organization is the ability of the membership to continue to earn a living, "grandfathering" is a preferred way of lowering the cost of agreement for the threatened group.

Of course, a defense of grandfathering on the grounds of protecting the ability of incumbents to earn a living does not get to the issue of the public interest. However, to argue that practitioners who have maintained an active practice do not have requisite qualifications to continue to perform is to deny the value of experience and the role of the market in separating competence from incompetence over the long run. So long as there is a reasonably free market with respect to choice of an accountant and access to information, the likelihood of public harm is significantly reduced.

Certification Evolves into Licensure

Pichler's other remaining concern is the profession's insistence on licensing as opposed to certification. We fail to share his concern on this issue since he is in favor of certification, and yet the only current distinction between certification and licensing is a work requirement. The effect of licensing, as it is practiced today, is not to keep certified persons out of the attest function but only to portpone entry for a short and specified period of time.[6]

Summary

AICPA behavior with respect to licensure, standards and grandfathering is consistent with the model of professional authority and behavior generally accepted as governing the actions of professional organizations. While all of Pichler's arguments might be valid if we were discussing occupations with no professional attributes, the nature of the attest function and its importance to the various external publics argue forcefully for the validity of the use of the professional model. The AICPA as a professional organization is obligated to take actions to protect its varied publics and we believe that the actions cited by Pichler were toward that end.

The Professional Code of Ethics

Again attempting to disprove his alternative hypothesis (that the sole function of organized market activities has been to protect clients and the public against unscrupulous practitioners), Pichler cites four aspects of the AICPA Code of Ethics: the restrictions on pirating employees, the limitations on advertising, restrictions on competitive bidding, and the absence of effective language on independence. Of the first three he says,

> It was argued that provisions against advertising and employee raiding cannot be justified on public interest grounds and that their existence is evidence of an attempt to reduce inter-practitioner competition. The recent District Court ruling nullifying the Institute's rule against competitive bidding was summarized as additional evidence of restrictive practices [Sec. 4]

Of independence he says, "How could an organization write 'public interest' regulations so detailed as to specify the permissible size of an advertising card and yet fail for three decades to formally prohibit relationships which pose an obvious threat to independence?" [Sec. 4]

We concur on the independence issue and we are willing to give him the no-raiding and competitive bidding arguments (although we fail to see how restricting inter-firm movement of personnel can restrict the quantity of accounting services; it only affects reallocation of existing resources as far as we can tell; with respect to competitive bidding, all professions are finding that their restrictions on competitive bidding are being attacked by the courts). We do not, however, agree with his interpretation of restrictions on advertising. Having described the operational interpretations of advertising restrictions as a "baroque delight" and having traced the origin of restrictions to professional ethics, Pichler observes,

> nevertheless, it is highly debatable whether professional self-regulation should wander into the area of esthetics when the prescriptions are *likely* to exert a restrictive economic impact. . . . Limitations on advertising reduce knowledge in the marketplace, reduce client awareness of alternative exchange partners, and increase the economic power of established practitioners over their clients. It is particularly difficult under such circumstances for clients to learn of new practitioners or of those who have expertise in a specialty within the profession. This *tends* to reduce competition, misallocate resources, and produce higher prices than would otherwise prevail for accounting services. [Sec. 3, italics supplied]

While the sentiment he expresses would be appropriate in the absence of any advertising, by his own admission the Code allows listings in the Yellow Pages.[7] Furthermore, at the margin, both quality and price information can be transmitted orally at social clubs, through industry associations, through lawyers, etc. Thus even if it can be shown that restrictions exist, it is doubtful that it can be shown that these restrictions have effectively blocked the flow of information in the market.[8]

Summary. Pichler argues that the references in the Code of Ethics to no-raiding, advertising, and competitive bidding and the lack of reference to independence raise serious questions about the extent to which the public can rely upon the Institute's judgment that legal and professional barriers to competition are necessary for safeguarding the common good. We would argue that, with the exception of the issue of independence, the issues he raises are not particularly relevant, primarily because the intent, as he interprets it, is not realized in practice.

2. AICPA RELUCTANCE TO MOVE TO NARROWLY DEFINED PRINCIPLES

Pichler contends that the accounting profession is "unlikely to develop [narrowly defined] operational principles because their establishment would be contrary to practitioner economic self-interest." [Sec. 5] He bases this contention on two separate assertions, (1) that narrowly defined operational principles "would substantially increase public accountants' legal jeopardy," and (2) that the development of such principles would precipitate a loss of professional prestige and thereby lead to a reduction in future fees. Both of these contentions are highly disputable and in part are inconsistent with available evidence. We will examine each assertion in turn.

Legal Jeopardy

Pichler is probably correct when he contends that the development of narrowly defined operational principles would make it easier to recognize and establish deviations from generally accepted accounting principles and that this, in turn, might increase the risk of suit for accountants who attest to statements that are not in conformity with these narrowly defined principles. However, Pichler overlooks that fact that the development of more specific principles, by reducing ambiguities, simultaneously decreases the risk of "error." That is, so long as auditors adhere to generally accepted auditing standards regarding "due professional care" and observance of "generally accepted accounting principles,"[9] the very existence of narrowly defined principles reduces the possibility of attestations which might precipitate legal liability. Thus, narrowly defined principles would, on balance, tend to decrease rather than increase the risk of legal liability *so long as audits were conducted in conformity with existing auditing standards.*

In arguing for the contrary position Pichler implicitly suggests that the existence of ambiguity in the interpretation of accounting principles provides the accountant with broader grounds for defending charges of non-conformity. But, in reality, a recent court ruling in the *Continental Vending* case (*U.S.* v. *Simon*, 397 U.S., 1006; 1970) contradicts this view. This ruling suggests that a jury need not give conclusive weight to an auditor's contention that statements under litigation conform to generally accepted accounting principles when the principles involved are non-specific. An attorney, writing in a recent *Journal of Accountancy* article, sees the implications of *Continental Vending* for the profession as follows:

> [The wording of the Court's decision] implies that in cases where there are specific rules or prohibitions they may be conclusive. . . . *For the profession the case points out once more the very real advantage, at least from the point of view of legal responsibility, in having professional standards spelled out.* Had there been specific rules or prohibitions governing the matters about which there was dispute among the expert witnesses in this case, to which the defendants could refer, it is quite probable the result would have been different. (Isbell, 1970: 36, italics supplied)

Since reduction in the ambiguity surrounding accounting principles can be expected to both (1) eliminate potential sources for attestation error, and (2) increase the legal defensibility of reliance on generally accepted accounting principles, we cannot support Pichler's first assertion; rather it appears more logical to suggest that narrowly defined operational principles would *decrease* public accountants' legal jeopardy.

Professional Prestige

Pichler asserts that a narrowed range of accounting principles would reduce judgmental latitude in the attestation process, thereby diminishing professional prestige and, eventually, fee differentials. Again, an equally plausible counter-assertion is possible.

To begin the argument, we must recognize that the attest function is of great importance for the efficient operation of capital markets. Since attestation is retrospective, its importance may be overlooked in the light of evidence regarding the rapidity with which the market impounds information and the apparent "staleness" of attested financial statements at the time of their distribution (Ball and Brown, 1968). But the fact that year-end attested reports may be largely stale at the time of distribution does not mean that such reports serve no useful purpose. On the contrary, attested results provide periodic benchmarks against which the market can measure the veracity of the unattested messages to which it reacted and also provide a basis for making needed corrections whenever the market misevaluates the financial impact of already impounded micro-events. Thus, attestation is seen to serve a policing and corrective function that is vitally necessary for the efficient operation of capital markets.

In his discussion, Pichler implies that a narrowing of accounting principles would transform attestation into a basically programmed activity. This, in turn, would make it "difficult for any practitioner to obtain a fee differential on the basis of presumed expertise regarding the attest function." [Sec. 5] Pichler fails to recognize, however, that the attestation process consists of far more than the mere determination by an auditor that financial statements are in accord with generally accepted accounting principles. While this conformity review may be the most visible element of the audit process, the bulk of the attestation effort is directed elsewhere.

In other words, Pichler reaches his particular conclusion because he concentrates on the end product of the attestation process—financial statements. What Pichler ignores is that attestation also encompasses a sampling and evaluative process designed to provide the auditor with a reasonable judgmental basis for corroborating the *existence* of the underlying events whose aggregate effect is portrayed in the financial statements. This corroboration dimension involves review of the structure and operation of the information system and related internal controls, as well as an examination of evidence supporting the underlying events themselves. Indeed, one can assert that as information systems continue to grow in sophistication and complexity, this corroboration aspect of the attestation process—with its required attendant judgmental dimension—will actually increase in importance.

Given this broader view of attestation, one can counter Pichler's assertion with the following somewhat more plausible contention: in a world in which information technology is continuously becoming more sophisticated, any decline in the need for judgment regarding choice of principles [10] will be balanced (or exceeded) by increases in the need for judgment in the design of audits of such systems. Insofar as professional accountants concur in this analysis, then there is no logical reason for them to resist a narrowing of accounting principles on economic grounds. Thus, we conclude that Pichler's second assertion, like his first, is highly debatable.

An Alternative View

In discussing the issue of narrowly defined operational principles, Pichler makes a crucially important observation. He states that

the public interest would be greatly served by consistent (and economically correct) accounting principles because they would increase comparability among statements, permit investors to choose among firms according to marginal rates of return, and improve the allocation of capital within the economy. [Sec. 4]

Indeed, there is little doubt that *valid* inter-firm comparisons are rendered difficult, if not impossible, by the multiplicity of available accounting options. For example, it is often not possible to state with any degree of confidence that a firm earning an accounting rate of return on equity of, say 15 percent is more profitable than another firm earning an accounting return of, say 10 percent. If accounting reports cannot provide meaningful ex post evaluative data for external users, they are not fulfilling one of their intended purposes. Indeed, many external users make this allegation; they contend that accounting reports possess attestation utility but very little decision utility.

If accounting principles were reformulated in order to generate reports possessing greater comparability, then not only would the public interest be better served but also (in contrast with Pichler's earlier statement to the contrary) the private economic interests of the accounting profession would also benefit. As matters now stand, accounting reports are provided externally in order to satisfy existing institutional requirements. But if these reports were designed to satisfy the legitimate information needs of external users, then new demand based upon decision-utility might be created. For example, if the information contained in restructured accounting reports was timely and afforded a legitimate basis for inter-firm comparisons, then users might clamor for attested quarterly reports, in addition to attested annual reports. By stimulating such latent demand, accountants could generate potentially significant new sources of revenue.

A Restatement of the Problem

We have already disputed Pichler's explanation for the profession's lack of progress in narrowing the latitude in accounting principles. Indeed, we argued that narrowed principles would *reduce* legal jeopardy and probably generate economic gains for the profession. Given these potential economic gains and the indisputable social benefits from increased statement comparability, it is necessary for us to provide some alternative explanation for the continuing diversity in generally accepted accounting principles. At least two explanatory factors should be cited:

1. There is a lack of awareness within the profession of the means by which comparability might be enhanced.
2. There is a lack of agreement regarding the objectives of accounting reports.

Lack of Awareness:

One of the prime objections to the development of greater uniformity in accounting principles is exemplified by the following argument:

The impossibility of presenting the accounts of different companies in the same industry on a completely comparable basis arises from the fact that physical and financial conditions and management policies are different, and this must be reflected differently in the accounts (Peloubet, 1961: 39).

Thus, efforts to reduce diversity in accounting techniques are resisted by appealing to differences in underlying circumstances. Over the years, this argument has largely prevailed despite the acknowledged difficulty that diversity introduces for financial analysis and interfirm comparisons.

What this argument fails to recognize is that much of this diversity is unnecessarily introduced by continued reliance on the historical cost measurement convention. For example, the selection of an arbitrary inventory cost flow assumption is necessitated by accounting's refusal to adopt a symmetric recognition of inventory price changes. Since accounting currently permits the same economic resource to be valued differently depending upon its time of purchase, it is obviously necessary to select some arbitrary rule for determining which of the potentially diverse values are to be removed when sales are made. And since there are numerous assignment rules available, comparability between firms is diminished. In contrast, this potential diversity could be reduced by the simple adoption of market value accounting for inventories. If this illustrative alternative approach were adopted, inventory carrying values and cost expirations would be reflected using then current market prices, and the need for selecting among alternative accounting techniques would be avoided.

The point of this discussion is that many of the alternative techniques which inhibit comparability are not inherent in the accounting process itself but instead are inherent in the historical cost convention that permeates accounting as it is now practiced. Were this convention to be selectively relaxed for various categories of assets, then many sources of artificial differences between the reported results of firms could be eliminated completely and others could be substantially reduced.[11] By contrast, many advocates of comparability have failed to recognize the essence of the problem—our continued insistence on the inflexible use of historical costs—and have instead adopted a "let's have everyone use FIFO" approach.[12] Such "solutions" have obscured the basic issue, generated understandable resistance, and impeded development of truly comparable financial reporting bases.

Lack of Objectives

Another explanation for the continued diversity in accounting principles relates to the current lack of agreement regarding the objectives of accounting reports and the associated information needs of various categories of users. The formation of the Accounting Objectives Study Group by the AICPA in 1971 represents an attempt to alleviate this deficiency. However, our inability to agree on what constitute the appropriate objectives of external reports has made it difficult to narrow the range of acceptable accounting principles. The reason is that alternative accounting principles often contain different assumptions regarding users' information needs. That is, one option may be intended to generate data for one implicit set of information needs while a competing option is directed towards satisfying a completely different set of information needs. Since the accounting profession is unable to specify which of these competing needs are more appropriate, it is not surprising that they have also been unable to specify which of the competing accounting options are more appropriate.

Summary

In summary, we suggest that the failure of the accounting profession to narrow the range of accepted principles can best be explained by a lack of awareness of the means by which comparability might be enhanced and a lack of agreement regarding the objectives of accounting reports. This explanation is in marked contrast to Pichler's contention that economic self-interest, legal fears, and the desire to retain latitude has helped perpetuate multitudinous accounting options.

3. POLICY RECOMMENDATIONS

Pichler bases his policy recommendations on an assumption that the public would best be served by "the provision of accounting services at the lowest cost consistent with some stipulated minimum level of quality . . ." (Sec. 5). Having shown, from his point of view, that "practitioners acting as a combination have augmented their economic power vis-à-vis clients through legislative and ethical provisions that decrease the supply of CPAs and restrict competition among them . . ." (Sec. 5), he then makes several policy proposals which would abandon licensure in favor of certification (maintaining the Uniform Examination as a minimum certification standard) and remove restrictions on raiding, advertising, and bidding in the ethical code and state laws.

We have argued alternatively that accounting, as a profession, has had a responsibility to establish and maintain standards, to police those standards, and to protect the public interest. We do not dispute that one effect of this may have been to restrict the number of accountants and raise the price of the attest function over levels that might have obtained under a free market system, but we do dispute that the price/quality trade-off Pichler suggests is as easy to resolve as Pichler would lead us to believe.

As an example of the complexity of the issues which Pichler attempts to paint in simplified economic terms, consider the arguments we have made on the question of why narrowly defined accounting standards do not exist. Pichler says it is a case of economic self-interest. We have argued that it is a matter of intellectual professional debate which can be resolved only through further investigation and thought.

The research question we would frame is this: what are the appropriate trade-offs to be assigned to free markets and the quality variable in formulating public policy with respect to the licensing of certified public accountants? To answer this question would require research along at least two dimensions in order to build a data base sufficient to support public policy recommendations. The first dimension would deal with an empirical examination of the economic structure of the accounting industry and a determination of the effect of supply and demand factors and any market imperfections on price. The second dimension would look at the complexity of the attest function and other accounting services as they have changed over time and relate these considerations to the criteria established for certification. Only after this kind of research would it be appropriate to propose recommendations for changes in public policy.

The accounting profession should be grateful to Pichler for opening these new avenues for research in the public interest.

NOTES

1. In Sec. 3 he talks of "accounting practitioners [constituting] an industry whose product line includes bookkeeping activities, data processing, management consulting, tax services, and the rendering of opinions on financial statements." In Sec. 4 he refers to the economic power of CPAs through their "virtual elimination of non-CPA sources of public accounting services." Yet in Sec. 3 he says that the AICPA favors a law which will require CPA licensure, and forbid unlicensed individuals from attesting statements but which *does* allow them to perform all other accounting work. We assume from the last statement that while public accounting services include all of the subjects mentioned in Sec. 3, the real object of investigation is the attest function, since there is no restriction of entry regarding the others, nor are any intentions along those lines imputed to the AICPA.

2. "An occupation is the social role performed by adult members of the society that directly and/or indirectly yields social and financial consequences and that constitutes a major focus in the life of an adult." (Hall, 1969: 5–6)

3. Kleingartner (1967) surveys the literature and shows that of seven prominent writers in the field, at least four agree that each of these characteristics must be present. Other attributes and their votes were: technique (1), ethical codes (3), community responsibility and sanctions (1), reward system (2), and professional culture (2).

4. Should the reader need a graphic distinction between professions and occupations, let him consider the response of garage mechanics and TV repairmen to client clamor for establishment of standards.

5. See Truman (1971). A contemporary example would be the potential interest group which coalesced on the ecology issue and led to the formation of the Environmental Protection Agency (EPA).

6. If, on the other hand, Pichler would allow both certified and non-certified persons to attest (a reading one might infer from his first policy recommendation in Sec. 5—although his precise meaning is unclear), then we would argue that this implies an attitude toward the price/quality tradeoff inconsistent with our alternative interpretation of his data. See our comments on his policy recommendations, *infra*.

7. The Wilmette, Illinois (population 32,000) telephone Yellow Pages list fourteen "accountants," eleven "public accountants," and nine "certified public accountants."

8. George Stigler (1961), whom Pichler cites, has argued that only if buyers have complete knowledge of all sellers' offers or all sellers have knowledge of all buyers' offers will there be a single price. Since these conditions do not obtain in the real world, buyers will undertake search in order to determine price dispersion and quality variance in the market. He shows that it is possible to compute the marginal cost of search and the marginal return from search. Presumably search will cease where marginal cost equals marginal revenue. Initially only a few observations should be required to determine the presence or absence of a single price and since those seeking attestation can be thought to be somewhat sophisticated, none of the restrictions cited by Pichler seem particularly restrictive to us.

Pichler also refers the reader to Lee Benham for "recent evidence regarding the price impact of advertising restrictions within licensed occupations." Benham (1972:

349) finds that restrictions on advertising did lead to increases in price but that "non-price advertising may also be a close substitute for price advertising." As we indicated above, we believe that consumers of attest services are sufficiently sophisticated to utilize the available information appropriately.

9. A recent codification of auditing standards issued by the Committee on Auditing Procedure (AICPA, 1973: 5) describes these two standards, as follows:

1. "Due professional care is to be exercised in the performance of the examination and the preparation of the report."
2. "The report shall state whether the financial statements are presented in accordance with generally accepted accounting principles."

10. Since it is unnecessary to our argument, we have not disputed Pichler's claim that more uniformity reduces judgment in the choice of principles. But some practitioners *have* argued that the judgment loss is illusory. For example, George R. Catlett (1964: 40–41) states:

The argument that the elimination of undesirable alternative practices will result in a rule book which will eliminate the exercise of professional judgment is ridiculous, but it is used frequently to play upon the pride of professional accountants. The fact is that it takes very little professional judgment to evaluate accounting practices if all that is involved is looking around to see what methods are being followed by other companies and are considered to be acceptable as reflected in their published reports. . . . Considerable ability, on the other hand, is required on the part of the profession to establish sound criteria in the form of uniform accounting principles. Professional judgment is required to apply those criteria properly in the wide variety of existing circumstances and conditions.

11. Continuing the example of selectively replacing (or supplementing) historical costs with market values, comparability would also be enhanced were this approach adopted in accounting for fixed assets. Existing accounting practices not only permit numerous arbitrary allocation patterns in depreciating such assets, but also take no cognizance of the dollar impact of differences in the timing of asset purchases. If market prices are available for such assets (an admittedly big "if"), then the situation is comparable to that of inventories insofar as we are willing to measure depreciation as the decline in market price. Even if market prices are not available, comparability may still be increased vis-à-vis historical cost accounting for fixed assets. That is, despite the fact that needed appraisals would introduce measurement error, the dispersion that results from applying "generally accepted" depreciation options to assets purchased at varying times (and prices) in the past.

12. Some might question how the advocacy of a market value approach differs from a "let's have everyone use FIFO" approach. There is an important distinction. FIFO, LIFO, weighted average cost, etc., represent detailed accounting procedures that are required because the broad measurement method in current use (historical costing) cannot be implemented without resorting to arbitrary computational rules. In contrast, market value approaches represent broad measurement methods that reduce the need for choosing detailed accounting rules. The market rather than the accountant is the valuer. Comparability would be achieved by market forces rather than by dictatorial imposition of a specified set of accounting procedural rules that cannot be unequivocally defended vis-à-vis available alternatives. (Of course, in areas where market prices are absent, then certain market value approaches—e.g., replacement costing—would also be forced to resort to arbitrary rules and comparability would accordingly be diminished.)

REFERENCES

American Institute of Certified Public Accountants (1973) *Statement on Auditing Standards* 1.

Ball, Ray and Philip Brown (1968) "An Empirical Evaluation of Accounting Income Numbers." *Journal of Accounting Research* 6 (Autumn): 159–78.

Benham, Lee (1972) "The Effect of Advertising on the Price of Eyeglasses." *Journal of Law and Economics* 15 (October): 337–52.

Catlett, George R. (1964) "Controversy over Uniformity of Accounting Principles." *Journal of Accountancy* 118 (December).

Greenwood, Ernest (1957) "Attributes of a Profession." *Social Work* II (July).

Hall, Richard H. (1969) *Occupations and the Social Structure.* Englewood Cliffs, New Jersey: Prentice-Hall.

Isbell, David B. (1970) "The Continental Vending Case: Lessons for the Profession." *Journal of Accountancy* 130 (August).

Kleingartner, Archie (1967) *Professionalism and Salaried Worker Organization.* Madison, Wisconsin: Industrial Relations Research Institute, University of Wisconsin.

Peloubet, Maurice E. (1961) "Is Further Uniformity Desirable or Possible?" *Journal of Accountancy* 3 (April).

Stigler, George (1961) "The Economics of Information." *Journal of Political Economy* 69: 213–25.

Truman, David (1971) *The Governmental Process.* New York: Knopf.

Vollmer, H. and D. Mills (eds.) (1966) *Professionalization.* Englewood Cliffs, New Jersey: Prentice-Hall.

Discussion

Lamden. The comment was made by Larry Revsine that if we assume that the percentage of those passing the CPA exam is constant, it still would not be an effective argument. I would like to point out that the percentage of those who pass is not constant. The Board of Examiners for the CPA examination reviews the cutoff with respect to quality and content. The very point that Pichler has missed is the fact that even if there is a percentage that is set—and there has to be a passing percentage based on some standard—he has failed to take re-examination into consideration. There are statistical analyses available. The state of California ran a study a few years back—taking all of the college graduates who had taken the examination—and found that 85 percent of those qualified had in fact passed. With the four-year college requirement in many jurisdictions such high percentages will be more common. In addition, the Board of Examiners is constantly reviewing, and has at the present time a study, of the content and quality of the examination. So the basic premise is wrong, in addition to the fact that as Larry points out, even if it were not wrong, it would still be irrelevant.

Pichler. The fact that people eventually pass merely indicates that the restrictive effects are somewhat lessened. Nevertheless, the fact that people must stand in a queue to get into the profession exerts restrictive economic effects for a period of time. Professor Stettler has conducted a similar analysis on the CPA candidates in Kansas. He found that a very high fraction of the candidates—upwards of 90 percent—passed. However, it took some of them sixteen years. This certainly constitutes a "temporary" restriction on entry.

Salmonson. I don't think that constitutes a delay on entry into the profession because many of these people are practicing now as junior or senior accountants in CPA firms without having passed the examination.

Pichler. It certainly restricts their upward mobility and their ability to establish their own competing practice.

Salmonson. Another factor that has been overlooked is that many of these people taking the CPA examination are engaging in a lark—they are taking a trial run.

Pichler. People engage in larks in teaching college, in becoming auto mechanics, and so forth. The market permits them to engage in those larks. The difference is that in accounting there is a restriction of entry.

Salmonson. I think you have to distinguish between candidates and serious candidates.

Pichler. When you have 95 percent of the candidates being college graduates and 10 percent being graduate students, I don't think you have too many larks.

Zlatkovich. I would like to speak about who passes and who doesn't pass the CPA examination. In my younger days I used to grade the examination, and I finally got elevated to the status of reviewing the grading. In my experience, the papers that didn't pass were absolutely atrocious. The passing grade of 75 points was a remarkably low figure because the number of potential points on subjects such as auditing and theory are far in excess of 100. I will point out further that in other professions, such as law, medicine, dentistry, architecture and so on, all of the candidates have gone through a professional school, whereas, in accountancy, frequently only a set number of hours with no specification of a major will meet the state statutes for sitting for the CPA examination. Hence, we are dealing with a less qualified applicant. Further, even in the case of the bar examination, a great many of the candidates do not immediately sit for the bar examination upon obtaining their J.D. or LL.B. Instead, they take a cram course or review course of some kind before taking the examination. All of these constitute explanatory factors for the higher passing percentages in the other professions than for accountancy. I would also point out that in my home state of Texas in the past twenty-five years there has been a sevenfold increase in the number of CPAs. We have a four-year requirement so I don't think that there has been an undue restriction.

Sterling. An *undue* restriction. Are you granting that there is *some* restriction?

Zlatkovich. There has been some restriction. I would point out that the problem in medicine is to get into school. We don't have that problem in accountancy—anybody can get in.

Pichler. That is a point that was also raised in the respondents' remarks. Accountants continue to use the analogy of the medical profession. I refer you to an article by Reuben Kessel in the *Journal of Law and Economics* in 1958. He points out that the medical profession has been one of the more advanced restrictors of supply because they have been able to choke off supply at the entry source [entering medical school]. Therefore, they don't have to worry about an examination. Accountants are raising the standard to five years of college-level education—a movement in a similar direction. You are not yet as successful as the doctors and lawyers.

Liggio. Since you seem to object to the standards being raised, how do you react to the increasing trend in a number of states to require continuing education for members of the profession?

Pichler. As I understand it, continuing education would not include re-examination. Is that correct?

Liggio. It doesn't include a re-examination, but as I understand it, if you don't meet the education requirements, you lose your certificate and then you must be re-examined.

Pichler. I am not familiar with whether or not the additional educational requirements are to involve a grading system or that it be sufficient just to take the course.

Liggio. It depends on the state. I believe that in California you have to put in forty hours of accredited additional work.

Pichler. I think this is an important issue because it speaks to the respondents' comments as well. I would be very much in favor of such a regulation. I am all for the public interest—who isn't? If public interest is served by continually increasing standards of education, then it should be applied to incumbent practitioners as well as to those trying to enter. If, in fact, you grant the argument that there has been a knowledge explosion in accounting—and I am willing to grant it—then the need to insure that everybody has that new accounting knowledge is in the public interest. It should be clear that those who are currently practicing will have to meet the same standards as those who are waiting in line trying to get into the profession.

Long. I have two points. First, I fail to see this tremendous queue waiting to get into the profession. You seem to attach a great deal of significance to the length of the queue, but I don't see it. I have never fired a man in my life for failing to pass the CPA examination. Second, I presume that with your theory of continuing education, and re-examination, you would be in favor of the same type of system for Ph.D. college teachers.

Pichler. Absolutely. And for medical doctors; and for lawyers, architects—

Sterling. For economists?

Pichler. Yes, even for economists. I was quite impressed with the AICPA figures which were shown in Table I. The number of people taking the examination has increased from 14,000 to 58,000.

Long. But you have assumed that those people are not in the profession or did not get in.

Pichler. All I know is that there were 58,000 people knocking on the door in 1972. I would be willing to alter my comment if I could get some more data. The AICPA won't give the data to me.

Long. How many people during that period of time actually engaged in the practice of public accounting as contrasted with those that passed the examination?

Pichler. That is a nice point. I would assume that the CPA certificate has some market value. In fact, I am sure of that since it is very difficult to establish your own practice and to compete with other firms. So the fact that unsuccessful candidates are currently engaged in accounting does not negate the restriction on competition because they are not free to go out and establish their own practice until they get that certificate.

Revsine. Bob, in responding to Professor Zlatkovich's comments, which I believe may be summarized by saying that there were probably not undue entry restrictions, you underscored the word "undue". I think this highlights the difference between Professor Pichler's approach and our paper. What we were suggesting was that he has examined the problems solely in economic terms, whereas our view is that there is a quality dimension involved. When we talk of undue entry restrictions we must consider the trade-offs between free markets and the quality dimension. Our point is that to make policy recommendations along this line we need empirical evidence which indicates how restrictive the current practices are, irrespective of their intent. We also need empirical evidence regarding the expected decline in quality and means for policing that decline in quality. Until this evidence is available, no defensible policy recommendations are possible.

Pichler. I have two points. First, I, too, would like to see some empirical evidence. Indeed, I tried to get it but was unable to do so. My view is that it would be in the profession's interest to publish figures on fractions of candidates passing the exam, and so on. Also it would be in the profession's interest to offer interpretations. At the present accountants seem to be overly concerned about how such statistics might be interpreted. The research staff of the AICPA should be large enough to provide reasonable interpretations.

Second, the question on the trade-off between quality and price is the key one. We want to achieve the benefits of competition with respect to price. The danger is that competition will occur along the quality dimension. The way to resolve that is to impose a constraint as we do in the economic sphere—a cost restraint on output. The constraint that is appropriate here is to set about standardizing accounting principles. We know that auditing principles have been standardized: at least I learned that from Professor Moonitz's article which talked about why it is so easy to standardize auditing principles and why it has been so difficult to standardize accounting principles. The reason seems to be that the accounting principles have some economic impact on shareholders and managers. Given that, and given the reasons I explained in the paper, I would like to see that constraint exist. However, I don't think it is likely to come from the profession. The only out I see is for the SEC to impose it. I don't like that solution, being a Chicago economist, but I don't see any alternative.

Vanatta. Where will they get the expertise to impose these standards?

Pichler. As I indicate, there should be full consultation with the AICPA, the AAA, and all professional organizations. Nevertheless, the argument has been going on for fifty-five years regarding the need for standards. I think it is time to get moving.

Carmichael. I would like to raise a few points that I don't think were dealt with in the analysis. One is that consumers have not solved the licensure problem. The point was raised that this is because of the lack of ability of consumers to mobilize themselves even where they have had that power. It should be pointed out also that the purchasers of the service are not the only consumers. Where the other consumers, as separate from the purchasers, have had the power, such as the Internal Revenue Service (which is now seeking a licensure for tax practice) and the federal government as a consumer of audit reports on various agencies, they have sought licensure. The other factor is in determining whether the supply has been restricted. The critical thing is not how many people are in the queue waiting to become suppliers, but how many consumers of the service are queued up waiting to get the service and cannot get it. In the area that you are talking about, the attest function, the profession seems to feel that it has a severe displacement problem—that is, CPA firms are being displaced, certain firms are losing work, to the advantage of others. This would give some indication that perhaps the supply is certainly adequate if we do in fact have the displacement problem that we believe we do.

Another factor that was overlooked is that outside the area of practice of large companies who are required to follow the requirements of the SEC and the stock exchanges, there isn't any mandatory requirement for these consumers to get the expression of an opinion on a financial statement. For unaudited financial statements they can seek non-certified practitioners, and they do. Also, even if they do want an audit they can get it from non-CPAs. So, in that area, there hasn't been any restriction on supply. Since the service is not mandatory in that area, I find it difficult to see that the restriction which you think exists does in fact exist.

Pichler. I would respond to two points. First, if one believes that demand curves exist, one wouldn't expect to find the queue on the buyer's side. What I would expect to happen is for the price to rise to the point of clearing the market. Second, with respect to the comments on the ability to obtain certain services from uncertified public accountants, you are quite correct. As I note in the paper, federal law does not require even registered firms to seek out certified public accountants. The only requirement is that they be independent. However, the Institute and the state Societies have been successful in obtaining state laws in forty-three jurisdictions that prevent the performance of the attest function by anyone other than a certified public accountant. While it is true that a corporation might go to one firm for the attest function and to another—a cut-rate firm— for other services, I think the cost of search would make that strategy prohibitive.

Burton. I would like to look at the question of the power of the individual practitioner versus the client in terms of the power expression you presented in your paper. There is one term that has not been explicitly discussed which I think is quite important. A device that is being used to increase the power of practitioner vis-à-vis client is the increase in transactions cost— the cost of changing auditors. This is an area that the Commission has been trying to work into. The Commission is not working it in strictly from the out-of-pocket cost of change, although that exists in the sense of additional audit time required in the case of a change in auditors, but also the cost of public disclosure. They are requirements that say we want to accentuate what might be called the social examination of the reasons for change to determine whether or not they are in the public interest. This type of addition to transaction cost, it seems to me, is one of the ways in which the power and authority of individual practitioner vis-à-vis his client can be enhanced, and to the extent that it is possible, should be enhanced.

Pichler. I was quite impressed, as I indicate in the paper, with the new SEC regulation requiring that when there is a change in auditor public notice be given as to the reason for the change, if it is based on a dispute regarding the application of generally accepted accounting principles.

Burton. This adds to the transaction cost of changing auditors.

Sterling. Right, and to that extent it increases the power of the public accountant vis-à-vis management but, from what I hear, management's sole reason for changing, according to their reports to the SEC, has been that the fees are too high. They never report a dispute over principles.

CHAPTER 3

The Accountant's Legal Environment For The Next Decade

CARL D. LIGGIO*

/72991

If at the start of the sixties I had been asked to describe the auditor's legal environment, I could have responded in slightly under one page of printed material. In fact in 1960 it was unlikely that I would have been asked to speak on the subject at length because there was nothing to say about it. Although some members of the profession were starting to evidence concern in 1960, the number of cases brought against the auditors were few and far between. If an accountant had then been asked to define the extent and scope of his liability, I believe that every accountant could have recited the holding of *Ultramares* v. *Touche* and also may have referred to a few other cases that had been decided. As a lawyer, I could have added a few sentences to that and probably would have named one or two other cases involving the accounting profession which had been decided; but nothing earth-shattering would have been said. Those were the happy days!

I think that anyone trying to predict the legal environment for the decade of the '60s would have been justified in relying on the then-existing limited exposure of the auditor. The predictions would have almost universally called for more of what had been. Oh, how we would have been wrong! I need not tell you that—you are all familiar with the *Continental Vendings*, the *Yale Expresses*, the *BarChrises*, and the literally hundreds of other cases that have been filed against the accountants

*A.B. 1963, Georgetown University; J.D. 1967, New York University School of Law. General Counsel, Arthur Young & Company. Member, New York and District of Columbia Bars.

The remarks and views expressed herein are my own and not those of Arthur Young & Company. Moreover, I do not necessarily believe that I am in favor of some of my predictions occurring, only that given the existing attitudes and social climates, they are likely to occur.

99

starting in the mid to late 1960s. I am told that in 1966 there were a *total* of 80 "lawsuits" against the profession (a number that seems high to me); today Lloyd's alone supposedly has over 170 "cases"[1] reported to it which have been brought against the profession—and this does not even begin to scratch the surface on the number of cases pending, let alone brought and resolved in one way or the other.[2]

The accountant today is living in a litigious environment where he can reasonably expect his every action—regardless of how right or wrong it may be—to be questioned in a court of law and possibly result in substantial damages being awarded against him. Whether the auditor will be sued or not will depend upon good luck more than good audit work—but once he gets sued all the luck in the world will not help; only having performed good auditing will.

Given this, I would like to divide my remarks into two areas. First, what has given rise to this "litigious" atmosphere, and second, what I foresee the environment to be in the coming decade.[3] As to the latter, I claim no omniscience; and as I would have been completely wrong had I been asked this question thirteen years ago, I can similarly be completely wrong today. However, our experiences of the past thirteen years are a good harbinger of what we can expect during the remainder of this decade particularly when viewed against the social mores of society. I hope that the profession as a whole takes my remarks to heart and helps prove some of my thoughts right and others wrong.

1.   THE CAUSE OF THE LITIGIOUS PLAINTIFF IN THE '60s

If I had to choose one word to sum up the cause of the change, I must necessarily choose "Money". Although it can be said there were other motivations in some cases and that the motivational impetus for the decade to come may not be as pecuniarily oriented, the fact still remains that money had been the primary cause of the litigious sixties.

A person suffers monetary loss. He seeks redress for that monetary loss and in the process enlists the aid of a lawyer. The lawyer seeks ways to make his client "whole" and in the process seeks to put a few (in most cases actually one third) of those "whole" dollars in his own pocket. I am sure I will be accused of being a cynic, but there is little doubt in my mind that in many, if not most of these cases, the only person who is interested in seeking redress is the lawyer; and in fact, he will be the only one that will benefit from this litigious exercise.[4] This attitude was "aided and abetted" by the contingent fee and class action devices[5]—procedural tools indigenous to the judicial system of this country alone.

As always, there were a few people who were willing to try new avenues to make a dollar and new people to sue in new fields. The '50s and early '60s had demonstrated to the Bar that there was much monetary reward in filing antitrust suits. Many plaintiffs' antitrust lawyers became millionaires within a short period of time and the electrical price fixing cases of the early '60s, with their monumental settlements and attorneys' fees, fed fuel to this fire.

The impetus to sue generated by large recoveries in other areas was also stimulated in the mid-'60s by increased regulatory activity in the securities area in general and against professionals in particular. What is now a landmark case, involving the Texas Gulf Sulphur Company, was brought by the Securities and Exchange Commission in 1965; and shortly thereafter criminal proceedings were filed in the now legendary *Continental Vending* case. These developments heralded the opening of a whole new lucrative area for the Bar. I am told that those eighty-plus lawsuits, that had been filed against accountants by the end of 1966 were filed principally within the prior eighteen-month period. Few of these cases, however, sought the astronomical relief that is commonplace today.

By the end of 1968 three cases had been decided which opened the floodgates of securities-oriented litigation and which caused the number of lawsuits (as opposed to cases—see footnote No. 1) pending against accountants to be multiplied manyfold. You all are aware of these decisions: *Fischer* v. *Kletz* (*Yale Express*) 266 F. Supp. 180 (S.D.N.Y. 1967), *Escott* v. *BarChris Construction Corp.* (*BarChris*) 283 F Supp. 643 (S.D.N.Y. 1968) and *S.E.C.* v. *Texas Gulf Sulphur Corp.* (*Texas Gulf Sulphur*) 401 F. 2d 833 (2d Cir. 1968).

Around this time we also started to see a new philosophy take hold in this country—whether you call it "Consumerism" or "Naderism" as I do,[6] it portended a new attitude on the part of the public as a whole. The acts of professionals, which heretofore had been considered sacrosanct, were now subject to scrutiny and criticism—but criticism that may have gone beyond the bounds of propriety. The public had accepted the "lawsuit" as a way of life.

By the end of 1969 we had experienced an economic reversal that had set the high-flying '60s back on the seat of its pants. Huge losses were incurred in the stock market—thus giving the plaintiffs' Bar much ammunition. The floodgates were truly opened.

Corporations and accounting firms that had been sued entered into big and small settlements, all of which added even more fuel to the fire. The incentive was surely present.

By the foregoing I don't mean to sound completely mercenary and completely cynical because I do believe that there are members of the plaintiffs' Bar who have brought the suits not just for their own personal aggrandizement but also for altruistic motives; and although the results that some of these lawyers have achieved have cost members of the profession money, I feel that benefits have resulted from these suits. I believe that they have helped to awaken the profession as a whole to their greater responsibilities; and in some cases have resulted in much needed change.

The litigation of the '60s has taught the profession lessons—lessons which I hope will not be forgotten or ignored. Although it is not my purpose at this time to act as your lawyer and to analyze in detail the cases that have been decided to date, I feel it will be helpful to briefly discuss some of the more significant cases in terms of what they stand for and their impact on the next decade.

The first of the new wave of cases was *Yale Express.* Here, the financial statements reported on by a firm of public accountants indicated a large net worth and a substantial net income for the prior year. As the result of "special studies" conducted following the issuance of the financial statements, the auditors discovered that the statements previously reported on were in fact wrong. Notwithstanding this, no mention was made of the errors contained in the prior statements for over one year after that. When the auditors issued their report the following year, they restated the prior year's statements. However, in the interim, while they knew the statements were erroneous, they sat silently by while *Yale Express*' management disseminated interim figures which the auditors were alleged to have known to be materially false. Prior to the time the case was to come to trial, a motion was made to dismiss the action on the grounds that even if the foregoing facts were true, there was no legal remedy against the auditors. The Court denied the motion and found that the auditors owed a duty not only to the client but also to the investing public, that a claim was made out under Rule 10b-5, and that the auditors had a duty to immediately recall their report if they believed anyone still relied on it. The profession of course responded to this with SAP 41 (now SAS No. 1-Section 561).

It should be noted that the Securities and Exchange Commission filed a Memorandum Amicus Curiae[7] in opposition to the auditors' motion to dismiss the case. The SEC argued that the accountant owes a direct and primary duty to the investing public to disclose any inaccuracies in the financial statement. The Court adopted substantial parts of the SEC's position and stated:

> In the instant case involving a failure to disclose after-acquired information, it is difficult to solve the "connection" issue in terms of [The Auditor's] "purpose." [The Auditor] had a very specialized and well defined task: to audit and to certify Yales's financial statements for the protection of

investors. In this sense, all of the Auditor's energies were directed toward investors.

Next in the line of cases came *BarChris*. After a lengthy trial to the Court, the late Judge McLean rendered an opinion in which he held that the auditors had not met the due diligence test of the Securities Act in that they did not have a reasonable ground to believe the truth of the financial statements at the time the registration statement became effective. Although he also held that "accountants should not be held to a standard higher than that recognized in their profession", he nevertheless found that they had not even met this standard.[8]

The last of the triad was *Texas Gulf Sulphur*. This case, probably the most often cited in the securities area, imposed substantial responsibilities upon corporate clients. Whether one views *Texas Gulf Sulphur's* standard of materiality and disclosure as a departure from the past or merely a court statement of what materiality and disclosure in the securities area always was and understood to be, the fact is that *Texas Gulf Sulphur* caused a radical departure in securities-oriented litigation. Although auditors were not involved in the litigation, the legal principles relating to materiality and disclosure enunciated by the Court in *Texas Gulf Sulphur* are just as applicable and pervasive as if the auditors had been directly involved. In a few words, it made *almost anything* that later was found not to have been disclosed a material item which should have been disclosed. I am not sure that the profession has fully come to understand the all-pervasive significance of this case.

Although there were other cases pending against accountants at the time, the Court's opinion in *BarChris,* followed so quickly by the landmark decision in *Texas Gulf Sulphur,* and the stockmarket downturn, opened the floodgates of accountants' litigation. The number of lawsuits that occurred subsequent to the *BarChris* decision was many times that of the lawsuits then existing. Each new lawsuit attempted to push further and further the bounds of the auditor's liability and responsibility. These I will turn to in a moment.

With the floodgates opened, more fuel was added to the fire. Until 1969 it was always felt that if it was shown that an auditor complied with GAAP and GAAS, there could be no liability on his part. In 1969 *Continental Vending* was decided by the Second Circuit Court of Appeals after it had been twice tried to a jury. *United States* v. *Simon* 425 F. 2d 796 (2d Cir. 1969). It has been argued that *Continental Vending* established a new standard for judging the auditor's liability. The charge to the jury, which the Court of Appeals approved, stated that the critical test was:

. . . whether the financial statements as a whole 'fairly presented the financial

position of Continental as of September 30, 1962 and whether it accurately
reported the operations for fiscal 1962'. If they did not, the basic issue
became whether defendants acted in good faith. Id at 805

The Court went on to note that "the proof of compliance with generally
accepted standards was evidence which may be very persuasive but
was not necessarily conclusive that the auditor acted in good faith and
that facts as certified were not materially false or misleading." Id at
805. Thus the Court seemed to be saying that the standard by which
the auditor would be judged in the future was not whether he complied
with generally accepted accounting principles, but whether in the
performance of his duties he acted in good faith.

> We do not think the jury was also required to accept the accountants' evaluation
> whether a given fact was material to overall fair presentation, at least not
> when the accountants' testimony was not based on specific rules or prohibitions
> to which they could point, but only on the need for the auditor to make
> an honest judgment and their conclusion that nothing in the financial
> statements themselves negated the conclusion that an honest judgment had
> been made. Such evidence may be highly persuasive, but it is not conclusive,
> and so the trial judge correctly charged.[9] Id at 806

All interpretations of the holding of *Continental Vending*, however,
must be considered in the context of what the case was—a criminal
proceeding where intent is a crucial element of the proof and good
faith would negate such a finding. Nevertheless, a year earlier, good
faith was found to be a defense to a civil securities act violation in
Texas Gulf Sulphur; Id at 862. However, its significance and importance
was not as crucial in a civil context and it has tended to be overlooked.
Some have argued that *Continental Vending* only added another
requirement to the then existing test. One member of the plaintiffs'
Bar who has sued several accounting firms has argued that as a result
of *Continental Vending*, good faith must also be found after it was found
that the auditor complied with the principles and standards of the
profession. Although such a position is arguable, I believe it is un-
supportable; I view *Continental Vending* as establishing a separate
test—good faith—which when applied to civil litigation will be taken
as an alternative test (i.e., to compliance with GAAP) for absolving
the auditor in questions of judgment.[10]
Following *Continental Vending*, the good faith defense was applied
in a civil suit. In *Colonial Realty Corp.* v. *Brunswick Corp.* 337 F. Supp.
546 (S.D.N.Y. 1971) Judge Palmieri said that the testimony of the
accounting firm demonstrated that the accounting judgments in dispute
in that case were made in "good faith" and based on generally accepted
accounting principles. Accordingly the claim was dismissed even though

it was found the reserves were very inadequate in light of what later happened in the bowling alley industry.

The reserves for bad debts assigned by Brunswick were reasonable and adequate and allocated in *good faith*. There is no evidence that the accounting judgment utilized in allocating the reserves was clearly wrong or misleading. (Emphasis added) Id at 557

Two other cases of recent vintage bear noting as they have in some respects helped limit the potential exposure of the auditor by requiring the court to look at the auditor's conduct in terms of the circumstances surrounding the case. In so doing, the courts have been unwilling to impose liability on the auditor for technical departures from accounting principles and auditing standards. These cases however, although beneficial to the profession, could also be interpreted to mean that under the "circumstances of a particular case" strict application of GAAP and GAAS by the auditor will not preclude a finding of liability.

In *Franklin Supply Co.* v. *Tolman* 454 F. 2d 1059 (9th Cir. 1971) the auditors had failed to disclose their alleged lack of independence with respect to the audit that they were conducting. Apparently the partner on the job was a statutory director of the corporation. The fact that the auditor was a statutory director was in accordance with the accounting practices of Venezuela where the audit was conducted and the report issued, and did not pose an independence problem under those standards of conduct. The auditors, a local practice office of one of the Big Eight, issued the report on their Venezuelan client but failed to disclose that under U.S. auditing standards it was not independent since its audit partner was a director of the client. The trial court found that this departure from U.S. GAAS should have been disclosed and held the auditors liable notwithstanding the fact that it was an audit conducted in Venezuela and Venezuelan auditing standards did not require separate disclosure. On appeal the Ninth Circuit, which did not consider the issue of which GAAS—Venezuelan or U.S.—applied, reversed and held that even under U.S. GAAS:

We can agree that this would have been better accounting practice. We cannot agree that under the circumstances of this case the failure to do so constitutes legal fraud. We have not had referred to us any cases so holding, nor have we found any. *Id* at 1064

A similar result was reached in *Wessel* v. *Buhler* 437 F. 2d 279, 283 (9th Cir. 1971) where the Court held that evidence must be adduced that the auditor did not prepare the financial statements "in accordance with good accounting practice *under the circumstances*."

Before I become Seer Liggio and gaze into my crystal ball I would like to borrow a passage from one of the leading English accountant's

liability cases which was decided half a century ago. Here Lord Justice
Romer stated:

> It is not easy to reconstruct the true position as it stood before the auditors
> when they were called upon to do their duty in the three successive years
> in which their conduct is challenged. It is also proper to remember that
> when a big disaster has occurred, such as the failure of this company, which,
> as I have said was a notable company in its day, there is on the part of
> some, a desire to find a scapegoat who can be made responsible and possibly
> make-good some of the losses which have occasioned disaster to so many.
> But it is the duty of the Court, as far as possible, to endeavour to ascertain
> what was the problem presented to the auditors, and what was the knowledge
> available to them at the time. *In re City Equitable Fire Insurance Company,*
> *Limited 1925 1 C.H. 407,503 (1922)*

Too often in the past the courts and Bar have ignored this admonition.
It is apparent from my vantage point that the vast majority of cases
are viewed solely with hindsight and that little attempt is made to
understand what were the circumstances surrounding a particular
decision or a particular set of facts. Recently when the Ninth Circuit
denied plaintiff relief in *Wessel* v. *Buhler, supra,* the Court recognized
this and held that "the exposure of independent accountants and others
to such vistas of liability, limited only by the ingenuity of investors
and their counsel, would lead to serious mischief." Notwithstanding
the Ninth Circuit's prophetic admonition, I can only say as one person
looking at both the trend in the law and the increasing attempts by
counsel to exercise ingenuity in the construction of the complaints against
auditors after the fact, that the vistas of liability will be tremendously
expanded in the next decade.

However, before there can be a finding of liability there must be
a correlative duty on the part of the auditor to do or not to do something
and that this duty has been breached. This can be more appropriately
termed the "Auditor's Responsibility" which leads me to the second
part of my discussion and that is, what I think may be found to be
the auditor's legal responsibility and environment in the next decade.

2.   THE AUDITOR'S LEGAL ENVIRONMENT IN THE NEXT DECADE

Last December while riding to work in the morning I was reading
an article in *The New York Times* which discussed a speech given the
night before at a meeting of the New York State Society of CPAs
by John C. Burton, my distinguished fellow panelist at this Colloquium
and Chief Accountant of the Securities and Exchange Commission.
Mr. Burton's comments were most enlightening and in some respects

most distressing because I see in them the vast vistas of liability that the plaintiffs' Bar seeks to impose upon the auditor. *The New York Times* reported it as follows:

> Furthermore, he told the New York society, "you have a joint responsibility, not a secondary responsibility and I think you had better recognize that fact, because that is the way the auditor's role is viewed in society and also, I believe, by the staff at the Commission."

> Yesterday, Mr. Burton described what he was asking as "quite an additional burden to put on accountants. Instead of taking a secondary point of view in preparing financial statements, accountants should recognize that they share primary responsibility. An auditor must ask himself: 'How would I have accounted for it?' "

> To make clear its position, the accounting firm should write an additional paragraph to the customary two-paragraph report it attaches to financial statements, Mr. Burton suggested.

> This procedure, he went on, "should come into vogue where the auditor . . . comes to the conclusion that the principles followed may fall within the purview of general acceptability but are not the principles he [the accountant] would have selected under the particular factual situation."

> Mr. Burton also warned accountants not to pay too much attention to their potential liability from shareholder lawsuits.

> If you let the fear of liability affect your willingness to innovate, to improve, then the cost will be far greater than the combined total expense of all the legal fees, settlements and unutilized partners' time, the S.E.C. accountant contended.

> An accountant's liability is something that can be budgeted and built into an auditing firm's fee structure, he argued. If accountants spell out in too much detail what they did not do in an effort to avoid possible lawsuits, corporations will begin to ask why they should pay large fees to accounting firms, he said.

I can truly sympathize with Mr. Burton's position and in many respects agree with him. I feel the profession must not be governed by the fear of lawsuits and the liability that could be imposed upon us in the performance of our duties. Nevertheless I think that the auditor should not be forced to live up to new responsibilities on an ex post facto basis as the plaintiffs' Bar and SEC seek to do; nor do I think as a profession we should be called upon to live by these new responsibilities until we know what they are. Yet the very thing that the SEC and the plaintiffs' Bar seek to impose upon the profession is a present determination of new standards and responsibilities applied on a retroactive basis.

This can be analogized to the good news-bad news jokes that have been making the rounds for the past year or so. First the good news—the public needs us and will look to us for help so our profession will continue to be a growing one, and as a result we do have a greater responsibility to the public as Mr. Burton has suggested and we should see to it that we fulfill this responsibility. Now the bad news—we don't know the limits or definitional bounds of this responsibility. We should have some guidelines. Maybe these guidelines have to be developed not by the profession alone, but in a joint effort with the legal profession, public interest groups, and by the SEC so that needs and expectations can be counter-balanced with what we are capable of doing.[11] But in any event this should not be left to the courts, the SEC, and plaintiffs' Bar to determine on an ex post facto basis. If we permit the existing system to continue to develop "our" standards of responsibility in the context of a litigious atmosphere while trying to impose a liability on the profession for a responsibility it did not know it had, the bad news will even be worse. It will result in the bankruptcy of the profession both intellectually and financially; more important it will cause capable young people not to want to enter the profession for fear of the vast vistas of liability with which they will be faced. (I already see some of the effects of this for when I speak on the subject of the auditor's liability today, I am told to tone down my remarks because the young people are getting scared out of the profession.) I think it is only equitable that the auditor know what the vistas of liability, which are the correlative of his responsibility, will be and that both the responsibilities and liabilities resulting therefrom be reasonable and within the auditors' abilities.

Unfortunately, to date, the legal liability of the auditor has been approached in a "cart before the horse" manner. Our courts have developed the liability before we as a profession, and for that matter anyone else, knew or understood what our responsibility was that gave rise to the liability. (This is ironic since there must be a known duty, i.e., responsibility, before a court theoretically should find a liability.) The SEC has been the greatest sinner in this regard. It has caused actions to be initiated on its own (or recommended to others that actions be initiated against the profession) where no set standards or rules previously existed. In some cases, the SEC has brought or threatened actions predicated on principles and procedures which are the subject of legislative recommendations made by it to Congress and then pending before Congress. In other cases, the SEC has reversed positions previously taken by it by either bringing an action or by filing an amicus brief in a civil proceeding. If the SEC feels there is a need for change, it should do so prospectively and by its rule making powers—not by ex post facto court determinations.

In some respects, I cannot fault the courts because as a profession we may not have acted as quickly as we should have in attempting to define our responsibility or to have defined the scope of our responsibility in a forum other than the arcane arena of litigation. We may also have been lax in educating the user of our work product as to what it means, what it should mean, its limitations, what we do and are capable of doing.[12] To the extent that we have been lax, only we can take the blame for it; and to the extent that we have failed to recognize responsibilities that actually exist when we do our work, only we can take the blame for that. Unfortunately many of the "responsibilities that actually exist" are known only in the minds of plaintiffs' Bar and the SEC.

Given the above, what can we expect in the next decade, if we continue to rest on the past and do nothing? What will be the responsibilities sought to be imposed upon us?

I believe that the scope of the auditor's liability will be increased dramatically in the next decade and the correlative responsibilities imposed upon the auditor will show a commensurate growth. This responsibility will increase as a result of three fundamental facts. First—what I have already spoken about—the pecuniary desire of the lawyer to plow new fields, to obtain new sources of revenue. Second the misconception of the auditor's function universally shared by the user of his work product. Unfortunately the general public and even many of the courts and people, whom you expect to know, consider the auditor a guarantor or insurer of the financial statements.[13] This misconception is as much the public's fault as it is the auditor's fault. The profession as a whole has been very lax in its attempts to educate the public as to what its role is; and in fact, as several commentators have suggested, may have permitted the public to bask in false delusions. Third, and the only legitimate reason I see for the increase and expansion of the auditor's responsibilities, all professionals are being asked to assume greater responsibilities with respect to the performance of their duties. I do not fault this. In fact I praise it and feel it is a desirable result. I also believe that as a whole the profession is continually attempting on its own to achieve this result. Where I do disagree, however, and where I do see potential problems for the auditor in the next decade, is the extent and bounds to which these responsibilities may be pushed as a result of a conbination of all three factors. Some of these areas of possible liability follow.

(a) *Everyman:* When the *BarChris* case was decided, *The Wall Street Journal* had an extensive article discussing the case. In the article, the writer stated:

The decision is likely to mean that everyone connected with a registration will be much more meticulous than in the past. It means that hardly anyone can safely take anyone else's word for anything. In theory, it means that nearly everyone involved must check every material fact himself by plodding through company records (*The Wall Street Journal*, May 14, 1968, page 1).

This will be one of the focal points of the auditor's increased responsibility in the next decade. He is being asked to be everyman, to make every determination. I try to read all the complaints I can get copies of that are filed against auditors to see what is being complained of and how it fits into our practice. As a trial lawyer I have participated in cases where issues of an accountant's liability have been raised. In both my studies and practical experience I see a definite trend toward attempting to make the auditor everyman and to require the auditor to judge the efficacy of the opinions of other experts, to make determinations which he himself may not be capable of making. These determinations which the auditor is being asked to make go to issues beyond accounting: they go to the correctness of the managerial decisions of the company, they go to legal opinions rendered by counsel, they deal with the propriety of engineering judgments and the correctness of oil and gas reserves estimated by independent petroleum engineers. If anything goes wrong in the company, the auditor is attacked immediately for not having foreseen this.[14]

Recently, a case was filed in California involving a company, its officers and directors, the attorneys, and the auditors. Two of the allegations of that complaint go directly to my point. The attorneys were charged with violating the securities laws because they failed in their professional duties to advise the auditors of a contingent liability and to require it to be disclosed in the financial statements. The auditors in turn, who had relied on the lawyers' letter that there were no contingent liabilities, were charged with being negligent and failing to detect the existence of a contingent liability. Without going into the particular facts of that case and the allegations of that complaint, I think I can say that the type of contingent liability which was not disclosed in that case is the type of contingent liability that would be particularly within the lawyers' bailiwick and that an auditor should not be expected to recognize that contingency in the course of his audit unless the auditor himself was a trained securities lawyer.

In another recent case, plaintiffs' counsel during the course of trial alleged that the auditor had a responsibility to determine the propriety of certain managerial decisions with respect to the running of the company, that the auditor should have known these decisions were improper or wrong, and had a duty to call the matter to the attention of the owners of the business. This same plaintiffs' lawyer suggested that certain engineering reports that had been rendered to the client were wrong and that the auditor had the responsibility to make that determination.

Now in hearing this, I am sure that you must all think that it could not be happening. How could anyone expect an auditor to make determinations as to engineering competence, or how or why or should the auditor be expected to make determinations as to the management decisions, the correctness, the propriety, etc. of those decisions? Yet it is happening. And it is going to continue to happen in this decade; and the courts, which already have been flooded with a multitude of cases against the auditor, are going to continue to be flooded with more cases where these very issues are called into question.

(b) *Reliance on others:* But even if the courts do not go as far as some of the plaintiffs' Bar now suggests and require you as auditors to be lawyers, engineers, actuaries, geologists, etc., I think you may be required, before being entitled to rely on the opinions of these other experts, to make independent verification as to some or all of the facts that underlie that expert's opinion. Such is not the law today, but may be tomorrow. In this respect the quotation I read to you from *The Wall Street Journal* back in 1968 after *BarChris* was decided is particularly prophetic.

A recent case involving an engineer suggests what I believe to be the responsibilities that will be imposed upon the auditor in this coming decade before he can rely on any independent experts or representations. In this case, involving the construction of a building on a filled area, the engineer went to the footings sub-contractor and was informed that the ground was control-filled of an area 8 to 10 feet deep and solid below that. Laboratory tests made after the suit was filed indicated that the soil was filled to depths varying from 13 to 28 feet. At the trial the engineer testified that if he had known it was a control-fill, he would not have approved the footings and foundations without requiring piers to extend down through the fill to the natural soil. The Court on appeal affirmed the trial court finding of negligence on the part of the engineer (Mr. Tobey). In so doing, the Court held:

> We concur in the finding of the Chancellor that Mr. Tobey was negligent in accepting the assurances from contractor Neal and/or subcontractor Edwards that the footings were being placed in a controlled fill without making any independent investigation to confirm the fact. He made no inquiry as to what laboratory made the testings of the soil as it was being compacted. He made no effort to get any reports from the laboratory or anyone concerning the density of the soil and did not determine nor attempt to determine by test borings or otherwise the degree and uniformity of compaction. He was guilty of negligent misrepresentation in certifying to the Planning Board and to Leader Federal that the foundations were sufficient to support the dwelling. *Cooper* v. *Cordova Sand and Gravel Company, Inc.* 485 S.W. 2d 261 (Tenn. 1972)

The Second Circuit Court of Appeal's recent decision in *Chris-Craft*

Industries, Inc. v. *Bangor Punta Corp.*, CCH Sec. L. Rpt. Para. 93,816.
(2d Cir. 1973) lends support to my prognostications. Here the court
held the investment bankers, First Boston Corp., liable for failing to
make *independent* verification of the facts. The Court held:

> The federal securities laws impose upon private parties the primary responsi-
> bility for verifying the accuracy and completeness of information provided
> to potential investor.

*   *   *

> First Boston is a skilled, experienced and well-respected dealer-manager and
> underwriter. It had an obligation with respect to the BPC exchange offer
> to reach a careful, independent judgment based on facts known to it as
> to the accuracy of the registration statement. Moreover, if it was aware of
> facts that strongly suggested, even though they did not conclusively show,
> that the registration materials were deceptive, it was duty-bound to make
> a reasonable further investigation.

*   *   *

> These minutes, if not sufficient in themselves to lead a reasonable person
> to believe that the registration statement was misleading, certainly would
> have impelled a reasonable person to explore further. The only additional
> investigation by First Boston was to question company officials about the
> possible sale of the BAR. First Boston did not seek verification of the officials'
> answer that a sale was not anticipated at that time . . . nor did it talk to
> officials at Amoskeag after it discovered from the minutes that Amoskeag
> was the likely buyer. Id. at pp. 93,510–93,513

*   *   *

The Court's holding will be equally applicable to the auditor in his
work when he relies on independent parties. The same rationale will
be applied to managements's representations which have so routinely
been relied upon to date. The auditor will eventually be called up
to verify each fact underlying the client's representation before he will
be able to rely on it.This will be a marked departure from the current
state of the law.

Consider in this regard The American Law Institute's proposed
Federal Securities Code, Tentative Draft No. 2 (March, 1973) which
provides that "A statement of fact within the meaning of [this new
code] is not a misrepresentation if it . . . is reasonably based on facts,
including whatever investigation is appropriate under the circumstances,
when it is made . . ." [Sec. 259(b)][15]

(c) *Proxies, Prospectuses and Press Releases:* Other areas in which I see
the auditor facing greater exposure relate to registration statements
and proxy materials. An alarmingly large number of cases allege that

the auditor has a responsibility for determining the correctness of every single line in a prospectus or proxy statement and not just those parts as to which he is admittedly expertizing. The effect of allegations of conspiracy and joint and several liability are resulting in the imposition on the auditor of a responsibility towards every part of the prospectus and proxy statement. (But see *Lanza* v. *Drexel & Co.* CCH Sec. L Rpt. Para. 93,959 [2d Cir. 1973] which may limit the expansion of the law in this area). Whether this is done wittingly or unwittingly by the courts, it is a fact of life which the auditor must be prepared for in the '70s and absent some form of legislative enactment to limit the scope of the liability as to those areas as to which the auditor has in fact expertized, the vistas of liability of the auditor will be unlimited.

I could spend a considerable amount of time enumerating many instances where I believe the auditor is being called upon today to take responsibility for things beyond his particular competence. I am sure each of you can recall situations in your practice in which you might be called upon to justify the work of others in subsequent litigation.

The areas of responsibility sought to be imposed upon the auditor are only limited by the business of his client and the ingenuity of the lawyer suing the auditor. For example, there are several cases in which the auditor is a defendant along with the client firm and its officers and directors where one of the allegations of the complaint is that the auditor failed to have misleading press releases issued by the client corrected. In those cases the auditor has been charged with aiding and abetting in not requiring the client to recall the false and misleading press release.

(d) *Lending the Good Name:* A recent case involving an accountant, several lawyers, and a financial advisor is particularly indicative of this increasing responsibility and liability. Here the annual report, the interim financial statements, and many press releases inaccurately described the company. The prospectus on which the sales of stock were initially made was deficient with respect to information concerning the business operations in the frozen meat department. The stock came out and went down. Everybody in any way connected with the stock was sued. One of the defendants was a person who gave general information about public offerings to the company and had been paid $2,500 by the company to provide financial advisory services. This person was not listed as an expert in the prospectus; nor was he an officer or director of the company. The Court held that since his name was associated with the company as a financial advisor, he had a duty to make an investigation into the accuracy of the prospectus. Since he had not done this, the Court held him liable "because he permitted another to use his reputation and goodwill to further a fraudulent

scheme." Auditors beware—you may become liable under this rationale
for anything a client does in which you can be associated. In fact the
only allegations of wrongdoing against accountants in several recent
complaints are that the accountants lent their good name to what was
a fraudulent scheme.

(e) *Knowledge from Other Parts of the Practice:* To the extent that the
profession continues to do management services and tax work for clients
and obtains information in the course of those activities and that
information is not conveyed to the audit staff (or visa versa), vast potential
areas of liability may be opened. The auditor (as well as the tax and
the management services personnel) will be presumed to have the same
knowledge as everyone else in his firm and the failure to have that
information communicated will not likely be an adequate defense to
a lawsuit. Thus as we as a profession continue to do work other than
audit work, the knowledge acquired as a result of these other activities
will of necessity have to be considered by the audit staff in the judgments
that they make and opinions that they render. The failure to do this
and to coordinate the activities of the three types of service that the
profession performs for its clients can only add to an increased exposure
of the auditor in the decade to come. The problem (and possible liability)
will be indigenous to all three areas of practice and not just the audit
side.

(f) *Interim Financials:* Another problem area for the auditor is the
interim financial statements of a company, which the auditor may see
only after issuance. The issue of the auditor's responsibility was first
raised in *Yale Express,* where the plaintiff argued that the auditor had
a duty to correct the allegedly misleading interim statements.[16] In ruling
on the auditor's motion to dismiss that part of the complaint that sought
to impose liability for the misleading interim financial statements, the
Court held:

> No similar independent duty can be found here by application of either
> statutory or common law principles. Contrary to plaintiffs' suggestion, issuance
> by Yale of the interim statements created no "special relationship" between
> the investors and PMM. In respect to the interim statements, PMM was
> not a statutory "independent public accountant" as it was during the audit
> and certification of the annual report. PMM made no representations which
> appeared in the statements, nor did it compile the figures contained therein.
> In sum unlike the situation in *Pettit,* there is absolutely no basis in law for
> imposing upon PMM a duty to disclose its knowledge of the falsity of the
> interim financial statements.

* * *

> As in *Pettit,* defendant's liability was premised upon the rationale that the
> failure to disclose constituted a breach of duty but, as indicated, no such

duty can be found in the context of those facts pleaded here. Absent such a duty, there is no basis for transforming silence into actionable aiding and abetting.

Notwithstanding the foregoing, the Court refused to dismiss the complaint at that time. Some court in the future in the context of different facts or different circumstances may well find that the auditor has a responsibility (duty) with respect to interim financial statements which he may not have seen until after they were issued—particularly since many plaintiffs' lawyers are urging this in pending litigation.

(g) *Forecasts:* Although we have yet to see our first case growing out of company's forecasts under the new liberalized policy of the SEC, I predict that as soon as the first forecast falls miserably on its face and the stock takes a big tumble, we will have one lawsuit which will allege that (1) the forecast violated rule 10b–5, (2) that the auditor knew or should have known that the forecast could not be met, and (3) he had a duty to call that fact to the attention of management and to the public at large. I also predict that such a claim will be made even if the auditor did not participate in the making of the forecast and even if the auditor did not do so much as check the mathematical accuracy of the forecast. Moreover, what I fear is that even where the auditor had no connection with the forecast, some court in an ex post facto manner will find a responsibility on the auditor's part to have determined the veracity of the forecast.[17]

(h) *Aiding and Abetting:* Some of the areas I just discussed will result in responsibilities (i.e., liabilities) being imposed on the auditor because of the legal doctrine that an aider and abettor can be equally liable. Under the aiding and abetting theory the auditor may well be held responsible for acts of others where it is found he knew or should have known something was amiss.[18]

(i) *Foreign GAAP:* We are living in the age of the multi-national corporation and the multi-national accounting partnership. This poses a whole new set of complex problems, responsibilities, and liabilities for the auditors in the decade ahead. What are the applicable accounting principles and auditing standards to be applied to engagements outside of the United States of multi-national or foreign corporations by multi-national accounting partnerships? The *Franklin Supply* case discussed earlier seemed to suggest that U.S. GAAP were to be applied. The issue was never resolved by the Appellate Court. In another recent case, *Koch Industries Inc. v. Vosko* (D. Kan. 1972) CCH Sec. L. Rpt. Para. 93,705, the issue was also raised . There, plaintiff's lawyers alleged that Arthur Young & Company, by signing a report on the Arthur Young & Company letterhead any place in the world, automatically was presumed to have applied U.S. GAAP and GAAS unless the report disclosed to the contrary. This argument was made notwithstanding the fact that the auditors were English chartered accountants (and so described on the letterhead), that the client audited was a Bahamian company operating out of Nassau with European subsidiaries, that it is the *Company's* financial statements upon which the auditor reports (see footnote 13), that it is the Company's accounting principles upon which the auditor reports, that all of its officers and directors were Bahamian residents and either Canadian or English nationals, and that the company conducted its business activities outside of the United States. Here also the Court never decided whether U.S. accounting principles and auditing standards were applicable to the engagement, as a favorable decision was rendered for Arthur Young without reaching the issue of whether U.S. GAAP and GAAS were applicable. (I should note in passing that not only were we completely successful in the case, but the Court awarded $450,000 in legal fees to Arthur Young under Bahamian law in defending this action).

Plaintiff in *Koch* also argued that one is entitled to believe that where the language of the report conforms to the "United States short form opinion" that U.S. GAAP and GAAS have been applied. The problem posed by what principles and standards are applicable to foreign engagements is further exacerbated by the conformity of language in the reports issued in countries whose accounting principles and auditing standards differ markedly. For example, the "short form" opinion as we know it is identical to the short form opinion used in the Caribbean, Latin America, South America, Canada and Japan. (See Appendix to Mr. Kapnick's paper presented at this Colloquium). In light of this, how can anyone rationally argue that the "form" of opinion tells the reader what GAAP and GAAS have been applied!

Thus the issue of which accounting principles and auditing standards are applicable to foreign engagements remains open. One of these days, possibly in the near future, this issue will be decided. In the meantime I fully expect it to pose more and more problems for accounting firms that engage in an international practice.

(j) *Fair Presentation and GAAP:* Another area in which I feel that auditor's responsibility will be substantially increased in the next decade involves the form of financial presentation itself. In fact, I believe this to be the most pressing problem the auditor will face in terms of his potential future liability. I am sure that everyone here is familiar with the continuing debate as to what the auditor's opinion does mean when he states that the financial statements are "fairly presented" in accordance with generally accepted accounting principles. Does this mean only that the statements comply with generally accepted accounting principles or does it mean that there is an overall fair presentation, a meaningful presentation, an adequate disclosure of the true financial position of the company?. I think the profession as a whole would view "fairly presented" as modifying only the question of whether the statements were in accordance with generally accepted accounting principles. One of my counterparts, Victor M. Earle, the dean of the accounting firms' general counsels, in speaking at a Seminar conducted by the New York Law Journal on Expanding Responsibilities Under the Acts posed the issue as follows:

1. Is there a distinction between fair presentation and compliance with generally accepted accounting principles?

   For the accounting profession, the answer is and must be no. See, for example, Accounting Principles Board Statement #4. This is not because strict compliance with generally accepted accounting principles leaves no room for professional judgment, but rather because professional accountants do not know how to make judgments which are subject to review by some super-professional "common sense" criterion of fairness. Their inability to function under such governance is demonstrated by its random application by judges and juries, laymen in accounting matters. No other professionals are held to such a standard. See also Judge McLeans's comment in *BarChris* that accountants should not be held to standards higher than those set by their profession.

   If the profession's view conflicts with Judge Friendly's opinion in *Continental Vending*, so be it. It should be remembered, however, in addition to the rather unique facts of that case, that the accountant defendants were there asserting, in a criminal proceeding, that compliance with generally accepted accounting principles is an absolute defense. The lower court took this request to charge to mean that, even in the presence of an intent to deceive, the defendants would have to be acquitted upon expert proof of compliance.

On the other the public probably views "fairly presented" to mean that the financial position of the company in question was fairly disclosed and that everything one needed to know about the company was set out in the financial statements. Clearly this is the interpretation plaintiffs' Bar has placed on it. In this connection we should consider that under generally accepted auditing standards the third standard of reporting mandates that "informative disclosures in the financial statements are to be regarded as reasonably adequate unless otherwise stated in the report." As S.A.P. No. 33 points out:

   The fairness of presentation of financial statements, apart from the relationship to generally accepted accounting principles, is dependent upon the adequacy of disclosures involving material matters. (See also S.A.S. No. 1 Sec. 430.02

From this it can be argued that, even when GAAP is complied with, additional disclosures may be necessary to make the financial presentation meaningful. Can it not be argued that fair presentation then is more than mere compliance with GAAP in light of S.A.P. No. 33?

The recent case of *Green* v. *Jonhop Inc., supra* is in point. There, the Company suffered four years of substantial losses because it expensed its R&D. In year five the Company decided to capitalize its R&D, and accordingly turned a handsome profit. The change in accounting policy was duly disclosed in the footnotes and the auditors gave a clean opinion, but noting, of course, the lack of consistency as disclosed in the footnotes. The Court found all of this was in accord with GAAP, but nevertheless held that given everything else that transpired (i.e., certain other activities of the company and the history of losses) the disclosure was not adequate enough. "Presumably" there was no fair presentation, and the company was found to have violated Rule 10b–5.[19]

The question of "fair presentation" will be the most pressing and troublesome question for the profession during the next decade. I am sure it will be argued that "fair presentation" means a presentation that may not necessarily comply with GAAP, and in fact may deviate substantially from GAAP in the particular circumstances in question. "Fair presentation" will be found to be a presentation which is meaningful to the person who uses the work product of the auditor. (*Compare:* The new Rules of Conduct which require departure from GAAP to avoid misleading presentation.)

This is purely a subjective test as to which reasonable minds can differ; and, in the heat of a lawsuit, after the fact, when substantial injury has been done and the public has suffered much in damages, it is very easy to argue that fair presentation was not there. Hindsight is infallible. Yet this is what the cases are leading to and this is what the auditor must face in the next decade. This will be the cross the auditor must bear since this standard is totally subjective!

I think Mr. Burton summed up the problem very well in a comment he made on a different matter—the AICPA's new audit guide for investment companies. I believe his comments may be universally applicable:

> It is apparent that neither the S.E.C. forms nor the AICPA audit guides have addressed themselves to the real issue—how do you tell investors how well their money is being managed? It is time that all of us began to do so. *B.N.A. Securities Reg. & Law Rptr.* #194, March 21, 1973.p.A4.

If we don't take Mr. Burton's admonition to heart as the plaintiffs' Bar has already done, then the courts may well do it for us in a manner which we do not like.

However, before such a subjective standard is adopted, we as a profession are going to need the help of both the courts and legislature to substantially limit our liability. If not, with such a subjective standard that the auditor must meet in each case, he will have unbounded absolute liability. If we are to meet the responsibilities and liabilities that I expect the courts and the public to impose upon the profession in the next decade, we must stop looking at the company's financial position from a 2 plus 2 attitude, but must start looking at it in terms of the business, the operations of the company, the economy as a whole, and many other complex factors that go into the makeup of a clients's business. (It may well be that the answer given in Mr. Briloff's apocryphal story to the question what is $2+2$ may be more true than "4" if we substitute "what should it be" for "what do you want it to be".) And in so viewing this, the auditor must try and examine the company's activities and financial statements in terms of these considerations. When he renders his opinion and looks to the adequacy of the disclosure in that opinion and the financial statements on which he is reporting, he should consider these other factors and try and step back from the opinion and from the financial statements and ask himself "What does this tell the investor?" And from my very cynical standpoint "What would a jury looking at this transaction, at this company, five years from now, in light of the company having suffered horrendous losses, have to say about the adequacy of the reporting and financial disclosure? What will the jury say we should have told the investor, but did not?"

If the auditor adopts this attitude, he may well satisfy the new responsibilities sought to be imposed on him in the decade to come and limit substantially those vast vistas of liability.

NOTES

1. Please note the distinction I draw between case and lawsuit. By case I mean one or more lawsuits involving the same subject—thus *Equity Funding* which reportedly has spawned over 50 different lawsuits is one case.

2. As an educated guess, I would suspect that the number of cases against accountants that either have been resolved or are still pending exceeds 300. (Harvey Kapnick in a recent issue of *Business Week* put the number at 500.) The number of lawsuits is greatly in excess of that. This, of course, includes claims ranging from a few hundred dollars to the multi-million dollar open-ended Securities Act claims. Although it is impossible to assess with any degree of certitude the total amounts sought by these complaints, it is fair to say that it is several billion dollars. For example, on paper the claims growing out of the Penn Central litigation are several hundred million dollars and one complaint in Equity Funding alone seeks $2.5 billion.

The issue of accountants' liability litigation today is directly tied to the ever-growing securities litigation. The April, 1973 issue of *Fortune* reports that in 1964 there were 267 lawsuits involving alleged Securities Act violations filed in the Federal District courts and that by the end of 1972 this had increased over sevenfold to 1,919 cases. (This latter figure seems low considering that over 50,000 cases were filed in the Federal courts in 1972.)

3. Part 2 of this paper does not speak of what has happened in the past, or what is the present, but rather what I see the evolutionary process of the law to be creating.

4. I do not mean to suggest by this that I feel securities litigation is without merit or that all members of the Bar seek only to pursue their own self-interest. On the contrary, I believe the threat of litigation and litigation itself in many instances serve a useful purpose; and from a social benefit standpoint there is much to say for it. However, as with all good things, it is abused.

5. This latter device has seen certain limitations placed upon it by the Courts in recent cases. Where in the past Courts were readily willing to make the determination that a case should proceed as a class action almost on a pro forma basis, they have recently shown considerably more restraint and denied class action status to litigants. (Fundamental questions as to the efficacy and use of the class action are finally being given the attention they deserve by the courts.) The Second Circuit Court of Appeals decision in *Eisen v. Carlise-Jacqueline*—F.2d—(2d Cir. May 1, 1973) ("Eisen III") is a landmark case that may help return sanity to this area. Although the effect of the Court's denial of class status, its rejection of the "fluid recovery" theory, and its requirement that those seeking class status pay the costs of notice will take a while to be felt, it cannot help but result in a more judicious use of the class action device, and, as such, further the interests of justice as it was intended to do.

6. Some call it "populism" revisited.

7. Amicus briefs filed by the SEC are a very fertile source of information for the SEC's thinking and policies. They afford a good overview of the direction in which the Commission may be moving.

8. *BarChris* also added to the profession's knowledge of materiality—but not as much as did the next case in my triad.

9. The Court's reference to "specific rules or prohibitions" suggests that compliance with GAAP and GAAS, if GAAP and GAAS are directly in point, will be a defense. Thus it is arguable that the Court merely adopted an alternative test and not a new test.

10. But cf. *Green v. Jonhop, Inc.* CCH Fed. Sec. L. Rep. Para. 93,940 (D. Ore. 1973)

11. Too often I have found we are expected to perform tasks we are not capable of performing.

12. I recently was told by a lawyer that he thought one of the accountants involved in a litigated matter should have told the lawyer's client, an investor whom the accountant did not even know existed, that an investment in a foreign REIT was not suited for him because this foreign REIT was highly illiquid. This is the height of folly!

13. *Compare:* Traditionally the Commission's philosophy has been that "the fundamental and primary responsibility for the accuracy of information filed with the Commission and disseminated among investors rests upon management." *Interstate Hosiery Mills Inc.*, 4 S.E.C. 706,721 (1939); And even more recently it has opined that "The financial statements are the responsibility of the client and all decisions with respect to them must ultimately be assumed by the client." A.S.R. 126 (July 1972). Notwithstanding this, the Commission's actions and those of its staff ignore these concepts and effectively seek to place on the auditor a greater responsibility than upon management whose stewardship of the company makes it privy to information that the auditor—no matter how extensive his audit procedures—will never have access to. Mr. Burton has expressed the view that this is a shared responsibility, which is contradictory to the foregoing policy pronouncements. (I personally believe that the distinction must be maintained and that the concept of "whose statements they are" is very real and not a fiction. Its import may not be as great in situations involving third party civil liability, but it does have important ramifications beyond issues raised in the context of third party cases.)

14. A recent example of this involved the ICC-IOS-Vesco litigation. Several private suits were filed immediately after the SEC filed its suit. The only difference between the SEC and private suits was that in the former suit the lawyers and not the accountants were named—while the private suits, which copied the SEC complaint word for word, typo for typo, substituted the accountants for the lawyers, who had been named by the SEC, and blamed the auditors for everything.

15. The Reporter's comment on this new section gives the following example: "An income statement represents that the depreciation expense on a straight line basis on a $1 million asset is $100,000. This implies an estimate of a ten-year useful life. The issuer certainly should be held to a reasonable investigation before making such an estimate. But, so long as the issuer's estimate is within the bounds of reason, it *could* be found that the *accountant* had no duty to make an investigation beyond *his general knowledge* of the lives of machinery" p.21 (Emphasis added). This implies therefore that unless the auditor has facts within his own knowledge to support the position taken, he has an independent duty of investigation which he must pursue. What "facts within his own knowledge" shall mean will probably only be defined after much litigation. Presumably, however, an auditor's general knowledge of industry conditions should suffice.

16. It is only now, some six years after *Yale Express*, that the profession has come to grips—and then only partially—with the issue of interim financials and the auditor's association therewith. See APB Exposure Draft Ref. No. 1097.

17. The trial of a case involving the forecasts of a large corporation made in 1966 will commence in Federal Court in New York on June 4, 1973. I have been advised that at the last pretrial conference in March one of the plaintiff's lawyers indicated that one of the issues to be considered was whether the auditors had a responsibility with respect to the company's forecasts.

18. One recent case involving officers and directors stands for the proposition that they have a duty "to correct statements and facts [presented by others] which they . . . should have known were erroneous or misleading." It is not too much to make the next step and apply this holding to the auditors for statements of others. Should this occur, the auditor may well have an impossible task which he is not capable of satisfying.

19. Notwithstanding what I have said above, I feel that a court would be hard pressed to find the accounting firm liable under these facts; and in fact to do so, would prostitute the purpose of the securities acts.

The Meaning and Implications of *U.S.* v. *SIMON* as to the Legal Role of Accountants

TED J. FIFLIS*

1. U.S. V. SIMON (THE "CONTINENTAL VENDING CASE")

The precise meaning of *U.S.* v. *Simon*, 425 F. 2d 796 (2d Cir. 1969), which is vitally crucial to a proper understanding of the legal role of the accountant, has been the subject of only limited analyses in the legal and accounting literature.[1] Hence, a fresh analysis is required.

The case involved a criminal conviction of three accountants for certifying false or misleading financial statements in violation of § 32 of the 1934 *Securities Exchange Act* (15 *U.S.C.* Sec. 6 78ff), the *Mail Fraud Act* (18 *U.S.C.* Sec. 6 1341), and a provision concerning false statements generally (18 *U.S.C.* Sec. 6 1001). Upon conviction, the defendants appealed on the ground that the jury had been given incorrect instructions as to the applicable rule of law and that the correct charge had been proposed by the defendants and refused by the judge.[2]

The facts were that Harold Roth, the president and controlling shareholder of Continental Vending, had been borrowing heavily from Continental and its sister corporation, Valley Financial, also controlled by him, to finance various stock market ventures of his own. At the end of the year in question, 1962, Continental owned a receivable of $3.5 million, owing from Valley, which had re-lent the money to Roth. Flowing in the other direction, Continental had borrowed $1 million from Valley, evidenced by notes. The notes thus received by Valley had been negotiated to two banks and therefore could not be offset against the debt of Valley to Continental. The prosecution contended that Continental's financial statement wrongfully failed to disclose: (1) that the $3.5 million receivable from Valley was uncollectable because Valley had re-lent it to Roth who was broke, (2) that 80 percent

*B.S. 1954, Northwestern University; LL.B. 1957, Harvard Law School. Visiting Professor of Law, University of California (Davis); Professor of Law, University of Colorado. Member, ABA Committee on Federal Regulation of Securities. Author, (with H. Kripke) *Accounting for Business Lawyers* (1972).

of the collateral for the Valley loans to Roth was Continental's own securities, (3) that the receivable from Valley could not be offset by the debt owing to Valley, and (4) that the amount receivable from Valley had increased by $400,000 since the year end. The Court held that the jury could reasonably have found that the defendants knew all of these facts at the time of publishing the financial statements.

When the market dropped almost immediately after publication of the financial statements, the collateral became valueless and bankruptcy ensued.[3]

Eight expert accounting witnesses testified that the financial statements treated the Valley receivable in accordance with GAAP and GAAS and fairly presented the year-end financial position except for the erroneous statement that the $1 million owing to Valley by Continental could be offset against the $3.5 million receivable from Valley. They specifically testified that nothing need be said about the 80 percent of the collateral being Continental's own securities, or about the $400,000 post-balance-sheet-date increase in the receivable, or that Roth was the ultimate recipient of the loans to Valley.

There were two crucial issues for the jury:

(1) Were the financial statements misleading?
(2) If so, had the defendants intentionally made them so?

On these two issues, the defendants' attorneys requested the trial judge to charge the jury that a defendant may be found guilty only if:

(1) (a) The financial statements did not fairly present the financial condition according to GAAP and (b) defendant knew it, and intended to deceive readers, and
(2) (a) The financial statements did not comply with GAAP and (b) defendant knew it and intended to deceive readers.[4]

Thus the defendants took the position in (2) above that financial statements cannot be misleading if they comply with GAAP and that the defendants cannot be guilty of intended deception unless they knew the statements did not comply with GAAP. The requested instruction described in (1) above is more ambiguous, but analysis of what the defendants had in mind there would not be fruitful.

The Second Circuit, speaking through Judge Friendly, upheld the refusal of these instructions and at pages 805–806 stated the crux of the opinion:

. . . Dealing with the subject in the course of his charge, [the trial judge] said that the "critical test" was whether the financial statements as a whole "fairly presented the financial position of Continental as of September 30, 1962, and whether it [sic] accurately reported the operations for fiscal 1962."

If they did not, the basic issue became whether defendants acted in good
faith. Proof of compliance with generally accepted standards was "evidence
which may be very persuasive but not necessarily conclusive that he acted
in good faith, and that the facts as certified were not materially false or
misleading." "The weight and credibility to be extended by you to such
proof, and its persuasiveness, must depend, among other things, on how
authoritative you find the precedents and the teachings relied upon by the
parties to be, the extent to which they contemplate, deal with, and apply
to the type of circumstances found by you to have existed here, and the
weight you give to expert opinion evidence offered by the parties. Those
may depend on the credibility extended by you to expert witnesses, the
definiteness with which they testified, the reasons given for their opinions,
and all the other facts affecting credibility, . . ."

Defendants contend that the charge and refusal to charge constituted error.
We think the judge was right in refusing to make the accountants' testimony
so nearly a complete defense. The critical test according to the charge was
the same as that which the accountants testified was critical. We do not
think the jury was also required to accept the accountants' evaluation whether
a given fact was material to overall fair presentation, at least not when the
accountants' testimony was not based on specific rules or prohibitions to
which they could point, but only on the need for the auditor to make an
honest judgment and their conclusion that nothing in the financial statements
themselves negated the conclusion that an honest judgment had been made.
Such evidence may be highly persuasive, but it is not conclusive, and so
the trial judge correctly charged.

Thus the lower court was upheld on the following instructions:

(a) The financial statements were not misleading if they "fairly presented
the financial position of Continental as of [the end of the period] . . .";
and

(b) If they were misleading, defendants could be held not to have intentionally
made them misleading only if they acted in good faith; and

(c) Compliance with GAAP is persuasive, but not conclusive, on either issue
of misrepresentation or intent.[5]

It has been said that the Court of Appeals' opinion stands for the
proposition that the statements must not only comply with GAAP but
must also be "fair". Although this is attractive for its simplicity, I would
choose to say that the case means that, even if the jury believes compliance
with GAAP and fairness in the opinion of experts is established by
expert testimony, it may independently find:

(a) The statements were misleading, regardless of the experts' view that
they are fair; and

(b) The defendants acted willfully, regardless of the experts' view that they
did not.

Thus the emphasis is not on whether statements are fair as well as in compliance with GAAP, but on whether the jury or the experts can determine misrepresentation and intent—and *Simon* says these issues are for the jury.[6]

A part of one sentence in the appellate opinion, although it seems to substantiate this view, is somewhat enigmatic and difficult to interpret. The full sentence reads:

> We do not think the jury was also required to accept the accountants' [the witnesses'] evaluation whether a given fact was material to overall fair presentation, at least not when the accountants' testimony was not based on specific rules or prohibitions to which they could point, but only on the need for the auditor to make an honest judgment and their conclusion that nothing in the financial statements themselves negated the conclusion that an honest judgment had been made (p. 806)

In the light of the jury instructions which were upheld, it appears that the appellate court was saying only that its holding applied, at least in the absence of "specific rules or prohibitions" constituting GAAP. One should be careful to note, however, that:

(1) The court did not say what its view of the law is when there is a "specific rule or prohibition" in point;

(2) It did not define what it meant by a "specific rule or prohibition". (E.g. is the historical cost convention "a specific rule"?)

(3) It did not mention the common problem of two alternative "specific rules or prohibitions".

The *Simon* result is defensible on several grounds:

First, the question of what is a fair communication of fact ought to be determined on the basis of what the intended recipients of the information could reasonably be expected to understand by the communication, and lay jurors can do this job better than accountants. (E.g. if accountants agreed in a duly promulgated APB Opinion that when a report is labelled "Report to Stockholders", it is fraudulent, and not to be believed, whereas, when it is labelled "Report to Shareholders", it is honest, we could not expect lay readers to know this perverse code and the courts would not charge them with such knowledge.)

Of course, if as some accountants argue, the layman cannot understand financial statements, an assertion with which I agree, then either the *raison d'être* for public accounting is in doubt, or accountants have a duty to make abundantly plain any facts casting material doubt on the viability of the firm or the values portrayed in the financial statements. The latter alternative seems more desirable.

Manifestly, this last statement at the same time suggests and ignores the crucial problem of accounting after *Simon*. If financial statements cannot truly be made fully comprehensible to the layman, just how much explanation is enough to make them "fair"? Clearly it is not incumbent on accountants to give readers of financial statements a mini-text on accounting, explaining the inherent misrepresentations in the use of the historical cost convention, FIFO v. LIFO, purchase and pooling accounting, and the like. On the other hand, where a year-end sale of appreciated fixed assets for little or no money down results in $20 million shown as "income", thus continuing an upward trend, when, without the transaction, income would be nil, more than the blessing of GAAP and an expert's opinion of fairness is required.

Perhaps this thinking is what Judge Friendly had in mind in his enigmatic statement about "specific rules or prohibitions" quoted in the text *supra*.

A second justification for the *Simon* result, permitting the jury to make its own determination of misrepresentation and good faith, is that almost always the jury must decide between the conflicting views of the plaintiff's and the defendant's experts as to what GAAP require;[7] and, presumably, the jury will frequently decide which to believe based on a comparison of the testimony with the juror's own views of what is fair.[8] The use of experts tends to be akin to the ancient trial by combat, where the object is to get the strongest men on your side and there is little concern for the merits.

Finally, in some cases, especially where accountants are themselves defendants, there is a code of silence which makes it nearly impossible for the prosecution or plaintiff to obtain expert accounting witnesses having the stature of the defendant's witnesses. In this circumstance, practical necessity should cause the courts to permit a plaintiff or prosecutor to go to the jury even without any expert testimony on its side—a result which the *Simon* case clearly permits.

One final word should be said about the principles established by *Simon* and the other authorities herein discussed. One frequently hears wails of anguish from accountants who bemoan the lack of understanding of accounting that necessarily underlies these evil legal opinions. In the student note previously referred to, this plaint appears throughout.[9] In that article, the theme is illustrated in terms that the rule had always been, prior to *Continental Vending*, that "fairness" meant "fairness in accordance with GAAP".

However, there is no evidence that accountants themselves have agreed on the issue. Indeed in the Report of the Select Committee established by the AICPA to study the Opinions of the Accounting Principles Board (1965), the first recommendation was that the APB "define such phrases in the auditor's report as 'present fairly' and 'generally accepted accounting principles.'" And just to make sure it was making itself clear, the Committee said:

. . . in the standard report of the auditor, he generally says that financial statements "present fairly" in conformity with generally accepted principles—and so on. What does the auditor mean by the quoted words? Is he saying: (1) that the statements are fair *and* in accordance with [GAAP]; or (2) that they are fair *because* they are in accordance with [GAAP]; or (3) that they are fair only *to the extent* that [GAAP] are fair; or (4) that whatever [GAAP] may be, the presentation of them is fair?

If the profession as late as 1965 did not know what its report form meant, can the courts be faulted for resolving the ambiguity by choosing among the alternatives?[10]

Moreover, some accountants had the same view as this aspect of *Simon*, long before that opinion was conceived. See Arthur Andersen & Co., *Four Cases in Public Accounting Practice, The Philadelphia Transportation Case* (1961) where in the preface it was stated:

> This case may well be a milestone in the development of sound accounting practices. It shows that the acceptance of accounting principles by the accounting profession is not conclusive unless these principles are supportable by logic and reasoning that will be persuasive to the judges in courts of law. It points up the fact that acceptance, approval, or prescription of accounting practices by State or Federal government agencies (in this case, the Pennsylvania Public Utilities Commission) does not, of itself, make them sound accounting practices. It demonstrates that accounting principles must produce accounting that is just and fair as among classes of investors. It shows that broad accounting principles are not mere theoretical concepts but that they have a significant impact on the actual cash income of the individual investors. It makes clear the responsibility of the independent public accountant to the public investors, and it emphasizes the importance of the function of the corporate trustee in safeguarding the interests of investors.

2. SOME FURTHER IMPLICATIONS OF *SIMON*

As in *Simon*, in other actions involving allegedly misleading financial statements, there are usually two issues at the heart of the case, one being identical with the first issue in *Simon*: whether there was a misrepresentation; and the other pertaining to the defendant's state of mind when he made the alleged misrepresentation. The issue of whether the statement is misleading, being the same in all of these cases, under *Simon*, expert testimony on this issue and compliance with GAAP will not be binding on the jury in any case.

In *Simon* the second issue took the form of whether or not the accountants acted *willfully*. But, in some other cases, the issue on state of mind is merely whether the defendant *negligently* made the claimed misrepresentation; e.g. should he, in the exercise of due care, have known that the statement was misleading?

Thus, for example, honesty is actionable under Sec. 11 of the 1933 Securities Act for misrepresentations in registration statements. Good faith is no defense. A pure heart is insufficient, absent proof by the non-issuer defendant of due diligence. [*See Escott* v. *BarChris Construction Corp.*, 282 F. Supp. 643 (S.D.N.Y. 1968).]

Similarly, for common law negligence actions by the accountant's client, or by a third party in states where privity is no longer required [e.g., *Rusch Factors* v. *Levin*, 284 F. Supp. 85 (D.R.I. 1968); *Rhode Island Hospital Trust National Bank* v. *Swartz, Bresenoff, Yavner & Jacobs*, 455 F.2d 847 (4th Cir. 1972)], the defendant will not be excused by honesty if he was negligent.

And in many, if not most, jurisdictions, actions under Rule 10b-5 may be brought for mere negligence: 'e.g., *Ellis* v. *Carter*, 291 F.2d 270 (9th Cir. 1961); *Vanderboom* v. *Sexton*, 422 F.2d 627 (8th Cir. 1970); *Financial Industrial Fund, Inc.* v. *McDonnell, Douglas Corp.* 474 F.2d 514 (10th Cir. 1972); Contra in the Second Circuit: *Shemtob* v. *Shearson, Hammill & Co.*, 448 F.2d 442, 445 (2d Cir. 1971); *Cohen* v. *Franchard Corp.*, CCH Fed. Sec. L. Rep. Para. 93,937 (2d Cir. 1973); *Lanza* v. *Drexel & Co., supra.* [11]

Finally, recent decisions have established that negligence is the appropriate standard for state of mind of beneficiaries of misleading statements under the proxy regulations. *Gerstle* v. *Gamble-Skogmo, Inc.*, CCH Fed. Sec. L. Rep. Para. 93,983 (2d Cir. 1973); *Gould* v. *American Hawaiian S.S. Co.*, 351 F. Supp. 853 (D. Del. 1972).

Of what significance is *Simon* in these cases? Does it mean that, in a case of alleged *negligent* misrepresentation, expert testimony cannot bind the jury on the issue of whether the defendant was negligent?

The answer requires some further analysis. There are at least two broad categories of negligence possible in misleading financial statements. In addition to negligent *presentation* of information, there are cases involving negligent *determination* of information. [12] An example of negligent presentation is the misleading press release in *SEC* v. *Texas Gulf Sulphur Co.*, 401 F.2d 833 (2d Cir. 1968). An example of negligent *determination* is the failure to ascertain the true facts in *Escott* v. *BarChris Construction Co., supra.*

The two classes are roughly defined, respectively, by the presentation function, guided by GAAP, and the audit function, to the extent it is guided by GAAS.

Does *Simon* apply equally to both types of cases?

As to negligent presentation because both willfulness and negligence are matters of state of mind, when *Simon* says a jury can make up its own mind on willfulness regardless of expert testimony to the effect that statements are presented fairly in compliance with GAAP, logically the opinion must mean that similar expert testimony is not binding on the issue of whether the defendant should have known in the exercise of due care that the statements as presented were misleading. Thus mere compliance with GAAP and expert opinion of due care is not enough if a jury finds that the statements are misleading and that the misleading presentation was the result of negligence in the use of words and figures. The jury may look at the words or figures used and, after finding them to be misleading, decide for itself whether the defendants negligently presented the facts.

But what of the other class of cases alleging negligent failure to properly *determine* facts? Will a court be correct in charging a jury that compliance with GAAS is merely persuasive, but not conclusive, evidence of due care, and that if the jurors find that the accountants failed to exercise due care in making an audit, it is no matter that all the expert witnesses testify to the contrary? The dictum in *BarChris* states a negative answer.[13] But it was only a dictum, and none of the profound difficulties with this view were considered because it was not necessary to do so.

One judicial opinion involving fault in both presentation and the audit, without citing *Simon*, appears to display a sensitivity to this issue. In *Rhode Island Hospital Trust National Bank* v. *Swartz, Bresenoff, Yavner, & Jacobs, supra,* a bank had increased the limits on a line of credit on the basis that capital improvements had been made which increased the borrower's ability to carry the larger amounts. Financial statements of the borrower were delivered by the defendant accountants to the bank with a covering letter, containing several reservations to the effect that adequate cost records of capital improvements constructed by the company had not been kept, and that estimates and management appraisals were used in capitalizing these costs. The accountant's report stated no opinion as to fairness could be given because of the "material nature of the items not confirmed directly by us."

In fact, the accountants had failed to discover that the improvements were never built and were wholly fictitious. The court found the statements negligently misleading, despite the fact that no opinion was given, because they gave the impression that some capital improvements had been constructed and that only the amount was in question.

The important point here is that the court found these statements to be negligently misleading, without referring to GAAS, and then *alternatively* held its conclusions were "reinforced by reference to industry standards." Furthermore the Court punctuated its apparent view that compliance with GAAS would not be conclusive by saying, "While industry standards may not always be the maximum test of liability, certainly they should be deemed the minimum standard by which liability should be determined."

Thus, to recapitulate, the Fourth Circuit panel in this case seemed to be saying that, regardless of expert testimony of compliance with GAAS, a fact-finder may independently determine whether an accountant should have discovered certain facts on audit, and GAAS are the minimum standard to be satisfied.

Many will recognize in this question a variation of the familiar question in the law of torts as to whether an expert, such as a medical doctor, may be found negligent by a jury applying its own standards.[14] Ordinarily, absent credible expert testimony to support a finding of negligence, the jury cannot so find.[15] However, even in medical malpractice cases, it is not necessary for expert testimony to support certain findings of negligence as when a surgeon amputates the wrong leg.[16]

Of course this is an exception for certain professionals that is denied to other groups. Ordinarily "[e]ven an entire industry, [other than those certain professions] by adopting . . . careless methods to save time, effort or money, cannot be permitted to set its own uncontrolled standard."[17]

But the special treatment for professionals is probably based on the "healthy respect which the courts have had for the learning of a fellow profession."[18] Is this healthy respect deserved when the question is whether careful observance of GAAS would have uncovered accounting errors? Doubtless the answer in many areas is, yes, but in others, perhaps, no. For example, is it excusable to permit computer frauds because the auditor on the scene had no understanding of computer systems and thus was unable to detect wrongdoing?[19]

Regardless of the answer to these questions, where an auditor in fact does not follow GAAS, it does not take expert testimony to substantiate a finding of negligence—the fact-finder can find negligence. For example, see the *BarChris* case where the court found a negligent audit from a failure to follow the audit program and other shortcomings. Expert witnesses are necessary only where the expert's testimony of GAAS and compliance with them is the exclusive reliable source.

In summary then, it would appear that *Simon* logically permits a finding of negligent misrepresentation in financial statements in which the negligence is in the presentation, regardless of compliance with GAAP and regardless of expert testimony. However, negligence in determining facts on audit is part of a larger question, and existing authority is not clear about whether a fact-finder may find negligence only if GAAS were not followed in the opinion of experts. Perhaps there are some limited exceptions, as in the case of the surgeon who cuts off the wrong leg or delegates the duty to count sponges. Whether accounting deserves the special privilege of making GAAS conclusive, or should be treated like other industries, is a question that has not been finally settled; but accounting, because of the present inadequate state of the art, is vulnerable.

3. SOME ADDITIONAL CHANGES IN THE LEGAL ROLE OF ACCOUNTANTS

In addition to the principles of *Simon* and the other authorities discussed above, numerous other developments in the law have made the accountant's world quite uncomfortable. Although they are beyond the scope of this paper, they should be mentioned.

Just as the myth of safety in complying with GAAP has now been exploded by *Simon*—and, as I have intimated somewhat superficially in footnote 10, the myth that change in the form of the report could protect accountants will be destroyed—so too, the illusion that financial statements are statements of management and not those of the auditors[20] has evaporated. Certainly one cannot read *U.S.* v. *Simon, Fischer* v. *Kletz*, 266 F. Supp. 181 (S.D.N.Y. 1967), or even *Ultramares Corp.* v. *Touche*, 255 N.Y. 170, 174 N.E. 441 (1931) and continue to believe that fiction.[21]

Further, disclaimers in accountants' reports will not be acceptable unless absolutely clear. See *Rhode Island Bank, supra.*

Moreover, even if the statements could be considered solely those of management, the concept of aiding and abetting, which was applied in *Fischer* v. *Kletz* and has since developed into full flower, will certainly cause accountants to be responsible for misrepresentations in the presentations in financial statements audited be them. Finally, as hinted in that case and the SEC's complaint in *National Student Marketing*, unaudited interim statements probably will be the accountant's responsibility, at least where they are part of SEC filings (such as "stubs" in a prospectus).[22]

4. THE NEED FOR GREATER "ACCOUNTING POWER"

Each of these notions expressed in Part 3 are beyond the scope of this paper and are not intended to be any more than a partial, largely unsubstantiated, outline of the legal role of accountants, which has been constructed by the courts. Rightly or wrongly, it is quite different from the way the accountants would structure it, or believe it to be structured.

Thus accountants are responsible for accounting statements as if their own; even utterers of misleading unaudited statements may be held to have been aided and abetted by the auditors; disclaimers or changes in the form of the report will not protect unless they result in fair disclosure; and, in any case, presentation must be not misleading in the eyes of a jury regardless of compliance with GAAP or GAAS or expert testimony. Perhaps even the audit must be in compliance with lay standards regardless of GAAS or expert testimony.

If most of this is true, the refreshing insight of Robert Sterling's article, "Accounting Power," becomes quite apparent.[23] As he states it, viewing accounting practice "logically," he is dismayed to find how far from the ideal it is. And yet, from his "sociological" point of view, accountants have done remarkably well in the face of the odds against them. As Dr. Johnson once observed about a dog struggling to walk on its hind legs, "It's a wonder that it walks at all." Sterling goes on to state that accountants know or have a pretty good idea of what good accounting is and can be, but, for various reasons, including perhaps fear of losing clientele and livelihood and the futility of insisting on their views, they have no power to enforce their notions. Thus he concludes that the real problem of accounting today is not to find better principles but to establish the institutional means to enforce those principles. This is akin to one concept of the substance-procedure dichotomy in the law, contemplated when variations are expressed on the theme that procedure makes substantive rules.

This logic leads Sterling to ask the right question—how can we increase the power of accountants to implement their views of what good accounting requires?

Having reached this hitherto unattained height, we can excuse him for not having a clear and convincing answer.

Perhaps there is no single answer. Maybe the solution lies in numerous measures. He suggests one—sanctioning of accountants by the profession for "competing by the flexibility of [their] accounting principles." The SEC already has power to bar or suspend CPAs from SEC practice. Perhaps the Commission should crank up its efforts in this area.

The Commission has taken other measures to attempt to discourage a company from changing its accountants, by requiring an explanation of the reason for the switch[25]—although this, according to rumor, has not been very successful.

As this paper was being edited, a settlement of a lawsuit by Laventhol Krekstein Horwath & Horwath, a large accounting firm, was announced in which the firm consented to the review of its supervisory and control procedures by an inspection team composed of other accountants.[26] Presumably this will discourage future untidiness for fear of embarrassment from exposure of dirty linen to the neighbors.

Perhaps the enlightened self-interest notion (the "stick" part of the carrot and stick concept) of *U.S.* v. *Simon, BarChris, Fischer* v. *Kletz,* and the like, ultimately will make accountants more independent—if only out of self defense.

One thing is clear, unless something is done to cause true independence, accounting will soon no longer be ambulatory.

NOTES

1. See the Note, "The Criminal Liability of Public Accountants: A Study of *United States v. Simon*," 46 *Notre Dame Lawyer* 564 (1971). The AICPA's counsel as Amicus Curiae in *Simon* wrote an account, "The *Continental Vending* Case: Lessons for the Profession," which appeared in 130 *Journal of Accountancy* 33 (August 1970). The article advocates a narrow view of the opinion.

Numerous short explanations of the case, not purporting to be full dress analyses, appear in several articles and books. See, for example, R. Sterling, "Accounting Power," 135 *Journal of Accountancy* 61 (January 1973); A. Briloff, *Unaccountable Accounting* 20–23 (1972); T. Fiflis and H. Kripke, *Accounting for Business Lawyers* 676–7 (1971); Sommer, "Survey of Accounting Developments in the 60's; What's Ahead in the 70's," 26 *Business Law* 209 (1970).

2. "Instructions" are the vehicle by which the jury is given the "law" to be applied to the "facts" as determined by the jury. As law, instructions are reviewable on appeal without deference to the lower court's views. Contrast a jury's finding of facts which are not reviewable unless a court finds that reasonable men could not have so determined the facts.

3. We must assume that the defendants did not successfully establish that publication of the financial statements itself caused the market drop—if it were so, the statements probably could not have been found misleading.

4. The full text of the two requested instructions appears in the Note, 46 *Notre Dame Lawyer* 595 (1971), as follows:

41 Thus, a defendant may be found guilty only if you find beyond a reasonable doubt that the financial statements as a whole did not fairly present the financial condition of Continental at September 30, 1962, according to generally accepted accounting principles, that he knew that the financial statements as a whole did not fairly present the financial condition of Continental at September 30, 1962, according to generally accepted accounting principles, that he participated in the certification with this knowledge and with the intent to deceive and defraud.

. . .

44 If defendants' certification of the Continental financial statements was rendered in accordance with generally accepted accounting principles, they must be acquitted without regard to any opinion you might otherwise form as to proper standards. Only if the defendants failed to comply with the generally accepted standards of their profession can there be any question of wrongdoing on their part. If they did fail in material respects, then the question is whether their failure was due to inadvertence, mistake, negligence, or a willful disregard of those standards with knowledge of falsity of the statements certified and with intent to deceive. Only in the last event may they be found guilty.

Of course, the portions of the instructions proferred by the defendants in this criminal action requiring proof of "intent to deceive and defraud" have no relevance with respect to civil liability.

The concept of "intent" in civil damage actions for fraud under the federal securities laws has been much watered down from the original requirement to show some intent to cheat. See *SEC v. Capital Gains Research Bureau, Inc.*, 375 U.S. 180, 192 (1963); *Lanza v. Drexel & Co.*, CCH Fed. Sec. L. Rep. Para. 93,959 at n. 98 (2d Cir. 1973). It seems that "scienter" now means something more than negligence in the Second Circuit. Even at the time of *Ultramares Corp. v. Touche*, 255 N.Y. 170, 174 N.E. 441 (1931), as that opinion states, knowledge of the misrepresentation or reckless disregard for the truth, or insincere profession of belief in the representation was sufficient to show the necessary intent.

Further, even a misrepresentation made with the sincere belief that it is for the victim's own good is deceit. "[T]he fact that the defendant was disinterested, that he had the best of motives, and that he thought he was doing the plaintiff a kindness, will not absolve him from liability so long as he did in fact intend to mislead." W. Prosser, *Law of Torts*, 538 (1955), quoted approvingly, *SEC* v. *Capital Gains Research Bureau, Inc.* 375 U.S. 180, 192 n.39 (1963).

For a case vividly portraying the difficulties of judges in defining intent, see the three opinions in *Chris-Craft Industries, Inc.* v. *Bangor Punta Corp.*, CCH Fed. Sec. L. Rep. Para. 93,816 (2d Cir. 1973).

5. It should be noted that a prior Second Circuit decision, *Kaiser-Frazer Corp.* v. *Otis & Co.*, 195 F.2d 833, 843 (1952), is in accord with Simon on the issue of whether a statement complying with GAAP could be misleading.

6. Under the new AICPA Code of Ethics, Rule 203, if financial statements are misleading, although in compliance with GAAP, full disclosure is required. Thus, although the accountants are less than lucid on the subject, it seems that they would not quarrel now with the position that statements must both be fair and in accordance with GAAP. More likely they are concerned only with the view of *Simon* that the lay jury may determine fairness for itself.

Counsel for the AICPA, writing as Amicus Curiae in support of defendants' petition to the Supreme Court for *certiorari*, characterized the holding at page 11 of their brief:

> The jury . . . was told that it might ignore generally accepted accounting principles and might evaluate the accounting presentation from the subjective viewpoint of what it thought "an average, reasonably prudent person" might wish to know.

(For the reproduced brief of the AICPA, as Amicus Curiae, see 129 *Journal of Accountancy* 69, May 1970.)

Contrast the much more narrow view of the holding, stated by one of such counsel in Isbell, 130 *Journal of Accountancy* 39 (August 1970).

7. Accountants will recognize that the problem here is twofold: (a) there really is no unified body of opinion as to the meaning or requirements of GAAP—see AICPA, APB Opin. No. 6 at App. A (1964), stating that GAAP may conflict; and (b) most of what are confidently referred to as GAAP are merely expedient inventions used to solve a particular problem of presentation or measurement. This second notion is illustrated by the frequent complaint of accountants that, usually when they have a problem of what GAAP requires, they can find nothing in the accounting literature. Thus, the argument goes, experts are bound to disagree and deserve not to be credited by a jury.

8. For an illustration of the tendency of a fact-finder to "decide for himself" when confronted with conflicting testimony of experts, see *Feit* v. *Leasco Data Processing Eqpt. Corp.*, 332 F. Supp. 544, 571 (E.D.N.Y. 1971).

9. See 46 *Notre Dame Lawyer*, especially 598 (1971).

10. Incidentally, I do not mean to suggest that the form of the accountant's report would dictate the applicable rule of law despite the popular misunderstanding of accountants that this is crucial. See R. Sterling, 135 *Journal of Accountancy* 65 (1973) recognizing the misunderstanding about this question. Probably little would result from alteration of the report form; but that is beyond the scope of this paper.

For this reason, APB Statement No. 4, Para. 189, published in October, 1970, after *Simon*, and purporting to define "fair presentation in conformity with GAAP" probably does not affect *Simon*, except as it establishes compliance with GAAP as the minimum standard. Even so, Para. 189 makes it clear that mere compliance with GAAP is not enough; the presentation must meet several somewhat amorphous requirements which may amount to "fairness" as an independent requirement.

At any rate, Para. 189 does not, and cannot, determine who, as between expert witnesses and the jury, has the final word on fairness.

Para. 189, in pertinent part, reads:

> . . . Financial statements present fairly in conformity with generally accepted accounting principles if a number of conditions are met: (1) generally accepted accounting principles applicable in the circumstances have been applied in accumulating and processing the financial accounting information, (2) changes from period to period in generally accepted accounting principles have been appropriately disclosed, (3) the information in the underlying records is properly reflected and described in the financial statements in conformity with generally accepted accounting principles, and (4) a proper balance has been achieved between the conflicting needs to disclose important aspects of financial position and results of operations in accordance with conventional concepts and to summarize the voluminous underlying data into a limited number of financial statement captions and supporting notes.

11. There are critics who argue that when a court says negligence is sufficient to hold a defendant liable under *Securities Exchange Act Rule* 10b-5 (17 C.F.R. 240.10b-5), if, in the critics' minds as armchair jurors, the facts are considered to amount to willfulness, all that the court said about negligence should be ignored. This rhetorical sport has reached fairly high into prestigious circles. See, for example, ALI Federal Securities Code Sec. 1404, comment (3) (b) (Tent. Draft No. 2 at 111, 1973); *Kohn* v. *American Metal Climax, Inc.*, 458 F.2d 255, 286 (3d Cir. 1972); *Lanza* v. *Drexel & Co.*, CCH Fed. Sec. L. Rep. at 93,831. For an article using this process of stuffing new thoughts into various judicial opinions, see Bucklo, "Scienter and Rule 10b-5," *Nw. U. L. Rev.* 562 (1972).

With all due respect, each of these authorities seems to ignore some fundamental notions as to who are the triers and reviewers of facts, as well as the difficulties of taking a judicial opinion, which itself can be but an articulation of "the skin[s] of . . . living thought[s]" and changing the writer's characterization of his own thoughts. Judge Friendly, in dealing with another matter, once devastatingly attacked this particular sport, which reached heroic proportions in some of the writing on *Erie* v. *Tompkins*. See Friendly, "In Praise of Erie—and of the New Federal Common Law," 39 *N.Y. U. L. Rev.* 383, 385 ff. (1964).

Some readers may recall Judge Friendly's own concurring opinion in *SEC* v. *Texas Gulf Sulphur Co.*, 401 F.2d 833, 868 n. 4 (2d Cir. 1968), in which he pointed out that certain of the defendants, held liable for negligence, had in fact been guilty of bad faith. But of course, Judge Friendly, in saying this, was not purporting to tell us what his colleagues were saying but what he was saying and thought they should have said.

Moreover, the policy reasons for permitting negligence as the standard in some cases are so powerful that no serious attention should be paid to the rhetorical argument. See Mann, "Rule 10b-5: Evolution of a Continuum of conduct to Replace the Catch Phrases of Negligence and Scienter," 45 *N. Y. U. L. Rev.* 1206 (1970).

I am forced to conclude that the Eighth, Ninth and Tenth Circuits could mean negligence when they say negligence, and the above-cited critics are engaged in argumentation better suited to Alice in Wonderland.

12. See W. Prosser, *Law of Torts*, 178 (4th ed. 1971) for a more generalized explication of these two types of negligent misrepresentation, citing no accounting cases. ·

13. It was "dictum" because the defendants were held guilty of negligence in not

complying with GAAS. If they had complied, then the court would have been faced
with the issue of whether compliance with GAAS established the requisite due care
of the defendant. (It should be noted that the opinion appears to be based on the
court's own determination of GAAS from documentary—not expert witness—evidence.)

14. See Prosser, *Law of Torts*, 161 ff. (4th ed. 1971).

15. See Prosser, *Law of Torts*, 164.

16. See Prosser, *Law of Torts*, 165; Cf. *Rhode Island Hospital Trust National Bank* v.
Swartz, Bresenoff, Yavner & Jacobs, 455 F.2d 847 (4th Cir. 1972).

17. See Prosser, *Law of Torts*, 167. Cf. the facts of *BarChris*, where the accountant
failed to observe his firm's audit guides (apparently, as I am informed, a common
practice) and, nevertheless, was held to be negligent. *Escott* v. *BarChris Construction Corp.*,
283 F. Supp. 643, 697–706 (S.D. N.Y. 1968).

18. See Prosser, *Law of Torts*, 165.

19. See Andrews, "Why Didn't Auditors Find Something Wrong with Equity Funding?"
Wall Street Journal 1 (May 5, 1973). Is it equally negligent for CPAs to permit unskilled
juniors to perform certain audits? For the medical analogue, containing more than
a verbal similarity, see the cases holding negligent the practice of surgeons in permitting
nurses to account for sponges. See Prosser, *Law of Torts*, 165.

For the classic case of accounting industry auditing standards being altered extramurally
to conform to a higher standard, see the summary of the *McKesson & Robbins* situation
in SEC, Accounting Series Release No. 19 (1940).

20. By this intimation that the statements are those of the auditors, it is meant that
the auditors are jointly responsible for them. Committee on Auditing Procedures of
AICPA, Statement on Auditing Procedure No. 33, 9–10 (1963).

21. See also *Restatement of Torts* (Second) Sec. 539, comment a.

22. *Fischer* v. *Kletz*, 266 F. Supp. 181 (S.D. N.Y. 1967), held *inter alia* that accountants
would not be considered to have aided and abetted publication of misleading unaudited
interim financial reports to shareholders merely because of their silence when they allegedly
knew the statements were false. However, the court based its holding on the lack of
any special relationship between the accountants and investors with respect to the financials
there, which were not part of any SEC filing. However, in this same case, the court
noted that there is a special relationship of accountants and investors when accountants'
reports on audited statements are contained in SEC filings. Clearly, if unimpeachable
audited statements are contained in a registration statement, and misleading "stubs,"
known by the accountants to be misleading, are also included, then there is no doubt
that accountants should be held as aiders and abettors. This would be one theory for
holding the accountants on the unaudited statements in *National Student Marketing*. See
complaint at CCH Fed. Sec. L. Rep. 1971–72 Tr. Binder, Para. 93,360 (1972), especially
Para. 48(h).

23. See Sterling, 135 *Journal of Accountancy*, 63, 64 (1973).

24. See Boswell's *Life of Dr. Johnson*.

25. See SEC forms 8K, Item 12; and N-1Q, Item 10; S.E.A. Release 34-9344, CCH
Fed. Sec. L. Rep. 1971–72 Tr. Binder, Para. 78,304.

26. CCH Fed. Sec. L. Rep. Para. 72,166 (1973).

Discussion

Liggio. Let me make two points in response to Ted. First, it is going to be the lawyers and the lay public that are going to judge the conduct of the profession and not the profession itself. In this respect, I have suggested to some of our practice office partners that what they ought to do when they have a set of financial statements that they are troubled by is to have their secretary read the financial statements and the footnote disclosures before they issue them, and see if the secretary understands the financial statements. There have been some comments made by some of the people at Arthur Young about that, but I think that if they do that they are going to find themselves in less trouble later on. The secretary type of person is going to judge whether or not the financial statements are a fair presentation at some future date if there is ever any litigation over it.

Second, I wanted to just briefly comment on Ted's discussion of the intent factor. He made reference to the new federal securities law. They try to do away with the concept of intent or scienter and have redefined it in terms of knowledge and what is a misrepresentation. I would like to read you both of those definitions because I think this is where the law is presently heading and you should try to appreciate that in how you act with respect to your professional practice. Knowledge is defined in the new code as follows:

> When reference is made to this section, a misrepresentation is known by a person to be a misrepresentation if he (a) knows or believes that the matter is otherwise than represented; (b) does not have the confidence in its existence or nonexistence that he expresses or implies; or (c) [and the (c) subpart is very important] knows that he does not have the basis that he states or implies he has for his belief.

Then, on misrepresentation itself they say,

> A statement of fact within the meaning of the liability section is not a misrepresentation if (1) it is made in good faith; (2) is reasonably based on facts including whatever investigation is appropriate under the circumstances when it is made; and [not disjunctive but conjunctive] (3) complies with any applicable rules so far as underlying assumptions or other conditions are concerned.

I think this is where the cases are heading right now if they have not already reached it. Judge Moore, whom Ted referred to in the

137

majority opinion in *Lanza,* in effect adopts the new knowledge requirements of the proposed securities code. I would hope that in your practices
you start looking at some of these things. Consider them in terms
of these new standards of knowledge or the codification of what may
be the existing standards of knowledge.

Defliese. I would like to comment on something that Ted said about
the *Continental Vending* case which I think underscores exactly his
inference of its importance. The fact that very few people know is that
no shareholder ever claimed to have lost a dime on the basis of those
statements. They had no opportunity to rely on them. Despite that,
the decision came as it did.

Sterling. There was no loss?

Defliese. Absolutely no one lost any money.

Fiflis. The statements were published on a Friday and then on Monday
trading was stopped and the facts came out. There was no possibility
of relying on those statements.

Defliese. The three defendants who were involved withdrew their
opinions the following week.

Sterling. As I recall, there have to be damages before there can
be a suit. What was the basis of this suit?

Fiflis. It was a criminal case.

Defliese. It was peculiar in that it involved this criminal intent question.
I think it underscores the fact that even though there is no loss, there
can be a problem—a criminal problem.

Grundeman. Carl, you mentioned the rather practical problem of
the ripple effect of people running from responsibility. What are you
doing with the lawyers' letters you are getting now? What approach
are you going to take on them?

Liggio. That is one of the biggest problem areas we have. If we
don't have a letter that responds both to a litigation and to a contingent
liability request, I tell our practice people that they are going to have
to do two things: (1) to try to make independent investigation through
the company files or other sources to see if they can satisfy themselves,
and (2) to go back and try to get the company to take some sort
of a position to force the lawyers to give adequate representation letters.
If they don't do that, then I think we are in a position of having
to give some sort of a qualified opinion, either subject to, if the lawyers
refused to respond, or a disclaimer of opinion based on a scope limitation
if, after having gone back to the client, the client will not take adequate
steps to get the lawyers to respond.

That is the threshhold problem. The next problem is that when
we get some of these letters they are worded as only lawyers can word
things. Some responses are inadequate—they don't really tell you

whether there are problems or contingent liabilities or really evaluate the litigation. When we get those letters I ask our people to try to read them to see what the letter really means, and if they are not satisfied with it, to come back to me, let me take a look at it, or on their own, go back to the lawyers for clarification. In one situation we wrote three or four letters to the lawyers before we finally got something that I felt was responsive to the questions of litigation and to the questions of contingent liabilities that existed.

Jackson. I wonder if we could go back to one of the things that Ted mentioned, and that has been brought up in several of the papers here. I refer to the "myth" about the responsibility of financial statements. I think most of us are aware that there is a responsibility as far as the auditing of the financial statements, and to what is in the financial statements, but from what I hear being said perhaps this means that the basic responsibility for these financial statements is being taken away from the companies and away from management—that we will not even be sharing this responsibility with the companies. The responsibility will be basically that of the auditors.

Fiflis. My statement is based on Holmes' "evil man theory". This theory says that the law is what the law holds a man financially or criminally responsible for. Therefore, if financial statements are published and are misleading, and if the accountants are held to have the requisite degree of culpability—they are held liable for damages or held liable criminally or held liable in some administrative or injunctive proceeding—who cares whose the statements are? The fact of the matter is, the accountants are just as responsible as if the statements were written, prepared, published, and fully documented exclusively by the accountants.

Jackson. Is that taking some of the responsibility away from the management?

Fiflis. There will be joint liability in most of these situations, in the sense that both parties will be held liable for damages. There is one other aspect of the *Continental Vending* case that should be mentioned because it is indicative of trends and pressures that are beneath the surface: there has been a great movement in the southern district of New York to press for convictions in white-collar crime areas. That, I think, was one of the basic reasons why that case was brought. A similar case may not ever be brought again for criminal conviction of this type. There is the notion that white-collar crimes have been a particularly sore social problem and ought to be taken care of.

If accountants are held liable in a damage action, much of the time the directors and officers will also be held liable, but they may often be excused because of bankruptcy or some other reason which accountants are not likely to seize. In the *Continental Vending* case, you may recall that the president of the company—the guy who was profiting in the sense that he was covering up his misuse of company funds for his personal stock market transactions—turned state's witness and was not fully prosecuted. So, in that sense, the accountants may be primarily and exclusively liable. Another reason, in addition to the concern about white-collar crime, is that I think I detect in SEC proceedings a new technique of getting private attorneys general to help enforce the securities law. That technique is to not go after specific individuals who have no professional status in the securities business, but to go after brokers, underwriters, public relations counsel, attorneys, and not their clients, because if you once convince these professionals that they are going to be held responsible and not the ultimate client, those people—accountants, public relations counsel, attorneys, etc.—will be more careful to act as a sort of private attorney general to make sure that these wrongs do not occur.

Ross. It does not make any difference at all who is basically responsible for the statements which prove to be misleading. When you are in trouble, it is just a technicality as to whether they are the accountants' statements or not. Nevertheless, that doesn't really settle this question. In the more normal case of statements which are not misleading, I think it is still very important to have clear agreement that they are the financial statements of the client, and not of the auditor. Whether you follow fair presentation or generally accepted accounting principles, there is still a wide range of presentations which are not misleading, or which are a fair presentation, or which are in accord with accounting principles. The exact picture depends on the degree of optimism or pessimism in making the many estimates that have to be made. I think that it is important to stick with the idea that it is the client who makes the statement up, and who decides what, within the range of reasonable results, he is going to report. All you can expect of an auditor is that he will report the statements are within the fair presentation range, or within generally accepted principles. The distinction is important quite apart from legal aspects.

Stettler. Isn't there support for this position also in the McKesson-Robbins situation, where the comptroller of the company was convicted of filing false statements, but there was no actual action taken against Price Waterhouse?

Fiflis. That case now is thirty-five or forty years old. I would expect that there has been substantial change since then.

Burton. I would think an accountant would have to be very, very careful about buying that philosophy. In fact, I would think he shouldn't.

If he is in a position where the financial statements represent a series of choices which he feels are not the best choices in the factual circumstances that exist, he should be very careful about putting his name on that statement without making sure that it is completely disclosed in his certificate.

CHAPTER 4

Accounting Principles—How They Are Developed

This paper selects a few areas in the field of accounting to see the process by which accounting principles are adopted and put into practice. In some of the examples the process succeeded: that is, an accounting principle was developed, adopted, and put into practice. In other cases, the process failed. We will see if we can detect any difference in the two patterns of success and failure with respect to the forces that helped or hindered the process. Special focus is on the type of organizational structure involved. Who organized it? Under what auspices? Was it ad hoc or formal, implicit or explicit?

Essentially this study is exploratory. It is loosely structured and makes no pretense of completeness. The cases selected are those which lie conveniently at hand, and were not chosen to fit a particular model. Nevertheless, all of the cases discussed are important in the present state of accounting. They are not ranked in order of importance. There may be other examples equally or more important. If you are familiar with other examples, please explore them and give the rest of us the benefit of your findings. Meanwhile, enough is presented here to serve the purpose of our mutual discourse at this meeting.

The sources of data are diverse and of uneven quality and completeness. For the most part I will refer to those on which I have relied as we move from area to area. We are fortunate in having two recent publications, however, which all of us may consult without excessive difficulty or extensive library resources. The first is John Carey's two-volume work, *The Rise of the Accounting Profession.* Carey (1969

*B.S. 1933, M.S. 1936, Ph.D. 1941, University of California, Berkeley. CPA, California. Professor, School of Business Administration, University of California, Berkeley. Member, Accounting Principles Board, 1963–66. Author, *The Entity Theory of Consolidated Statements* (1944); (with R.T. Sprouse) *A Tentative Set of Broad Accounting Principles* (1962). Contributor to accounting periodicals.

and 1970) focuses on the organized profession in all of its manifestations, not just the area of accounting principles. Nevertheless he gives us a lively, well-written, reliable account of the interplay between the profession and its environment.

The second is Stephen A. Zeff's *Forging Accounting Principles in Five Countries.* Zeff's book (1972) is almost exclusively a history of the attempts by independent auditors in England, Scotland, Canada, Mexico, and the United States, through their professional organizations, to reduce to writing the principles underlying accounting practice. Its explicit aim is to "review the actual experience with various program configurations." About half of the book is devoted to the United States, and gives us a solid factual basis on which to build, similar to Carey's contribution, but more directly involved with the formation of accounting principles.

The description in each case is limited to the period since the end of World War II. Most if not all the important agencies were active in that period—the Committee on Accounting Procedure (followed by the Accounting Principles Board), the American Accounting Association, the Securities and Exchange Commission, and other government agencies established in the New Deal period.

Limiting the period covered in this way prevents me from discussing a fascinating case like LIFO in which a principal industry (nonferrous metals) pressed for a change in the mode of calculating its taxable income, and prominent accountants like Peloubet developed a new formula for inventory pricing; in which the U.S. Treasury resisted the change in order to "protect the revenues," and the U.S. Congress was finally prevailed upon to amend the income tax law to include the new formula, but at a price which the accounting profession later regretted it had to pay, namely, the requirement that the formula (LIFO) must be used in all published financial statements if the "elective method" is to be accepted for tax purposes; in which the Treasury still resisted the new method by insisting it could be used only by those taxpayers who complied literally with the law and the regulations; in which other prominent accountants like McAnly devised further refinements on the formula (dollar-value LIFO), the courts accepted the refinement, and the Treasury acquiesced; and finally in which further attempts to bring LIFO under the umbrella of "cost or market" were firmly resisted by Congress. But we will have to forgo the pleasure of examining a case like LIFO in order to get on with our task.

The first part of the paper deals with areas where the organized profession has not been overly active, at least not until recently, in attempts to develop the applicable accounting principles. These areas are nonprofit organizations, cost accounting standards, public utilities, and financial institutions.

The second part of the paper deals with areas in which the organized profession has a long record of active interest—the impact of inflation on financial reports; income tax allocation; private pension plans; business combinations; the investment tax credit.

The concluding section pulls the different parts together to see what we have found.

1. NONPROFIT ORGANIZATIONS

The organized profession has voluntarily stayed out of the nonprofit field as far as accounting principles are concerned. Paragraph 5 of ARB No. 43, for example, concludes with the following two sentences:

> The committee has not directed its attention to accounting problems or procedures of religious, charitable, scientific, educational, and similar non-profit institutions, municipalities, professional firms, and the like. Accordingly, except where there is a specific statement of a different intent by the committee, its opinions and recommendations are directed primarily to business enterprises organized for profit.

The nonprofit area was not entirely neglected. When the Accounting Research Division of AICPA was established, accounting for nonprofit organizations was one of eight research projects initiated in 1960. The Division was unable to complete the study, however, and the APB did not press the matter. Meanwhile, activity is observable at the grass-roots level, as the following examples attest.

The state of New York and the county of Los Angeles, among others, require financial reports from *voluntary health and welfare organizations* soliciting funds from the public. "In general, accrual-basis accounting is required . . . although depreciation may not be reported as an expense unless the charity is permitted to report it as an expense to another New York agency. The law requires that the annual report be accompanied by an independent accountant's audit report," containing the standard reference to compliance with generally accepted accounting principles.[1] The organized accounting profession, mainly through its state societies, played a key role in framing the rules and regulations in this area.

Close cooperation is also evident in the case of *colleges and universities.*

For many years the authoritative accounting guide for colleges and universities has been Volume I of *College and University Business Administration,* . . . published in 1952 by the American Council on Education. *The AICPA appointed a special committee on college and university accounting to cooperate with the National Committee* [that prepared this publication]. A second volume relating primarily to matters of administration was published in 1955. Recently the American Council on Education published a revised edition of these two volumes in a single publication entitled *College and University Business Administration* (Revised Edition). . . . *The writers of this article, who served on the earlier AICPA committee on college and university accounting, were designated by the AICPA to serve as consultants to the National Committee* [that prepared the revised edition of CUBA] (Johns and Withey, 1969: 55, italics supplied).

To judge by our experience in California, the organized profession interacts at many points with governmental agencies. The interaction stems from the requirements for audits of these agencies. For example, 58 counties, 400 cities, over 1,000 school districts, and over 4,000 special districts are required to have audits performed by independent accountants. And the auditor needs guidance when he composes his opinion. I have seen evidence of interaction among the State Board of Accountancy, the AICPA, and the California Society to establish auditing standards. The emphasis in California is on joint activity with groups outside the organized profession. One example: an accounting manual for counties was developed jointly over a period of eight years by a committee of the state Society and a committee of county auditors, published by the state controller, and adopted as law in the government code. Another example: several manuals on accounting for schools were written into the education code through the state Department of Education.

Things may be changing, however, at the highest levels. The proposed rules of procedure of the new Financial Accounting Standards Board state that the mission of the FASB

. . . is to develop and issue standards of financial accounting and reporting for industrial and commercial corporations, partnerships, proprietorships, *institutions, not-for-profit organizations, and other entities* (*Journal of Accountancy*, 1972: 75, italics supplied).

If the FASB does in fact enter this area, it will find "standards of financial accounting and reporting" already established by a host of different agencies. In some sense the task of the FASB may be easier in this area, where the concept of "net income" is of little importance, than in the profit-seeking sector of the community where the concept is so crucial and critical.

2. COST ACCOUNTING STANDARDS

A few years ago, the U.S. General Accounting Office recommended to Congress that a set of *uniform cost accounting standards* be developed for use in government contract negotiations. The AICPA responded promptly, urging Congress to stipulate that the pronouncements of the APB be the starting point for the cost standards envisioned by the GAO. The AICPA representative explicitly referred to the relationship between the SEC and the AICPA over the years, and urged the new Cost Accounting Standards Board to adopt a policy similar to that of the SEC, namely, to permit the AICPA to take the lead in establishing accounting principles (Journal of Accountancy, 1970: 9, 10, 12, 14, 16). Predictably, the Financial Executives Institute, speaking for management, opposed the development of a set of cost standards. Leonard Savoie, speaking for the AICPA, testified that such standards were "both feasible and desirable."

The CASB was established by an act of Congress, is an agent of Congress (not a part of the executive branch), and is financed by Congress. Its standards have the full force and effect of law after sixty days of exposure through publication in the *Federal Register*. During that period of time, Congress can reject a proposed standard by a joint resolution which does not require the signature of the President. After the sixty-day period a proposed standard that is not rejected by Congress is printed once more in the *Federal Register* and becomes law.

By administrative regulation the standards promulgated by the CASB will apply to all federal government procurement, not just to Defense Department contracts. A number of state and local governments have already expressed an interest in the adoption of the standards.

By the time of its first "Progress Report to the Congress" (August 15, 1972) the CASB was almost fully manned with about twenty full-time professional staff and an impressive agenda of projects. Its first two standards became effective July 1, 1972.

In March 1972 Commerce Clearing House announced the

> imminent availability of a looseleaf COST ACCOUNTING STANDARDS GUIDE, in recognition of the profound impact that the work of the Cost Accounting Standards Board promises to make on the accounting practices of United States businesses and government agencies. I believe they have correctly assessed the situation.

3. PUBLIC UTILITIES

In its Opinion No. 2, "Accounting for the 'Investment Credit,'" the APB included an addendum relating to regulated industries. The first paragraph of that addendum states:

> The basic postulates and the broad principles of accounting comprehended in the term "generally accepted accounting principles" pertain to business enterprises in general. These include public utilities, common carriers,

insurance companies, financial institutions, and the like that are subject to regulation by government, usually through commissions or other similar agencies.

The part played by the AICPA in recent years to establish accounting principles in two regulated industries is summarized below:

1. Uniform accounting seems to exist in the *electric utility* industry. According to Commissioner Lawrence J. O'Connor, Jr., of the Federal Power Commission:

> The general objectives of federal and state regulatory statutes are similar. Accordingly, over the years the state and federal commissions, especially with respect to electric utilities, have been able to develop uniform systems of accounts for use in the various jurisdictions. The virtually identical National Association of Railroad and Utilities Commissioners and the Federal Power Commission systems of accounts have been prescribed one or the other by almost all of the commissions. . . . utility accounting substantially, at least, approaches uniformity and a framework for a national standard of consistent reporting (O'Connor, 1966: 62ff).

How did this system of accounts develop? The federal and state regulatory commissions developed the system on a cooperative basis. O'Connor makes no mention of assistance or cooperation from the AICPA. It is no surprise then to find that "utility accounting" differs somewhat from "generally accepted accounting principles."

2. On January 25, 1962, the Interstate Commerce Commission issued an order, effective July 1, 1962, permitting a *railroad* to issue financial reports prepared in accordance with generally accepted accounting principles:

> Sec. 25.1 *Financial statements released by carriers.* Carriers desiring to do so may prepare and publish financial statements in reports to stockholders and others, except in reports to this Commission, based on generally accepted accounting principles for which there is authoritative support, provided that any variance from this Commission's prescribed accounting rules contained in such statements is clearly disclosed in footnotes to the statements.

This action followed a long struggle initiated and carried on primarily by Arthur Andersen & Co., against the passive or active opposition of the AICPA. In 1957 a subcommittee of the House of Representatives investigated railroad accounting practices, after which the ICC modified some of its rules and issued the one quoted above.

4. FINANCIAL INSTITUTIONS

The specific reference here is to commercial banks and insurance companies. In each case the business entities are subject to control at state or federal level by regulatory authorities. As a result, their accounting principles were developed initially outside the orbit of the AICPA or related organizations. But things are changing.

Commercial Banks

The Securities Acts Amendments of 1964 extended disclosure, solicitation of proxies and insider trading requirements to banks and other corporations not listed on national securities exchanges . . . . As a result of the 1964 legislation, the Federal Reserve Board and the Federal Deposit Insurance Corporation adopted identical codes, generally known as Regulation F, in late 1964. . . . On May 1, 1967, the Comptroller of the Currency issued new regulations for national banks aimed toward uniform accounting procedures and full disclosure (Mills and Luh, 1968). In essence these regulations extended accrual accounting concepts to the financial statements of banks.

At this point the AICPA enters the picture openly and publicly. The March 1968 issue of the Journal of Accountancy reported that a bank audit guide prepared by the Institute's committee on bank accounting and auditing was ready for distribution. It later appeared under the title "Audits of Banks." "The bank audit guide is being issued against the background of a re-evaluation by publicly owned bank management of the traditional concept that financial presentation should be designed primarily for the benefit of depositors . . . " A year later, in March 1969, the APB issued its Opinion No. 13, making its earlier Opinion No. 9, "Reporting the results of operations," apply to commercial banks. At the reporting level the process continued in the appearance of the 1969 annual reports of banks. They conformed to the new regulations, including a restatement of the previously-reported 1968 figures on the new basis. As a further development, the SEC required banks, bank holding companies and life insurance companies to be audited by independent auditors, thereby bringing the banks more directly under the influence of APB Opinions.

Meanwhile a related development had occurred. On February 1, 1966, J. Howard Laeri (1966: 57), of the First National City Bank, addressed the American Bankers Credit Policy Committee. His subject was "The Audit Gap." Among other things, Laeri recommended a joint effort of bankers and auditors to agree upon "generally accepted auditing principles and related reporting practices" applicable to the financial statements, not of the banks themselves, but of "loan applicants." Since "loan applicants" covers the entire spectrum of economic activity, the AICPA would have to agree upon a set of accounting principles to carry out Laeri's recommendation. What did the AICPA do? It did take up part of Laeri's recommendation and formed a National Conference of Bankers and Certified Public Accountants. This Conference issued a joint publication in September 1967, entitled, "The Auditor's Report—Its Meaning and Significance." According to the October 1967 issue of the *Journal*, "the booklet was designed to explain clearly and concisely the CPA's responsibilities in issuing audit reports and opinions on financial statements." I find no subsequent mention of this National Conference in the *Journal of Accountancy*, and no indication of any other joint publication.

In summary, the federal government, acting through the SEC, brought the banks as separate business ventures into the mainstream of financial reporting in 1964. The AICPA responded promptly with an audit guide to assist its members in examining the financial statements of banks. With the assistance of the regulatory authorities, the banks were brought into the fold of accrual accounting and conformity with generally accepted accounting principles.

But the project to assist the banks by formulating standards for loan applicants never got off the ground. Such a project clearly must await adoption by the AICPA of a comprehensive set of accounting principles and related reporting standards.

Insurance Companies

The Committee on Auditing Procedures issued a "Guide for audits of fire and casualty insurance companies" in 1966. It has been working on a "Guide for audits of life insurance companies" but such a guide is not listed in the 1972 Catalogue of AICPA Publications,

The SEC accepts financial statements prepared in accordance with the state regulatory requirements, provided there is a reconciliation with generally accepted accounting principles of capital share equity and net income, with certain exceptions for life and title insurance companies (Regulation S-X, Rule 7-05 (2)).

To date, the state regulatory commissions have neither required nor permitted the insurance companies to use generally accepted accounting principles in financial statements issued to shareholders. Apparently the best that can be done is to reconcile certain key figures in a supplemental schedule.

5. PRICE-LEVEL ACCOUNTING

The Study Group on Business Income

Throughout the period since World War II, the business community has been seeking ways to neutralize the impact of inflation on reported financial position and results of operations. One of the most imaginative projects was the Study Group on Business Income. Its moving spirit was George O. May, who had also been active in the collaboration between the American Institute and the New York Stock Exchange in the late 1920s and early 1930s. Both projects reflected George O. May's conviction that the accounting profession should not presume to act alone in setting accounting principles but should work through and with other organizations.

The Study Group was set up in 1947 with joint financing from the American Institute and the Rockefeller Foundation. Percival Brundage, senior partner of Price Waterhouse, acted as chairman, with May as a research consultant. The expressed purpose of the Group was to make "a survey and a historical study of the uses of the word 'income' and terms associated therewith in accounting and in business, economic and political fields." The Group deliberated for some five years, after which its report was published by MacMillan under the title *Changing Concepts of Business Income.*

Between forty and fifty persons were active in the Group, including the research director of the Congress of Industrial Organizations (now part of the AFL-CIO), the chief accountant of the SEC, a partner in a leading Wall Street law firm, the head of the Department of Stock List of the New York Stock Exchange, the director of the National Bureau of Economic Research, the chief accountant of the Federal Power Commission, and a number of CPAs in practice, in industry, and in academia.

In addition to its final report, the Study Group published a monograph by Arthur H. Dean on the legal aspects of business income, one by George O. May on its accounting aspects, and one containing five studies of business income by four prominent economists—Sidney S. Alexander, Martin Bronfenbrenner, Solomon Fabricant (two studies), and Clark Warburton. No one can doubt that the Study Group had adequate research support for its task. Despite its eminent sponsorship, its research support, its broad-based representation, and ample time to deliberate, Carey points out

> The discussion in the report was generally conceded to be of great value in bringing diverse minds to bear on the problem of defining business income and in reaching some areas of agreement, as well as in providing a basis for further studies. However, the report did not bring about any immediate change in accounting practice (Carey, 1970: 69).

Why the lack of success in the face of substantial, high-quality input? No one can be sure, of course, but here are some observations and suggestions:

1. Eight of the forty-four members who were still active at time

of publication of the report dissented to its recommendations. One of the dissenters was Solomon Barkin; organized labor was suspicious of the motives behind a recommendation that would reduce reported business income in a period of rising prices and probably also reduce the tax burden on business. Of more importance to accountants, the chief accountants of the Federal Power Commission and of the SEC dissented to any change from historical-cost based accounting. So did the two former chief accountants of the SEC. The regulators, in other words, would have none of it.

2. In October 1951, as the final report was being drafted, the Committee on Concepts and Standards of the American Accounting Association published its recommendations on price-level accounting in the *Accounting Review*. The AAA Committee agreed with the Study Group that recognition ought to be given to the impact of inflation on financial reports. The AAA Committee recommended a complete recasting of the accounts in supplemental statements by the use of a general index of changes in purchasing power. The Study Group by contrast concentrated on the charge for depreciation in the income statement (to be restated by the use of a general index), with no restatement of other expenses or of any balance sheet accounts.

My own interpretation of the record is that the Study Group was in too much of a hurry. It offered to settle for too little. Cost of goods sold was under control through the availability of LIFO, and the monetary items needed no adjustment in the balance sheet. Depreciation was the only major recognized income-measuring magnitude not reflecting current costs or some close approximation thereto. The AAA report echoed a deep-felt suspicion of partial solutions, such as LIFO and price-level depreciation. The Study Group never had the support of the academic arm of the profession.

3. The U.S. Treasury has consistently opposed the use of price-level depreciation for tax purposes. Without a tax benefit, the business community would not use it for general reporting purposes.

Subsequent Developments

In 1954 the Internal Revenue Code was amended to permit the use of two forms of accelerated depreciation. This concession was in no way an answer to the impact of inflation on reported net income and reported financial position, but it did relieve the pressure, at least for a time, on the working capital position of those companies with heavy investments in depreciable property. The business community, accordingly, relaxed its pressure for some form of price-level accounting. So did the American Institute.

The American Accounting Association, representing the academic arm of the profession, continued to push ahead. It published the studies of Ralph Jones and Perry Mason in 1956, studies based on the 1951 report of the Committee on Concepts and Standards.

In the late 1950s and early 1960s, some parts of the economy began to feel restive again. The steel industry in particular found that it had "run out of depreciation" and began to move for relief from some quarter. At one of the early meetings of the APB in 1960, several representatives of the steel industry were luncheon guests of the Board. The steel men urged the APB to change generally accepted accounting principles relating to depreciation. They were told politely but firmly that they were really not talking about accounting principles relative to depreciation but about tax relief, and that the proper forum for their request was the U.S. Congress. (Incidentally, late in 1960 the APB discontinued the practice of having industry representatives as guests.)

Shortly thereafter, the APB discussed the price-level problem. At first the Board thought the problem could be handled as part of the research studies on basic postulates and broad principles. But it soon became evident that the problem was too complex to be treated as part of another study. As a result, the APB authorized the Research Division to move ahead with a separate project on price level. In 1963 ARS No. 6 appeared: "Reporting the Financial Effects of Price-Level Changes." In 1969 the APB issued a technically sound Statement (No. 3) urging the presentation of supplementary restated financial statements, but it did not require them for fair presentation.

All during this period many prominent accountants in practice were trying to spur the cause of price-level accounting. Paul Grady, for, example, included an extended plea for it in his "Inventory of Generally Accepted Accounting Principles for Business Enterprises" (ARS No. 7). He also published articles on the subject. Arthur Andersen & Co., among the large national firms, mounted an active campaign among its clients for the adoption of supplementary reports, restated for the effect of price-level changes with modest success. I have also heard of a few local or regional firms that attached clean opinions (with adequate explanations, of course) to financial statements similarly restated.

Meanwhile price-level accounting is used extensively in many foreign countries, and some of our larger firms learned about it first-hand, because some of their domestic clients had subsidiaries or other affiliates overseas. In every case that I know of, however, the use of restated financial reports abroad is linked to the acceptance by the local government of tax returns containing similar adjustments for price-level changes.

6. TAX ALLOCATION

This area is a most interesting one. The profession, both practicing and academic, is deeply split over the soundness of comprehensive tax allocation, yet its adoption can be traced in a clear trail over the years. The story starts with Accounting Research Bulletin No. 2, issued by the Committee on Accounting Procedure in September 1939 under the title, "Unamortized Discount and Redemption Premium on Bonds Refunded." During the 1930s the long-term rate of interest was dropping. Many refundings of bond issues took place, especially among the public utilities of the country, who were under pressure from the regulatory authorities to reduce the burden of interest charges.

The Committee noted three methods of dealing with unamortized discount in case of refunding:

1. A direct charge to earned surplus. The Committee found this method "permissible." Incidentally, APB Opinion No. 26, issued in October 1972 ("Early extinguishment of debt"), makes this method the required one.

2. Amortize over the remaining life of the original issue. The CAP found this method permissible, indeed, "preferred."

3. Amortize over the life of the new issue. This method, the CAP decided, was "not acceptable in the future."

The "preferred" method is the one that disturbs the customary accounting for income the least, a desirable state of affairs for a public utility. But it collides with the income tax rule.

This point was covered in ARB No. 18, issued in December 1942 as a supplement to ARB No. 2:

Unamortized discount is deductible for tax purposes in the year in which refunding takes place and in no other year. If rates are high, charging the entire unamortized discount to surplus and the reduced income tax to income may result in serious distortion.

Where unamortized discount on bonds refunded is written off in full in the year of refunding, it is sound accounting to show such charges as a deduction in the income statement in the year of refunding in harmony with the treatment required for income tax purposes. Where any write-off is made through surplus it should be limited to the excess of the unamortized discount over the reduction of current taxes to which the refunding gives rise, and there should be shown as a deduction . . . in the income statement for the year of refunding an amount at least equal to such reduction in current taxes.

If the alternative of spreading unamortized discount over a future period is adopted, a charge should be made . . . in the income statement in the year of refunding equal to the reduction in current income tax resulting from the refunding.

After backing into the tax allocation problem, the CAP tackled the problem head-on in ARB No. 23, "Accounting for Income Taxes," issued in December 1944. This Bulletin laid down some of the principles that are operative today:

> Income taxes are an expense which should be allocated, when necessary and practicable, to income and other accounts, as other expenses are allocated.

> Where an item resulting in a material reduction in income taxes is charged to or carried forward in a deferred-charge account, or charged to a reserve account, it is desirable to include a charge in the income statement of an amount equal to the tax reduction . . . . If it is impracticable to apply such procedures the pertinent facts should be clearly disclosed.

With regard to allocation of taxes among periods (the timing differences), ARB No. 23 cited "amortization of emergency war facilities as an outstanding example of difference between the tax return and the income statement" that needs to be dealt with formally in the financial statements. The reference to "emergency war facilities" was expanded in November 1952 in ARB No. 42, "Emergency Facilities—Depreciation, Amortization, and Income Taxes."

Meanwhile the SEC had issued its Accounting Series Release No. 53 (November 16, 1945), "In the Matter of 'Charges in Lieu of Taxes'—Statement of the Commission's Opinion Regarding 'Charges in Lieu of Income Taxes' and 'Provisions for Income Taxes' in the Profit and Loss Statement." This case involved an electric power company. The specific issue concerned items charged directly to retained earnings in the financial statements but deducted as allowable in the tax return. The Commission insisted that "the amount shown as provision for taxes should reflect only actual taxes believed to be payable under applicable tax laws" but that "it may be appropriate, and under some circumstances such as a cash refunding operation it is ordinarily necessary, to accelerate the amortization of deferred items by charges against income when such items have been treated as deductions for tax purposes." In brief, the SEC won on form, i.e., with respect to the captions to be used. The registrant and auditors won on substance, i.e., the amount of net income to be reported.

The Committee on Accounting Procedure issued ARB No. 44 (October 1954) on "Declining-balance Depreciation." It urged the extension of tax allocation to the "accelerated depreciation" cases, but contained the following sentence:

> However, the committee is of the opinion that in the ordinary situation, deferred income taxes need not be recognized in the accounts unless it is reasonably certain that the reduction in taxes during the earlier years

of use of the declining-balance method for tax purposes is merely a deferment of income taxes until a relatively few years later, and then only if the amounts are clearly material.

The Committee revised ARB 44 in July 1958. It narrowed the exception just quoted:

. . . accounting recognition should be given to deferred income taxes if the amounts thereof are material, except in those rare cases . . . where there are special circumstances which may make such procedure inappropriate. (Para. 4)

The "rare cases" are specified in Para. 8:

. . . where charges for deferred income taxes are not allowed for rate-making purposes, accounting recognition need not be given to the deferment of taxes if it may reasonably be expected that increased future income taxes, resulting from the earlier deduction of declining-balance depreciation for income-tax purposes only, will be allowed in future rate determinations.

Finally, in APB Opinion No. 11, "Accounting for Income Taxes" (December 1967), comprehensive tax allocation became the basic principle. Public utilities continued to be special problem. "This Opinion . . . does not apply (a) to regulated industries in those circumstances where the standards described in the Addendum to APB Opinion No. 2 are met . . ." Incidentally, Opinion No. 11 was preceded in 1966 by the publication of Accounting Research Study No. 9, "Interperiod Allocation of Corporate Income Taxes," by Homer Black and others.

A year or so later the profession was caught between the public utilities and the regulatory authorities. The Bell System in particular had consistently used straight-line depreciation both in its books and in its tax returns. Regulatory commissions also used straight-line depreciation in setting rates. Some commissions, however, began to insist on the use of accelerated depreciation in the income tax returns of the regulated companies in order to reduce the amount of tax currently payable. The reduced tax was to "flow through" to the benefit of the consumers by way of reduced rates.

To meet this problem, the Tax Reform Act of 1969 changed Sec. 167 of the Internal Revenue Code with respect to a "reasonable allowance in case of property of certain utilities." As to pre-1970 property, the method already in use for tax purposes has to be continued. No change can be made. As to post-1969 acquisitions, accelerated depreciation is permitted provided "normalization" (i.e., tax allocation) is used both for reporting and for regulatory purposes. "Flow through" is out, or so it would seem, for regulated utilities.

The Senate Finance Committee explained the reasoning back of this provision:

The Committee amendments provide that the requirement of normalizing is not met by simply normalizing the regulated books of account of the utility if these books of account may be ignored by the regulatory agency in setting rates. Under the committee amendments, while the regulated books of account are to be used as the basic source of information, these books are not to control if the current rates of the utility are set by reference to the flow-through method. This is done because the use of flow-through in setting rates would produce the revenue loss the bill seeks to avert (S. Rept. 91–552, 91st Cong., 1st Sess.: 173–74).

The preceding recital calls for some comment:

(a) For a public utility, income taxes are an operating expense, so recognized by the regulatory authorities in setting rates. As a result, a public utility is especially sensitive to any changes in accounting procedures that may result in a change in the basis on which its rates are set. Apparently, ARBs Nos. 2 and 4 were drafted to meet a special problem of the utilities, namely, a reduction in operating expenses flowing from a debt-refunding operation. Instead of dealing with the situation as a special problem of the utilities, however, the Committee on Accounting Procedure enacted a rule or principle of general applicability. The APB has followed suit.

(b) In the non-regulated sector of the economy, no simple, direct relationship exists between income tax expense and the price or rate to be charged for output. The pressure for tax allocation should, therefore, be less from management in that part of the economy. Nevertheless, tax allocation has an appeal, once it is established, to many accountants and to some managements because it is conservative in effect. In practice, tax allocation reduces reported net income below what it would be in the absence of allocation. To many, this is virtue enough.

(c) In the Tax Reform Act of 1969, the U.S. Congress enacted an accounting principle to support the regulated companies against their regulators. Congress shaped the specifics of accounting for income taxes in response to a special problem in the utility area. The immediate result is in accord with generally accepted accounting principles, but the precedent leaves many accountants uncomfortable. And the story is not ended, because some regulatory commissions (e.g., California's) assert that Congress cannot tell them how to set rates for services supplied intrastate. The U.S. Supreme Court will probably have to resolve the conflict.

7. BUSINESS COMBINATIONS

This section draws heavily on Arthur Wyatt (1963) for historical background and technical details.

Relationship to the Combination Movement

Three distinct periods of merger or combination have occurred in the United States in the past seventy-five years: (1) 1890–1904, the period following the passage of the Sherman Act, which outlawed the formerly popular "trustee" device, (2) 1918–1930 which covers the boom period following World War I, and (3) 1945 to date, the period of expansion following World War II. Against this backdrop, consider the fact that a distinction between a purchase and a pooling was not even discussed in the literature until 1928 (Wildman and Powell, 1928: 224), was not operative until 1943[2] and was frowned on as improper in the same year (Paton, 1947: 1019). The first mention by an Institute committee was in 1945 in the "Blue Bulletin" of the Committee on Accounting Procedure. The subject does not appear in a formal bulletin until ARB No. 40 was issued in 1950.

It is true that the three periods of the merger movement differed in certain important respects. Still they all involved basically the combination of two or more formerly independent businesses by the use of cash or of debt, or by an exchange of securities. Why the relatively late recognition by accounting and accountants of the distinction between a "purchase" and a "pooling"? I have no definitive answer, but one surmise is that no one was aware of any special or distinctive financial or accounting problems in this connection in the first two periods that required special or distinctive treatment. If so, the problem before us really becomes one of identifying the factors present in the third period that were absent in the first two.

Three factors seem to furnish an explanation for this lag. There may be more than three, but these will do for the present:

(a) Since the close of the second period (about 1930), corporate income tax rates have become high enough to be a significant factor in business planning and policy.

(b) Since the early 1930s, accountants have stressed the income statement increasingly, relative to the balance sheet, with the spotlight focused on "net income for the period."

(c) In recent decades, all interested groups seem to have agreed upon the range of acceptable accounting procedures with respect to property generally and intangibles in particular, and to have observed those limits in practice.

Relationship of "Principles" to the Income Tax

The *Internal Revenue Code* identifies six types of corporate reorganization which are "tax free" at the time. Three of these six are pertinent to a discussion of business combinations; namely, a statutory merger or consolidation under state law; an exchange of voting stock for the shares which control another corporation; and an exchange of voting stock for the properties of another company. The availability of a "tax free" transaction is of immediate and obvious interest to the owners of the company going out of existence (or becoming a subsidiary of another), but less so to the owners or management of the surviving or dominant company. It is therefore probably not a major factor in the decision to merge except in the case of the owners of closely-held companies who will usually be more willing to merge and at a lower price if the transaction is "tax free." Also, if the merger is actually accomplished on a "tax-free" basis, there will be some pressure to keep the property accounts unchanged and thereby avoid a difference between book and tax basis.

Even if there is no objection in principle on the part of management to a difference between book and tax basis, the device of tax allocation is probably not appropriate in a situation of this type to reconcile the two bases. The difference in basis in these cases is a permanent difference, not merely a temporary shift between years. Tax allocation fits well in those cases where the item giving rise to the difference appears both in the books and in the tax returns, albeit in different years.

The difference in basis points up a deeper-lying issue. On the one hand, if the merger is "tax free" but the properties involved are recorded at a figure higher than tax basis, the excess cannot be amortized for tax purposes, although it should be for financial statement purposes. On the other hand, even if the merger is not "tax free," the use of a new basis may require the recording of intangibles of a type which are not amortizable for tax purposes but, again, should be amortized for business accounting purposes. What is involved here is a conflict between (1) a tax law which does not recognize the deductibility of certain types of costs, and (2) generally accepted accounting principles applicable to property accounts, which require their recognition. The most important example is that of goodwill. The distinction between "type a" intangibles (limited life) and "type b" intangibles (indefinite life) was first explicitly drawn in formal fashion in ARB No. 24, "Accounting for Intangible Assets," issued late in 1944, just about the time the distinction between a "pooling" and a "purchase" came into prominence. (APB Opinion No. 17, "Intangible Assets," issued in August 1970, eliminated the distinction between "type a" and "type b" and made all intangibles subject to amortization.)

Relationship of "Principles" to Business Policy

The managements of two or more companies contemplating a merger must take into consideration all relevant factors, including the tax and accounting consequences. They are not at that time concerned with the principles of taxation or the principles of accounting as separate problems of investigation and analysis. They are of course interested in what the practical impact of taxes and accounting will be on their situation, and especially, on the options available to them. Without getting into the subtleties of tax planning, we can readily identify one choice open to them: to choose a method which will result in a taxable transaction now, with probable benefits in future years, or to choose a method which will result in a transaction which is not taxable now but which probably will be to some extent in one form or other in the future. The managements can weigh the advantages and disadvantages and decide to go one way or the other or even to conclude that the tax consequences make the merger unattractive.

Is anything similar possible as far as accounting principles are concerned? In the years before the accounting recognition of a distinction between a purchase and a pooling, probably not. If all transactions involving a transfer of property require a new basis of accountability in the hands of the surviving unit, as they used to, the only point of flexibility open to the parties involved is in the determination of the fair value of the consideration given or of the property received. In many cases, fair value will be higher than book value, and subsequent reported earnings will be diluted, with an adverse effect on the market price of the shares involved. The proposed merger may be dropped as a consequence.

In the presence of a distinction between a purchase and a pooling, however, an option is available to the managements. In a nutshell, a purchase requires a new basis of accountability, a pooling does not. If the distinction between them is substantive and is at least as clearly described as the distinction in the tax law between taxable and "tax free" transactions, the managements can evaluate the results of taking one route or the other and be guided accordingly.

We now turn for a brief look at APB Opinion No. 16, "Business Combinations," and No. 17, "Intangible Assets," both issued in August 1970. Prior to their issuance, an exposure draft was circulated, proposing to eliminate "pooling-of-interests" as an accounting device, and requiring all mergers to be accounted for as "purchases." The Financial Executives Institute objected in no uncertain terms, and launched an intensive nationwide campaign to forestall its adoption by APB. As we know, APB did leave poolings in the picture. These two Opinions are improvements over what we had before, but they change nothing fundamental. The story of these two Opinions and the outside interest they generated is told in some detail by Steve Zeff in a section of his book (1972: 212–16) aptly subtitled, "Vesuvius erupts"!

Comments. The case of business combinations deals with an old problem that suddenly acquired new aspects. The "urge to merge" was observed and commented on by Adam Smith in 1776, and has been an integral part of western economic development ever since. In this instance accountants had apparently worked out a satisfactory solution by treating practically all mergers as though they were purchases. Accountants yielded grudgingly to the pressures from management for a new interpretation. The research bulletins on the subject of business combinations clearly call for the burden of proof to be borne by those who wish to interpret the merger as a pooling. In fighting this rear-guard action, however, the research bulletins did not adequately allow for the interplay of the tax law and accounting principles relative to property and its amortization. Management itself is never of much help in situations of this type because it is not interested primarily in the development of accounting principles. Instead, management views accounting principles as aspects of the environment in which it must operate and therefore looks upon these principles as factors to which it must adapt or to its needs, as the circumstances permit.

8. INVESTMENT TAX CREDIT

Much of what follows on this topic is taken from my article, "Some Reflections on the Investment Credit Experience" (Moonitz, 1966).

In December 1962, the Accounting Principles Board issued its Opinion No. 2, "Accounting for the 'Investment Credit'" in which the required two-thirds of the Board's membership recommended the use of a single method: the spreading of the benefit from the investment credit over the useful life of the property whose acquisition gave rise to the credit. In March 1964 the Board issued its Opinion No. 4 (amending No. 2) withdrawing its recommendation for a single method of accounting for the credit and concluding that "the alternative method of treating the credit as a reduction of Federal income taxes of the year in which the credit arises is also acceptable." With the issuance of Opinion No. 4, the Board acknowledged that it was powerless to take advantage of the golden opportunity presented to the accounting profession by the investment tax credit.

The Novelty of the Investment Credit

Why did the investment credit represent such a golden opportunity to the accounting profession? By all odds, the most important reason is that the investment credit as of the date when Opinion No. 2 was issued was absolutely new in the experience of the financial community in the United States. Three foreign countries—The Netherlands, The United Kingdom, and Belgium—had enacted similar provisions in the 1950s, but the U.S. investment credit was not identical with any one of them. For example, the U.S. credit was a "credit against tax," to be taken after the tax liability for the year had been calculated. The others were "credits against taxable income" to be deducted before calculating the tax liability for the year. As a consequence of this unique situation, no one in this country had had any prior experience with the investment credit. No alternative accounting procedures existed already embedded in accounting practice. "Substantial authoritative support" did not exist for any single method or practice or any group of practices or methods. The references by the Securities and Exchange Commission in its Accounting Series Release No. 96 and by some members of the Accounting Principles Board to "substantial authoritative support" covered testimony before Congressional committees, and to letters written to the SEC and the AICPA. But there was no "substantial authoritative support" of the type the SEC and others had relied on hitherto, namely, actual practices of regulatory commissions, actual practices embodied in published financial statements approved by outside auditors, or alternatively, serious, detailed research studies published in textbooks, manuals, treatises, or journals, analyzing the problem, marshalling the evidence, and examining the alternative solutions. In a nutshell, the slate was clean. For the first time, certainly in recent history, an authoritative body in the field of accounting had a clear chance to *establish* a principle of accounting, not merely to sort out among practices already in existence to indicate a preference among them.

A second important reason, in addition to the opportunity presented by the historical circumstances in this country in 1961 and 1962, is the nature of the problem posed by the investment credit itself. To determine how to account for the investment credit is almost entirely an exercise in pure theory. Virtually no practical problems are present as they are, for example, in accounting for the depreciable assets which give rise to the credit. In the depreciable asset case, both the length of useful life and the rate of utilization must be estimated. These estimates require the skill, knowledge and judgment of experienced men. As a result, competent men can arrive at different answers as to a proper depreciation rate for a given asset. Not so with the investment credit. The data are virtually all given. The only open question of any substance is the nature of the credit from an accounting point of view, and that is a question for theoretical analysis.

Both the Accounting Principles Board and the Accounting Research Division failed to anticipate the difficulties of getting agreement on the problem in time to meet the deadline imposed by the enactment of the Revenue Act of 1962. The academic arm of the profession stood by and offered absolutely no assistance, probably because it too could not visualize the issues that would arise. We apparently have neither a recognized theory nor a professional organization capable of coping with problems as simple as the ones posed by the investment credit.

One manifestation of the lack of a recognized theory is the reliance by the Board and others on "legislative history" as sanction for their conclusions. The "authority of persons" is substituted for the "authority of reason." The line between the two has not even been generally recognized, much less drawn clearly.

The Role of the SEC

The SEC had little or nothing to do with the formulation of Opinion No. 2. The members of the Board did receive copies of a letter from Andrew Barr, Chief Accountant of the Commission, but not until the morning of the meeting of December 10, 1962, the meeting at which the Board adopted Opinion No. 2. Barr's letter was in response to the "exposure draft" (dated November 1, 1962) of the Board's proposed Opinion, and was received too late to be of much influence. At any rate, the Board clearly did not vote the way of the SEC.

External Influences

The accounting profession was poorly equipped to handle the investment credit. The APB itself had no basis in a set of explicitly stated principles on which it could proceed. The academicians had not supplied a theory adequate to the subject. The SEC was clearly unwilling to take strong leadership. But management was not. As in other cases, the interest of management in accounting principles is on their impact on the financial position and reported earnings of the company they direct. Some (e.g., the electric power companies) wanted a rule or procedure that would increase reported net income immediately; hence, they opted for treatment of the investment tax credit as a reduction in taxes otherwise payable. Others (e.g., the telephone companies) were fearful of any method that would disturb the customary mode of calculating "operating expenses"; hence, they opted for the treatment that would spread the impact of the investment credit over a large number of years. The resolution of the issue, in brief, turned on the outcome of a power struggle among different groups within management.

The sad story continues with the revival of the investment credit by President Nixon in 1971 under the new title of a "job development credit." Once more, APB tried its hand at reinstating its Opinion No. 2, enthroning the "deferral" method as the sole acceptable method. This time APB had the support of SEC. Late in 1971, however, the U.S. Senate acted. In the words of Steve Zeff (1972: 221):

> . . . the Senate amended the tax bill to allow taxpayers to use whatever method they wished in accounting for the credit. These actions were taken notwithstanding intense lobbying efforts by Institute representatives to keep a provision on accounting practices out of the bill. The Senate amendment . . . passed both houses . . . the Board withdrew its exposure draft . . . and issued a statement deploring Congressional involvement in the establishment of accounting principles. The financial press also criticized the Congressional intervention.

So, twice in recent years, once in 1969 in connection with tax allocation for public utilities and once in 1971 in connection with the investment tax credit, the U.S. Congress has taken a hand in using the coercive power of government to establish an accounting principle.

9. COSTS OF PRIVATE PENSION PLANS

Private (i.e., nongovernmental) pension plans provide retirement income to large groups of workers in the United States. They have grown rapidly since the *Inland Steel* case (1949) established the rule that pensions are a proper subject for bargaining under the National Labor Relations Act. The accounting principles with respect to the employer's cost under a pension plan apparently developed as the result of the activities of various groups, among them (1) management, assisted by their attorneys and actuaries, as a by-product of negotiations with trade unions and the establishment of specific pension plans, and (2) the income tax law in granting concessions to certain types of arrangements for "deferred compensation." The accountants, both professional and academic, seem to have been passive bystanders, awaiting developments before acting.

We can understand the reluctance of accountants to move in this area. At the technical level, I find pension costs the most difficult of all the major issues we have tackled in the last quarter-century. Not only are the technical (actuarial) features difficult, in and of themselves, but the underlying institutional arrangements are still obscure. The law of pensions, so to speak, is still in process of development. I refer to such matters as the locus of equitable title to a pension fund, the right of employees to redress in case an employer moves his plant or becomes insolvent, the right of an employer to protect himself in case of a change in the tax provisions relative to deductibility of pension costs, etc., etc.

Many were immobilized by the difficulties I have just referred to. When we started work on the pension project in New York about ten years ago, I talked to a partner of one of the large national firms. He told me he had never inquired of a client's actuary concerning the formula used by the actuary, the interest rate assumed, or whether, in fact, any changes in basic actuarial assumptions had been made. He was disturbed because the client's charge to operations for pensions had varied greatly from year to year. Still, he did not know what to do about it because the actuary had assured him that all the figures in the accounts were sound.

The first formal attention to pension costs in the professional literature is ARB No. 36, "Accounting for Annuity Costs Based on Past Services" (November 1948). This bulletin was later reproduced with merely editorial changes as Chapter 13, Sec. A. of ARB No. 43. The Committee concluded that:

> (a) Costs of annuities based on past services should be allocated to current and future periods; provided, however, that if they are not sufficiently material in amount to distort the results of operations in a single period, they may be absorbed in the current year.

> (b) Costs of annuities based on past services should not be charged to surplus.

Note that the opinion relates entirely to past service costs, with no mention of normal or current costs. Someone must have been treating past service costs as corrections of past periods' reported profits. Here is one bit of evidence, from Fiflis and Kripke (1971: 352):

> In a public utility rate case accountants took the position that expenditures by the employer for past service benefits were not current expenses, and could not be figured as current expenses in the computation of the rate schedule. New England Telephone & Telegraph Company, 53 F. Supp. 400 (D. Mass. 1943). The accountants' position prevailed in that case, but they have since come to recognize, along with everyone else, that provision for past service benefits is a necessary part of sound labor relations, and that the cost thereof when properly distributed is a current expense. . . .

In September 1956 the Committee on Accounting Procedure issued ARB No. 47, "Accounting for the Costs of Pension Plans." It did try to deal with all the major issues, normal or current costs, as well as past service costs. It attempted to move away from cash-basis accounting (i.e., expense equals cash paid out on account of pensions) to accrual basis (i.e., expense is a function of the growth in the obligation to provide deferred compensation). It did this by making a distinction between "funding" (i.e., the financial arrangements necessary to meet the obligations under the plan) and the manner of recognizing the expense properly attributable to each accounting period. The pace of events was apparently already too swift, however, because the committee had to admit that:

> . . . opinion as to the accounting for pension costs has not yet crystallized sufficiently to make it possible at this time to assure agreement on any one method, and that differences in accounting for pension costs are likely to continue for a time. Accordingly, for the present, the committee believes that, as a minimum, the accounts and financial statements should reflect accruals which equal the present worth, actuarially calculated, of pension commitments to employees to the extent that pension rights have vested in the employees, reduced, in the case of the balance sheet, by any accumulated trusteed funds or annuity contracts purchased.

In the mid-1960s, the APB swung into action. Its Opinion No. 8, "Accounting for the Costs of Pension Plans" (November 1966) was preceded by the publication in 1965 of a research study by Ernest L. Hicks under the same title. In grappling with this Opinion, the APB experienced its finest hour. Let us see what Zeff (1972) has to say on this topic:

> . . . Hicks and his actuarial consultant attended meetings of the Board's subject-area committee as well as meetings of the Board itself. For the first time, the subject-area committee held numerous informal meetings with interested organizations. Moreover, here was an area . . . which had technical ramifications that had until then not been fully understood by Board members with many years of practical experience. Contrary to many problem areas in accounting, where technical considerations and arguments for and against various methods are already too well known to most Board members, the subject of pensions could be discussed with educational advantage to the Board. It was also a subject which unlike the investment credit or tax allocation (for example), admitted of many intermediate compromise positions. For these reasons, it is believed that in the area of pension accounting the Board came closest to utilizing research, consultation, and interchange among Board members as was probably contemplated by the Special Committee on Research Program.

I concur.

Opinion No. 8 still left a considerable degree of flexibility, but it did succeed in making the crucial distinction between accounting for the cost of a pension plan and for the method of its funding. It also set forth formulas to determine an upper and lower limit for the current charge to income. These formulas are in accord with the income tax regulations on the calculation of the allowable deduction for pensions in the tax return. Other features of the tax law, incidentally, also helped because they defined the type of plan that qualified for tax benefits to an employer. A strong tendency obviously exists for the pension plans in operation to be drawn up in order to meet the tax test. Accordingly, the range of possibilities is greatly reduced. The metes and bounds of the problem can be more readily defined. While much remains to be done in the pension area, and while accountants themselves did little to forge the principles in use, APB did succeed in narrowing the areas of difference existing in this most important field.

10. CONCLUSIONS

Here is a summary of what we have found, organized by the major topics discussed:

1. Nonprofit organizations. Not much activity at the national level primarily because the AICPA elected to stay out of the field for many years, probably in order to give its attention to the more pressing problems in the profit sector. But at the grass-roots level, there has been considerable cooperation between the profession and such nonprofit organizations as voluntary health and welfare organizations, colleges and universities, school districts, and counties.

2. Cost accounting. Another area in which the profession, at the national level, elected to stay out of the arena. Because of the importance of the federal government as a customer, the vacuum has been filled by a government agency, the Cost Accounting Standards Board.

3. Public utilities. The profession has clearly had an interest in the area, but the accounting systems in use were developed primarily by the regulatory commissions. We will comment on the influence of the public utilities in another connection later on.

4. Financial institutions. Once more the profession at the national level was primarily a bystander, until these institutions began to finance by "going public." The pressures for improved financial reports came from various government agencies, such as the SEC, and the bank regulatory bodies. The profession cooperated in what seems to have been a successful partnership.

5. Price-level accounting. The Study Group attempted to change the business concept of income to allow for the impact of inflation. It failed. Both the American Accounting Association and the AICPA have been interested in the topic so that we have adequate knowledge of

the technical problems involved. But the impact on practice has been negligible in this country.

6. Tax allocation. Here the record clearly supports a finding that the process was a success. Although there were difficulties along the way, especially after the introduction of accelerated depreciation in the 1954 tax code, the successive pronouncements of the AICPA exhibit a widening of the net until we now have comprehensive tax allocation firmly embedded as an accounting principle, at least in the nonregulated sector of the economy. What still bothers me is why the process should have worked so well in a controversial case like tax allocation and so poorly in others.

7. Business combinations. A frustrating story of a steady retreat before the onslaught of management, with the organized profession continually underestimating the magnitude of the problem or the strength of the opposition.

8. Investment tax credit. Another case of an organized accounting profession too lightly armed to operate successfully. In recent years, even with the help of the SEC, we are frustrated. The U.S. Congress has taken the options away from us.

9. Pension costs. A success story, at least in terms of making measurable progress from a clearly unsatisfactory situation to one more in line with fair presentation. In this area success seems linked in large part to the technical and institutional complexities of the subject. As a result, the actuaries and the accountants were left in relative quiet to work out the formulas, the guidelines, and the jurisdictional dispute.

* * * * * *

Let us move away now from the mental grooves created by the manner in which this paper is organized. Let us back away from the nine neat tidy packages summarized above. One of the rewards of research is to find something you did not expect to find, to see aspects of the scene hidden or obscured before. And I did find one or two things I did not expect to find. One is the influence of various organs of government in the formulation of accounting principles.

Even in the relatively few cases we examined, the influence of the U.S. Congress is marked. Back in the 1930s, Congress had to amend the tax law for LIFO to become acceptable. Much more recently, Congress intervened directly in the tax allocation problem by outlawing "flow-through" accounting for public utilities. It also intervened directly in the investment credit situation by legislating choice on a taxpayer's part as to the accounting he wishes to follow. A few years ago Congress authorized the creation of a Cost Accounting Standards Board as a governmental agency, not as a private agency with certain delegated powers. I find it more than a coincidence that a year or so later the organized profession established a *Financial* Accounting Standards Board. The accounting world (U.S. version) is now divided into two parts. Will these two parts live in amity or in enmity? Will they be rivals or partners? Will a federation emerge?

Other government agencies have been active. The independent regulatory agencies such as the ICC, FPC, and FCC (and their counterparts at the state level) have always used accounting as a principal instrument of control, and have not permitted the private sector much leeway. The clear success of the profession in bringing the commercial banks into the mainstream of accrual accounting is attributable to an active partnership among the SEC, the bank regulatory authorities, and the AICPA. As a group the partnership was able to overcome the opposition of bank management and its desire to continue its customary mode of accounting. In the examples I cited from California (duplicated no doubt in many other states) the local CPA organization cooperated with governmental agencies, but it was the governmental agency that put the principles and standards into effect.

Something else I did not expect to find is the influence of the public utilities. On at least two major occasions, the special problems of the public utilities crop up, this time not from the standpoint of the regulators (the Commissions) but from the standpoint of the regulated (the companies themselves). In order to operate effectively under regulation, the management of a public utility needs to be especially alert to changes in accounting procedures that may disturb the customary basis on which the company's rates are set. So, we find utilities mentioned in connection with tax allocation (and the predecessor problem of unamortized discount on refunded bond issues), and with the investment tax credit and the split over that issue within the utility industry itself. The utilities were also of some importance in the early stages of the pension problem.

Other findings are not so much of a surprise, but it is well to note them, if only for the documentation now available. For one thing, the impotence of the Study Group on Business Income tells us that ad hoc groups are not likely to be worth their cost. The Study Group itself was well conceived, well staffed, and well served by its research consultants. It included representatives from all the influential groups in the economy with an interest in financial reporting. But it led nowhere. It had no impact on practice, or, for that matter, on theory.

It was also no surprise to find management cropping up again again as an influence and a force to be reckoned with. We have already referred to the management of the public utilities and their interest in tax allocation, the investment tax credit, and pension costs. With respect to the investment credit, they were joined by management in the nonregulated sector. Management's impact is clear in the business combinations area, in the cool reception to proposals for price-level accounting, and in the opposition to change in the reporting practices of the financial institutions. We also note here that two major topics not discussed in this paper but formerly high on the agenda of the APB have been set aside. I refer to the APB's proposals in the areas of marketable securities and intangible drilling costs. The insurance industry blocked APB action on the former; the oil industry on the latter. Perhaps the FASB will be able to do something with them.

And finally the scorecard of the APB itself (and the predecessor CAP) is no surprise—strong in the areas of tax allocation and pension costs, weak in the case of business combinations and the investment tax credit, and showing much activity but no impact to date in the case of price-level accounting. And we refrain from mentioning the areas where the APB should have spoken but did not. But for some reason, a refrain does run through my head. It is the words of a graduate student after studying the record of the APB—"YOU GOTTA HAVE CLOUT!"

NOTES

1. See Paul Pacter (1970: 71–72) and also AICPA (1967). The legal provisions regarding reporting are summarized in Marion R. Fremont-Smith (1965).

2. See *Niagara Falls Power Co. v. Federal Power Commission,* 137 Fed. Reporter, 2d series, p. 794.

REFERENCES

American Institute of Certified Public Accountants (1967) "Audits of Voluntary Health and Welfare Organizations." New York: Committee on Auditing Procedure.

Carey, John L. (1969) *The Rise of the Accounting Profession from Technical to Professional,* 1896–1936. New York: American Institute of Certified Public Accountants.

Carey, John L. (1970) *The Rise of the Accounting Profession to Responsibility and Authority, 1937–1969.* New York: American Institute of Certified Public Accountants.

Fiflis, Ted J. and Homer Kripke (1971) *Accounting for Business Lawyers.* St. Paul, Minnesota: West.

Fremont-Smith, Marion R. (1965) *Foundations and Government—State and Federal Law and Supervision.* New York: Russell-Sage Foundation.

Johns, Ralph S. and Howard A. Withey (1969) "Authoritative Accounting Guide for Colleges and Universities." *Journal of Accountancy* (March).

Journal of Accountancy (1970) "Institute Offers Assistance in Setting Cost Standards." (May).

Journal of Accountancy (1972) "Financial Accounting Standards Board Proposed Rules of Procedure." (November).

Laeri, J. Howard (1966) "The Audit Gap." *Journal of Accountancy* (March).

Mills, Robert H. and Frank Luh (1968) "Financial Reporting of Commercial Banks." *Journal of Accountancy* (July): 49–54.

Moonitz, Maurice (1966) "Some Reflections on the Investment Credit Experience." *Journal of Accounting Research* (Spring): 47–61.

O'Connor, Lawrence J., Jr. (1966) "Accounting and Reporting Uniformity for Utilities." *Journal of Accountancy* (August).

Pacter, Paul (1970) "Annual Reports of Charities Soliciting in New York State." *Journal of Accountancy* (February).

Paton, W. A. (1947) *Accountants' Handbook.* New York: Ronald Press.

Wildman, John and Weldon Powell (1928) *Capital Stock Without Par Value.* Chicago: A. W. Shaw.

Wyatt, Arthur (1963) *A Critical Study of Accounting for Business Combinations.* New York: American Institute of Certified Public Accountants.

Zeff, Stephen A. (1972) *Forging Accounting Principles in Five Countries.* Champaign, Illinois: Stipes.

Comments on
Accounting Principles—How They are Developed

STEPHEN A. ZEFF*

Maurice Moonitz's paper is, as he says, exploratory. His aim is to discover generalizations or hypotheses which could explain the successes and failures of the process by which accounting principles are established in the United States. He concludes his episodic narrative with few such explanations. Yet read in conjunction with other articles he has written in the last five years, Moonitz would draw the following generalizations:

1. The clear successes of the APB are principally in the area of the *form* of financial reporting, the extent of detail, the amount of disclosure (Moonitz, 1971: 344).
2. The process is less likely to succeed when the APB attempts to alter accounting measurements (e.g., net income, assets, liabilities) in a manner which corporate management or other powerful groups interpret as threatening their interests (See Moonitz, 1968: 627–31 and 1970: 58–60).
3. When the process appears to be on the brink of failure owing to the active intervention of corporate management, it may be saved through the collaboration of "allies" such as the SEC, the bank regulatory agencies, and the New York Stock Exchange (See Moonitz 1972: 124, 133).

A fourth hypothesis which has been suggested by Moonitz but perhaps not in the words I would use, is the following:

4. The informal relation existing between the SEC and the American Institute has promoted the success of the process when other affected parties, such as corporate management or other government agencies, have not also intervened. When this intervention has occurred and the SEC's position either was unclear or appeared to be subject to change, the accounting profession was effectively undercut.

When political pressures were largely absent, in the relatively tranquil 1940s and 1950s, the American Institute's committee and the SEC could exchange signals that would be accepted as valid indications of their

*B.S. 1955, M.S. 1957, University of Colorado; M.B.A. 1960, Ph.D. 1962, University of Michigan. Professor of Accounting, Graduate School of Business Administration, Tulane University. Author, *The American Accounting Association—Its First Fifty Years*(1966); *Forging Accounting Principles in Five Countries: A History and an Analysis of Trends* (1972); and *Forging Accounting Principles in Australia* (1973).

respective points of view. Now, in the midst of political cross-currents, such signals are tinged with strategic and tactical considerations, which themselves may be subject to change once new special interests and resulting pressures are brought to bear. When the APB is unsure of where the SEC stands, but knows only that the SEC may endorse one of several solutions, depending on how the political forces coalesce, the Board is likely to be defeated before it begins. It is not as if an apolitical panel were to submit a firm recommendation on a highly politicized subject, such as civil rights or drugs, to a legislature for approval. Here the political body which possesses all the statutory authority, the SEC, is shifting the ostensible onus of decision to an expert body which is apolitical and entirely lacking in legal stature. This arrangement is particularly vulnerable when both the expert body and the SEC are being buffeted by strong political winds. Neither body knows what the other regards as (a) desirable and (b) politically feasible, and the opportunity for a disastrous signal-mixing is great, raising serious questions of credibility, intellectual honesty, and political leadership. In these conditions, the apolitical expert body will necessarily be guided by its own assessment of the political feasibility of alternative solutions. It is dangerous to assume that both the APB and the SEC will arrive at the same assessment, or that this assessment will not alter in the time that elapses between the issuance of the APB's pronouncement and the moment at which the SEC makes its formal decision to support, modify, or reject the APB's recommendation.

If the APB (or the Financial Accounting Standards Board) is going to be subjected to intense political pressures, thus imposing on its members an enormous accountability to a pluralistic constituency, a larger share of the decision-making authority should be allocated to the Board. In this respect, both Canada and the United Kingdom seem to have arrived at better solutions. Last December, Canada's provincial securities commissions announced that they will accept the pronouncements of the Canadian Institute of Chartered Accountants as the authoritative source of "generally accepted accounting principles" (*CICA/ICCA Dialogue,* Jan. 1973: 1). Thus, the Canadian Institute is on notice that its decisions will automatically be endorsed by all the provincial securities commissions. The Canadian and American securities laws, however, are not parallel enactments, as there is no reference in the Canadian acts to a source of authority on accounting principles. In the Commonwealth tradition, the Canadian securities acts lay down minimum disclosure requirements and are silent on accounting principles. The provincial securities commissions have used their discretion to vest this authority in the Canadian Institute. If one forgets for the moment the SEC's enormous indirect influence on the accounting practices of both the Canadian subsidiaries of U.S. corporations and the Canadian companies which have issued securities in U.S. capital markets, the Canadian Institute of Chartered Accountants is potentially in a more powerful and secure position to determine accounting principles in Canada than is the APB in the United States. This is particularly true regarding highly contentious issues which might arouse political animosities.

In the United Kingdom, the London Stock Exchange announced last year that the directors of its listed companies will be required to explain departures from accounting standards established by the leading accountancy bodies in circumstances where the independent auditor has cited such deviations in his report to the shareholders. Like the American Institute, the U.K. accountancy bodies require their members to disclose departures from their councils' recommendations.

In both Canada and the United Kingdom, therefore, the accountancy bodies know in advance that their recommendations will be widely applied. These understandings do not relieve the accountancy bodies from negotiating acceptable solutions with powerful interest groups, both within and without government. But at least the profession knows where it stands. The discussions between the Accounting Standards Steering Committee and the Bank of England, the Inland Revenue, the Department of Trade and Industry, and the Confederation of British Industry on the subject of inflation-adjusted accounts are a potent reminder that the profession must sell its policies. It is significant, moreover, that the powerful London Stock Exchange made known its policy on accounting standards at the height of the Steering Committee's protracted and difficult discussions on this contentious subject. Seven months following the Exchange's announcement, the Steering Committee felt it had sufficient support to issue an exposure draft.

Moonitz (1972: 131) has elsewhere endorsed Leonard Spacek's proposed amendment of the Securities Act of 1933 (and by extension, the 1934 Act) to require that financial statements be prepared on the basis of "uniform accounting standards and principles determined by the accounting profession. . . ." He also recommends that the New York Stock Exchange be enlisted as an active ally of the accounting profession. It would seem that a minimum commitment which the New York and American Stock Exchanges could make to improved financial reporting would be to adopt the policy of the London Stock Exchange. While the New York and American Exchanges are not such potent forces as is the London Exchange in their respective capital markets, the two U.S. exchanges could nonetheless exert considerable influence in financial and business circles. Recent news reports indicate that the New York Stock Exchange, at least, intends to play a more active role in financial reporting.

A fifth hypothesis concerns the kinds of questions on which the SEC has sought "substantial authoritative support" from the accounting profession:

5. The SEC has been principally interested in correcting abuses, closing loopholes, and narrowing the range of alternatives, rather than in expanding financial disclosures and experimenting with new approaches. The emphasis of the SEC is on disclosures that are "not misleading" rather than "informative." The two are not necessarily compatible.

The SEC's long-standing opposition to departures from traditional historical cost is well known. When examining the accounting profession's alleged antediluvian attitude toward alternatives to traditional historical cost, it is seldom recalled that in 1950 the American Institute's Committee on Accounting Procedure unanimously approved a bulletin on upward quasi-reorganizations. But the bulletin was never issued. The SEC advised that its contents were unacceptable. This is the only instance in which a pronouncement which already had been adopted by the Committee on Accounting Procedure or the APB was withdrawn owing to SEC opposition.

Moreover, when discussing the fate of the APB's attempts in 1971–72 to gain acceptance of a form of current-value accounting for marketable securities, it must be remembered that the SEC's Chief Accountant announced at the APB's public hearing in May, 1971 that "Generally, at this time, we believe a market or fair value basis for general practice is not desirable or feasible." (Arthur Andersen, 1971: 370) How successful would the insurance industry have been in thwarting the will of the APB if the SEC had given the proposal its full-throated support?

Even allowing for the usual reluctance of the accounting profession to require the use of general price-level accounting or of current market values, the root cause of the lack of any significant expansion of corporate reporting beyond traditional historical cost has been the undeviating opposition of the SEC. In Britain, no securities commission exists and there seems to be a more flexible accounting environment. The Accounting Standards Steering Committee decided in 1971 that a supplementary statement containing inflation-adjusted accounts was a required disclosure in the face of persistently rising prices. Following strenuous discussions with powerful government and private bodies, enumerated above, the Steering Committee won the support of the Confederation of British Industry and made bold to issue an exposure draft in January of this year. We know that the controversial draft secured "virtually unanimous" approval of the 21-member Steering Committee, not a mere two-thirds support (Leach, 1973: 566). Britain thus appears to be at the threshold of adopting general price-level accounting. Will the United States follow Britain once the latter implements the new accounting standard?

It would not be the first innovation in financial reporting which the United States borrowed from Britain. The London Stock Exchange first broached the subject of diversified reporting in 1961, and four years later a requirement was added to the Exchange's listing agreement. In 1967, the U.K. Companies Act was similarly amended. It was not until 1966 that a comparable trend began in the United States. In May 1966 the SEC chairman publicly called for diversified reporting, but it is at least arguable that he was strongly influenced by pressure from a committee of the U.S. Senate. In his public addresses, he cited the earlier experience in Britain. The APB was less than enthusiastic, and the Financial Executives Institute and National Association of Accountants happily commissioned research studies on the subject. By the close of the decade, the SEC had amended its regulations to provide for such disclosures.

The publication of profit forecasts accompanied by the opinion of a reporting accountant originated in Great Britain in 1969, at the insistence of an extra-legal panel which supervises the conduct of parties to take-over bids. In the United States, by contrast, the SEC had always prevented the publication of profit forecasts in comparable circumstances. In late 1971, the SEC chairman, again borrowing from British experience, began to advocate the publication of profit forecasts on this side of the Atlantic.

The United States has taken the lead in funds statements, although the New York Stock Exchange seems to have done more to secure this advance than either the APB or the SEC.

Why does innovation in financial reporting occur more frequently in Britain than here? First, the U.S. securities laws, still less than fully tested in the courts, actively discourage experimentation with disclosures that might be adjudged "false and misleading," "untrue," or "deceptive." The penalties for transgression are harsh. Second, the SEC has evolved into a conservative, if not a reactionary, institution on matters of financial reporting. There are signs, however, that the SEC's attitude toward new approaches to financial reporting may be undergoing a change. Third, the British accounting profession enjoys a higher standing than its U.S. counterpart among government officials, businessmen, members of the financial community, and the public (See Seidler, 1969: 493–500). This fact, coupled with the British genius for quiet diplomacy and the quest for viable solutions, surely has lessened the likelihood of American-type confrontations on accounting principles. At the same time, the British have not pushed as hard and on as many fronts as the Americans, and the SEC has been a major factor in impelling the profession forward.

I can find little fault with Moonitz' catalogue of attempts to reform accounting practice. I can best serve this conference by suggesting, as I have, some hypotheses which fit the data. In passing, I would like to comment on a few additional points. After reviewing the work of the 1947–52 Study Group on Business Income, Moonitz concludes that "ad hoc groups are not likely to be worth their cost." I doubt that its ad hoc-ness had much to do with its small impact. An obdurate SEC also prevented a standing committee, the Committee on Accounting Procedure, from issuing a unanimously approved bulletin which also recommended a departure from traditional historical cost.[1] Further, it should be mentioned that the Study Group, unlike the Trueblood Study on Objectives, was probably not a project which had the enthusiastic support of the Institute leadership. The Study Group on Business Income owed its origin more to the pertinacity and resourcefulness of George O. May, its guiding spirit, and one can characterize the Institute as no more than a willing collaborator. Finally, in 1953, when the Committee on Accounting Procedure reaffirmed its earlier opposition to replacement-cost and general price-level depreciation, six members of the committee filed dissents. The 1952 report of the Study Group was cited by the dissenters. It is true that George O. May's ad hoc Study Group failed in its mission, but nothing else was working either.

As a final remark, I must confess that I do not share Moonitz' apparent belief that the opinions and theories of individual accounting educators and academic organizations are significant elements in the process of developing accounting principles. Twice [Sec. 5 and Sec. 8] Moonitz refers to academicians as if their views were important variables. A study of the U.S. experience suggests that the academic literature has had remarkably little impact on the writings of practitioners and upon the accounting policies of the American Institute and the SEC. Too often, accounting theory is invoked more as a tactic to buttress one's preconceived notions, rather than as a genuine arbiter of contending views. This circumstance, which is hardly unique to the United States, is much to be lamented. It surely places accounting, as a professional calling, below both law and medicine.

NOTE

1. In the same year, 1950, the American Institute succeeded in persuading the SEC not to insert a section into Regulation S-X which would have required that historical cost be the basis of accounting for all assets.

REFERENCES

Arthur Andersen (1971) *APB Public Hearings on Accounting for Investments in Equity Securities not Qualifying for the Equity Method, Cases in Public Accounting Practice*. Chicago 8.

Leach, Sir Ronald (1973) "The Role of the Accountant: Independence and Auditing Standards." *Accountant* (April 26): 565–67.

Moonitz, Maurice (1968) "Why is it So Difficult to Agree Upon a Set of Accounting Principles?" *Australian Accountant* (November): 621–31.

Moonitz, Maurice (1970) "Accounting Principles—Some Lessons from the American Experience." *Journal of Business Finance* (Winter): 51–64.

Moonitz, Maurice (1971) "The Accounting Principles Board Revisited." *New York Certified Public Accountant* (May): 341–45.

Moonitz, Maurice (1972) ". . . To Advance the Written Expression of What Constitutes Generally Accepted Accounting Principles . . ." pp. 121–33 in Alfred Rappaport and Lawrence Revsine (eds.) *Corporate Financial Reporting: The Issues, the Objectives, and Some New Proposals*. Chicago: Commerce Clearing House.

Seidler, Lee J. (1969) "A Comparison of the Economic and Social Status of the Accountancy Profession in Great Britain and the United States of America." *Accountant's Magazine* (September): 489–500.

Discussion

Lamden. I want to comment with respect to the not-for-profit area. There have been developments in accounting principles in that area. They have come through the audit guides rather than through APB pronouncements. The first one came out as early as 1966. The hospital audit guide, in presenting a reporting format, indicated depreciation should be included. Of course that changed the accounting principle as compared, for example, to educational institutions. I think there was a Union Fund audit guide that came out about a year or two ago. Then the educational institutions have a guide that has just come out. There are two now, I believe, that are in exposure draft which have gone before the APB on health and welfare organizations and on pension funds. These do more than just tell you how to audit. They tell you what accounting principles in these areas should be.

Moonitz. I am grateful for the suggestion. I was aware of some of the developments, but it is too late to work them into the paper. I will look them over. However, what puzzles me for the moment is whether this constitutes a breach of what I understood was the policy at the Institute that the APB is the sole authority on accounting principles. Now you are telling me it is not true. I know these things have to be cleared with the APB, but this is a procedural matter that I can check out later on. But on the hospital guide, isn't it true this would be the introduction of depreciation accounting into hospitals as a response not to any pressure from the American Institute, but from the changed environment in which hospitals operated? That is, the growth of prepaid plans or hospital insurance. This called for reimbursement formulas on a cost-plus basis. It forced the hospitals as operating units to consider their own accounting systems and they found them deficient if they didn't include an allowance of some sort for capital consumption. The audit guide in effect codifies or summarizes what had already been developed. The question in my mind is whether something similar happened in other cases.

Lamden. As you know, of course, the educational institutions' guide does not recommend depreciation, so if you have a situation where you have a university hospital you have a conflict.

Moonitz. This is tied in with government contracts for research; that is, the big centers like Princeton and Berkeley and Chicago faced this problem during and after World War II—the formula under which they were going to be reimbursed for the work they were doing for the federal government. It was this reimbursement formula problem which forced them to think through the problem of overhead allocation in general, identified within an educational, institutional setting. What you are saying, Chuck, is valid. I appreciate it. But the question is, To what extent has the organized accounting profession taken the lead in formulating accounting principles? I find evidence that in many areas either by default or by lack of ability we have not formulated those principles. At best we have rubber stamped what others have provided. In many areas I think they are getting away from us.

Horngren. Steve commented that accounting theory has not had much usefulness in the accounting policy-making groups—that the academicians' influence has been small. I was wondering what evidence there is for that particular remark. The reason why the question is prompted is that it seems to me that the policy-making groups, notably the Accounting Principles Board, when they begin a topic always start with accounting theory. They don't worry about implementation problems or feasible alternatives. They start at the right place, by and large, trying to come up with the best possible answer without considering political constraints. From there they move to implementation problems. And sometimes the implementation problems aren't so awesome, and the political problems aren't so awesome, and they come up with, I would think, expressions of theory which by and large have been developed in the academic world. The interest on receivables and payables is the thing that comes to mind most readily. Early extinguishment of debt is another one which relied heavily on what was in the academic literature. So I would like you to elaborate, Steve, on your comments.

Zeff. I think the principal source for my conclusion, Chuck, is the interviews I have had with practicing accountants and others who have been members of bodies such as the Accounting Principles Board, discussing with them, to be sure in an *ex post facto* way, what factors were significant in the evolution of a particular opinion or position of the Board and of the Committee on Accounting Procedures.

Horngren. I can think of business combinations and goodwill where the early discussions, in fact an early draft of an opinion, was based on what I would consider a doctoral seminar kind of discussion of the issues using the research studies that had been generated. So at least the preliminary positions were influenced strictly on what one might call academic or theoretical grounds.

Zeff. I think it would be fair to say that the research studies that were published by the Accounting Research Division of the Institute seem to have had little proximate impact on the decisions that were later taken. This doesn't mean that if accounting theory is to be successful the decisions have to follow all of the recommendations of a given researcher. But I think we have a fair amount of evidence that the research studies didn't have any impact. I think board members themselves will attest to the general impotence of the research process in generating solutions that otherwise might not have been produced.

Horngren. My point is that it isn't *all* a political arena. I recognize that it is a political arena, but there is a place for academic research, and sometimes the academic research dominates. I cited two cases where it did.

Zeff. I will take those as data.

Defliese. I would like to support Chuck in that respect. I think that it is easy for critics to emphasize one of the very many influences that the APB has suffered from, and I think we have recognized all of these impacts, and there has been a constant interplay. I should set the record straight on the marketable securities issue which seems to have been laid at the SEC doorstep. While it is true that the insurance industry put pressure on the SEC to influence the marketable security opinion, it is also a matter of fact that within the Board there was not a clear consensus. In fact there had never been an exposure draft ready for publication. The chairman of the sub-committee, who had dealt with that subject for three years, reversed himself and backed away from using market. It is quite possible that without that influence from the SEC the Board would never have come up with the opinion that was being formulated at that point. As you say, it started from a very academic viewpoint, but then the practical implementation of it soon became evident to many Board members—some who saw it in the early stages and resisted it, and others who saw it as we went along—so it is hard to say which one influence is greater, but certainly they all have an effect.

Zeff. Wouldn't you say, Phil, that there would have been a fairly comfortable majority behind some opinion in that direction?

Defliese. No there would not have been. They did not ever have a two-thirds majority.

Zeff. That wasn't my reading of it.

Sterling. What do you mean by the practical implementation, Phil? Do you mean the resistance by the insurance companies?

Defliese. Yes, that is part of it. But part of it is that the business community would not have accepted the yoyo effect on earnings per share in a situation like that. It just wasn't practical from the standpoint of what the insurance companies were attempting to portray. Many held a strong theoretical view that the market was not necessarily the evaluator because you couldn't liquidate the entire portfolio at that time and receive those dollars. Secondly, when is income realized in a situation like that? Is it realized as the market fluctuates, or is it realized over a period of time with a smoothing of the yoyo? The element of smoothing was something that many, particularly the academicians, felt was a bad thing. Yet we smooth a lot of things in accounting, notably pension costs.

Sterling. Let me pose a hypothetical case. Suppose that you had been convinced on a theoretical basis that market values of marketable securities were 100 percent correct. What do you think your chances are of implementing it?

Defliese. Well, we might have had the same chance we had with investment credit. In that case you had a similar situation where a strong majority of the Board (15 to 3) felt that this was the only answer, and practically all our clients were opposed to it. We attempted to do what we could in that situation. That of course emphasizes again the fact that all forces have to be reckoned with in the environment in which we operate. We can't just ignore these forces.

Burton. There you made the mistake of defining the accounting before the law was passed.

Defliese. That was a very bad mistake. We learn by our mistakes. We thought we had to have it ready, and that was unfortunate.

Horngren. I have a second part to my question. This one is directed really for information to flesh out some of the remarks that Maurice made regarding the bank situation, and I would like to put Len Savoie on the spot only in terms of the description. I was very impressed by the fact that here was an industry that was almost 100 percent opposed to a promulgation, and yet the government's forces and the APB united in one battle. I know that you played a role in that, a very active role, and I was wondering if you could contribute to this discussion by describing what you did, because perhaps the FASB should do some of the things you did when they have a similar problem.

Savoie. That has been some time ago, Chuck, and it was a most trying experience. An Institute of the committee on banks was attempting to get out a net income format for banks and was meeting with very strong resistance from the various banking groups and also from the bank regulatory agencies—the Federal Reserve Board, the Comptroller of the Currency, and the Federal Deposit Insurance Corporation. It took a long time even to get agreement within the Institute committee. In addition, the subject was debated before the full Accounting Principles Board on a couple of occasions because audit guides require the approval of the chairman of the Accounting Principles Board, and on substantive issues each chairman has sought to consult with the entire Board. We finally did arrive at a format which would produce a net income figure and would include the gains and losses on security transactions. This was much to the distress of the banking group. The real catalyst in getting this put together, however, was not myself and not the Institute. It was the chief accountant of the SEC who finally got the various groups together—representatives of the committee, of the Accounting Principles Board, of the regulatory agencies and the American Bankers' Association. We had a long discussion as to just how the problems could be worked out. It was a compromise on the precise format, which is securities gains and losses being shown after a figure which was labeled "income before securities gains and losses," so that it was almost what the banks wanted, but it still produced a net income figure such as the accountants wanted. This was finally agreed on after about three meetings in Washington. Isn't that right, Phil?

Defliese. I think the emphasis there was again the compromise that was reasonably accepted both by the industry as well as by the government agencies and the accountants. It is certainly far from what the accountants wanted, or the SEC wanted, but it at least has been able to furnish a net income figure. I think that had we continued with the marketable securities issue, at some point a similar compromise would have been reached. The only reason we dropped the ball on marketable securities was the imminent advent of the FASB. We just weren't going to have the time. That is true of several other things that we put aside principally on the basis that with our remaining tenure we wanted to get through those things that we thought we could and get as many of them done so that there wouldn't be this hiatus before the FASB comes up.

Sterling. I might read that another way. As an outsider I would interpret what Len said as that the Institute *and* the SEC were on the same side and that they were overcoming management's resistance; whereas in the other case, it was the Institute versus the SEC and management, and they weren't able to do anything.

Savoie. That's right. We were solidly in line with the SEC. However the opposition was from the agencies as well as from the industry. The agencies don't like to argue with their banks over something like this and it took a lot of convincing. But I would like to add a footnote to that—something that I have never mentioned publicly before. After the guide was adopted, which was early in the year, as the months went by we learned that some of the banks weren't going to follow it anyway, and some of the accounting firms were going to give them a clean opinion. I went back to the agencies who had been part of the agreement and asked what they would do if they received statements like that, and they said "probably nothing." At which point we went back into discussion, and I was able to convince them that they had better honor the agreement that we had and support the pronouncements of the profession. Each of the three agencies issued a memorandum to all their member banks stating that their financials had to follow the audit guide format. That is the way it came out. It was sort of a cliff hanger at that point. There again the chief accountant of the SEC assisted and stayed together with us.

Liggio. I would like to have either Steve or Maurice comment on what they feel is the role of the court in the development of accounting principles. That's a subject near and dear to my heart.

Moonitz. I am trying to think of an instance in which the courts have done this. Have they enacted an accounting principle? I can't think of an instance. I think it is a poor way to establish principles. That is, as a by-product of an adversary proceeding. You see all kinds of special circumstances of a particular case before the courts. So I would think—ideological preferences aside—it seems to be an inefficient way to do it and a hazard. Is it still true in our court system (it was true when I was a graduate student) that in the Anglo-American system we don't like declaratory judgments? We can't go to a court ahead of time and say that if you do thus and so we will be all right. Maybe there are a few special cases where this can be done, but generally speaking this is not permitted. Just to wait for the ax to fall on some poor devil in order to get the principle enacted doesn't seem fair. I can't think of any case where a principle was established by the courts.

Liggio. What about *Continental Vending*, especially the disclosure requirements there? Whether you consider that an accounting principle or a standard of auditing, isn't that a place where the courts in effect have established a principle or standard?

Moonitz. Perhaps. But I would suppose that no one in that case disagreed on the accounting issue that there should have been disclosure of the facts.

Zlatkovich. I expect you will regard these as a low order of principle, but I think our doctrine on such things as stock dividends and treasury stock has come largely from the courts.

Moonitz. We could debate that. Certainly our stock dividend rules didn't come from the courts. That statute came from the New York Stock Exchange. That is, the idea that you charge retained earnings for a market value and not a par value.

Zlatkovich. The idea that they are not income to the recipient came from the court.

Burton. That is really a tax rule.

Moonitz. It is also generally accepted in accounting.

Stettler. How about *Gerstle, Gamble-Skogmo?*

Zeff. Wasn't that a case where the intent of the company was to dispose of the depreciable assets within a short period? I think that was the actual situation, was it not?

Stettler. Wasn't this the start of new principles, so far as certain specific situations were concerned?

Burton. It has always been demonstrated that where you are in a liquidating mode your traditional cost based financial statements are not appropriate. I don't think that is a new principle.

Moonitz. In this paper and in this discussion I am using principles in a very loose sense. So I would accept Charlie's citation as a principle. In some other discussion I would like to be more precise. Whatever is accepted or adopted or asserted to be a principle and believed by the group. That is, it is all right as far as the problem of who is establishing the principles, how they are developed, what their expected impact is, this type of thing.

Fiflis. Now that you have *Continental Vending* to be reckoned with, the courts will say, "We don't care what existing principles call for in certain circumstances at present." It might be that the courts will now step in. I can envision a case, for instance in the natural resources area, where a company on full costing is the subject of a suit for misrepresentation and the court determines that as a matter of law full costing is or is not misleading. I can see that *Continental Vending* may open the way for a court to settle the issues that have been much debated in accounting circles.

Zeff. I would say that the series of court decisions on auditors' liability has caused the U.S. profession to become much more conservative when considering departures from traditional practice, for fear of the tremendous consequences of becoming subjective in totally untested areas. I find this a wholly understandable behavior. The only case I can think of that really deals with generally accepted accounting principles (but even it did not deal with the merits) is the famous challenge from American Electric Power: back in 1958 when Donald Cook took the American Institute all the way to the Supreme Court level. It said that the Accounting Principles Board of the American Institute had a right to advise their members of what best practice was. But none of the courts dealt with the substance of the question, only that the American Institute had the right. I can't think of any cases to which one could look in this country that would be determinative or even very strong guidance as to what are generally accepted accounting principles *generally*.

Moonitz. My mind is beginning to function a little bit, because some years ago I published a short note, I remember, called "Can Laws Coerce Accounting Principles?" and I think my answer at that time was "yes." But I reached for such things as the Prohibition Amendment, the Eighteenth Amendment to the Constitution, the one which clearly affected valuation of distilleries. It takes something of that sort. Public utility regulation, or a regulatory body, if you include their regulations in the legal framework, clearly can dictate whether particular kinds of property—using that term loosely—are includable in the asset list or not because it affects the valuation. It has to be at that level, I think.

Liggio. That is of prospective nature. I am more interested in the retrospective nature of such a situation growing out of *Continental Vending* and some of the other cases. I know there are a number of cases right now involving firms on computer leasing—the lives of computers. There are a couple of cases where this issue has been put directly into effect. Whether we will ever have a resolution of it, I don't know.

PART II
ISSUES OF PROFESSIONALISM

CHAPTER 5

Public Accounting: Guild or Profession?

THOMAS R. DYCKMAN*

Interest is growing in the sociological and institutional structure of the public accounting profession. Since I am not a professional accountant or even a behavioral scientist, but rather (if anything) an interested observer by virtue of being an educator, it may be appropriate for me to pontificate concerning matters of someone else's expertise.

The thesis in this paper is that public accounting as practiced today has many attributes of a guild; that on the continuum between profession and guild it often seems to be moving toward the latter and does not yet qualify for the dignified title of profession. Contributors to this unhappy state are legion but foremost among them are management, accounting educators, and practitioners.

1. SOME DEFINITIONS OR CHARACTERIZATIONS

In order to have a reference point, we need a definition or two. At most, we assert that these are reasonable and appropriate. Each of you may have a different characterization of the terms profession

*B.A. 1954, M.B.A. 1955, Ph.D. 1961, University of Michigan. Professor of Accounting and Quantitive Analysis, Cornell University. Author, *Long-Lived Assets* (1967); (with S. Smidt and A. McAdams) *Management Decision Making Under Uncertainty* (1969); (with H. Bierman) *Managerial Cost Accounting* (1971); (with J. Thomas) *Calculus and Algebra for Business and Economics* (forthcoming). Contributor to accounting periodicals.

The author is indebted to Professor D. H. Pletta, who is worried about the issues of professionalism in engineering and whose ideas stimulated my own thinking in this area. I also wish to thank Professor Thomas Hofstedt for his many helpful suggestions.

189

and guild, and we commend you to follow the logic of your own definitions if you find ours wanting.

By guild we will mean an association of persons engaging in the same business or plying the same craft. Membership reflects the trade practiced, and a primary function of the guild is to establish control over the practice of that trade by setting standards of workmanship. Guilds also hope (or hoped) to protect the organization from competition, and, thereby, assure the economic security and public status of their members. Historically, the regulatory activities of guilds were an important aspect of their operations. These activities involved rigorous controls and an emphasis on stability and quality of workmanship in conformance with set standards. Guilds tended to guard their monopolistic position jealously and to oppose change. As time passed, the guild system became increasingly rigid and the trend toward hereditary membership grew very marked.

Two aspects of this description are particularly important. First, the focus on the well-being of the members is paramount. Second, there is no recognition of the dynamic process that one typically associates with the learned arts such as law and medicine, where practice continuously adjusts to reflect the inputs from theoretical and empirical analysis.

A profession, I submit, is quite a different animal. Alfred North Whitehead (1955) defines a profession as "an avocation whose activities are subject to theoretical analysis, and are modified by theoretical conclusions derived from that analysis." This description of inquiry and the adaptive reaction of practice to theoretical and (I would argue) empirical investigation is quite contrary to that implied by a guild.

Another aspect of a profession is suggested by Roscoe Pound, a former Dean of the Harvard Law School. Pound (1953: 5) writes: "*Pursuit of a learned art in the spirit of a public service is the primary purpose [of a profession]*." Benjamin Whichcote (1753) once wrote, "every profession does imply a trust for the service of the public." The implication I wish to draw is that a professional has as his prime responsibility service to the larger community through the practice of his expertise. Such an outward-directed perspective would suggest that the responsibilities of the CPA to his client, the profession, his firm, his fellow members, and himself, are secondary. These residual responsibilities are not unimportant, but, rather, of a lesser priority. The order of responsibilities of a profession are, then, quite different from those of a guild.

Let us now turn to a view of the accountant's world and see how he fares against these characterizations. To do so, we will explore several attributes raised by the above characterizations as they relate to a guild and a profession. A schematic of the attributes selected is given in

FIGURE 1

SCALES FOR

SOME ATTRIBUTES RELEVANT TO DISTINGUISHING

A GUILD FROM A PROFESSION

Attribute	Profession ←————→ Guild	
1. Responsibility	To Society ←————→ To Members	
2. Adaptability	Creativity ←————→ Stability	
3. Authoritative Basis	Judgment Through	Sanctioned
	Personal Competence ←——→	Rules
4. Ethical Responsibility	Self-Imposed ←————→ Regulatory	

Figure 1. We hasten to add that no claim of exhaustiveness can be made for the attributes selected. We do believe them to be among the more important ones on which the data suggest accountants may fall short of professional stature. The list is therefore biased, but perhaps sufficient to establish the hypothesis.

2. DIRECTIONAL RESPONSIBILITY

Perhaps the most important distinction between a guild and a profession is the responsibility of the profession to society while a guild's responsibility is toward its members. To some extent this responsibility is being recognized by the courts. In *Rusch Factors, Inc.* v. *Levin* (1968), for example, the court said:

Why should an innocent reliant [third] party be forced to carry the weighty burden of an accountant's professional misconduct? Isn't the risk of loss more easily distributed and spread by imposing it on the accounting profession, which can pass the cost of insuring against the risk onto its customers, who can in turn pass the cost onto the entire consuming public?

In the *Rhode Island Trust* case, the court held this rule to be that "an accountant should be liable in negligence [not just fraud] for careless financial representations relied upon by actually foreseen and limited classes of persons" (Quoted in Isbell and Carmichael, 1973: 41). So far this rule has not been applied to the more general class of "unforeseen" third parties but it seems only a matter of time. Thus, in *Yale Express* the court stated that the accountant "must report fairly on the facts as he finds them whether favorable or unfavorable to his client."

The AICPA publication *Horizons for a Profession* (Roy and MacNeil, 1967: 194) makes a similar point. "The CPA not only has an obligation to his client, the firm whose affairs he audits, but he also has a

responsibility to third parties, the investor-creditor public." The statement seems, however, to imply that the client responsibility takes
precedence.

But is the behavior of accountants consistent with this dimension
of responsibility? Let's look at some selected cases from the record
that would suggest that "at least not all the time" is the appropriate
answer.

A relevant incident is provided by data uncovered in the case of
the Penn Central. The ICC found that the Penn Central took various
steps in 1968–70 to divert public attention from the railroad's precarious
financial condition. Among others, these steps included: recording sales
of property to subsidiaries under whichever accounting treatment was
most favorable to the Penn Central; listing certain dividends from
subsidiaries totaling at least $19 million in 1968 and 1969 as income,
although no cash gain to the Penn Central was involved; writing down
passenger facilities to eliminate depreciation expenses supportable only
if these facilities had a zero value); and reporting a $21 million gain,
deemed extraordinary by the ICC, as ordinary income. (See *Wall Street
Journal,* 1971a.)

The *Penn Central* case involves actions by the firm's accountants as
well as by their auditors. The reporting manipulations of the Penn
Central and its subsidiary, Great Southwest Corporation, in regard to
the transactions involving the Six Flags Over Texas Amusement Park
are well documented in Abraham Briloff's recently published book,
Unaccountable Accounting. Since the same firm of independent auditors
certified the reports of both the Penn Central and Great Southwest
and were also listed as the accounting experts in the Six Flags prospectus,
it seems they must have known the situation. Yet no disclosure was
made on the Penn Central's statements. Surely this is a sorry chapter
in a "profession's" history.

But if it were the only chapter it might be forgivable. Alas, this
is not the case. There are the franchising manipulations of Minnie
Pearl, the misuse of percentage completion methods by National Student
Marketing, leasing and revenue recognition irregularities in the compu-
ter industry by Telex, Memorex and Leasco, failure to report on
anticipated losses when they were known in the case of Lockheed.
The roll continues with such names as Continental Vending, American
Express and the salad oil scandal, Westec, BarChris, Yale Express, GAF
Corporation, Commonwealth United, Mill Factors, Liberty Equities,
Major Realty, Rhode Island Trust, and Ampex, to name a few where
the facts are known.

Were the accountants who acted as independent auditors unaware of the facts when they certified the statements of these companies? I believe one must conclude with Briloff (1972)

> that the auditors in each of these instances knew, or as responsible professionals should have known, that the particular statements were not telling the story really fairly; they knew, or should have known, why and how the relevant principles were being distorted or stretched—they must have known what it meant.

Settlement of claims amounting to about $5 million by one of the Big Eight public accounting firms arising from its role in the *Mill Factors'* case suggests some did indeed know what it meant. Provision of a million dollar "settlement fund" by the auditors of Yale Express reflects at least the auditors' unwillingness to take the issues to court. Conviction of the auditors of Continental Vending for violation of the Federal Mail Fraud Statute and the Securities Exchange Act of 1934 indicates that the courts occasionally knew, too.

A reading of these cases suggests that CPAs at times have viewed their responsibility to their client as more important than their responsibility to society in the large. Indeed, public accounting firms have, in general, articulated the position that their primary loyalty is to their client, apparently even when they knew or should have known that the public was not being given an accurate picture. In a dated study, the AICPA (1957) found that the CPA was highly respected for, among other things, "his genuine interest in promoting the financial success of his clients."

To some extent the problem is compounded by the fact that the auditor lacks economic independence from his client. This creates an unequal balance of power in favor of management, which may wish for selfish reasons to play a different tune on their accounts. As Leonard Savoie, Executive Vice President of the AICPA, remarks (Briloff, 1972: 14–15):

> This fact becomes especially significant when a company is, as you might say "shopping" for the accounting principles which best suit its game plan. The company's present auditor may stand adamant against what the management wants to do, so management begins looking for an accounting firm that they hope will be more accommodating. [The use of the word "may" by Savoie is striking.]

As Kapnick (1972) remarks, "the appearance of independence, as well as independence in fact, is crucial in maintaining the public's confidence." To this we might add even the potential for lack of independence in the attest function.

There is no way of knowing whether the incidence of situations such as those alluded to in the cases cited earlier are increasing or not. That they have not ended is suggested by the recent indictment of a number of firm officers, several members of a major financial underwriter, and three members of a major public accounting firm in connection with the case of the Four Seasons Nursing Centers of America, not to mention Equity Funding.

While it is true that the cases described above represent only a very small fraction of the audits conducted, we maintain that it is in just such situations that public accountants earn their credibility to the public. If such failures severely diminish this credibility, the public accountant's value to society will be substantially diminished.

Now every profession has its rascals. That's why there are codes of professional ethics and boards to enforce them. Public accounting has such a code and such a board. We will return to this issue again when we look briefly at ethical responsibility.

There is also the possibility that CPAs may place loyalty to their firm before their obligation to society. An example of the relative importance of the firm in a CPA's loyalty structure, this time for a CPA firm, is provided by *The First Fifty Years, 1913–1963*, published by Arthur Andersen. This publication argues for the importance of a "one firm" concept and it discusses the steps taken by the firm to achieve and strengthen such a concept. This concept stresses the goal "to operate as a *firm*, rather than as an amalgamation of individual practices."

To some extent the loyalty of an accountant to his firm reflects the identification of his long-run economic well-being with the firm's prosperity and his continued association with the firm. This inevitably creates conflict between the accountant's "professional autonomy" (his freedom to discharge responsibilities in accordance with his individual judgment) and his need for security. Lengermann (1971) found an "extremely strong positive relationship between position and professional autonomy." One interpretation of this finding is that lower-echelon accountants do not feel free to exercise the independence of evaluation that is prerequisite to professional stature.

Lengermann goes on to argue that professional autonomy depends on profession-related factors provided they are associated with a professional community identification. Unfortunately, Lengermann finds in preliminary analysis that few CPAs possess such a professional community identification. This does not augur well for the interests of accountants (at least CPAs) in the concerns of a larger society.

In an earlier study of bureaucracy and professionalism in a CPA firm, Sorensen (1967) finds that the orientation of the firm's members becomes increasingly bureaucratic and less professional with more years of experience. This empirical finding also has negative implications for the position of the professional accountant on the responsibility scale.

A study by Solomon (1970) of one thousand randomly selected citizens resulted in over 90 percent of the respondents identifying the medical and legal groups as professions. Less than 30 percent labeled the CPA as a professional. Apparently the public is not yet ready to bestow upon the accountant the professional status he claims.

3. ADAPTABILITY

An organization that serves society should be able to evolve with the changing needs of that society. It should be creative, ready to tackle new problems, concerned with research and education. A guild, on the other hand, would promote stability and the status quo.

This is perhaps one area in which accounting has made substantive strides. Accounting is now a recognized subject worthy of study in most colleges and universities. This is a relatively new phenomenon. Practicing and academic accountants through their respective societies have encouraged research into new issues of theory and application. Yet all is not well. Even in light of such a positive record much remains to be done, as we shall see. But some disturbing reactions by accountants suggest a timidity more appropriate to a guild than to a service-oriented profession.

For example, we find the accountant reluctant to take on a host of admittedly difficult measurement issues now confronting him. These include the areas of quarterly reports, management forecasts, and managerial performance evaluation. As Donald Bevis (1972: 57) notes in discussing forecasts, "Whether we like it or not, decisions *will* be made based on forecast data. The decisions *will* be made whether the forecast data are reliable or not."

A prime stumbling block to extending the attest function is the concern over the legal liability potentially created if the forecast proves to be in error. Clearly, the public accounting firms are reacting to the recent history of increased liability the courts have forced them to assume in light of questionable published data. Meigs, Larsen, and Meigs (1973: 106–107), in a larger sense, suggest a thorough investigation of prospective clients to avoid the risks of court cases. But is this the direction in which a socially responsible organization should move?

The issue raises again the question of independence, in the sense that the auditor may feel committed to realizing the forecasts. Perhaps attesting only to the forecast method is a workable alternative.

And shouldn't we, and I mean educators as well as practicing accountants, also be devoting more time to societal issues, the solutions to which depend on good accounting data at both the macro and micro level? How can valid decisions be made on resource allocation issues at the organization, industry, or national level without some attention to many accounting issues that have not been adequately addressed as yet, such as the costs of unemployment, pollution, measures of human capital, and so on? Isn't it important to measure these variables if intelligent decisions are to be made, involving both programs and their interactions at the community level, including crime prevention, housing, pollution control, and unemployment, to name only a few? Have accounting practitioners and educators done an adequate job of measuring these phenomena? The present flurry of activity on these difficult issues is encouraging.

Nor does our teaching of accounting typically reflect the uncertainty typical of professional problems and the creativity necessary to resolve them. Traditionally, the student is given problems to work, problems which are written with the goal of being as clear and unambiguous as possible. Is that how most problems arise? The problems typically contain everything the student needs to work them, but they seldom include any superfluous information. Is that realistic? Further, the student knows that nine times out of ten he can find the proper solution somewhere in the chapter to which the problem related, if he is persistent. Finally, not only does he not have to seek out the relevant data, but also he seldom if ever has to implement his findings or deal with the personnel issues involved. We have done a reasonably good job of training technicians. But technicians are the stuff guilds are made of, not professions. To some degree, the programs offered by the public accounting firms may help correct this imbalance between technical and professional education. A list of the professional development courses offered in 1973 by the AICPA is not particularly encouraging, however. The bulk of the coverage appears to be of a technical variety.

And what of research? Accounting research has for years proceeded on two different and seldom intersecting paths: that of the practitioner and that of the academician. The former was usually concerned with applications, the latter with theory. A good example of the one-sidedness of the practitioner viewpoint is articulated by Douglas Carmichael of the AICPA (1972). Striking examples of academicians' work abound in any issue of the *Accounting Review*.

Even when a topic with potential application is addressed, the academic researcher's game plan is to dress his idea in clothes, often of a mathematical variety these days, designed to gain his paper entrance to the most academically prestigious journals in his field. If the researcher were willing to extract the kernel of his idea and write about it in legible form for one of the practitioner-read journals, the problem would be alleviated, but this is not standard operating procedure for several well-known reasons. We educators usually write to each other rather than to the practitioner, and I suspect the latter do the same.

Theory and application are the opposite sides of the same coin. One cannot flourish without the other. Although the path of joint practitioner-academician research has much to commend it, little progress has as yet been made. Perhaps the most one can hope for is that we learn instead to write for each other's trade publication. That way we could at least share results and problems, if not research projects.

The tendency for accountants to move away from accepting the broader range of responsibilities offered them is reflected in the increased emphasis on compliance with generally accepted auditing standards and the Code of Professional Ethics, articulated by public accounting firms in both the defenses offered in court proceedings and in the writing of those concerned with auditing issues. (See Meigs, Larsen, and Meigs, 1973: 79, for example.)

4. AUTHORITATIVE BASIS

A profession should be characterized by the evolution of practice through improved theory. Practice should reflect the exercise of logic and judgment in determining proper treatment. In a guild, on the other hand, we would expect to find that a set of rules sanctioned by some organizational hierarchy would define appropriate treatment. The extent to which the latter description dominates the former in accounting will be left for the reader to judge.

Let us turn instead to an issue that illustrates the failure of accounting to measure up on this dimension. A recent and excellent example is supplied by management's (and, sadly, some public accountants') opposition to the APB's draft opinion which would require the valuation of marketable securities at market and the inclusion of the value difference in income.

To paraphrase Professor Sterling (in press): In short, the APB wanted to issue an Opinion that was in accord with accepted research findings and whose logic is not at issue. But the resistance of management and a large number of public accountants forced the Board to retreat.

Sterling believes, as does Moonitz, that management is vitally interested in accounting principles but that their objective is to maximize the alternatives available to them. Further, management has the power (of the purse?) to secure their desires. Quoting Moonitz (1968), "Management as a class has sought [and apparently has accomplished its desire] to consolidate its power." Sterling concludes, "whenever we look at the progress of accounting in the context of a power struggle [management versus the accountants], the explanation is obvious. The accountant could not reform a deficient theory because the dominant institution opposed that reform" (Sterling, 1973: 65). Now this is perhaps too one-sided a view of the world. We have already suggested that accountants themselves are not simon pure and further that educators have contributed. However, there is more than enough logic in this position to justify our concern. (One may wonder, though, why a countervailing power does not arise from within public accounting.)

Other instances which we will not expand on include leases and the so called "full cost method" of accounting for dry wells by oil companies. The retreat by the APB on accounting practice in the latter area is due principally, it seems, to industry pressure. (See *Wall Street Journal*, 1972.) This inaction is important regardless of whether the "full cost method" is good accounting or not. It is worth mentioning that management alone is not the only constraint. The SEC played an important restraining role in the case of marketable securities, and Congress was a factor in the case of the investment credit, for example.

Sterling and Moonitz are in fact arguing that accounting theory is not sufficient to support good practice, or, perhaps, that practicing accountants have not adopted enough of existing theory to do so. (The second interpretation is my own and may be in accord with their beliefs. The first reflects more accurately their words.) Assuming they mean what they say, should we accept the argument that present accounting theory is deficient? Do examples of bad accounting practice support a claim of deficient theory?

Although bad practice may follow from deficient theory, it does not necessarily follow that the former implies the latter. Now we still may be willing to accept the statement that accounting theory is deficient, but the supportive argument is not trivial. It would first be necessary to define, operationally, and agree to the purpose (could there be more than one?) of accounting, as well as to specify what constitutes accounting theory before we could evaluate its deficiencies. Further, we would need some cost-benefit measures for evaluating the desirability of proposed improvements even in a supportive management environment. But having parted this curtain, let us close it again, since the issues are beyond our ability to resolve here. Let us suppose that accounting theory is deficient for whatever purpose and by whatever criteria are appropriate.

Given the premise, could the "problem of deficient theory" be rectified if management restrained the exercise of its power or alternatively, if a countervailing power arose in the public accounting area? Sterling (1973) suggests that it could. The empirical data do not seem, however, to be conclusive. Academicians, with apparently little management influence, have failed to resolve a number of relatively simple issues through theory although they have grappled with them for some years. As examples one could offer: accounting for inventories, depreciation, tax deferrals, price-level adjustments, human resources, and many more. The more complex issues raised by the time-value of money, risk and uncertainty, among others, have also raised their theoretical horns without definitive resolution.

Would all this yield to logical analysis if only the alleged institutional power discrepancy were removed? If accountants were willing to accept the edicts of an single man or group, we could obtain closure, but this does not assure the "reform of a deficient theory." Perhaps the search for "a better" theory must proceed concurrently with the implementation of workable procedures which necessarily lag behind the theoretical development. This lag may even be desirable as well as inevitable since the time-trend toward better theory development inevitably consists of cyclical and irregular movements. No one has yet demonstrated that an alternative system would be superior, although we commend and encourage those who seek this Holy Grail.

Those who work on developing better theory should do so in the spirit of pure inquiry. The search could, for example, carry one to a fundamental position whose logical implications would lead to different accounting treatments of the same item, for example depreciation, across firms. After all, comparability, not uniformity, is the desired goal. Some such suggestions and their theoretical development are in a rudimentary form already. If this were the case, though we are not suggesting that it is but only that it might be, given a presently deficient theory, then the efforts by Chasteen (1971), for example, who allegedly demonstrates that differences in circumstances as justification for using different accounting techniques is pure hokum (see Sterling, 1973), are beside the point. His research is inevitably tied to his definitions and these would not be relevant to the issue. Thus, it is dangerous (as well as fallacious) to suggest as Sterling does (1973) that someone has proved this or that, using empirical data and statistical tests.

We may eventually find that the key to improved theory lies in the predictive ability criterion advanced by Beaver, Kennelly, and Voss (1968), or through the yardsticks provided by efficient market theory, or in the estimation methods discussed by Brief and Owen (1970), or in the measurement approach suggested by Chambers (1966) in his book, or in the events approach advocated by Sorter (1969), or in an analytical approach to theory, or through some as yet to be suggested approach. But no single road to truth has yet revealed itself. And even an improvement in accounting theory may not lead to better practice. In part this may be due to the power position of management to which we have alluded.

We have argued here that if theory is deficient, accountants must accept their fair share of the blame. Further, accountants may also be partly responsible for another set of problems. Given the supposed power of management in securing the availability of alternative treatments, it may come as a shock to some to learn of the problems sometimes created for management decisions by the existence of generally accepted accounting principles (GAAP).

There is a good deal of evidence to indicate that GAAP can and do at times lead to measurements that can be inconsistent with the methods and models used for making management decisions. When true, the result is that measurement errors are introduced into managerial decision models and this can lead to inappropriate decisions. We shall propose a theoretical example first and then recount some admittedly anecdotal evidence in support of this contention. (It is worth noting that the existence of these problems is consistent with other than just client responsibility on the part of public accounting firms.)

One theoretical model that could be applied to the valuation of a firm is suggested by the Miller and Modigliani (1961) valuation model. Using this model, total firm value is shown to be a function of several variables, including what the authors call total net profit and the firm's investment or increase in physical asset holdings. The maximization of stockholder wealth in this model is equivalent to maximizing the rate of growth in earnings. Earnings represent the *cash* flows over and above those necessary to meet the required rate of return. Now suppose management takes maximization of the current shareholder's stock market value as its working criterion for capital investment (and other) decisions. Suppose, further, that they are supplied with accounting data on earnings growth, *as reported in the firm's financial statements* using GAAP, for making and evaluating capital investment (and other) decisions. Then all the ingredients for measurement error in the management decision-making process are present.

In this example, the accounting system introduces measurement error into the decision model through the medium of measuring variables substantively different from those used in the valuation model. Of course the fact that the accounting measurement process provides data different from that required by the normative decision model may merely indicate that the normative model is incomplete and that, if the total model were properly formulated, the present accounting measurement methods would in fact be optimal. Although it is not possible to reject this explanation on the basis of empirical evidence, I, for one, find it, at best, unappealing.

For a specific example, consider the increasing use of cash flow analysis in capital budgeting decisions. The variables and their measures considered in the cash-flow capital-budgeting model are unlikely to be the same ones used in either internal or external performance measurement due to the intrusion of non-comparable data based on GAAP at the performance measurement stage.

Does this actually happen? As an example of the effects that can occur, consider the remarks made by Orville R. Mertz, Vice President for Finance and Central Service of the Koehring Corporation, on the use of accounting data in decision-making. Mertz (1966) stated,

> The basic measurement of divisional success at Koehring is the net profit in proportion to the assets employed. . . . Monthly, each division's return on assets employed is calculated and the divisions are ranked according to return. . . . Our standings have a pay-off: the only system of incentive bonuses we have for management is based on return-on-employed performance.

We are all aware of the inappropriateness of using single performance measures and in particular the difficulties in using return on investment as the only performance measure.

Let's look at some more cases where GAAP contribute to inappropriate management decision-making. A vice president of a major firm with an extremely rapid growth rate indicated a few years ago that his firm planned to reject an investment that everyone concerned believed was sure to provide a return on investment of over 50 percent. The reason he gave was that generally accepted accounting methods would require an almost immediate expensing of the investment while the return would be recognized gradually over a ten-year period. The effect on the externally reported financial condition of the firm would be such that the firm felt compelled to reject the investment.

Several corporations have the alternative of leasing or selling expensive equipment. There are a number of considerations that are relevant to this choice. It is apparent from discussions with several executives from these firms that the impact of the accounting alternative, elected on reported income patterns over time, is an important factor in their choice to lease rather than sell. The external reporting issue may also influence the pricing policy selected. Related disclosure issues are present in the decision to lease rather than buy as well.

As another example, consider the following quotation from the *Wall Street Journal* of May 4, 1971:

McCulloch Oil has had year-to-year gains in net income of about 30% for 14 or 15 consecutive quarters . . . and the same gain has been realized for seven years in a row. . . . The company will match that growth goal again this year . . . the Executive [the President Mr. C. V. Wood] said the figure of 30% is tattooed on everyone's brain.

He explained that "the company can fairly closely predict ahead of time what it will earn from its oil and gas operations, and then it sells just enough land to reach the 30% increase." We do not know if any operating decisions made by McCulloch were in error because of this strategy but the possibilities abound. Another case is suggested by the desire of International Multifoods to obtain a growth rate of "10 percent per year in earnings per share . . . over an extended period of time." (See Foy, 1973.)

The area of acquisitions and mergers provides another case in point. Consider the following specific example of acquisition strategy based on published reports. According to Rex Brown (1970), the Inmount Corporation uses computer simulation techniques to evaluate potential acquisitions. "The computer prints out detailed information as to the cost to Inmount and the return to individual shareholders of the acquired company, including a pro forma balance sheet and income statement. . . ." The discussion suggests that alternative financing and operating strategies for the proposed acquisitions are evaluated in terms of projected accounting income and balance sheet statements and that these statements then provide the basis on which final acquisition decisions and the choice among alternative financing strategies are made.

One of my colleagues at Cornell in finance suggests that, according to his experience, one important factor influencing the decision of whether to refund existing debt is the resulting leverage position of the firm. Furthermore, the leverage position is typically measured using the accounting figures as they appear in the firm's financial statements. But these figures seldom adequately reflect the market value of the securities, let alone the firm's total assets or other relevant variables that typically go into the ratios used as measures of leverage. Hence, again the decision-making process may be impeded by the externally dictated accounting measurement process.

Even corporate organizational decisions may be significantly influenced by external accounting measurement pressures. Copeland, Wojdak, and Shank (1971), report that "at least one member of *Fortune's* top 50 companies is known to be working on a corporate reorganization, involving holding companies, so that it can stay on LIFO for tax purposes while adopting FIFO for its financial reports." (In this instance the tax law is a contributing problem.) The same issue was a factor in some of the leasing company operations such as Memorex's, mentioned earlier.

One final example of the problems partially created for management by public accountants is worth sharing with you. Just recently a change in life insurance accounting allows insurance companies to pay agent commissions early and then write off this cost over several years. In the past, agent commissions were written off against premiums. The result is that firms are paying commissions earlier and hiring more agents. Again an accounting technicality is having a significant impact on how business is done. (See Meyer, 1973.) The relevance of these examples for us is that the perceived importance of certain kinds of final accounting reports to outsiders has now become a significant variable in the internal decision process. This would not cause us great concern if the accounting measurement process were consistent with optimal decision models and techniques, but this is often not the case.

5. ETHICAL RESPONSIBILITY

The cases enumerated in an earlier section of this paper suggest that the ethical standards embodied in the Code of Professional Ethics for public accountants have not always been approached, let alone met. Perhaps this is to be expected, but then we would also expect the Code's Enforcement Board to act. But one finds little, if any, evidence that this Board has acted in any of the above cases to discipline its members except, possibly, for the defendants in the *Continental Vending* case, who were apparently censured anonymously.

While this is not a record designed to instill confidence in the public accountant, it is understandable. In part it simply reflects the Board's reluctance to act until all legal recourse has been exhausted. This can take years. The Board also includes a substantial number of representatives from the eight largest public accounting firms. As Briloff concludes, "when a major fiasco is presented for their awesome deliberations: 'Let him who is without sin cast the first stone.'" This is the type of member protection we would expect in a guild, not a profession.

Professions select those who aspire to practice by establishing criteria for admittance and continued good standing. Not only does there seem to be no *operating* means by which accountants who fail to adhere to the profession's standards are stripped of the right to practice, but the apprentice period during which some of the important professional standards could be imparted by its elder statesmen is under attack. Furthermore, it appears that this apprentice period is now used primarily to fine tune or adjust the technical proficiency of the candidate rather than to imbue him with professional standards. When we should be expanding both the use and concept of an internship, we seem instead to be going in the opposite direction. And support for the experience requirement again appears to be based on technical rather than professional arguments (For example, see Porter, 1971). One may wonder if such admittance, progress and continued acceptance does not more nearly reflect the narrow responsibility of the guild to its members than of a profession to society.

Once again we in the educational arena must bear our share of the guilt. To my knowledge little is done academically to instill ethical standards. Apart from a portion of the traditional auditing course, is anyone aware of a sustained effort to foster ethical responsibility through the educational process? Isn't it important for an aspiring professional to be exposed to such values? I would venture to observe that the ethical and moral fiber of our raiment seems to be at least tattered if not torn.

A profession, in contrast to a guild, might also be expected to regulate itself internally rather than require imposed regulation. Yet we see an increasing degree of change in the standards of conduct being legislated by the courts.

The auditors (and others) of the BarChris Corporation were found to have failed to exercise due diligence in conducting the "S-1" review, covering developments between the audit date and the effective date of the registration statement. This case, together with the Yale Express Company fiasco, was paramount in the issuance of SAP No. 41, which extended the auditor's responsibility for facts uncovered at a time subsequent to the initial audit.

The *Continental Vending* case was perhaps historic in its emphasis on "fair presentation" versus compliance with GAAP. Full and fair disclosure, not compliance with generally accepted accounting principles, was considered paramount. Accountants can no longer hide behind the due exercise of these generally accepted principles but must make whatever additional disclosures are necessary for full and "fair" presentation. This doctrine has been reinforced by several recent cases, including *Ryan* v. *Kanne, Gerstle* v. *Gamble-Skogmo Inc.*, the *Rhode Island Trust* case, and *SEC* v. *Bangor Punta Corporation.*

The activities of the courts have been in part responsible for what Arthur Andersen (1972: 125) calls, "the mischief created by the disciplinary approach." The idea is that a proposed accounting rule becomes attractive because it may eliminate an abuse regardless of its logic. But, as Andersen observes,

> This effort at detailed rule making to prevent abuses may also lead to . . . a premium on cleverness in financial reporting. The rules may become a substitute for professionalism, and an underlying mood develops that any procedure is appropriate that is not prohibited by the rules.

Self-imposed ethical responsibility has never been the complete answer in any of the professions. Yet effective concern and impact in this area is a distinctive characteristic of the learned professions of law and medicine. A somewhat disquieting note on the position of the Professional Ethics Division of the AICPA was offered by Wallace Olson, speaking when he was Chairman of the Division:

> Where litigation is pending against an auditor, he is understandably reluctant to disclose any information to the ethics division since it is not privileged, and the information might well be subpoenaed and used to his detriment. Because the ethics division does not have subpoena powers, it has little choice but to defer its investigation until the litigation has run its initial course. To discipline a member for failing to disclose all the necessary information prior to the completion of litigation would not seem to be a satisfactory alternative. In most instances the litigation extends over a long period of time, and by the time disciplinary action can be taken the public has long since concluded that the profession is not interested in policing its members (reported in Briloff, 1973: 72).

The Code of Ethics is not and possibly cannot be effective in matters affecting the interests of society. Legal processes may continue to provide the only effective enforcement.

A subsidiary issue here is the ability (and desire?) of accountants to communicate to third parties. The development of technical jargon is inevitable and indeed often economical in communicating with the initiated. But it may impede communication with the larger society. As A. A. Sommer, Jr. (1972) put it in interpreting recent statements by the SEC and the courts:

> It is not enough to prepare financial statements in a manner that would permit intelligent interpretation only by trained accountants or the investment banker. Above everything else, they [the SEC and the courts] are demanding that the statements *disclose* and that this disclosure be intelligible and helpful to more than a handful in understanding the financial condition and the operations of the company.

The failure of accounting reports to do an adequate job of communication is suggested by a recent extensive study made by Georgeson and Company, an investor relations firm. The study found that 15 percent of stockholders don't read the firm's reports at all, 40 percent spend five minutes or less, and an additional 26 percent give the firm's annual report only six to fifteen minutes. (See Foy, 1973: 49.) That something can be done is suggested by the recent annual reports of Koppers and International Multifoods. The appearance of APB No. 22 is an encouraging sign.

The importance of communication has long been given lip service by accountants. Recent confirmations of this apparent concern can be found in the AICPA committee on long-range objectives, which stated "communication must be intelligible to the user." (AICPA, 1962: 54) Even more recently there is APB Statement No. 4, which includes understandability as one of the seven desirable characteristics of financial accounting.

The position of the major firms seems to be that this means reports must be understandable to the "reasonably knowledgeable investor." Defliese, managing partner of Coopers and Lybrand, and Chairman of the APB, states: "Can financial data be simplified to the point where the man on the street can understand it? The answer is clearly negative. . . . Instead, the emphasis should be on telling a story that a reasonably knowledgeable investor can analyze" (Defliese, 1973: 9, 18). Arthur Andersen (1972: 155) seems to go somewhat further in taking the position that statements should be "understandable to those who may use them." This statement is qualified in the next paragraph by the sentence, "Disclosure should be restricted to what is comprehensible to as broad a range of users as is practicable." I submit that it is still not clear just how far accountants are willing to go to achieve the objective that "Financial statements are first and foremost a vehicle for communication of information" (Andersen, 1972: 125).

On this count it is interesting to note that the medical profession has a problem here too. In January of 1973, the American Hospital Association sent a letter to its seven thousand member hospitals. Among other items, it urges that the patient or a responsible relative is entitled to complete information concerning diagnosis, treatment and prognosis *in terms that can reasonably be expected to be understood.*

Perhaps this again suggests the type of professionalism that is still lacking in public accounting. Communication is not an easy task even when both parties try. When there exists the opportunity to bury important facts in close-written, small-type, extensive and vague footnotes, as appears to be the case in the 1969 annual report of the Lockheed Corporation; or to exclude facts entirely, as seems to have happened in the same year for the Penn Central, one could well ask whose interest is being served. In the later case, the situation was exacerbated by the very positive statements of the Board Chairman included in the annual report. The Ampex case provides another and more recent example of a failure to adequately communicate (via disclosure), this time in the income statement.

Certainly one of the major ethical issues of the day is the question of independence. Can the auditor whose fee is paid by the audited company exercise truly independent judgments? Can the auditing firm engaged in actuarial services, executive recruiting, acquisitions, and consulting activities with the firm it is expected to audit be expected to act independently and in the best interests of society? Most of the firms involved maintain that no conflict of interest exists; and argue (at times persuasively) for their comparative advantage and the purely advisory capacity of their consulting work.

But again there is evidence that suggests the situation may be otherwise. Examples where a serious breach of audit independence may or did occur include Yale Express, National Student Marketing and Orvis Brothers among others. These cases reflected the consulting activities of the auditing firms. Indeed, many of the cases mentioned earlier may in part reflect the lack of independence due to economic factor of who is paying the fee. At least some public accountants are beginning to admit to these problems, as the remarks of Marvin L. Stone (1972) indicate. (See also Kapnick, 1972.)

6. CONCLUSIONS AND RECOMMENDATIONS

The evidence suggests that there are several dimensions on which accountants may have failed to achieve a satisfactory level of professionalism. There seems to be much that is more in keeping with the guild than the profession.

The ingredients for a profession, however, appear to be present. Societal need and the technical expertise to service this need are available. But it has not worked adequately yet and those of the Efficient-Market School remind us that if accounting does not fulfill the information needs of society other systems will emerge that will do so.

Some recent developments are encouraging, including the formation of the FASB, which is, at least nominally, divorced from the direct control of public accounting. But there are many other steps that need to be taken. Briloff (1972) suggests several possible structural changes. Others include the need for better educational approaches, the expanded use of the apprentice period to develop professional attitudes, and attention to the issues of improved organizational design.

At the same time care must be exercised to prevent further erosion of those professional attributes already attained. Hence, we should do a better job of meeting our attest responsibilities and enforcing the ethical code, where possible, rather than yield these responsibilities to the courts or perhaps even to government. New challenges need to be accepted rather than resisted. And vigilance must be exercised lest some unfortunate changes take place that would seriously impact on future efforts to achieve increased professional stature.

An example of this last point is the growing trend toward unionization in professions. This trend is very strong in the unionization of teachers;

and accountants may not be immune: their academic brothers certainly are not.

The growing unionization of faculty is an ominous specter. Already over 15 percent of college faculty members on 10 percent of college campuses have been unionized. The economic situation together with the lesson supplied by elementary and high school experience suggests this trend will continue.

What is worrisome is that a union's goals are inverse to those of a profession, although not to those of a guild. Its primary responsibility is to increase benefits to its members and itself. Service to society is claimed to be a result of securing these benefits: an "invisible-hand" argument. But service to society is, at best, a residual goal to a union, whereas to a profession it must be primary. Furthermore, unions do not typically have a code of ethics nor do they concern themselves with disservice to the public by individual members. Perhaps there are other factors we should consider but these are not encouraging signs to a profession. (They do seem appropriate to a guild.)

The significant question raised in this paper is where do we stand and in what direction are we moving on whatever are the appropriate attribute scales. Possible scales are suggested. In my opinion, public accounting has neither achieved what it should nor is it presently moving in the right direction as practiced today. Perhaps we are fortunate that things are as good as they are. But things can and must be improved. The problems are extensive and solutions interdependent. We do not pretend to have dealt with all the issues, and much of the evidence is admittedly anecdotal, yet things are not what they should be. Our house is not in order and it will take a forthright and herculean effort to turn things around. This is an effort to which management, public accounting, and accounting educators must give allegiance, else it will fail. In the long run, public accounting will survive as a private institution only if it attains the full professional status which it now claims.

REFERENCES

American Institute of Certified Public Accountants (1957) *Small Business Looks at the CPA.* New York.
American Institute of Certified Public Accountants (1962) *The Accounting Profession—Where Is It Headed?* New York.
Arthur Andersen & Co. (1972) *Objectives of Financial Statements for Business Enterprise.*
Arthur Andersen & Co. *The First Fifty Years 1913–1963.*
Beaver, W. H.; J. W. Kennelly; W. M. Voss (1968) "Predictive Ability as a Criterion for the Evaluation of Accounting Data." *Accounting Review* (October): 675-83.

Bevis, Donald J. (1972) "Future Extensions of Audit Services; Meeting Investors' Future Needs," pp. 55–66 in Howard Stettler (ed.), *Auditing Looks Ahead.* Lawrence: University of Kansas.

Brief, R. P. and J. Owen (1970) "The Estimation Problem in Financial Accounting." *Journal of Accounting Research* (Autumn): 167–77.

Briloff, Abraham J. (1972) *Unaccountable Accounting.* New York: Harper and Row.

Briloff, Abraham J. (1973) "Quo Vadis." *Financial Analysts Journal* (March–April): 34ff.

Brown, R. V. (1970) "Do Managers Find Decision Theory Useful?" *Harvard Business Review* (May–June): 83-84.

Carmichael, D. R. (1972) "Future Directions for Auditing Research," pp. 101–11 in Howard Stettler (ed.), *Auditing Looks Ahead.* Lawrence: University of Kansas.

Chambers, R. J. (1966) *Accounting Evaluation and Economic Behavior.* Englewood Cliffs, New Jersey: Prentice-Hall.

Chasteen, L. G. (1971) "An Empirical Study of Differences in Economic Circumstances as a Justification for Alternative Inventory Pricing Methods." *Accounting Review* (July): 504–508.

Copeland, R. M.; J. F. Wojdak; J. K. Shank (1971) "Use LIFO to Offset Inflation." *Harvard Business Review* (May–June).

Defliese, P. L. (1973) *The Objectives of Financial Accounting.* Coopers & Lybrand.

Foy, F. C. (1973) "Annual Reports Don't Have to be Dull." *Harvard Business Review* (January–February): 49–58.

Isbell, D. B. and D. R. Carmichael (1973) "Disclaimers and Liability—The *Rhode Island Trust* Case." *Journal of Accountancy* (April): 37–42.

Kapnick, Harvey (1972) *Return to Professionalism.* Arthur Andersen.

Lengermann, J. L. (1971) "Supposed and Actual Differences in Professional Autonomy among CPAs as Related to Type of Work Organization and Size of Firm." *Accounting Review* (October): 665–75.

Meigs, W. B.; E. F. Larsen; R. F. Meigs (1973) *Principles of Auditing* 5th ed. Homewood, Illinois: Richard Irwin.

Mertz, O. (1966) "The Use of Internal Accounting Data in Decisions at Koehring Company," pp. 213–25 in T. J. Burns (ed.) *The Use of Accounting Data in Decision Making.* College of Commerce and Administration, Ohio State University.

Meyer, P. S. (1973) "Accounting Change Enables Life Insurers to Pay Out Agent Fees Over Fewer Years." *Wall Street Journal* (March 6).

Miller, M. H. and F. Modigliani (1961) "Dividend Policy, Growth and the Valuation of Shares." *Journal of Business* (October): 411–33.

Moonitz, Maurice (1968) "Why Is It So Difficult to Agree Upon a Set of Accounting Principles?" *Australian Accountant* (November): 621–31.

Pletta, D. H. (1972) "Professional Conflicts in and a New Dimension of Engineering Education." Virginia Polytechnic Institute and State University.

Porter, W. T. (1971) *Higher Education and the Accounting Profession.* Haskins and Sells.

Pound, R. (1953) *The Lawyer from Antiquity to Modern Times.* St. Paul, Minnesota: West.

Roy, R. H. and J. H. MacNeill (1967) *Horizons for a Profession.* New York: American Institute of Certified Public Accountants.

Solomon, K. (1970) "The CPA's Public Image." *Bulletin of the National Association of Hotel-Motel Accountants* (April): 3–11.

Sommer, A. A. (1972) "What are the Courts Saying to Auditors," pp. 23–25 in Howard Stettler (ed.), *Auditing Looks Ahead.* Lawrence: University of Kansas.

Sorensen, J. E. (1967) "Professional and Bureaucratic Organization in the Public Accounting Firm." *Accounting Review* (July): 553–65.

Sorter, G. H. (1969) "An Event's Approach to Basic Accounting Theory." *Accounting Review* (January): 12–19.

Sterling, Robert (1973) "Accounting Power." *Journal of Accountancy* 135 (January): 61–67.

Sterling, Robert (in press) "Accounting Research, Education, and Practice." *Journal of Accountancy.*

Stone, M. (1972) "The Problem with Auditing Is . . ." pp. 121–35 in Howard Stettler (ed.), *Auditing Looks Ahead.* Lawrence: University of Kansas.

Wall Street Journal (1971a) "I.C.C. Inquiry Says Penn Central Hid Financial Straits." (April 20): 2.

Wall Street Journal (1971b) "McCulloch Oil Says 1st Quarter Net Climbed." (May 4).

Wall Street Journal (1972) "Accounting Board Eases Rule Plans for Oil Units." (March 24).

Whichcote, B. (1753) *Moral and Religious Aphorisms.*

Whitehead, A. N. (1955) *Adventures of Ideas.* New York: New American Library.

Public Accounting: Guild or Profession?
A Homiletic Response to Professor Dyckman

ROBERT K. MAUTZ*

Whatever the intent of Professor Dyckman, his paper comes through as a slashing attack on the public accounting profession, using any weapon at hand. As such, it is unlikely to convince our members of any genuine need for improvement, but will, no doubt, give aid and comfort to other attackers. My principal reaction is one of disappointment because this is a curious paper to come from the pen of a research scholar. Even a casual acquaintance with research techniques and procedures is sufficient to raise questions about both its conclusions and approach. Specifically, (1) the conclusions rest heavily on a questionable premise; (2) the evidence cited is of uneven quality and some of it is downright unreliable; (3) the rationalization running from the cited evidence to the conclusions is occasionally devious and often less than valid; (4) and finally, the author doesn't seem sufficiently interested in the stated issue to perform at the level one expects of him.

1. THE DEFINITION OF A PROFESSION.

Let us look more closely at some of the elements in the paper which support these criticisms. A major premise in any argument that public accounting is a guild rather than a profession is the definition of a profession on which the rationale relies. No real definition appears in the paper but the argument relies heavily on throughts expressed as follows:

> Another aspect of a profession is implied by Dr. Roscoe Pound, a former Dean of the Harvard Law School. He defined a profession as the pursuit of a learned art in the spirit of service. Note the emphasis on service in

*B.S. 1937, University of North Dakota; M.S. 1938 and Ph.D. 1942, University of Illinois. CPA, Illinois, Ohio, Louisiana. Partner, Ernst & Ernst, Cleveland, Ohio. Author, (with H. A. Sharaf) *The Philosophy of Auditing* (1961); *Fundamentals of Auditing* (1964); *Effect of Circumstances on the Application of Accounting Principles* (1972). Contributor to accounting periodicals.

this definition. The implication is that a professional has as his prime responsibility, service to the larger community through the practice of his expertise. This outward directed perspective suggests that the responsibility to his client and to the profession is secondary. In a residual position, we would find the professional's responsibility to his firm, his fellow members and himself. These residual responsibilities are not unimportant, but, nevertheless, of a lessor priority. The order of responsibilities of a profession are, then, quite different from those of a guild. [This quotation is taken from the original draft. The final draft was slightly altered—(ed.)]

Service to the larger community as a responsibility greater than service to the client is a theme dominating the paper. I find nothing in the assertion attributed to Pound that places service to the community before service to the client. Indeed, with rare exceptions professionals utilize their expertise for the good of the community only through the service they provide to their clients. A lawyer is expected to represent his client's interest as fully as he possibly can. Our legal system holds that if he does so, and if other attorneys do the same, the cause of justice will be served. Some of us find that in specific cases we have reservations about whether the cause of justice is well served by such an approach, but we do not then rail at the legal profession and tell its members to put their clients in second place and to seek some as yet unspecified way of placing community interests first.

Members of the medical profession treat individual patients, not a community. Conceivably, a doctor who devotes himself fully to the needs of a crucially ill patient may be neglecting opportunities to draw to the attention of the general public matters of great interest. But since he is a professional, we expect him to treat, not neglect, his patient. Were he to do so in the cause of some unspecified service to the larger community, he would have failed in his professional responsibilities.

If we accept the definition of a profession espoused in the Dyckman paper, public service lawyers and medical missionaries will meet his standard, but few, if any, others can do so. The conclusion that public accountants do not measure up to such an unrealistic standard does not seem to be significant.

As a matter of fact, Pound takes an entirely different position from that proposed in the Dyckman paper. Pound insists that service to the client is primary, and that it can be assured only by strong professional organizations which promote high standards of practice, screen out incompetents and undesirables, and discipline members. The following direct quotation accurately suggests Pound's views on the subject:

Effective service to the public, such as is assured by the tradition of duty of the physician to the patient, to the medical profession, and to the public, and the tradition of the duty of the lawyer to the client, to the profession, to the court, and to the public, authoritatively declared in codes of professional ethics, taught by precept and example, and made effective by the discipline of an organized profession, cannot be had from unorganized individual practitioners, responsible to no one, not bred to a professional tradition and motivated, as in a trade, solely by quest of pecuniary gain. Even less can the professional tradition be replaced by a political tradition of office holders owing primary allegiance to political parties and depending for advancement on the favor of political leaders. Professional organization and professional tradition are also to the general public interest because of their effect on the learned arts which the professions follow as callings. (Pound, 1953: 355)

2.   CONFLICTING RESPONSIBILITIES

Perhaps Dyckman's point is of another kind. Perhaps he is pointing out that the nature of the independent accountant's work adds a unique feature not equally characteristic of other professions, a special kind of responsibility to those who read and rely on his report. This is a valid contention, yet one whose total implications are unclear.

A distinction between the independent CPA's responsibility to his client and his responsibility to third parties is not easily verbalized. A first consideration is that without the client relationship, an accountant may be independent but he is not practicing his profession. An independent accountant has no responsibility—or opportunity—to examine financial statements, for example, until a client relationship is established. In this sense, the client is primary. The professional practitioner owes no responsibility to anyone other than his client until he affixes his opinion to financial representations. At that point he does assume some responsibility to others, a duty which at times may run counter to his apparent duty to his client.

It is in the natural order of things for an accountant to be concerned with the welfare of his client. Why else would the client seek him out? Why else would he accept the client relationship? The accountant's intent is to serve the client as effectively as he can within the bounds of professional propriety. The relationship is not one to be taken lightly. Yet an independent accountant never owes his client any responsibility to be dishonest, to compromise his professional standards or personal ethics, or to be subservient in any way.

Ideally, an accountant would never favor his client to the detriment of the general public; neither would he favor the general public to the detriment of his client. But what about those cases in which the interests of the client and the general public conflict? Dyckman's contention is that the general good must dominate. But is the general good always so apparent?

If the accountant is asked to misstate, to conceal, or to overlook, he must refuse. He has no choice and he has no problem. Take another kind of question. Inferring from the words spoken by some of the loudest voices, one concludes that the public believes its good would be well served by additional financial disclosures. Financial executives representing client companies argue that excessive disclosure can harm their companies and the interests of their shareholders in a number of ways. So there is a cost-benefit decision to be made and not an easy one. To resolve it fairly in specific situations, one must identify and measure both the benefit to the public and the cost to the client. If every practicing CPA possessed the wisdom of Solomon, the total task would still be an overwhelming one. Not every practitioner has such grounds for confidence that he can recognize the good of the community in all times and seasons. So although I have difficulty with Professor Dyckman's conclusion, he has drawn attention to an important problem.

3. THE NATURE OF THE EVIDENCE

The evidence cited throughout the paper is a collection of such sterling primary sources as *Forbes,* the *Wall Street Journal, Associated Press* news items, and discussions with unnamed executives. Weak as such evidence is, some of it is also irrelevant. For example, he cites one *Forbes* item criticizing treasurers for allegedly improper write-downs of assets and another indicting a vice president for the same practice [Sec. 2]. What these have to do with whether public accounting is a profession is not at all clear, but the paper implies they constitute a "damning indictment" of CPAs.

Indeed, even rumors and superficial surmising by writers and speakers who themselves appear to be careless of their facts are included. For instance, we find:

> Let us turn instead to an issue that illustrates the failure of accounting to measure up on this dimension. A recent and excellent example is supplied by management's (and, sadly, some public accountants') opposition to the APB's draft opinion which would require the valuation of marketable securities at market and the inclusion of the value difference in income.

> To paraphrase Professor Sterling (1973): In short, the APB wanted to issue an Opinion that was in accord with accepted research findings and whose logic is not at issue. But the resistance of management and a large number of public accountants has forced the Board to retreat. [Sec. 4]

What "accepted research findings" and whose "logic?" I wonder if either Professor Sterling or Professor Dyckman read the letters and studied the testimony presented to the APB on this issue. Was the question as neatly black and white as here described? Should not one present evidence more substantive than this before directing such harsh criticism at the APB?

4. THE QUALITY OF THE RATIONALIZATION

At another place, we find this remarkable sentence:

> The tendency for accountants to move away from accepting the broader range of responsibilities offered them is reflected in the increased emphasis on compliance with generally accepted auditing standards and the Code of Professional Ethics. [Sec. 3]

Now how in the name of heaven can an increased emphasis on compliance with audit standards and ethical conduct in itself reflect a tendency to move away from the acceptance of a broader range of responsibilities?

We find another non sequitur in Section 5. In it, a study by Georgeson and Company is cited which

> . . . found that 15 percent of stockholders don't read the firm's reports at all, 40 percent spend five minutes or less and an additional 26 percent give the firm's annual report only six to fifteen minutes.

This is offered as evidence of "The failure of accounting reports to do an adequate job of communication. . . ." Millions of newspaper readers in this country never read the *New York Times.* Does that fact mean the *Times* fails to do an adequate job of communication? Surely an experienced researcher can conceive of any number of reasons why stockholders might not read annual reports other than that those reports fail to communicate. The charge may be a fair one, but it cannot stand on the evidence offered.

Section 4 includes a quotation from the Vice President for Finance of Koehring Corporation, part of which reads as follows:

> Mertz stated, "The basic measurement of divisional success at Koehring is the net profit in proportion to the assets employed. . . . Monthly, each division's return on assets employed is calculated and the divisions are ranked according to return. . . . Our standings have a pay-off: the only system of incentive bonuses we have for management is based on return-on-employed performance."

Based on that quotation, Professor Dyckman concludes: "We are all aware of the inappropriateness of using single performance measures and in particular the difficulties in using return on investment as the only performance measure."

But is that what Mertz said? If I read his remarks correctly, he states that return on investment is the "basic measurement," not the only measure. He states his cómpany has but one system of incentive bonuses which is based on return on investment. He does not say that the company's bonus system is based solely on any single measure. To reach the Dyckman conclusion, one must take liberties with Mertz' words. Incidentally, the reported discussion following Mertz' presentation shows such liberties to be unjustified.

The point is made in Section 4 that the management decision-making process may be impeded by externally-dictated accounting measurement procedures. Section 4 also cites with approval the arguments of Sterling and Moonitz that management dominates accounting. Which is it to be? If management is the dominant institution, why is it then constrained by externally-dictated accounting requirements? If management is unduly pressured by externally-dictated accounting requirements, how can it be the dominant institution? Can Dyckman have it both ways?

Another inconsistency is found between Sections 3 and 5. In the first sentence under "Ethical Responsibility," Dyckman criticizes public accountants with these words: ". . . the ethical standards embodied in the Code of Professional Ethics for public accountants have not always been approached let alone met." However, in Section 3 he finds "the increased emphasis on compliance with generally accepted auditing standards and the Code of Professional Ethics" to be evidence that accountants are not accepting their broader responsibilities as they should. Apparently, public accountants cannot win on this one. Emphasis on their standards gets them into trouble; so does alleged failure to meet those standards.

5. THE NATURE OF THE SUBJECT

So I find this a very curious paper indeed. Why does a man of Professor Dyckman's reputation fail so badly in making his case? I can only surmise an answer, but it occurs to me that the subject assigned to him did not capture his interest. It did give him an opportunity to criticize public accounting, which he apparently enjoys in an off-hand sort of way, to display academic license, and perhaps to expound on other favorite topics such as the lengthy digression in Section 4. But he seems to have little real interest in the question of guild versus profession.

Another surmise is that the topic was selected by the director of this Colloquium and deliberately intended to be inflammatory. Nothing adds spice to a colloquium quite as much as a subject that arouses emotions and results in controversy. The difficulty here, however, is that the topic is really not all that important. Many practicing CPAs, if assaulted with the charge that they were members of a guild rather than a profession, would respond "Who, me?" and go on about their work. The more important question is whether public accounting is providing a useful service as efficiently, economically, and professionally as that service can be provided.

Dyckman finds to the contrary. There is no question but that he is seriously disturbed about the quality of public accounting performance as he understands it, just as he is concerned about the performance of his academic colleagues who provide the recruits on which public accounting depends. He cites a good deal of "evidence" to support his views. Even if much of that evidence is not very reliable, in the mass the total effect is impressive and perhaps difficult to counter. I will not attempt to do so. What may be useful, however, are a few simple conclusions gleaned at some cost over a good many years of association with accounting. They are not impressive conclusions, nor do they provide any easy solutions to the ills that trouble Professor Dyckman. They are proposed because they suggest ways to avoid significant waste of time and energy in endless and fruitless argumentation. And although they are offered here gratis, they came to me only at the price of many lengthy committee meetings and some harrowing personal experiences.

6. SOME MINI-HOMILIES

First, ultimate truth in accounting, if any exists, is not equally discernible to all. Some select few are confident that they perceive it more clearly than the rest of the world, but their claim to such inspired insight is at least questionable. Theorists tend to criticize practitioners because practitioners refuse to accept "sound theory" as asserted by theorists. But theorists disagree among themselves, and more than that, practitioners may have access to relevant information not known to the theorists who pronounce their conclusions so authoritatively. Of course, theorists may also have access to information, to argumentation, to evidence not available to many practitioners. So who is right?

I think that in most cases the evidence is not all in. Until it is, there is room for doubt that anyone has the final answer. Should we not therefore be hesitant to accuse anyone of bad faith, or even lack of progressiveness, just because he disagrees with a position we favor? The failure to agree is no evidence of cupidity or chicanery. Should not the person who cherishes academic freedom be reluctant to accuse others of improper motives for no fault greater than that of disagreement? Until we have standards which assure us of the quality of research, we cannot expect practitioners to accept every assertion by a theorist as if it were gospel truth.

Second, no group should be condemned for the errors or deficiencies of a few of its members. Without exception, the cases cited in Dyckman's article received attention because they were unusual. This is not to say that they were any the less undesirable, only that they do not provide a basis for drawing broad conclusions about all public accountants. Illustrations of thoroughly professional work, of CPAs standing up to clients, of carefully thought-out conclusions insisted upon in difficult situations are not likely to come to light, given the confidential nature of the work which public accountants do. And in any large organization, quality control is a problem. Both the public accounting profession and the firms which make it up recognize this. On investigation, you would find a surprising effort to obtain that quality control, an effort far surpassing that exercised for the same purpose by our critics.

The situation is not very much different from that of a university or a large department within a university. My own experience tells me that educational institutions also have problems of quality control. How would you like all professors to be judged by the least competent faculty member at your own institution?

Third, even men of high principles sometimes find ideals difficult to attain. Certain decisions are very easy because they are obviously right or obviously wrong. We have little difficulty with these. In between these extremes, however, are some very troublesome borderline cases. Accounting decisions are often a factor in obtaining equity in important financial relationships. A strict "hew to the line" decision may do great harm to innocent shareholders and others. In a classroom, accounting decisions may be isolated so that one can deal with them in a pure and sterile state. They are never isolated in practice, and many of them have distressing ramifications. As suggested previously, balancing the general public's right to know with the corporation's need for confidentiality can pose great difficulties. Determining the nature and extent of disclosure desirable to present fairly a complex and as yet uncompleted transaction, without at the same time revealing corporate strategy or perhaps inviting litigation, is a far different matter than solving an accounting problem in the abstract.

Fourth, a single breach of standards should not in itself brand any person as beyond redemption. Let me give you an interesting illustration, from a talk by Robert R. Sterling.

> Lanny Chasteen recently published a piece in which he demonstrated that
> the revered notion of "differences in circumstances" as a justification for
> using differing accounting techniques is pure hokum. That is, as you know,
> when we accountants discuss the existence of alternative accounting techniques,
> we have argued that like events ought to be accounted for in the same
> way and that unlike events ought to be accounted for in different ways.
> Thus, the existence of differing circumstances calls for the existence of
> different accounting techniques. Now Lanny went out and proved that this
> is hokum. He examined a bunch of different firms that used different
> accounting techniques and tried to correlate them with the differing circum-
> stances in those firms. He found that there was no correlation. I think that
> is a very significant piece of research. (Sterling, 1973: 62)

Note that Sterling's statement is unequivocal, unqualified, and unlim-
ited. The research apparently covered all "differences in circumstances."
Now turn to the fine-print footnote immediately following that column.
Here we find that Chasteen's research is described as "An Empirical
Study of Differences in Economic Circumstances as a Justification for
Alternative Inventory Pricing Methods." Now that's interesting. Chasteen
did not study all differences in circumstances; he studied only "Differences in Economic Circumstances as a Justification for Alternative
Inventory Pricing Methods," a much more limited subject. Does such
limited research justify so broad a conclusion? Now I suggest to you
that if a practicing CPA were to so qualify by footnote assertions in
financial statements carrying his opinion, he would be accused by some
of our academic friends of deception—not of bad judgment, not of
a simple careless error in wording, but of outright deception. As a
matter of fact, if one reads the Chasteen article carefully, it provides
little support for Sterling's extravagant assertion. Can you imagine what
Professor Briloff could do with a case of this nature?

But you and I both know Professor Sterling. We know him to be
a man of honor and integrity who would never deliberately mislead
all the innocent readers of this publicly distributed article. So we conclude
that the misleading statements are probably not material to the conclusions drawn. We not only judge him leniently, we honor him as chairman
of this Colloquium. Shouldn't we treat practicing CPAs as kindly?

There is an ancient and honorable principle of justice that a man
is innocent until proven guilty. I think at times we might expand that.
There may be some men who are innocent even after they have been
"proved guilty." I, for one, would rather err on the side of generosity
in this respect.

These little homilies are offered in the hope that they will discourage
counter-productive extravagances and encourage us to follow a more
sensible course of action. Let each of us try to be a little more tolerant

of others. It may be that they are possessed of information and have reasons that we cannot know. It may be that had we been in their position, we might have made the same judgment. Until we have all the facts before us, judgment is not only unkind but subject to error.

Let us hold ourselves to as high standards as possible. Whether it is in the preparation of a paper for a discussion group such as this or in the practice of our respective professions, and I use that term deliberately, let us hold ourselves to standards higher than we expect of others.

Let us all strive to professionalize public accounting more effectively. I particularly appeal to the professors on this score, because I think a great deal of help could come from an effort to provide students with truly professional education in preparation for entrance into public accounting. I do not mean merely gathering present programs in a professional school of accounting. Rather I mean a much greater interchange between practitioners and educators and the introduction into the formal educational process of materials and ideas that are essential to the adequate practice of public accounting.

Finally, let us, by all means, continue to urge the profession to mend its ways, to improve its practices, to increase its standards, and to accept its public responsibility. We have much need for internal discipline within the public accounting profession. Like any group, to some extent we are the beneficiaries of historical developments over which we had little control, and we must find ways to overcome some of these. Thoughtful and responsible criticism can help us. But criticism that is irresponsible or dismissible on the grounds of inadequate evidence and faulty reasoning is unlikely to be effective.

REFERENCES

Pound, Roscoe (1953) *The Lawyer from Antiquity to Modern Times.* St. Paul, Minnesota: West.
Sterling, Robert R. (1973) "Accounting Power." *Journal of Accountancy* 135 (January): 61–67.

Discussion

Dyckman. I thought Bob's response was a very cavalier treatment of some rather significant issues that I tried to raise. I have read Pound's work and I used his definition specifically in terms of raising the issues that I wanted to raise. I wonder whether Bob accurately read mine. I hope that his published paper will speak in *specific* to the points that he is unhappy about so people can evaluate both what I have to say and what he has to say. I do not get satisfaction from what I have seen, even as non-penetrating perhaps as my analysis may have been. I do not obtain satisfaction from observing that things are not as they should be and that they could be better. Let me end only by saying that I want to absolve the host of this conference, who in no way set the subject, who in no way tried to dictate what I would do, and who in no way tried to control or make this particular discussion what it did become.

Sterling. I just want to say that the two of you agree on one thing, namely my hyperbolic statement about Chasteen's findings. Tom also criticized me for that so both of them agree on at least one point. Not only do you both agree, you are both right. It was an overstatement.

Montagna. I think there are some important implications that Tom has raised with regard to the idea of what is a profession in terms of this continuum idea. I feel that this is an excellent way to look at a profession. As a matter of fact the American Institute had a committee work on just such a project several years back. It resulted in Roy and McNeals' *Horizons for a Profession,* in which they attempt to state the requirements or the attributes of the profession. Among them were listed:

> A body of knowledge which is formulated in a systematic theory or set of theories, has a developed intellectual technique, and an established and formalized educational process;
> Imparting of a body of knowledge which the professional group decides is necessary and a standardized formal testing of the body of knowledge for admission to the professional group;
> Formal recognition of the profession by the society through means of state and federal licensing, plus limiting entrance into the professional group;
> A code of ethics governing relations with colleagues, clients, and other external organizations;
> Professional associations to facilitate colleague relations and communications

and act in concert in aiding the development, maintaining or changing the above attributes;

A set of values in which there is an idea of a career or calling in the service of the public;

An authority in the sphere of knowledge, not in all matters related to its service, and objectivity in its theory and technique for advanced social progress.

I think in arguing this point there are two main factors—the service to the public and a body of knowledge—that we have been alluding to and many of the papers refer to.

I think that the concept of ideology is important in that all the public has to do is to believe that there is a developed body of abstract knowledge, that the profession has some important contribution to make that other people cannot handle—some technical expertise that is important in which some kind of complex activities take place. In service to the public we don't have to *be* altruistic. All we have to do is *act* altruistic. That is an important distinction. It is not necessary that we build up to the ideal type that exists here or the "null situation" or whatever that term was that you used. All that is important is that it is believed by the public and by accountants themselves that they are going in this direction. I think the important factor here is that *is* the accounting profession going in this direction, or do people believe that it is moving in this direction? I think by taking this wider point of view we get a different picture of how the profession is developing.

I realize this doesn't touch upon the more pragmatic, day-to-day events of the profession and how different organizations within the profession and those who relate to it deal with one another. Nevertheless this is a very important point to consider. I don't think that that was made very specific in the analysis.

When I interviewed a stratified random sample of five of the Big Eight firms and three medium-sized firms in other areas of the country—I used a questionnaire with a total number of 141 people—I came up with the responses as follows in terms of what they thought of the profession. They felt that most important was a code of ethics, followed by formal recognition through licensing, followed by a formal testing procedure, followed by a body of knowledge, followed by the importance of the professional association in maintaining and developing these other attributes, followed by personal qualities of a professional practitioner going beyond the technical competence, such as commitment to the profession to work in its associations, good judgment and poise in social relations at work and in civic activities, followed by, finally, a set of values—an idea of a career, a calling in service to the public. At this point in time, which was of course several years ago, this is the way the practitioners felt about these attributes of a profession, and I think they are very important to consider in terms of the development of the profession.

Buckley. I want to ask Tom a question that deals with the profession and the bureaucratic organization. Many of these time-honored definitions of the professional—for example, things like personal competence and personal altruism—were defined in an era when the individual interacted with other individuals, or with other small units. I would venture to say that today there are more professional people employed by formal organizations, be they government or business organizations of one sort or another, than operate under the traditional mode. Does this framework that you set forth in Figure 1 really cater to that new variable of professional activity?

Dyckman. A very quick response is merely to say that I think the institutional factor you have raised may make it more difficult to attain those objectives. I don't think it changes the objectives or their importance. I think they are just as relevant today as they would be in a more individualistic society.

Buckley. You will concede that in sociology today that whole area is fuzzy and ill defined. The question is "How do the attributes of professionalism change, when professionalism is now incorporated in bureaucratic organizations?"

Montagna. I don't think they change much at all. I think that the effect of the large organizations in terms of bureaucratic elements that touch people every day are of considerable importance. When I was able to look at the largest accounting firms, I found that CPAs handle it extremely well. They are much better than professionals in other occupations, such as law, social work, and other groups that have very large organizations. (Accountants have the largest professional organization.) They do this by keeping people away from the bureaucratic process and the administrative process as much as possible. There are very few people who spend full time in accounting firms on administrative work.

I don't think that organization affects this that much in the accounting profession. I think what is important here is the ideas that accountants can get across to the public and other important groups in our society, whether they be other professional groups or regulatory groups, in terms of what they think they are trying to project as an image. In other words, this is partly public relations. That is what I am concerned with.

Mautz. I want to respond to that part about client service and public service. If I am wrong correct me, but I believe it is in the nature of any profession to be concerned with the public only by serving through a client. There is no other way you are called upon to do anything. Now it is true that a CPA in practice could go out and decide that what he is going to do is measure the pollution for the local power company. But if he were doing that, he would be doing it in an extra-professional capacity. As a professional he is called upon by clients to help them in some way—perform some service. If he performs that service adequately and it is a service that is desired or useful to the client and the client is in an activity that is useful to society (all these are presupposed), then he serves society, he is serving the community good. But he is not called upon to serve the community good directly. Now if the city were to come to him and say "We would like you to make a study and compute the social costs," the city would automatically become his client and he would serve the city. The only services he is called upon to perform, except in some cases where it is on a charitable basis, are through a client, and if he refuses to serve clients, he refuses to be of any service.

In a given case it is possible that when you are helping your client you are actually causing harm to the community. If a professional has to make that kind of a judgment, he is in a difficult position, because it presumes that he knows in all cases what the community good is. I don't know that we call upon any other profession to make the same kind of decision. The court system is set up on the basis that the lawyer is an advocate for his client—he does the best job he can for the client—and we assume that justice will result. The doctor doesn't neglect his patient in order to go out rendering public service to the community at large, giving lectures on public health or whatever. He serves his patients as best he can and by healing his patients he helps the community. I think the accountant has the same kind of relationship with a client. His service to the community is through the client.

Pichler. As you have just indicated, if the doctor sews the sponge up in the patient, it is the patient who dies. If he serves the patient ill, then the bad effects don't go beyond the corpse. I believe public accounting is a different kind of profession. A small potential stockholder, not directly related to the client, relies upon the accountant's judgment and upon his application of generally accepted accounting principles in order to make financial decisions. There are cases, as you have just indicated, in which service to the client—broadly considered as administrators of the firm and the current shareholders—would conflict with the welfare of an individual about to make an investment decision. The problem I see is as follows: the lack of operationalized accounting principles gives the CPA and the client a rather wide basis for negotiation, if you will, as to which principle to apply in a given case. I was impressed by arguments in the *Journal of Accountancy* on depreciation, mergers and poolings, and other contentious issues. Given this range of negotiations in serving the client, one accounting firm may choose to serve the client—in so far as the client sees that his best interests are served—in a manner that will raise earnings per share higher than they would be if a different principle were accepted. I, as a reader of a financial statement, have no way of knowing what the possibilities were and what the range of possible earnings per share might have been had some other generally accepted accounting principle been applied. It seems to me that this area of negotiation raises a problem, that the accounting firm can be pressured to some degree to apply a principle that perhaps would not have been its first choice, even though it falls within the area of generally accepted accounting principles. I see the accounting profession as somewhat different from the medical profession or the legal profession in that I think a potential investor should come to expect that the independent accountant is serving them, as well as the more narrowly defined client group.

Mautz. I recognize the problem. I think it is interesting that you define the good of the public as the good of the purchasing shareholder. I am not sure that is the good of the public. It may just exchange from one individual to another individual, with no good or harm to the community at large.

Pichler. The reason I chose that definition is that Spacek, Moonitz, and Sterling agree convincingly that the interests of current shareholders and administrators are parallel, since both would like to see the earnings per share stated in the most favorable way. So there is no conflict of interest, or little conflict of interest, on that particular point. It seems to me that the basis for regulating *any* occupation is that the occupation's performance produces substantial "neighborhood effects"; that is, effects which go beyond immediate client-practitioner relationships. Unless you are going to define public interest that broadly, the real question is raised whether or not any form of regulation is appropriate.

Holstrum. I have a question for Tom that arises from my view of the fact that what we are calling "the profession" involves at least two separate topic areas: auditing and accounting. I wonder if you go down through your spectrum of dimensions, if we separate those two we would have less trouble with auditing as a profession. First of all, items 1 and 3 may not be mutually exclusive. For example, if you take the separation between auditing and accounting and talk about the authoritative base or adaptability, it seems to me that in regard to auditing, personal competence, creativity, or both are fairly important attributes and ones that do exist regardless of whether or not stability of accounting principles exists. Was this a distinction that you purposely left out?

Dyckman. I was more concened with the auditing side than with accounting per se. I hadn't gotten to that yet. It seems to me we certainly do come up with different positions on what you have properly indicated are not mutually exclusive ideas.

Burton. I am a little concerned about one of the points Bob made, particularly because I have heard similar arguments given before, and that is that where we look at a relatively few number of cases and compare them with the broad number of situations where auditors serve their clients well, we draw the wrong conclusions. I am a little concerned about the implications of that. In the first place, I wish I had great faith that the cases which we read about are the only cases in which a bad job was done by the auditor or the professional accountant. It seems to me that for a case to be publicly noted and to come to the attention, as perhaps twenty to thirty cases have in a dramatic way over the last decade, it has to have three attributes. First, it has to be a large company, or a reasonably large company; second, there has got to have been a bad job done by the auditors in a professional sense; and third, a major loss must have occurred. Now I suspect that if one were to examine the files of the inter-office review teams of public accounting firms, one would find that the number of cases where you have this particular combination is a small part of the cases where one of these three situations exists.

I am a little concerned with the rationale that has been offered by representatives of the profession on a number of occasions that what we are looking at is merely a very small number of exceptions to the normally superb job done by public accountants and auditors. By this I don't say that in the overwhelming majority of cases a good job isn't done, but I don't think that the conclusion that is drawn necessarily follows. Related to that, I think that there is another factor that just has to be recognized. When auditors are looking at their social function, which is, in my judgment, very much a third-party function as Joe suggested, what is expected of them and what they accept by accepting this responsibility is a rather high standard. I think we all would agree that in the academic world if someone scores 99 percent he gets an A. I think we might also, if we think about it, agree that if an auditor scores 99 percent he fails. I don't think that is unreasonable given the reason that the auditor is hired, the number of people who are involved, and the need for quality control that exists. When you have that situution the normal response is to say that a quality-control system must be devised which, even though it is costly, reflects the cost of failure. Where 1 percent error is a failing grade, it is necessary to design your quality control system so that the tolerances are less than that. I am a little concerned as to whether or not the quality-control systems of the individual firms or of the profession as a whole are consistent with the concept which is being applied in the social environment that 99 percent is a failing grade. So I just express a concern in terms of what you said, particularly at the end of your talk.

Mautz. I guess if I have any response on that, it would be that I am not sure there are enough competent people available who can bat 100 percent. We have to use people like you and me to get the total amount of work done that needs to be done. Otherwise I have to accept what you say. There is a responsibility. We are obligated to do the very best we can. I don't think there is any question about this. My response to Tom is that you do not indict an entire profession because there are x number of bad cases.

Defliese. I think I would like to soften somewhat the comments that Bob has made. I think that as we do in accounting altogether too frequently, we try to draw analogies, and there just isn't an analogy you can draw with other professions. Whether we like it or not, practitioners have three masters: their client, the SEC, and the present and prospective shareholder. Their duty is to all three. We are just not going to find anything like it elsewhere in the world, so we should stop trying to draw comparisons with other professions and decide whether we are a profession.

It is not a question of are we a guild or a profession. The question is, is everyone within our profession a professional? I think this is something we ought to analyze very carefully. I have been close enough to the scene for the last twenty years to recognize that the story that Carl Liggio told earlier would be equally appropriate if it were the accountant who was given professional courtesy by the sharks. I am sure he did not imply that the lawyer is not a professional, nor am I implying that an accountant is not a professional; but the question is whether or not the people within the profession are always what they should be in the professional sense. When the head of a major firm says that he may not like the accounting principles that his clients are applying, but by God he is going to let them apply them because he is going to give his clients every break possible, the question is whether or not that is professional. We need to direct ourselves to acting professionally. That is the real crux of the problem. The constant striving to be number one is not something that is professional. There has been a lot within the last twenty years to prove that. With a constant decline in business morality, which I think is a sad commentary on which I think we can only agree and I think that is in sharp contrast to the situation in Great Britain, we have to recognize that in such a decline the effort should be to direct ourselves to acting as professionals.

CHAPTER 6

The Nature of Professional Responsibility

HOWARD ROSS*

Let us start at the beginning. A profession is a body of practitioners who are granted a position of prestige and the responsibility of self-regulation. They are expected to do something useful in return. Accountants are recent arrivals in this league, and it is probably not too clear to the public what contribution to the general welfare we are supposed to be making. This confusion in the public mind is sometimes attributed—by the accountants—to a failure in public relations; but I cannot help suspecting that it is more a question of our failure to decide for ourselves precisely what our function is.

We are essentially hangers-on of the Establishment; and it is our humble but useful function to encourage those receiving reports, emanating from within the Establishment, to rely on them when trying to figure out what is going on. In this we hope to accomplish two things:

1. to discourage those outside from getting in on the act, by asking nasty questions and even, in extreme cases, from agitating for a change of management; and
2. to provide some acceptable financial data for those who, in making an investment, like to do a certain amount of preliminary financial analysis—instead of relying on alternative approaches to investment—such as astrology, tea-leaf reading, spiritualistic seances, or hot tips from customers' men in brokers' offices.

This is the function usually described by the old-fashioned, but quite adequate, term of "auditing"; although recently we have tried to make

*B.A. 1930, McGill University; M.A. 1932, Oxford University, LL.D. 1964, Queens University, 1965, Sir George Williams University. C.A. Dean of the Faculty of Management, McGill University. Partner, Touche Ross & Co., Chartered Accountants, 1942–1969. Author, *The Elusive Art of Accounting* (1966); *Financial Statements—A Crusade for Current Values* (1969). Contributor to accounting periodicals.

what goes on more explicit (and more impressive) by referring to the "attest function," or to the task of "adding credibility to financial data." It is not the only function of members of the accounting profession—but it is still the most important service performed by public accounting firms and, moreover, it is a highly distinctive function involving considerations of independence and performance standards. For these reasons, a study of the nature of auditing suggests itself as the proper approach to an appraisal of the role of the accounting profession in society.

Our study can be further narrowed down. While auditing is useful in businesses of all sizes and in non-business operations, the crucial tough problems tend to arise in the audit of the annual reports and prospectuses of publicly-owned corporations. It is in this area that most of the crunch issues are encountered; and it is therefore in the audit of these corporations that the profession does its trail-blazing. This is where the action is. It is an area inhabited by large (often multi-national) businesses, audited by large (often multi-national) audit firms; and it is to the complex relationships between these huge organizations that I intend to confine myself in this paper.

1. GOD BLESS THE ESTABLISHMENT

In a society of any complexity—and goodness knows we live in a society that's complex enough—someone must run things. In a participatory democracy everyone, up to a certain point, has an opportunity to get in on the act—by occasional balloting, and demonstrating and general hell-raising. But there is always a relatively small group who really makes the important decisions; and has the responsibility of trying to carry them out. In our society, this small group is composed of leaders in government and in business. We sometimes behave as though leaders in government and industry should confront each other as natural adversaries. A certain amount of this does go noisily on, but it is a hangover from the old nineteenth century ideological battles— which were based on the notion that there was an essential conflict between free enterprise and communism; one of which was bound ultimately to drive the other out of existence. It should be obvious that we have now, in the Western world, settled down to the uneasy compromise of the "welfare state," in which we live by a combination of market forces and centralized control.

One must, then, always have a group of insiders running things. Every one of the great revolutions—American, French, Russian or Chinese—has demonstrated conclusively that if you ever do throw the rascals in power out, you simply get a new gang running things. Not only history but common sense tells us that this must be so.

What we can hope for is not a society which runs itself in some Arcadian fashion, by a sort of spontaneous exercise of the general will, without anyone pushing anyone else around, but a society run by a good establishment. A good establishment may be defined as one that is reasonably efficient, that reports fairly what is going on; and to which access by new men and women of talent is not too difficult. It is also, of course, desirable that there should be some way of getting rid of incompetent or senile performers without too much bloodshed.

Judged in all these respects, I believe any fair-minded critic must say we have quite a good establishment. It is of course far from perfect. Important basic reforms are urgently required but, at least compared with anything anywhere in any previous epoch, the sort of regime we now have (say in Western Europe or North America) is, with all its shortcomings, relatively enlightened. This sweeping and rather smug generalization is ventured with at least an attempt at historical perspective. All things are relative. Certainly terrible injustices still persist; and we may expect them to continue to persist when we reflect that, after the gospel of the brotherhood of man and the basic importance of the individual had been proclaimed, so eloquently and persuasively, at the dawn of the Christian era, it took over eighteen hundred years for slavery to be abolished on this continent.

Well, we finally have got rid of slavery, which must surely be the grossest of all social injustices. And we have also, to all intents and purposes, got rid of the almost equally unjust distinctions of a class society. We have now progressed to the relatively less invidious distinctions of rich and poor. We have even gone some way towards coping with inequities of wealth—to a point at which a visitor from any other country, or any other age, would probably conclude that the distinction was between the rich and the not so rich.

2. COMMUNICATION, CONSULTATION AND DECISION-MAKING

As we have to have an Establishment, it is clear that there must be good communication—both between the individuals and organizations that constitute the managing group, and also between the managers and those outside the Establishment.

The managers and decision-makers in the large corporations, that are such important units in the Establishment, are constantly dealing with each other—buying, selling, borrowing, lending, investing, merging, spinning off, extending credit, foreclosing and so on. Each business corporation needs to know what is going on within other corporations. And the government needs information for purposes of taxation, tariff policy and coping with other aspects of fiscal control. Moreover, while the general public are not in on the large management decision-making in an intimate way, they are not exactly disinterested by-standers either. They play a part by investing, buying, saving, estate-planning and carrying on other activities for which they require some knowledge of what's going on.

The need for information is obvious enough, but any group which feels it has some sort of mission to help operate the communication system should be prepared to explain why they believe they have an essential, socially useful, part to play. There is such a continuous outpouring of news and comment from newspapers, magazines, TV and radio, that anyone who wishes to broadcast more data should expect to have to explain why he thinks he has a contribution to make.

The trouble with the communication of information through the media is in its quality—certainly not in its quantity. By the sort of standards by which the accounting profession judges the adequacy of information, the press and TV both fall short in three essential respects—skill, due care, and independence. A word on each of these. (a) You don't have to pass any exams to be a reporter, or a columnist, or an editorial writer, or a TV commentator. Nowadays you do not even have to have any experience. It used to be that a newspaperman would expect a lengthy apprenticeship, as a reporter, before he was granted the coveted privilege of a "by-line," and was permitted to toss around his opinions. Now we have arrived at a stage of instant punditry, and raw recruits to the newspaper staff write by-line articles pontificating on every subject under the sun. (b) To the reporter or columnist, "due care" means, not a sufficient examination to warrant the venturing of an opinion, but merely cautious drafting to avoid the possibility of a libel action. (c) It may seem, at first blush, that the media are at least in a position of independence; as newspapers and broadcasting stations are unlikely to be directly connected with those on whose activities they report—but they live by readership and audience ratings; and this means they must concentrate on the sensational which, alas, means the derogatory and the critical. This is not a criticism of the media, so much as a criticism of those of us who attend to them when they are being exciting and critical, and ignore them when they are being fair and dull. This has been described as an age of rising expectations. But in view of the way anyone who tries to do anything is reviled, and jeered at, and spat upon, it might perhaps be more precisely described as an age of rising expectoration.

3. THE REGULATORY SYNDROME

It is not only the media that tends to be obsessed by bad cases. Even the most sophisticated and knowledgeable professional men tend to give undue weight to cases of demonstrated fraud and error. *McKesson & Robins, Penn Central, Continental Vending,* and such spectacular debacles, loom large in the minds of those responsible for keeping us on the straight and narrow path—like members of the APB or SEC. The danger here is that the thousands upon thousands of satisfactory financial statements published in recent years will get less consideration than a dozen or so intriguing cases of fraud. And this can only mean that our accounting principles are likely to develop in the direction of preventing an occasional fraud—rather than in the direction of facilitating freer communication between those attempting honestly to keep each other informed. The hesitancy of the accounting profession to sanction professional audit opinions on forecasts—or indeed to allow auditors to become involved in any way with future probability—is clear evidence of the danger of concentrating on atypical dishonesty.

It may sound naive to stress the essential decency of most people's motives. But it has been pretty well demonstrated that crime pays only rarely. Undoubtedly there are people out to make a fast buck—and we should not ignore them. But it is even more important not to base our accounting principles on the false premise that everyone will be dishonest if he gets a chance. Most of those who achieve positions of responsibility, in the hierarchy of business, take a reasonably long-term view both of their own careers and of the prosperity of the corporation that employs them. If this is so, the temptation to "pull a fast one" is not as strong as one might suppose—even if one takes the most cynical view of human motivation.

We live in a world of uncertainty, and this must mean that any attempt to predict the future can turn out to be wrong. But what this really means is that the predictions should be accepted cautiously and in the knowledge that they may not work out. It does not mean that there should be no attempt at prediction. Without any doubt, the profession, and all agencies concerned with investment regulation, have tended to discourage forecasting by the very people most likely to do it competently and honesty. Perhaps this may be put in more general terms, by saying that concentrating on the rare bad cases, in drafting our accounting principles, will inevitably lead us to restrict the use of judgment—whereas we should frankly recognize the inevitability of judgment in any form of financial reporting. Our basic objective should be, not to restrict the use of judgment, but to promote good judgment.

If the food industry paid as much attention to cases of food poisoning, as accountants pay to cases of fraud, we would no doubt have had such severe food inspection procedures that far more people would have starved, or suffered malnutrition (because of delays in food distribution or increased food costs) than have actually been poisoned.

4. OUR SOCIAL OBLIGATION

To get back to our auditing—the published financial statements of large business and financial corporations clearly provide a basically important contribution to the communication system. It is presumably self-evident that the more informative and reliable these statements are, the better our economy should perform. Thus the essential task of the accounting profession, in its auditing function, is to improve the quality of corporate financial reporting, so that our society will operate more efficiently.

In these days of rampant righteous indignation, the promotion of business efficiency is apt to be dismissed as a somewhat sordid preoccupation—far less commendable or heroic than concerning oneself with the great problems of pollution, poverty, social inequity, race discrimination, and other aspects of our unjust society. But however unglamourous it may seem, one of the fundamental problems our civilization faces is the allocation of scarce resources. If this is done ineffectively, there will be more poverty and more inequity. If costs are miscalculated, pollution control will be harder to accomplish. It is fine that more and more attention is being paid to unfairness in the sharing of wealth—but it will not help in the battle against poverty to forget that producing wealth is a necessary prerequisite to sharing it fairly. I once witnessed an embattled Dean of Engineering under cross-examination by sociology students, who were explaining to him that today's students were concerned about the gross evils of society, and felt engineering was rather an "unaware" sort of discipline. The Dean replied in words to this effect: "Well, if you want to confine yourselves to protest meetings and righteous indignation, just go right ahead; but if you ever get concerned enough about pollution and poverty, to want to do something about them—then enroll in our Faculty where you may learn how to tackle such problems."

This ponderous kind of analysis of our problems is supposed to support the contention that producing reliable financial statements is a contribution to the good life. Of course we should be socially conscious as a profession. But this does not mean we should turn from our traditional role, as custodians of the art of financial reporting, and spend our time re-cycling sewage, or holding protest meetings about the fact that fewer corporation presidents are members of some racial minority group than the size of such group would seem to justify. There is still great merit in the old maxim that a cobbler should stick to his last.

5. FINANCIAL REPORTING

A tradition has developed—notably in these United States, in certain Commonwealth countries and in the Netherlands—for the information about what is going on in our major business corporations to be disseminated in periodic statements, prepared and issued by management, and accompanied by words of comfort and reassurance from a professional accountant in public practice.

Theoretically, I suppose, the financial statements of a corporation could be produced by someone other than the management of the corporation—by some government inspector or some independent outsider. However, anyone who has ever been closely involved in the complexity and pressures of producing such statements, will be well aware of the practical impossibility of anyone but management doing the job. About the best one can do is to stipulate that the statement-producing process be reviewed and reported upon by a competent professional man, acting as independently as possible.

In this respect, the responsibility of the accounting profession is two-fold. First, we must produce the ground rules under which financial statements will, by agreement, be produced—so that those having recourse to the statements can safely make certain assumptions about what the figures mean. We purport to fulfill this function by pronouncements on generally accepted accounting principles. Second, we must provide an auditing service through which we can assure the readers of a financial statement that it has indeed been prepared carefully under these ground rules.

Both these professional obligations require comment.

6. GENERALLY ACCEPTED ACCOUNTING PRINCIPLES

This part of our task has been so widely discussed, that I may perhaps be permitted to deal with it somewhat lightly on this occasion—in favour of a fuller discussion of points that usually get less attention.

In our extensive discussions of generally accepted accounting principles we tend, in my opinion, to give undue attention to two criticisms which are of doubtful validity—by which I mean, in my cautious accountant's way, that they are utter nonsense. The first of these criticisms is to the effect that we should have something more authoritative than the rather vague notion of general acceptance. It would of course be great to have something more solid—but there is just no possibility that we ever will have much more precise guidance. We are fortunate in having a number of excellent accounting textbooks which attempt, at very considerable length, to set forth the principles upon which statements should be prepared. In the course of a long career in professional practice, I have many time been deep in doubt and uncertainty on a point of accounting principle. At such times I have turned to our standard texts for guidance—and I do not recall a single instance in which I found the answer I sought therein. I say this, not as a criticism of our standard texts, but to emphasize the impossibility of producing an explicit code in sufficient detail to answer the enormous variety of questions that arise in the process of actually producing financial statements. Of course such bodies as the Accounting Principles Board can continue to do useful work in clarifying some moot points. But I have no confidence in any project for a complete codification.

The second general criticism of our accounting principles is that we permit alternative accounting procedures, thereby enabling management to slant their reports by switching from one procedure to another and obtain results more to their liking. In my opinion, an attempt to insist upon standard procedures would do far more harm than good. A full development of the arguments against standardization would take up a good deal of time. Perhaps for our present purposes, one illustration might suffice. Let us take the case of a company with two plants—one of which is brand new, and the other an unsatisfactory old building being used only pending sale. It makes no sense at all to me to require that both these plants should be carried in the balance sheet on the same basis. Cost would seem the most sensible and appropriate basis for the new building, and estimated sale price for the old. Often a large public corporation has many plants in various stages of usefulness, and there should always be a great deal of scope for the exercise of judgment in selecting the procedure that is most appropriate in each situation.

7. THE INEVITABLE INTRUSION OF JUDGMENT

The real argument against an insistence on standardization of proce-dure is that it would not accomplish what it is supposed to accomplish— that is, the production of unslanted statements. Without making any change in accounting procedures, there is lots of scope for producing alternative reports indicating different degrees of profitability and wealth. For example, consider the valuation of receivables. Judgment has to enter here. If a company has $50 million in accounts receivable, there is just no way of specifying valuation procedures which will guarantee that different officers (or the same officer in different moods) will come within, say, a million dollars of the same conclusion on valuation. Or consider inventories. It is all very well to stipulate that inventories must be at the lower of cost and market, calculated on the FIFO "principle"—but questions of condition and saleability enter the picture, and no general rules could ever be expected to cover such factors. When we come to warranty reserves, or pending legal cases and such matters, the scope for judgment is wider still. It is not the ability to switch from one accounting procedure to another that enables management to slant its reports; it is the essential element of judgment that must always enter into financial reporting.

The accounting profession has, I believe, been seriously at fault in not making this basic point clearer. We have encouraged the public to believe that the financial statements we produce are far more authoritative and unchallengeable than any such statements could possible be. The meticulous balancing of debit and credit adds to the illusion. We might perhaps have done better to insist less on the professional competence we have achieved in devising a reporting system and to emphasize more how tentative and imperfect even the best reports must always be.

The fact that there is always scope for judgment in valuing assets and liabilities means that different net income may legitimately be reported over a range, sometimes quite a wide range. If the income reported falls within this range, the auditor has no alternative but to report that the statements present fairly the result of operations—even though he himself, had he been producing the statements, might have reported a somewhat different figure. A clear audit opinion only means—and can only mean—that the statements show the results within a reasonable range of accuracy. To make this clear, it has sometimes been suggested (usually by academicians, I believe) that statements should not show net income at $128,000 but should report that it was in the range of $100,000 to $140,000. This would lead to devastating confusion. We must have a definite amount agreed upon as representing such basically important results—otherwise endless arguments would inevitably arise in statement analysis and negotiations.

8. FAIR VALUATION

The really legitimate criticism of our accounting principles is that we have clung obstinately to "cost," as calculated by certain arbitrary rules, in the determination of asset values (and thus in the determination of net income) even where there are obviously more appropriate way of estimating relevant values. As Professor Sterling tells us (and he just couldn't be righter):

> As I read these cases [*Continental Vending* and *Pacific Acceptance*], the courts are telling us that we can no longer defend ourselves on the basis of accepted accounting theory and practice. Instead, we must assure ourselves that the statements are true, correct and understandable by non-accountants. (Sterling, 1973: 65)

It is hardly surprising that the profession is in a state of shock as a result of the outburst of major law suits against auditors. This is not conducive to a mood in which practitioners are likely to welcome new and untested accounting rules—but the fact remains that the auditor will always be threatened by giant damage judgments and criminal convictions, so long as, in defending himself, he must lead lay judges and lay jurymen through an endless labyrinth of our accounting pronouncements. The definitive lay view on financial statements may be taken as the comment of the learned Justice Walter in the case of *Randall* v. *Bailey,* when he said:

> I see no cause for alarm over the fact that this view requires directors to make a determination of the value of the assets at each dividend declaration. On the contrary, I think that is exactly what the law always has contemplated that directors should do. (Quoted in Fiflis and Kripke, 1971: 365)

This has always seemed to me an eminently fair and reasonable view. Professional accountants may immerse themselves in arguments about procedures, and may persuade themselves that a balance sheet is not really supposed to be a valuation document—but I don't believe they will ever convince non-accountants of this. And if they ever do, won't that be the end of accounting? I have always felt myself that if the balance sheet is not supposed to be a valuation document—then to hell with it.

The only way out of the morass of unfair law suits, which threatens to bog us down, is through the production of statements which at least attempt to set forth the fairest current values that it is feasible to produce. The accountant, in defending himself, will then have the task of demonstrating why he accepted the valuations he did—instead of having to explain why he used techniques which a skilled prosecutor suggests are in conflict with some esoteric pronouncement of an Australian accounting body, or the confused verdict of an Ontario jury.

9. THE AUDIT FUNCTION

The second important social function of the profession is, having formulated acceptable ground rules, to provide a professional reviewing service through which the public can be assured a statement is indeed prepared under such ground rules. The three basic requirements in reaching a professional audit opinion are well known and beyond dispute. The auditor must have adequate skill; he must have made an appropriate examination of the statements and supporting data; he must be independent. The first two of these would seem to present relatively few problems. We do seem to have generally satisfactory training and screening procedures in most North American jurisdictions; and the typical audit is searching and well organized, however vaguely we may state our standard audit procedures when it comes down to detail.

Independence is quite another matter, and it requires extensive comment. It has always seemed to me that, while we have spent a great deal of time worrying and talking about independence—and insisting on its vital importance—most of our energy has been absorbed in wild goose chases. Notable amongst these has been our preoccupation with share ownership by the auditor or his relatives. If we expect investors to use financial statements when deciding on share purchases, there is naturally something to be said, in theory, for disqualifying any auditor who, as a potential vendor, may find himself on the selling side. However, any professional man signing an opinion has so many basic pressures and problems to worry about, that even a quite large stake in the company's shares is most unlikely to be a decisive influence. A relatively modest share holding (in relation to his total wealth) could hardly be a factor at all.

When we pursue the ownership investigation to relatives of the auditor, we often make ourselves quite ridiculous. On other occasions, I have confessed that I have a wife, a brother, two sons, and almost as many sisters and cousins and aunts as Sir Joseph Porter, K.C.B., of Pinafore fame. These are a pleasant group with most of whom I am on excellent terms. However, it never occured to me in approximately forty years of public practice that I should worry, when reaching an audit opinion, about investments they might have. I had always many other things to worry about on such occasions. When I was in practice, the Seattle office of the American firm with which we were associated was questioned about independence when someone discovered that one of my brothers-in-law was a director of a client company. This was one of my favorite brothers-in-law, but I only see him, for brief visits, about once every ten years. Our other contacts are confined to an exchange of Christmas cards. When I heard of this, I could not help reflecting on the position of the Seattle partner who was in charge of this audit. I am sure he must have had many other things to think about when signing the auditors' report—without worrying about the financial interests of the several hundred partners in our American firm, let alone the activities of a brother-in-law of a partner in our Montreal office.

But independence is no joke. It is, in fact, one of those problems which is basically insoluble. All we can do is to promote it as far as practicable—which means that we must face up frankly to the various jeopardies to independence, see them in proper perspective, and try to mitigate them as best we may. Perhaps our failure to cope intelligently with the independence issue is partly due to the fact that we have never emphasized sufficiently that, if you take the issue literally, independence is a will-o-the-wisp. It is of course possible to produce some very simple statements with complete independence—with disregard of the consequences of showing a more or less favourable picture. This is the sort of thing one may do in the classroom—when a certain number of transactions are enumerated, and the student is required to draft statements to record them. But this is not at all what it is like actually to produce the statements of public corporations.

It would be nice if such statements could be produced by someone who was completely disinterested in the effect of publication on the corporation, or on anyone connected with it. But the idea of a horde of totally disinterested persons descending on a corporation and producing a reliable statement of operations sufficiently promptly to be of any use to anyone is too ludicrous to contemplate. Any person sufficiently knowledgeable to help in producing a financial statement must somehow be involved enough to be concerned about the effect the issuance of the statement will have on the corporation—*and therefore cannot be said to be absolutely independent.*

10. SUBJECTIVITY

In practice, all statements are selling documents. Those responsible for issuing them must have some interest in the effect they are likely to produce. Independence therefore presents the sort of serious problem that cannot be solved by regulations—such as those requiring disclosure when the wife of some distant partner owns one hundred shares in the corporation. We should of course emphasize, by every means we can, the fundamental importance of personal integrity in financial reporting. But the really important thing is to speak a great deal more frankly about the inevitable limitations upon what it is practical to accomplish in preparing a statement.

We keep worrying about the general public not understanding our statements, but what really shatters me are the comments by serious accounting theorists that one keeps coming across which raise doubts about their grasp of the accounting process. Consider for a moment the following quite typical quotation from an article in a recent accounting research journal. The author advocates a new mathematical approach to the measurement of materiality. He starts by referring to the view that materiality is essentially a matter of judgment in each case and comments:

> The main deficiency of this approach, which relies on professional education and experience, is that it does not provide any benchmark for determining whether an item is material or not. Moreover such an approach does not strengthen the image of the profession but rather weakens it, since it introduces subjectivity into the process of preparation of financial statements. (Barlev, 1972: 194)

What makes this quotation so terribly alarming is that it is not a casual and thoughtless aside, taken out of context—it is the basic reason for the whole article, in which an elaborate mathematical formula is developed for settling all questions of materiality. For the purpose of the present discussion, it is irrelevant whether the formula is useful or not—the point is the serious contention that, if it works, we could produce statements without introducing subjectivity.

If statements are prepared by management and reported upon by professional auditors, our real concern should be to explore the extent to which one may guard against subjectivity.

To begin with, it begs a lot of questions to say a statement is prepared or issued "by management." Modern corporate management is complex. The final legal responsibility for statements (at least in Canadian practice) is always with the Board of Directors. Behind their formal approval, decision-making responsibility spreads through the staff of the corporation. This deserves further study—but, for purposes of the present discussion, the situation may be simplified by taking an anthropomorphic view of management—as though all important decisions really were made by the chief executive officer.

11. THE MANAGEMENT WISH

The points of view of management and auditor are usually grossly over-simplified. Management is often thought of as determined, at all costs, to show the most optimistic picture—the highest net income and the strongest current ratio and net assets, whereas the auditor tends to be thought of as the cautious pessimist, who spends all his time trying to bring management down to earth. There is something in this view. Managers often do tend to be optimistic (or they would not be in business). And auditors certainly tend to be conservative—being hopelessly addicted to understatements of assets and profits.

But in my experience, it is just not true that management always presses for favourable results. High profits and asset strength are of course desirable in attracting new investment or obtaining credit. While these are important considerations, they are not the only ones that occupy management's attention. There are important pressures in the contrary direction. To report high profits encourages demands for higher wages to the staff, and for higher dividends to shareholders—both of which management often wishes to resist. Moreover under a system in which the government snatches away some fifty cents out of every dollar one rings up as net income, there is the strongest temptation to moderate any enthusiasm one might have to report profit on the high side.

It may be forgotten that, while there is not a formalized profession of management, modern managers are really professionals. We are far from the days of the owner-manager. In fact the great importance of published annual statements still rests on the fact that they are management's report to the owners on stewardship. This being the case, let us consider what slanting we may expect in statements prepared by management. The wish uppermost in the mind of management must surely be to be left in peace to carry on the enormously difficult task of running a large complex operation. This must mean that they hope readers of the statements will be reassured, and will conclude that the corporation is being well run, and thus preclude the possibility that anyone will want to fire management, or even to interfere by criticisms and demands for greater disclosure.

In the managements I have audited over the years, this had not always produced a desire to show the brightest picture possible. What is supposed really to reassure shareholders is not dramatically higher earnings, but rather a steady growth in market value earnings and dividends. In a disappointing year, this does suggest the desirability of scraping around to make as good a show as possible. But in a year of prosperity, it produces exactly the opposite tendency. Management are far-sighted enough to ask themselves, when they have had an outstanding year—"What on earth will we do next year for an encore?" In short, this year's reported net income must be higher, if possible, than last year's—but it must also be lower, if possible, than next year's.

The natural prejudices of management are therefore generally directed to "rounding out." This should mean that they are unlikely seriously to distort long-term reporting of results—even though they do tend to slant the results of individual years.

In the light of this analysis, we may conclude that the essential function of the auditor—apart from the obvious task of detecting fraud and error—is to restrain, within reasonable limits, management's propensity to round out. When you think of all the terrible sins that can be committed in the name of financial reporting, a tendency to rounding out is certainly not the most hideous crime that comes to mind. It can even be argued that it is desirable—on the grounds that to report very high profits, which result from some good fortune which is unlikely to be repeated in future, is almost certain to mislead shareholders or investors. However, like any other tendency, it can get out of hand, and it will always be an important function of the auditor to fight against exaggerated recourse to it. Most of my own serious arguments over the years, with clients, were in this area.

12. THE AUDIT WISH

We might now consider the independence of the auditor himself. The question of the financial interest of the auditor, his kith and kin, have perhaps been adequately dealt with. The real threat to independence is, of course, the fact that the auditor gets a fee for his work from the client, and hopes to get reappointed again in future years. He should ideally be completely free to "tell it like it is," without fear of loss of income or non-reappointment. In order to emphasize the auditor's essential impartiality, his position is sometimes described as judicial. There is some value in an analogy between auditor and judge—but it must not be pressed too far. Professor Sterling has pointed out that a judge does not have to rely on one of the litigants, appearing before him, for his livelihood. Nor does he suffer loss of income, or subject himself to the threat of a damage suit, if his conclusions are found to be wrong in a higher court. His decision is simply reversed.

While an auditor can never be considered to be in an ideal state of independence so long as he must rely on the client for his remuneration, there are very serious difficulties in any other arrangement; and there are also very strong forces operating to prevent him from giving a servile opinion. Let us consider some of these.

In the first place, an auditor's whole career depends on maintaining a reputation for integrity. Nothing much else is expected of him. He is not supposed to be intellectually brilliant or creative or sexy. But he is expected to be honest. Thus every time he signs an audit opinion, his whole reputation rides on it. I must have signed several thousand such opinions over my years in practice, and I don't believe I ever signed one without reflecting on the devastating consequences that could follow if it should prove that the statements were wrong.

It is always nice to please a client and gain acceptablity in his eyes. But the retention of even the biggest of clients is not a matter of great importance compared to the havoc caused by loss of professional reputation—either by becoming involved in a law suit or by emerging doubts about one's integrity. Some audit fees today are very large indeed, but such fees are always paid to very large auditing firms; their importance to the firm should be judged with relation to total firm revenue. Moreover, while the firing of an auditor is admittedly tough on the auditor, it is apt to be tough on the client too. We have developed a tradition of extending audit connections for very long periods in normal circumstances; and one of the good aspects of this tradition is that a change in auditors is rather a sensational event. It usually means the corporation concerned has some explaining to do; and most managements would prefer not to find themselves having to explain they are firing the old auditors because they refused to provide a clear opinion.

The position of the auditor is then apt to be a good deal stronger than it might appear at first sight to be. Nevertheless, it would clearly be in the public interest to strengthen further his position; so that he could play his role of watchdog and critic more effectively still. Several measures could fairly simply be taken to increase his effective authority—and these should be embodied in appropriate legislation forthwith.

For example:

1. The auditor should always be appointed by the shareholders and have an obligation to report to them. (This is already a standard requirement in Canada's various company acts.)
2. An audit committee of outside directors should be standard practice—assuring the auditors of direct contact with members of the Board not on the management team.
3. It should be stipulated that, when an auditor resigns, or does not stand for reappointment, he must report to the shareholders explaining fully the reasons for his action. If there was a dispute on accounting presentation, the auditor's side of the case would be explained in this report. (Naturally management would have every opportunity to present its case.) At present, when an auditor-management dispute occurs, it is probably the usual course for the auditor to resign without formally presenting his reasons for doing so to the shareholders—a sort of concession to nice-chapmanship.

13. OTHER SOLUTIONS—ROTATION OF AUDITORS

We happen to live in a world where many of the important choices are not between the obviously right and the obviously wrong. Often the problem is to find the solution that approaches most closely the result we desire—that has most good features and fewest bad. And a final judgment on the social usefulness of the audit function, as we practice it, really boils down to the question of whether or not there is some better alternative.

There do not seem to be many options to consider. One relatively mild change that gets suggested from time to time is that we should retain the audit profession much as it is now, but stipulate that every corporation must switch audit firms regularly—say every five years, or even annually. There is undoubtedly something to be said for this notion. It would reduce concern about losing an audit through taking a stand unpopular with management—and thus enhance the auditor's independence. On the other hand, it would greatly increase the cost of auditing. On a first appointment an enormous amount of work must be done to familiarize the auditor with the operations. Once done, much of this work has a carry-over value. Moreover, doing an audit for a period of years can enable the auditor to accumulate an ever deepening and broadening knowledge of the client's affairs, and this should make it possible to do a better and better audit. Certainly in audits I went back to, year after year, I would have been very disappointed unless I felt a better examination had been done each time. The larger modern corporations are almost unbelievably complex. To understand their operations well enough to plan and direct an intelligent audit requires reasonable familiarity with all their important operations, and this can only be acquired by many hours of hard work, for which someone must eventually pay.

In weighing the advantages and disadvantages of frequent audit changes, it is well to remind ourselves that, when we speak of "the auditor," we are really alluding to a large and well organized team, often carrying out their work in several countries—with all the problems of communication and foreign legal requirements that this involves. It takes a great deal of planning to organize and train such a team. Most audit firms naturally attempt to get a balance of experience and fresh insights in building up the team. This in itself provides the virtual certainty of a rotation of personnel which at least makes it unlikely that too palsy-walsy an atmosphere will develop. Another argument in favour of our present tendency for long-standing audit appointments is that, just because changes of auditor are so infrequent, the decision to change is one which no management relishes. At best a change calls for explanation and this, in itself, gives strength to the auditor in a case of conflict.

Another aspect of auditing that we should consider is the growing emphasis on cyclical tests. As computers are churning out more and more data, as industrial units are getting larger and larger, and as information is required more and more promptly, it becomes increasingly difficult to devise adequate tests in reaching an audit opinion. It is never possible to test the data as thoroughly as one could wish, and the auditor needs to use all possible devices to make his restricted tests effective. One solution is to select certain aspects of the work to concentrate on each year. By planning changes in emphasis each year, the auditor can assure himself that, in time, he will cover all important aspects reasonably throughly. With this kind of approach, an audit ceases to be strictly an annual affair. It is only with some assurance of reasonably long tenure that the auditor can plan properly in such circumstances.

On the whole, I would be against any mandatory requirement for the rotation of auditors. Audit firms are well aware, in their own interest, of the danger of leaving staff too long on an audit; they can be counted upon to aim at an optimum balance between experience and freshness of approach.

14.   OTHER SOLUTIONS—AUDICARE

In searching for possible alternatives to present practice, there remains to be considered the possibility of audit by a government-appointed official. This had a certain plausibility, and is supported by the analogies, sometimes drawn, between auditors and the judiciary. However, as previously suggested, this analogy is misleading. The judge sits in his court, while skillful lawyers attempt to tell him what happened, and to explain to him the law he is supposed to apply. He may spend several weeks deciding whether or not the butler really was at the movies when someone slipped the arsenic into Lady Ormond's Ovaltine. Decisions are normally reached years after the event; whereas in auditing, tough points must be settled within a week or two of the balance sheet date. The great advantage of government inspection over our present system is, of course, that the inspector would be paid by the government and not by the corporation whose statements he is examining—but this is achieved at great cost. To begin with, civil servants have their hang-ups too. In issuing opinions, they would be under somewhat similar pressures. Civil servants, too, need friends, as the Watergate disclosures (in the midst of which this paper was presented) would seem to emphasize.

Some of the serious problems that might arise in a government inspection system may perhaps be foreseen in the tribulations of Canada's Auditor General, now getting extensive coverage in our press. Our Auditor General is an experienced accountant of unquestioned professional competence. His appointment is well designed to ensure maximum independence. He is responsible to and reports to Parliament itself, and not to the Cabinet—which, under our system, is the executive branch. He performs an annual audit of government departments and of some of our crown corporations. As one might imagine, the Auditor General is a highly popular figure with Opposition parties in Parliament and with the media. To both of these, his reports provide ammunition for attacks on the government, by setting forth the various improprieties he has discovered. Understandably, for the same reason, he is less popular with the government in office, and with departmental officials whose unauthorized actions and mistakes of judgment he describes in his reports. In spite of his theoretical independence he consistently complains of major budgetary troubles in his department—leading to inadequate staff. These have been sufficiently serious in recent years to occasion long delays in completing his reports.

15. THE PROPER AUDIT ATTITUDE

The more you think about independence, the trickier it becomes. It is clear that we do not want the auditor to be subservient to management, but a hostile opinion is just as likely to be misleading as an overindulgent one. Management is a tough and demanding task. What we can hope for from a management team is the maintenance of a reasonable batting average rather than a flawless performance. Modern management involves a good deal of risk-taking. The last thing one would wish would be to place so much emphasis on mistakes that reasonable risk-taking is discouraged. This is the sort of thing that one suspects can develop in a harsh and rigid bureaucracy. The significance of an error in judgment can only be properly appreciated by someone who can see it in perspective and can weigh it against other actions which are creditable. How many batters would we have in baseball's Hall of Fame if only strike-outs were recorded?

In other words, in the professional opinion we expect from an auditor, we should not look for the maximum disclosure of every bit of grief discovered during the examination, but rather a fair disclosure which will enable those using the statements to interpret the data intelligently, and to minimize the likelihood that they will arrive at wrong conclusions.

If I am not too worried about the weakness of the auditor's position in disputes with management, it is perhaps because I believe the scope for the exercise of power and authority in life tends to be very much exaggerated. To those who observe the higher executive officers in action, it may appear that they are able to throw their weight around in a carefree manner; but in my experience, it all looks quite different when you actually attempt to exercise the authority you are supposed to have. The fact is that, when observing some brilliant and decisive leader in action, it is impossible to tell whether he had the great gift of persuading people to do what he wants them to, or whether he is simply good at sensing what people want to do and "leading" them in the direction they want to go. The age old story of the two politicians chattering by a window at the height of the French Revolution has always seemed to me beautifully accurate. When a howling mob with pitchforks and torches rushed past the window, one of the politicians ran off hastily, explaining over his shoulder—"Excuse me. I must follow them; I am their leader."

I have always believed practically everything in business life is accomplished by persuasion rather than by authoritative pronouncement. A good auditor must, if he is to do his job properly, gain the complete confidence of his client. He should be able to accomplish a great deal by giving sound advice. I am sure no one has spent more time worrying about losing clients than I have, but I still insist that in dealing with clients I have never felt like a slave facing his master.

16.   OTHER ACCOUNTING FUNCTIONS

This paper has dealt only with the audit of large business and financial corporations. I believe much the same conclusions would be reached by a study of the audit of smaller businesses or of the increasingly important category of non-profit organizations. There is also much of interest that might be gleaned from a study of those services performed by the public accounting profession which do not involve the attest function. These areas should be studied too, but are beyond the scope of this commentary.

REFERENCES

Barlev, Genzion (1972) "On the Measurement of Materiality." *Accounting and Business Research* 7 (Summer).

Fiflis, Ted J. and Homer Kripe (1971) *Accounting for Business Lawyers.* St. Paul, Minnesota: West.

Sterling, Robert R. (1973) "Accounting Power." *Journal of Accountancy* 135 (January): 61–67.

Comment on
The Nature of Professional Responsibility

LAWRENCE L. VANCE*

The subject of Dean Ross's paper might as well have been *apologia pro vita sua,* since it seems to be almost entirely a defense of the status quo in public accounting in the English-speaking countries, and Ross took part in this as partner in a large public accounting firm. As usual, there is much merit in Ross's statements, but my task, I presume, is to appraise his remarks critically, and I shall try to do my duty; after all, Ross is not paying my fee in this case, so I can be extremely independent, although, of course, I may be subject to some "civil service" or perhaps "academic" hangups.

Since we are looking at the problems of the accounting profession from the vantage point of social and political theory I will first look at Ross's presentation from that viewpoint. In adopting this viewpoint we recall that the functioning of social and political systems reflects the value systems of their members. If you do not believe this, you should recall the story about the McGovern campaign in which the candidate made a strong pitch for soaking the rich by means of income tax reform while talking to a group of union members. The candidate is said to have been unable to understand the cool reception the unionists gave his proposals. Others have explained, however, that the unionists reacted not on the basis of what might be considered their economic interests, but on the basis of their values, which include an adherence to the idea that everyone should have the chance to get rich and, if successful, to enjoy it. In Europe, including Great Britain, the value system still includes, to some degree, an acceptance of class status based on birth and on tradition. In terms of Ross's requirement for a satisfactory society of reasonable access to the Establishment, those who succeed are granted the status even if birth does not provide it. This appears

*B.A. 1932, M.A. 1933, Ph.D. 1947, University of Minnesota. CPA, Minnesota and California. Professor of Accounting and Associate Dean, Graduate School of Business Administration, University of California, Berkeley. Author, *Scientific Method for Auditing* (1950); *Theory and Technique of Cost Accounting* (1952, 1958); *Accounting Principles and Control* (1960, 1966, 1972). Contributor to accounting, economics, and business periodicals.

to be the case in Britain. A popular word of address used by persons of low status in approaching those of higher status in England— "Guv'ner"—illustrates the lingering influence of such attitudes. I have the impression, furthermore, that a substantial amount of this attitude has been transplanted to Canada, in contrast with the United States, where a more egalitarian ideal, nurtured by Puritanism, free land, and the American Revolution, predominates. It is therefore not surprising that Ross should caption one of his paragraphs with the words "God Bless the Establishment," or that he should rationalize the status quo. The temptation to defend the Establishment is of course stronger when one is a member of it. Perhaps those of us who have thought of Ross as something of a revolutionary, because of his espousal of what I call current cost accounting, suffer a mild surprise when we find him defending professional practice as it exists rather than suggesting far-reaching improvement. However, his consistency becomes clear when we notice that his espousal of current costs in accounting is advanced in the belief that it is necessary to enable accounting and the profession to maintain its credence with other groups and so to preserve its place in the Establishment. Professor Montagna's paper in this colloquium referred to such efforts as this one as a means of maintaining professional status and power. But alleging that Ross's conclusions are the product of his social conditioning or his economic interests does not directly confront his arguments on their merits. Let us look at some of those arguments.

Ross suggests that there is always a relatively small group running the society, including civil servants and businessmen. The part about civil servants applies, as far as I know, to Canada, but not to the United States. Here civil servants are restricted to functions well prescribed by rules and regulations, and policy is indeed set by politicians, who set it, as a rule, by finding out, or trying to find out, what policy promises to obtain or hold the most votes—which is as it should be. However, the conclusion that throwing out one set of the Establishment and substituting another would not change anything significantly is not acceptable as a general proposition. This idea may apply in a smoothly functioning democracy where conflicts are restricted to questions of relatively minor change. For example, it has been alleged in this country that the Democratic and Republican parties often offer only a choice between Tweedledum and Tweedledee. In fact, if either departs from this pattern it is likely to find only disaster, as the Goldwater and McGovern campaigns well illustrate. But if we think of a radical change in the Establishment, of the sort that some of our own radicals would like, or of the kind the Russians got in 1918, the effects, of course, are tremendous. Perhaps we should merely agree that Ross's viewpoint here assumes a stable democracy with no really far-reaching conflicts; but we must then address the problem of how serious our conflicts are and how much must be done to reduce or accommodate them. I do not propose to enter upon that task at this time.

Ross has warned against the regulatory syndrome, pointing out that most people are decent and that it costs too much to have a policeman looking over everyone's shoulder. This is indeed a social-political question. From one viewpoint it is essentially a cost-benefit problem: how much we are justified in spending to save how much in misleading information or possible fraud? If we leave cost-benefit aside, we can look at it as a question of values. How much are we willing to do to prevent widows and orphans from being robbed, even if the probability of any widow or orphans being robbed is very small? This is not a new problem for the accounting profession in this country. The profession faced it in 1939 when the *McKesson-Robbins* case broke. It was the conclusion of the Committee of the AICPA (then AIA), appointed to make recommendations in light of the case, that two important changes in what had been considered normal audit procedure should be made. I well recall that the partner in charge of the public accounting office in which I worked at that time said, in professional meetings oriented to the case, that general rules should not be made on the basis of unusual cases. The decision of the official committee no doubt was a political one; the SEC was investigating the case at the same time and the profession wanted to have the initiative in setting auditing standards, so it preempted the SEC. It was a successful effort. Incidentally, we could stick to a more rigid cost-benefit viewpoint and provide for the defrauded widows and orphans by means of an insurance scheme, as we have done with regard to bank accounts. To take another tack, it is a bit odd for auditors to argue against anything on the grounds that most people are essentially decent and can be relied upon to report fairly. I refer to the fact that if we could indeed rely upon everyone as being essentially decent we would not need auditors at all. An independent audit is required only because third parties, by sad experience, have found that the human race is inclined to cover up its mistakes, especially when knowedge of them militates against the continued prosperity of the perpetrator. The question of how far to go in assuring an honest report, of course, remains; but it well may be that public pressure—that is, political considerations—will determine the issue.

Ross has suggested that the essential task of the profession is to improve the quality of financial reporting, and that the profession must produce the ground rules under which, by agreement, financial statements will be produced. I believe that the value system most of us follow in Canada and the United States is showing here. Our belief in private enterprise and individual initiative encourages us to prefer a private sector control of accounting to any alternative. Perhaps even more important is the need to keep the profession in high status. The belief has been expressed that if we only check compliance with a set of rules promulgated by someone else we lose status. But in a complicated system the alleged loss of status may not occur. I have the impression that able tax accountants do not lack clients, status, or income, yet they work with a set of tax laws enacted by legislatures and with administrative rules set by tax administrators. Dean Ross has pointed out that it is not always easy to decide how to treat a particular transaction or condition in the light of received accounting principles; this complexity would no doubt remain even if accounting rules became as detailed and voluminous as the tax laws.

There is another interesting aspect of this matter of the regulatory syndrome. Society has not entrusted the determination of laws to lawyers, though lawyers participate. Incidentally, I was told a few years ago, while in England, that the largest vocational group in Parliament were university instructors. We all know that lawyers make up the largest legislative group in this country. Evidently, the British give lawyers even less participation in determining what the law will be than we do. Similarly, society does not leave the regulation of medical practice entirely to the medical profession. Certain drugs may be prescribed only under certain circumstances as a matter of law, and others may not be prescribed at all. It was only recently that abortion was left to the medical profession and its patients in this country, and that came about by action of a court—most legislatures were too timid to change the law on this point. If society does not leave law entirely to lawyers or medicine entirely to doctors, why should we expect it to leave accounting entirely to accountants? I see no reason why it should, and we have much recent evidence that it will not. We may console ourselves in this connection with the thought that neither the lawyers nor the doctors seem to have suffered unduly from loss of status as a result of this situation, and we probably won't either.

In line with his general reliance on a benevolent Establishment Dean Ross has suggested that there are two pieces of nonsense going around about accounting. One is that we should have something more authoritative than a vague notion of general acceptance as to accounting principles that are to be required, and the other is that allowing alternative procedures permits accounting reports to be slanted. As to the first idea, Ross feels that an explicit set of rules that would cover all situations is impossible, so we should stay with the vagueness we have. This argument says in effect that if we cannot achieve absolute perfection we should not try for any improvement, which is an obvious non-sequitur. It is, of course, true that it is not possible to describe every transgression in detail in advance, but it definitely is possible to set standards that require acceptable performance even in unforeseen situations. The general law has the same problem; it is solved by use of such standards as the conduct of a reasonable man attending to his own business. The jury may have to decide what reasonable conduct is in a particular case, but the rule nonetheless circumscribes conduct more effectively than would be the case without it. Accounting rules can be formulated along similar lines.

As to the second piece of alleged nonsense, namely, that permission of alternative accounting methods allows reports to be slanted, Ross suggests that standard procedures would do more harm than good. This is a popular argument; everyone who wants to indulge in a choice of accounting procedures advances it. One cannot escape the conclusion that most advocates want it for the manipulative tools it provides, since the back-up for the argument is never convincing. Ross's illustration, for example, points to a company with two buildings, one old and kept only while seeking a favorable disposal price and one new, intended to be used in operations for the foreseeable future. He says that cost is sensible for the new building but estimated sale price would be appropriate for the old one, so that these cannot be carried in the balance sheet on the same basis. This is a remarkable definition of "the same basis"; as a matter of fact, current practice would require the old building to be depreciated sufficiently to reflect its actual status quite apart from any new or improved standard—the example does not fit the problem. I can think of only one important case in which an alternative method might be considered justified, and that applied to one or a few special industries, for a limited period of time, and it was a situation in which the use of an alternative accounting principle was the wrong way to solve the problem. That is the case of last-in, first-out inventory costing. This method was invented primarily to solve a tax problem of extractive industries such as copper mining that had widely fluctuating price structures and long processing times. This combination produced wide swings in income—large profits in some years and large losses in others. At the time the inventory question was first vigorously promoted the income tax law in this country did not allow carry-forward or carry-back of losses, so concerns in this situation paid taxes on the profits, got no adjustment on the losses, and so paid a higher rate on the average earnings than other concerns did. The use of last-in, first-out, by smoothing net income, helped alleviate this problem. But the problem should have been solved by introduction of carry-back and carry-forward, as did happen later; the warping of accounting principles was the wrong way to do it. Furthermore, the unfortunate accounting method is still with us and has spread widely for two reasons: it permits postponement of some tax and it offers some small opportunity for income smoothing even in industries more stable than copper mining. The fact that alternative accounting methods allow slanting of reports is well documented: switches from accelerated to straight-line depreciation in this country a few years ago present a well known case. Furthermore, leaving a choice between capitalizing or not capitalizing leases, for example, can be useful only to people who want to use it to make their accounting reports reflect their wishes rather than their performances. Ross suggests that a certain amount of "rounding out" of income may be a good thing. There is a tradition of this sort in Europe but it says, in effect, "just let the Establishment look after things and everything will be all right." Unfortunately, the Establishment is not that competent, and, of course, individual performances within it vary too much from the norm.

I have said enough about Ross's arguments, although there are others that I might comment upon. However, we need to notice the positive suggestions Ross has made for improvement. He has suggested that (1) auditors be appointed by shareholders and be required to report to them; (2) that an audit committee of outside directors deal with the auditors on behalf of the client; and (3) that an auditor who separates from a client be required to report his reasons to the stockholders. Similar suggestions were made by the SEC in this country when it reported on its investigation of the *McKesson-Robbins* case in 1940. Corporations in this country that want to put on as good a public face as possible have adopted the suggestion that auditors be elected by the stockholders and report to them. The procedure is meaningless because the proxies that re-elect the management also re-elect the auditors, so nothing is changed. The use of a non-officer committee of directors (indeed, outside directors) is helpful, but I suggest we may have to rely on governmental compulsion to get it, especially in view of the fact that certain corporations prefer to have no outside directors. A full and frank report from departing auditors would also be helpful, but it seems to me unlikely that we can reasonably expect this, even with governmental prompting. The auditors are, after all, a part of the Establishment, and expecting them to say very disparaging things about a management with whom they have parted company would be equivalent to asking them to put themselves in a bad light with unrelated managements. One does not advance one's standing with the Establishment by attacking any of the members of the club, even if they deserve it. Witness, for example, the fact, which some people consider odd, that when some courts have found some auditors guilty of offenses which the profession considers not to be offenses, no action has been taken against the auditors by the professional bodies. To get thrown out by the profession you have to do something less equivocal, such as bribing a tax officer.

In summary, it would be pleasant if all the members of the Establishment were of the character of Dean Ross; in which case we could relax, secure in the knowledge that our financial affairs were being properly managed. Unfortunately, this seems not to be the case. Furthermore, we live in an age of sufficiently rapid change so that any Establishment is hard pressed to find good solutions to the new and complex problems and conflicts that face us, bound as it must be to methods that must give way. In these circumstances we must all participate in the effort to find new and better methods, if for no other reason than the same for which Dean Ross has advocated current costs, namely, to maintain the usefulness of the profession we represent.

Discussion

Holstrum. I sympathize with you with respect to looking at the literature on social accounting and saying it seems to be such a hodge-podge of unrelated articles. There really has not been a good codification of the various articles in social accounting, and I think that this perhaps leads to disagreements as to what people are attempting to accomplish. But I think if we look at the nature of what is being attempted and the needs that we have, they are very much related to your opening comments when you said, "We look at the goods and we look at the bads, and if the goods outweigh the bads, well then we go ahead and produce the goods." But we can't really do that unless we have some measure of the bads, or some estimate of the bads. It seems to me that is what social accounting is about, at least one aspect—how can we measure the bads?

You maintain that we are dealing with something which is not only a measurement problem but which is immeasurable, and I would maintain that there is sufficient evidence in the literature to suggest that there are aspects of social cost—air pollution and water pollution are two that you mentioned—which are measurable and have at least as much reliability, validity, and objectivity as our generally accepted accounting measurements. The problem is in trying to monetize the cost of pollution. But, to take your two examples, I am somewhat disturbed by them. In re your example of air pollution, there are standard ways of measuring it. The standard ways of measuring it are now being applied to evaluate the amount of pollution. The fact that there are numerous companies within a small locality does not prevent the measurability of the pollution coming as an effluent from one factory. The same thing applies to water pollution. That can be measured. The units are not in monetary terms, and the difficulty comes in trying to say the dollar cost to society is x amount. But, nevertheless, it seems to me that since it can be measured and it has a sufficient degree of reliability, that is relevant information for financial statements, relevant information for the annual reports, and it is important information for a potential investor or a present stockholder to have. It seems to me that that is very relevant information, and we do have the degree of reliability there sufficient to report it.

Ross. I disagree with you on about four or five points. First of all, I think these measurements, so called, these indexes of pollution, are entirely experimental. If you read the literature on them there are dozens of different kinds; it is a question of what you take in and how you weight the different pollutants, how the gradual build-up of lead in the system compares with the instant threat of carbon monoxide. There have been some attempts to measure the amount of air pollution. You get a formula which is useful in a kind of general way, but the experts will tell you that the first thing you want to do when you get one of those indexes is to break it down to find out what it is made up of, before you can really find out how serious the situation is.

Think of your other problems. First of all, there is no reason for bringing in the estimate of the cost of pollutants unless you can estimate the increased cost of prevention and what it is going to do to employment and whether remedial action is going to have other effects. There is not much use in measuring the cost of a national park unless you measure the cost of what the picnickers lose by not being able to go there and have their type of fun. There are too many intangibles: I don't object to philosophic speculation and I have read some interesting articles, but to get down seriously to produce financial statements, you have to agree on the amount of pollution, and find out how much of this is attributable to one of forty plants, say, in a certain area—and how much to automobiles, and to other polluting agents.

If the ordinary, humdrum business of getting out a set of financial statements is not challenging enough, there are all sorts of reasonably soluble problems to tackle—for example, the measurement of human resources. Working on some of these problems is far more likely to yield results than this social cost business. I am not saying it is entirely a waste of time. It is intellectually interesting, and maybe you will get somewhere someday. But for the profession, with audit deadlines coming month by month, we have to do the practical things first. What Larry said about this being a rather conservative paper for somebody he thought was more or less of a hell raiser is perhaps true. My experience as a hell raiser has discouraged me a bit because, first of all, professional people don't have the slightest interest in what you are writing about, and academics don't really want to talk about practical statement production problems. They want to talk about social costs. What I would like to sell is somebody who will do something practical—so we will actually issue better statements. That is our number one priority. If somebody's tastes run in other directions and they want to write about what is going to happen in the year 2000—that's fine; but that is not the top priority the profession has, as I see it.

Kissinger. Would you change your opinion if one of your clients asked you to measure social cost of the pollution his plant puts out?

Ross. In my paper I confined myself entirely to the attest function on published financial statements of commercial enterprises. Now, on your question, if in addition to that, somebody says to you, "We would like you to do a survey of the smoke coming out of our plant," we could do a survey and make an estimate of the cost. I can see an accounting firm doing some kind of investigation, and making a report using what data they can get, as they do in management consultant assignments. But this to my mind has nothing to do with financial reporting, which is what I was talking about.

Participant. You asked if it is better to be vaguely right or precisely wrong. It seems to me, from my viewpoint here in the United States as compared to Canada, that what we have is some people looking at the basic objectives of institutions. You ask the question, is the increase in wealth the sole and overriding concern of our institutions? Can we operate under that kind of a premise? We have evidence to suggest—like in Japan where they have followed that premise—that these non-monetary concerns become overriding when you don't have good water or good air. If you could conceive of India as having the standard of living that we have and the kind of pollution that they would then have with their population, this is the kind of problem that some of us think we will face. I agree with you that there is a lot of nonsense written on social measurement. Yet at the same time, I think that has got to come first before we have some relevant thinking. I also think that probably some poor decisions are being made if we talk about allocation of resources. We dig up coal and leave the surface there to spoil and leach for fifty years. While it is not the prime function of accounting, it is a function which is closely related and presumably on which information gathering and development ought to have something to bear. We ought to have some more rational decisions made by someone else. So I guess that is a point for your viewpoint. I would rather see a viewpoint of permissiveness and encouragement to find measures for making better decisions, because I get back to the fundamental decision of earning wealth and how it seemed fine a hundred years ago, or fifty years ago, in this country, and how it might be fine today in Canada, where you don't have the problems that are here. That is the overriding consideration.

Ross. I would be disappointed if anything I have written gives the impression that the great goal in life is making money. What I am talking about here is the accountants' job of producing reports, which show what actually is going on, for the benefit of decision-makers. I don't think accountants should attempt to provide, in the annual statements of a corporation, all the information a decision-maker needs. He is likely to have all sorts of other sources of information. I am saying that we should stick to the kind of data we can really handle professionally and do something effective about. I agree with Bob Mautz that if somebody asks you: "Can you do a job here?" you may be able to help him in some special project. But that is not the attest function and it is not financial reporting. I don't want to just maximize profits but I do want us to do our essential job of reporting them in reliable terms. It was said here by Joe, a little while ago, that shareholders and management all want to show the most favorable picture possible. This is not, in my view, true at all. What management want to report is a steady progress—so people won't want to fire them. Management's interest is not necessarily parallel to shareholders'! If it has been a terribly good year, management doesn't usually want to show the highest profit possible. Normally they want to report more than last year—but not set too tough a target for next year.

I think Larry's comments on my paper were well taken and fair. He did, however, quote every extreme remark I made without the qualifications that went with it. What I really would like is a bit of perspective on problems. When you can't even get agreement on how to value marketable securities, you have got troubles. When you consider recent debates on this topic, how much hope have we of measuring goodwill, human resources, and the evils of pollution. I simply suggest we learn to walk before we try to run.

Pichler. In order to avoid being misquoted on my own extreme statement, I did not intend my comment to be interpreted that reporting maximum earnings was necessarily the most favorable reporting. If the firm feels that it should show a steady rise that is sufficient. If there are numerous accounting procedures such that there is one that will show a maximum, another that will show a steady rise, the firm would opt for the latter.

Ross. Joe, you said that the shareholders' and management's point of view was the same—showing favorable earnings. This is not necessarily the case. We have had cases where the shareholders would hope earnings would be shown as high as possible because they want dividends; while management want them lower so they won't have to pay dividends or excess wages. You get all sorts of differences between shareholders and management. You said, I think, they had the same view.

Bentz. I think we might take a slightly different tack here. I don't see us going anywhere in terms of suggesting changes in the profession or that sort of tack. Let me say it this way: the public sector of the economy is growing. There is a new interest in cost benefit analysis for education, administration of universities, in public sectors generally. My experience is that these people don't know very much about cost accounting; they don't know very much about accounting in general.

It seems to me that there is a possibility for great contributions in developing informational systems that are designed to reflect cost information as well as benefit information that will assist in making decisions.

All that the people outside the profession are saying is, "Here is an area where you can contribute a lot. We wish you would." All that the people in academia are saying is, "Here is an area where some of us would like to do some work. We would like the support and tolerance of the leaders of the public accounting firms." These statements are incorrectly interpreted as: "We think you ought to be going out in this direction," but I don't think that is the issue.

Ross. I agree entirely. Incidentally, my paper was just on commercial accounting, and this is a little late in the day to get me on university accounting. I am very, very critical of university financial reports. I think it is an entirely different problem, and I think the tragic thing is that most attempts to revise and bring university accounting up to date, have been based on the premise that university statements should be more like commercial reporting. This to my mind is basically and absolutely wrong; but I won't get into that more deeply at this late hour.

Pichler. I would like to state my agreement with you on one point. You just mentioned, in your remarks for the record, commercial accounting. I think that is quite an important distinction. In general I would expect the accounting professionals to make their living by responding to the market. If their clients are asking for cost analysis for social welfare situations, they would respond to that. I agree with you on that point. However, it is important to distinguish that core from what we do at universities. We enjoy what has been called the leisure of the theoried class. It is a good thing to address these kinds of abstract questions. They may not be of imminent importance to the profession, but hopefully long-over gains will be achieved by this abstract theorizing.

PART III
THE SEC VIS-A-VIS THE PROFESSION

CHAPTER 7

The SEC and the Accounting Profession:
Responsibility, Authority, and Progress

For nearly forty years, the Securities and Exchange Commission and the accounting profession have constituted a highly effective partnership for progress in improving the quality of public information about the economic activities of corporations who came to the capital markets of the United States for financial resources. As a result of their joint and several efforts, investors in the United States have the most comprehensive and well-understood financial data base that exists or has existed anywhere in the world. This data base is one of the pillars of our capital market system, which is also without peer.

While it is true that neither our system of financial disclosure nor our system of financial measurement is without fault, it is incumbent upon critics to note the accomplishments of the accounting world as well as to emphasize the failures and deficiences which currently exist. It is easy to point to the dramatic fraud or misstatement, the accounting aberration, the case of the undisclosed asset or liability and even, in a few limited cases, the case of the disclosed asset which isn't an asset. As long as such situations exist, efforts at reform continue to be needed, as do enforcement actions, when appropriate. It is important, however,

*B.A. 1954, Haverford College; M.B.A. 1956, Ph.D. 1962, Columbia University. CPA. Chief Accountant, Securities and Exchange Commission. Professor of Accounting and Finance, Graduate School of Business, Columbia University, 1962–72. Author, *Accounting for Business Combinations* (1970); (with W. T. Porter) *Auditing: A Conceptual Approach* (1971). Contributor to accounting periodicals.

The Securities and Exchange Commission, as a matter of policy, disclaims responsibility for any private publication by any of its employees. The views expressed herein are those of the author and do not necessarily reflect the views of the Commission or of the author's colleagues on the staff of the Commission.

265

to place these actions in the perspective of a system of reporting which is largely successful and to be certain that attempts to improve do not destroy the strength of what does exist. The creation of a few waves is healthy, even if they produce a temporary queasy feeling in the stomach, but a full scale storm does not seem to be needed.

If one concludes, as I do, that our reporting system has evolved in a largely satisfactory manner, it is perhaps worthwhile to examine it to see why this is so and to study the roles of the various participants in it. From such a review, it may be possible to gain an understanding of the institutions which have developed and to predict the ways in which they may interreact and change in the future.

There are a wide variety of perceptions of the way in which the SEC and the accounting profession have related to each other, although most people do agree that the SEC and the accounting profession have been the principal players in the drama of developing reporting standards for the past forty years. Some see the Commission as the top manager in this process, while the minions of the accounting profession are subordinates who may occasionally be allowed to manage a decentralized "profit center" under the broad control of the top manager. Others view the profession as the principal advocate of change and improvement, responding to the demands of the market place, while the Commission, by establishing a floor which becomes a ceiling, unwittingly serves as a check on the good deeds that could be done and contributes to the inefficient bureaucratization of the reporting environment. Still others view the accounting profession as the leader (or laggard) in developing reporting standards, while the SEC largely stands aside and ignores its statutory responsibilities, so captured by the profession in this important part of its activities that it regulates only for the benefit of the regulatees rather than the general public.

In most cases, when making an effort to describe this relationship, one must resort to analogy. This is an attempt to liken the interaction between the Commission and the profession to other better understood relationships. The danger in analogy is that while some part of a relationship may be accurately reflected thereby, other parts may not and, yet, if the analogy catches on, there is a strong tendency to apply it totally, and thus misunderstand the reality of the institutional environment that is being described and analyzed. This is particularly the case when the analogy is made to a formal power structure.

One of the great strengths of the American political and economic scene is its pluralistic nature. There are many decision centers which operate with large degrees of autonomy. Even the governmental structure is formally pluralistic with the constitutionally directed separation of powers. Where independent decision-makers make decisions which impinge on other groups, conflicts inevitably will arise which must be worked out among the parties involved. At the same time, actions take place which reinforce the goals of others, and a series of floating and informal coalitions arise on various issues. Government in the broadest sense is the ultimate arbiter since its source of power is the collective will of the people, but this power is not easily applied, nor can it be realistically viewed as simple line authority.

The relationship between the SEC and the accounting profession must be viewed in this framework. The fundamental goal of the Commission, which is a fair and efficient capital market, and the fundamental goal of the accounting profession, which is the existence of a prosperous and respected group of professional practitioners of accounting, are generally consistent. Thus, it is likely that coalition will exist between the two groups far more frequently than conflict. The groups can generally rely upon each other since their interests are likely to be similar. Where parties are moving in concert, the question of which will be the more dominant force generally is answered in terms of the particular persons involved, and on the basis of the relative importance of individual issues to the ultimate goals of the organization.

While accounting and auditing issues are of considerable importance to the Commission, they are not as dominant to its objective as they are to the accounting profession. Thus, it is not surprising to see the Commission devote fewer resources to these areas than does the profession and to observe that the profession has generally been in a leadership position in these areas. While Congress assigned statutory authority over many aspects of accounting and financial reporting to the Commission in the Securities Acts, the delegation of this authority to the accounting profession has been consistent with the goals of both groups.

Some authority was assigned directly to the accounting profession under the Acts. This was done in the provision that requires financial statements to be certified by independent public accountants. Thus, the responsibility of the profession arises from authority delegated both directly by Congress and by the Commission. Such delegation is quite real, and has been reinforced by the actions and attitudes of the Commission over the years. Any assertion that responsibility was assigned without authority is inconsistent with the historical record.

It is also not appropriate to suggest that the responsibility and authority of the accounting profession came solely from the SEC or the Congress. As early as 1910, when the accountant was primarily a bookkeeper, the profession made its first attempt to gather and define accounting terms in usage.

In 1914 the newly created Federal Reserve Board and Federal Trade

Commission both indicated interest and concern over the diversity in quality of financial statements. The FTC, in particular, expressed the desire to set up uniform accounting systems for all principal industries. The FRB's interest stemmed from the fact that banks in their lending capacity were in the position of relying on financial statements.

As a result of these pressures the American Institute of Accountants (now the American Institute of Certified Public Accountants) agreed to prepare a memorandum on auditing procedures. This was published in the Federal Reserve Bulletin as a tentative proposal and was also published in booklet form. This statement was updated on several subsequent occasions. It was the first semi-official pronouncement about the meaning of audited financial statements.

As the Institute emerged as the spokesman of the profession, it sought alliances to further its aims. Cooperation with the New York Stock Exchange led to the formulation of five broad principals of accounting which had won general acceptance. Members of the Exchange were required to submit financial statements which were in conformity with the basic principles of the Institute.

Thus, before the Securities Acts, the Institute had taken its first steps to formulate generally accepted accounting principles and had gained recognition of its authority from the leading stock exchange.

At the time when Congress was considering the Securities Act of 1933, Colonel Arthur Carter, representing the accounting profession, testified that the bill should include a requirement that financial statements be audited and reported on by independent accountants. Such a provision was ultimately added to the Act before passage. In addition, the Act did not follow the example of companies' acts throughout the world—which generally define required financial statements in considerable detail—but rather gave authority to an independent agency to set forth accounting and disclosure requirements. Thus Congress created the necessity of the partnership between agency and profession that has since existed. In the years since its creation, the Commission has looked to the profession to be the leader in the setting of accounting principles. Authority and responsibility have been delegated by the Commission and have been accepted by the profession.

The first Chief Accountant of the SEC, Carman Blough, expressed the position of the Commission in its early days as well as in the present when he argued that the development of accounting principles should be left to the accounting profession. He recognized that the accountants faced the problems of the profession on a daily basis and thus should be responsible for their solution. At the 50th Anniversary of the American Institute of Accountants in 1937 he stated the following:

As a matter of fact I think I have emphasized at numerous times that the policy of the Securities and Exchange Commission was to encourage the accountants to develop uniformity of procedure themselves; in which case we would follow. We expect to be able to follow the better thought in the profession and only as a last resort would the Commission feel the necessity to step in.

Throughout its existence the Commission has been active in supporting the efforts of the profession to articulate principles. It encouraged the Committee on Accounting Procedure, and when it became apparent that a new approach was needed, the Chief Accountant of the Commission served on the committee which recommended the creation of the Accounting Principles Board. Fourteen years later when the institutional structure was changed again, a former SEC Commissioner, Francis Wheat, was chairman of the task force established by the profession to recommend a new framework, and the Commission endorsed the proposals made by the task force. These proposals led to the creation of the Financial Accounting Standards Board. In each of these cases, the Commission's role was supportive of the efforts of the accounting profession.

Perhaps more important than the SEC's assistance and support of the establishment of institutions for defining accounting principles has been its support of the principles established by these bodies. Long before the accounting profession bound its members to support pronouncements of its own principle-making bodies, the Commission was enforcing these statements. With only one significant exception, the Commission indicated by word and deed that it would not accept financial statements in filings which were prepared in a fashion not in conformity with the authoritative pronouncements of the profession. The conspicuous exception—accounting for the investment credit—was one in which the Commission concluded that it would not support an opinion when representatives of leading accounting firms had not only voted against it but indicated that they would not require their clients to abide by it. In this case; the Commission was not enforcing a view contrary to that of the Board but rather refusing to enter a dispute among major firms on the side which the Board favored. In retrospect, it is the judgment of most parties involved that the Commission made an error in declining to support the Board. It is certainly clear that neither the profession nor the Board benefited from the episode which ultimately culminated ten years later in an act of Congress which enshrined the diverse practices which had been used. Since that time, both groups have worked to avoid recurrence.

The means by which such situations have been avoided has been a carefully developed program of communication between the Accounting Principles Board and the staff of the Commission. This is the process which has been identified by some as the means by which the Commission works its will on the Board. Such an analysis reveals a misunderstanding of the decision-making process in a pluralistic society.

Where two groups, both with elements of responsibility and authority over a field of endeavor, and both with a similar overall view of the objectives of the field, seek to exercise their authority, coalition is the natural result. In such a situation, each group recognizes the power and authority of the other but does not seek to test it, because conflict under such circumstances nearly always represents a negative-sum game. Thus it is with the SEC and the accounting profession. In setting accounting principles, neither side wishes to put the authority of the other to the test. This does not make the authority of both groups any less real. In those situations where conflict has developed, each group has won its share. The recent example of land sales accounting is only one case where the Board has had its way against the expressed wishes of the Commission. In that case, communication broke down and confrontation developed. Other less publicized cases could be cited where strongly expressed views of one or the other group caused a full or partial surrender.

Much more frequently, however, the two organizations work in harmony. The Commission staff provides input to the Board's deliberations on the basis of their continuing experience with individual problems of registrants. They express their views on the accounting issues informally as an opinion is being developed. These views are seldom in substantial conflict with those of most Board members. Differences are usually compromised.

An analysis of this process does not lead to the conclusion that authority rests on one or the other side. Both groups have real authority but neither wishes to push the other to the extreme. At such an extreme, each group could inflict much damage on the other but at substantial cost. It is far more efficient to exercise authority jointly. Successive Chairmen of the Commission have articulated this approach. Chairman William Cary, responding to a 1964 congressional question as to who had the primary responsibility for determination of accounting principles, said:

> I think I can say quite truly that we have cooperated with the accounting profession very carefully on this subject over a period of years. I would take it as a joint responsibility.

Chairman William Casey identified the relationship as a partnership in his 1972 speech to the AICPA annual meeting.

As we now move into the era of the Financial Accounting Standards Board, there seems little reason to expect any basic change in relationships. The Commission supported the creation of the Board. In a letter to the AICPA on May 4, 1972, it set forth its views as follows:

> The Commission believes that the structure for the development of standards of financial accounting and reporting recommended in the "Report of the Study on Establishment of Accounting Principles" will foster the continuation of the longstanding policy of cooperation between the Commission and professional accountants. Of equal importance, the recommended structure appears to be responsive to the need expressed in many quarters for improvement of investor confidence in accounting principles and in financial reporting generally.

* * *

> In conclusion, we wish to reaffirm our strong conviction and our policy, dating back to 1934, that the development of accounting principles within the private sector is consistent with the public interest.

To the extent that the FASB is able to obtain more inputs from diverse groups and undertake more meaningful and controlled research, its authority will increase, since it will be able to defend its viewpoint in the ongoing dialogue on accounting principles. The Board and the SEC, however, will have to operate on the principle of mutual non-surprise if their joint efforts are to be maximized. It appears that both entities are moving in this direction in their early contacts.

The relationships between the accounting profession and the SEC are by no means limited to the establishment of accounting principles. A second area that requires attention is auditing standards.

In many respects, the relationship between the Commission and the Committee on Auditing Procedure (now the Auditing Standards Executive Committee) parallels that with the bodies responsible for accounting principles. The Commission's statutory authority over the auditing process is not so clearly defined except in terms of the form of audit reports which will be considered acceptable. Nevertheless, the Commission staff and the Auditing Committee have generally cooperated in the creation of published standards, with the profession again in the leading position.

The Commission's approach to auditing standards was put to its most rigorous test in the *McKesson & Robbins* case in 1938. The record in this case raised many questions as to whether or not the generally accepted auditing procedures in use were adequate to assure accuracy of financial statements. It was revealed that an elaborate set of records had been forged by corporate officials (using fictitious names) and that a substantial amount of recorded assets were fictitious.

In the SEC hearings regarding the case, the testimony of many accountants, acting as expert witnesses, revealed weaknesses in the auditing procedures. Several professional groups immediately took steps to correct these weaknesses, including the Institute, which issued *Extensions of Auditing Procedure*. This statement became the first of a series on auditing practice.

In recognition of the profession's attempt to strengthen auditing standards, the Commission concluded its report as follows:

> We have carefully considered the desirability of specific rules and regulations governing the auditing steps to be performed by accountants in certifying financial statements to be filed with us. Action has already been taken by the accounting profession adopting certain of the auditing procedures considered in this case. We have no reason to believe at this time that these extensions will not be maintained or that further extensions of auditing procedures along the lines suggested in this report will not be made. . . . Until experience should prove the contrary, we feel that this program is preferable to its alternative—the detailed prescription of the scope of and procedures to be followed in the audit for the various types of issuers of securities who file statements with us—and will allow for further consideration of varying audit procedures and for the development of different treatment for specific types of issuers.

In the last decade, public accountants have again come under criticism for defective auditing. There are several dimensions to this criticism. Some relates to cases where auditors have done a defective job of fact finding in terms of professional auditing standards currently in existence. Here the Commission has undertaken disciplinary procedures, sought injunctions and made criminal references depending on the seriousness of cases involved.

Another set of problems relates to cases where the audit fact-finding was adequate but poor judgment was used in appraising the measurement principles used by the client so that presentations inconsistent with accounting or economic reality were blessed with unqualified auditor's opinions. In one such case (*Penn Central*), the staff of the Commission has publicly criticized the auditors. Some disciplinary actions have also been undertaken. The staff of the Commission, in its review of documents filed with it and in conferences with registrants and their auditors, attempts to reduce the incidence of such items before they become part of the final financial statements. In many cases, items of this sort have indicated an area of weakness in the application of accounting principles currently in existence, which has led to an Accounting Series Release (as in the case of real estate—ASR No. 94; pooling of interests—ASRs Nos. 130 and 135; and leasing—ASR No. 132) or to actions by the Accounting Principles Board.

A third type of case which has led to criticism is one in which accepted auditing procedures have not proved adequate to uncover a serious problem with financial statements. Here the question that must be dealt with is whether the situation is so unique that it constitutes an aberration that does not warrant a change in basic procedures or whether it reveals a significant weakness in procedures which the profession should seek to remedy. The Allied Crude Vegetable Oil fraud led, for example, to new procedures on auditing procedures for goods in public warehouses (Statement on Auditing Procedure 37). The *Equity Funding* debacle is also leading to a re-examination of auditing standards in the areas of fraud detection, computer auditing procedures and insurance auditing, although it is too early in the investigation of this case to draw conclusions as to why the fraud was not uncovered.

In each of these situations, the profession has been responsive to the public need, and the joint efforts of profession and Commission have led to improvement. Once again, both responsibility and authority have been delegated. The relationship is a legitimate partnership, not a superior-subordinate relationship.

There are some areas in the partnership where the Commission has definitely played a leadership role and is likely to continue to do so, even though cooperative efforts with the profession are important in these cases as well. One is the area of independence of accountants. The Securities Acts provide that financial statements shall be "certified by an independent public or certified accountant." While the profession has dealt with independence as an auditing standard, it has been slow to impose firm rules and guidelines. This is partly due to the structure of the profession, which includes many small practitioners who service their clients in many ways and have been concerned with the implications of a number of specific rules directed primarily toward the appearance of independence, which the Commission has felt to be essential in dealing with auditors of public companies. The Commission has, therefore, set forth specific rules on independence in Regulation S-X and it has publicized in three Accounting Series Releases a number of individual decisions of the staff on particular independence problems. The AICPA Ethics Committee has taken an active role in developing independence standards for the profession, and in most respects the profession's standards are now consistent with those of the Commission. It seems likely that cooperative effort will continue to narrow areas of difference.

A second major area in which the Commission has taken a leading role in the partnership is in the development of standards of disclosure. In the various registration forms and in Regulation S-X, the Commission has fulfilled its legislated responsibility of defining information required by investors. Both accounting principle-making and other professional bodies have worked closely with the Commission by providing inputs and public comments on proposals, and in some cases by including disclosure requirements in APB opinions, but the Commission has not hestitated to take the first step. Recent proposals on disclosure of details of unusual charges and credits to income, liquidity and compensating balances, quality of earnings, impact of alternative accounting principles and components of tax expense indicate that the Commission remains willing to innovate in the disclosure area.

The Commission's partnership with the profession cannot be viewed simply on a profession-wide basis. An important part of the relationship must be examined in the framework of the responsibility and authority of individual firms in fulfilling their auditing and reporting functions in individual client situations. The responsibility of representing the public while being paid by a client was assigned by Congress at the behest of the profession, which said that their members could handle the difficult problems posed by the economic relationships involved.

The Commission has traditionally taken all possible steps to support individual auditors in resisting client pressures. This has been done informally in meetings and telephone conversations in which the client has been advised of staff support for the position taken by an independent auditor. While the Commission staff does not like to be used as a no-sayer in cases where an auditor knows the right answer but prefers not to be the one to tell it to the client, it is supportive in cases where the auditor is prepared to exercise his authority and responsibility.

Even beyond individual situations, the Commission has sought to improve the position of the auditor in dealing with his client. For example, the Commission's traditional refusal to accept "except for" opinions or opinions which indicate major scope qualifications in filings has strengthened the hand of the individual auditor in difficult situations. In addition, Accounting Series Release No. 123 advocated the establishment of audit committees which would establish a direct relationship between auditor and board of directors and thus improve the auditor's situation.

In 1971 the issuance of a revised Form 8-K requirement called for timely public disclosure of all auditor changes, together with letters from both client and auditor indicating whether or not in the past eighteen months there had been any disagreements between auditor and client on accounting or auditing matters which would have led, if not resolved, to a qualification in the auditor's report. This requirement was designed to discourage clients from employing new auditors simply to obtain a more favorable accounting treatment by exposing such changes to the full glare of public disclosure. In addition, the Commission staff routinely follows up in cases where significant disagreements are reported to determine the full facts and to be sure that the interests of investors are being protected.

Summary

In summary, the record indicates that the Commission and the accounting profession exist in a legitimate partnership for the protection of investors. Both have authority and responsibility. This partnership is a logical and expected result of a social setting in which parties with authority and related objectives are created or develop. Because this result is a natural one and because it is generally perceived to have worked effectively, it is highly likely that the relationships established will continue and will continue to serve the best interests of investors, accountants, and an efficient capital market.

Comments on the SEC and the Accounting Profession: Responsibility, Authority, and Progress

CHARLES W. LAMDEN*

Mr. Burton has presented an excellent analysis of the ways in which the SEC and the accounting profession have related to each other and have cooperated in the development of reporting standards for the past forty years. The advantages of the cooperation between the SEC and the accounting profession, and the many joint efforts he describes, which have led to more comprehensive and better understood financial data, are indeed worthwhile and impressive. Nor can one disagree with the philosophy of the SEC, as stated and restated over the years, that the development of accounting principles should be left to the accounting profession. Overall, this commentator has no major disagreements with the factual or historical data set forth in Burton's paper.

1. IS IT REALLY A PARTNERSHIP?

Like Charles Horngren,[1] this commentator cannot accept the partnership concept. It is true, as Burton indicates, that in the pluralistic structure in which both the accounting profession and the SEC work, actions have taken place where mutual goals were reinforced, and "floating or informal coalitions" arose on various issues. This does not result, however, in a long-term coalition or partnership.

The function of the SEC is to carry out the duties of a regulatory agency. There cannot be a partnership between regulators and those being regulated. They operate on different levels of authority. It is, of course, true that the delegation of authority related to accounting principles has been consistent with the goals of both groups. But the final regulatory authority—the right to enforce the rules—has not been, and probably cannot be, delegated.

*B.A. 1937, M.A. 1939, UCLA; Ph.D. 1949, University of California, Berkeley. CPA, New York, California, et al. Partner, Peat, Marwick, Mitchell & Co. Contributor to accounting periodicals.

This in no way denies the fact that the cooperative arrangement described in Burton's paper has worked effectively and is highly likely to continue in a way that will serve the best interests of investors, accountants and an efficient capital market. As also clearly pointed out in the presentation, the precedent for this position was established by Carman Blough, the first chief accountant of the SEC. It has continued to the present time because of the high degree of knowledge and understanding of the chief accountants that followed Carman Blough— William Werntz, Earle King, Andrew Barr, and the current highly knowledgeable and articulate chief accountant.

In passing, it should be noted that while the authority and responsibility for establishing accounting standards have been delegated and have been accepted by the accounting profession, this is not entirely a result of altruism on the part of the SEC. The difficulty of establishing accounting standards that will give the "right" answers is well understood. Shifting the responsibility, even though considered a wise decision on the part of the profession, relieved the SEC of an arduous and onerous task.

2. FORMULATION OF ACCOUNTING PRINCIPLES

In the course of his presentation, Mr. Burton refers to the formulation of accounting principles. If he means identifying and formulating *statements* of the principles then there can be no disagreement. But the implication, as it is in much of the literature, is that the principles are created.

Perhaps this is merely polemics based on terminology. Yet the concept of developing or modifying accounting principles in the sense of the creation of the principle itself does not seem appropriate. It is the *statement* concerning a principle that is established, developed or modified—not the principle itself. Rather standards and rules are established, developed or modified in order to implement the underlying principles.

This position is based on the concept that a principle is a fundamental truth—primary or basic. A standard, however, is defined as that which is set up or established by authority, custom, or general consent as a basis for measuring procedures, techniques, or quality. Or a standard may be thought of as a model or example against which one can test or measure what he does.

While underlying principles must be identified, most of the cooperative work of the SEC and the accounting profession (through the efforts of the Accounting Principles Board) related to standards, rules and procedures rather than principles. At least the name of the new organization which has been established to develop or modify the standards will be the Financial Accounting Standards Board.

3. ACCOUNTING AS AN INSTRUMENT OF PUBLIC POLICY

In evaluating the activities of the SEC as described in the paper, it is important to note that accounting practices and procedures (including related disclosures) have two functions, which are:

1. measuring the results of operations
2. effecting the results of operations.

The way accounting procedures are implemented will determine whether they have a passive function—that is, they serve as a yardstick, or whether they have a positive function—that is, they serve as a tool of policy and control.

To the extent that the SEC uses the conventions, standards, procedures and rules established by the profession, accounting assumes a passive role. But when the SEC shapes accounting procedures and concepts to fit requirements which it defines, accounting becomes an active element in regulation.

The use of accounting to arrive at taxable income by the Internal Revenue Service, and the use of accounting to establish rates by federal and state regulatory agencies, are clear-cut examples of accounting as a positive force in regulation. Nor does there seem to be any doubt that when the SEC requires corporations to present their financial statements regularly and requires certain methods of presentation and disclosure, it is exercising substantial control over the various phases of the operations of business.

In its early development accounting was regarded as peculiarly the tool of private business enterprise. In recent years the determination of standards, rules, and procedures for the reporting of assets, liabilities, and income is no longer primarily determined by business enterprise. At least for external reporting, the emphasis has shifted almost entirely to the needs of third party users of financial statements.

The purpose of the Congress in passing the securities acts and in establishing the Securities and Exchange Commission was to protect corporate investors. In carrying out this function, it is clear, as stated in the paper, that it was the intention of the SEC to utilize the standards, rules, and procedures promulgated by the accounting profession. It is also agreed that it was not a primary objective of the Commission to prescribe detailed accounting or reporting methods. Yet almost from its inception the Commission laid down specific rules from which deviation could be made, and it continues this kind of control with even increased vigor today.

With protection of investors as its keynote, the SEC takes positive action each time it sets forth specific requirements for changes in the accounting procedures it will accept. This reflects more than leadership, as Burton describes it. It should be noted, also, that many of the changes in accepted standards and procedures made by the accounting profession can be directly related to the fact that the SEC does not place its emphasis on the passive use of accounting as a yardstick. Rather, the modified standards and rules emphasize the positive use of accounting as a tool of public policy.

This in no way denies the progress that has been made in improving financial reporting for protection of investors, but it does give a different perspective to the relationship between the SEC and the accounting profession from that presented by Burton.

4. THE ACCOUNTING PROFESSION, ACCOUNTING PRINCIPLES, AND THE FUTURE

A brief comment may also be appropriate about the term "accounting profession" as used in the paper. It apparently refers only to Certified Public Accountants. But the total accounting profession includes others—management accountants, internal auditors, governmental accountants, and accounting educators.

The long-range dream of a small but growing number of accountants is for a true profession of accounting, supported by a recognized common body of knowledge and disseminated through professional schools of accountancy. Such professional schools would then be the centers of basic, meaningful, and relevant accounting research in all the areas of accounting.

A joint committee of the American Institute of Certified Public Accountants and the National Association of State Boards of Accountancy, charged with the responsibility for studying ways to improve the recognition and regulation of CPAs, has recently issued its report recommending the establishment of professional schools of accounting. Also, a statement of the AICPA Education Committee encouraging the establishment of professional schools of accounting at qualified and receptive colleges and universities has been approved by the AICPA Board of Directors.

The significance of these developments as related to the subject of Burton's paper, "The SEC and the Accounting Profession: Responsibility, Authority and Progress," is most profound. The end objective of the cooperative effort between the SEC and the accounting profession, which he describes, is to achieve ". . . progress in improving the quality of public information about the economic activities of corporations who [come] to the capital markets of the United States for financial resources." Regardless of where the responsibility and authority rest, or are delegated, it is the opinion of this commentator that neither the SEC nor the accounting profession has devoted sufficient attention to the identification of the underlying principles of economics, finance, and accounting upon which the standards, rules, and procedures can be based. The kind of basic research that is needed can be done best by academic researchers working in the milieu of a professional school.

The relationships established between the SEC and the accounting profession should, of course, be continued. Significant progress will come in the future, however, when the SEC carries out its enlightened regulatory activities on the basis of the standards, rules, and procedures promulgated by the accounting profession (in conjunction with the Financial Accounting Standards Board); and the FASB, in turn, carries out its work on the basis of the underlying principles identified by academic researchers working in the environment of professional schools of accounting.

NOTE

1. See the discussion by Horngren in his paper in this volume entitled "The Marketing of Accounting Standards." See also Charles Horngren (1972) "Accounting Principles: Private or Public Sector?" *Journal of Accountancy* (May): 37–41.

Discussion

Burton. In looking at the SEC and considering the extent to which it is a regulator of the accounting profession, I guess I would first say that I am not sure that history indicates that regulators and regulatees cannot join in partnership. In fact I think the history of, for example, the ICC and the CAB indicates that there has been a partnership of interest. But I think the thing that the SEC has as its principal objective is not the regulation of the accounting profession, but rather the regulation of the capital markets. In achieving its principal objective, an efficient capital market, accounting is an important component, but it is not the principal focus. So I think that, while it would be difficult to conceive of a partnership between the SEC, if you will, and Investment Company Institute or even broker-dealers, it does not seem very hard to conceive of a partnership between the SEC and the accounting profession because of the fact that the SEC's objective runs toward an efficient capital market, and accounting is a vital tool for this purpose.

Liggio. Sandy, whether you view it as a coalition or a partnership, it seems to me that there is some form of co-equality there. One thing that has disturbed me about some of the papers and the comments that have been made at the Colloquium today, is that there seems to be an abdication to the SEC of the accounting profession's role in the making of standards or principles. I think there was more than one speaker yesterday who suggested that this was the area where the SEC should take the lead. It seems from my standpoint that maybe it should be the profession that takes the lead in some form of a coalition with the Commission. I was wondering what your views are on that.

Burton. Chairman Casey said it quite well when he said that he identified this relationship as a partnership, and that it was not the Commission's desire to be senior partner, but that if it turned out to be necessary that might be the way in which it worked out. I think that is a fair statement of our position. If the accounting profession does not respond to the demands made upon it, it seems clear that there is going to be a variety of different steps that it is going to have to face from the point of view of external impact. The courts certainly have been one of them up to this point. The Commission is certainly likely to be another. Congress is likely to be a third. There are various different groups and outside influences that are going to be brought to bear on the profession to the extent that it is not moving in an expeditious fashion to meet its responsibilities as perceived by the public. If the profession's view of its own responsibilities is substantially different from the public's view of its responsibilities, I think you can feel confident that the public view is the one that is going to be imposed upon it in a fashion that may not be what the profession wants. It is far better for the profession to take the lead. We have asked the Auditing Standards Executive Committee to look at a variety of areas—for example, the whole question of standards associated with interim reports, with the accountant's responsibility for interim reports, and the question of standards associating the auditor with summaries and other data of this sort. We may be the trigger that started them going on the subject of standards for interim reports and the auditor's responsibility for interim reports. I think there are other cases where the profession will be urged to develop standards. The public sector is anxious to have the profession not just respond to specific requests, but to innovate in a variety of different ways. I think the Commission, for one, will be responsive to innovation. So I guess the answer is, that if a void or a vacuum develops, various groups will move to fill it. If there is a perceived need which the profession is not willing to fulfill, either it will be pushed to do so, or else other groups may move in its place.

Mautz. Sandy, could I ask by just what mechanism you view, or the Commission perceives, what the public demands?

Burton. This represents an ongoing dialogue. We have a very substantial number of people who are continually telling us what the public demands. Some of these people are on Capitol Hill; some of these people are in the analytical community; some of these people are in the financial press. There is a wide variety of different inputs. We also get letters from stockholders asking why certain things have been done or not been done. The mail that comes across my desk has substantial elements of all these things. I guess that is part of how we perceive what is being demanded. Then I suspect also, that since there are a number of professionals in the agencies, we may also have some ideas as to what should be.

Kapnick. Sandy, I have heard Chairman Casey mention this partnership several times. I never really had the opportunity to ask either him or you the one question that bothers me about this line of reasoning. That is, if it is a real partnership, why shouldn't the public know, then, that the SEC has approved the accounting principles that apply in the financial statements?

You still insist upon the disclosure that the SEC takes no responsibility for the contents of the registration statements. It seems to me that if you are talking about protecting the public and you feel there is a partnership in the establishment of accounting principles, then the public should know that the accounting principles used in the statements have been approved by the SEC—not the application of them, but at least the identification of the accounting principles.

Burton. There are two dimensions to what you ask. One is the question as to whether the SEC should take in some sense formal action accepting pronouncements of authoritative professional bodies. The second goes to the question, should the Commission in some specific way associate itself with these in registration statements. To deal with the second first, I think the problem of misunderstanding would be substantial were the Commission to make statements that they approved of the accounting used. In the first place, in selecting accounting principles the auditor and the client both must appraise a factual situation about which the Commission may not be fully aware, so that while the accounting principle per se might be an appropriate principle in the absolute sense, it might not in the particular application. To make a statement associated with registration statements would almost inevitably imply that the application in this particular case was appropriate. I don't think that would be useful. I think it would be more inclined to mislead in terms of what the Commission has actually done.

In regard to the Commission approving the pronouncements of the Board, I think that again might create not an impression of partnership but a creation of a superior-subordinate relationship. To follow Chuck's analogy, the profit center produces the budget which the chief executive officer approves. I don't think that that is the image which the Commission wishes to communicate. As a practical matter, I think that most readers of financial statements who have a knowledge of institutional environment are aware that the Commission is involved cooperatively in the establishment of accounting principles and that we are not totally passive in this respect. On the other hand, if the Commission should take a positive position, my own inclination is to think that it might create the wrong rather than the right impression of what is being done.

Fiflis. I want to follow up on this point. I think that maybe there ought to be a reconsideration by the Commission. I understand that formalized principles and standards are not any more than a very small percentage of the rules and principles that accountants have adopted. It seems to me that now is a very appropriate time for the Commission to reconsider Mr. Kapnick's suggestion. There are several reasons for this. First of all, as Homer Kripke once said, it may be that it is legally required by the Administrative Procedure Act that before the Commission adopt any rule, it must be subjected to the hearing and notice provisions of that Act. That is a formalized reason why it might be desirable to have the Commission formally adopt the statements.

There are other reasons, it seems to me, that would be more powerful. Accountants would be especially interested, for instance, in gaining the immunity of Section 19 of the 1953 Act, and Section 23 of the 1934 Act, which say that anyone who relies upon a rule of the Commission, even though it is later held to be invalid, is free of liability under the 1933 and 1934 acts. Presumably it would be fairly easy to have such a summary provision enacted under the 1934 Act and perhaps some of the other Securities Acts, so the purpose of having the Commission formally adopt the statements would be the creation of immunity.

Burton. I have the feeling that if you start down that road, there is only one place where it is going to lead you. It is going to lead you to a full, formal Commission rule-making procedure which is going to take over the establishment of accounting principles.

Fiflis. That may be a good thing. It seems to me that one of our greatest difficulties is the lack of general acceptability on the part of the public. If you did comply with the administrative procedure, then that would mean that formal notice would be available to lawyers, accountants, managers, and other representatives of different groups, so that they would be harder put to later complain that a small group of people, a private organization, is implementing rules of law which are adopted whole hog without any procedure or hearing. I would think it would be to our great advantage and should be studied very seriously.

Burton. I can understand how an attorney representing a client would prefer it that way in terms of minimizing an exposure to liability. My feeling is that the direction that would lead would be to a very rapid termination of the existence of a body such as the Financial Accounting Standards Board. One of the ways in which it has been set up is to be sure that there are adequate inputs, adequate exposure, so that—while it is in the private sector—to simply call it a private body is not reflective of the way in which it operates. I don't personally believe that the Commission should directly adopt as part of rule making the pronouncements of the Board because I think that would lead to a result which might be beneficial in terms of the liability constraints on particular clients, but it would, in my judgment, be a poorer result in terms of the kind of financial information being presented and how measurement standards are being developed.

Zeff. Sandy, in view of the procedure that the Financial Accounting Standards Board said it is going to use, which closely parallels what the SEC does in establishing its own rules—exposure drafts, hearings, etc.—what would be your reaction, assuming the law could be changed accordingly, to adopting the Canadian approach, by which the Commission would say that those practices which had been recommended by the Financial Accounting Standards Board are regarded by the Commission as generally accepted accounting principles?

Burton. In the first place, that would have to be a congressional determination. It would seem to me to be not inconsistent with the way in which we are presently acting. The question as to whether Congress wants a body that is involved directly in the capital markets to be involved in the process of establishing accounting principles in a somewhat greater fashion than might be the case otherwise would be a decision for them to make. It would not be my inclination to oppose such a thing, but I can't speak for how the Commissions feels.

Kapnick. Before I am misunderstood on this point, Sandy, the reason for the question was that it is hard for me to see this as a partnership. I would be violently opposed to the SEC's setting standards. We went down that road two years ago and developed the FASB, which I believe is the appropriate answer at this moment in time. It seems, though, that the SEC does have the clout as far as the public is concerned. If they don't like what the private sector is doing they can always object. It isn't really a partnership. It is, whether you like it or not, a superior relationship to the profession because they can always overrule the profession. So long as the Commission has that club I don't see how we can really talk about a partnership in the true sense of the word.

Burton. When you say "the Commission can always overrule the profession," I think you are looking at the legal structure rather than the realities of the process as it operates. I don't believe that as a practical matter the Commission has the alternative of overruling the Financial Accounting Standards Board more than once, if you will. I think that if the Commission comes to the conclusion that a particular principle that the Board has adopted is not consistent with the public interest, before it moves it has to look at the question as to whether or not to exercise this authority. Once it is exercised, it seems to me that that is going to have the impact very quickly of making the FASB wither away, and a vehicle which the Commission believes on a long-run basis is the right vehicle for establishing accounting principles is going to become ineffective. The moment we overrule the Board you are going to find a great number of people routinely trotting down to Washington the moment an opinion comes and trying to re-fight the same arguments that were fought before the Board. I don't think it is a practical alternative to overrule the Board. While in a sense the

Commission has the ultimate authority to overrule, it is a little like a nuclear deterrent approach. Once we exercise it, there is not going to be much left. So that would have to be something we would consider with great care.

I think the experience that we have had in situations where the SEC has not supported the Board has been very unfortunate for both parties. At the same time, I think the Board would be foolish if it wasn't aware that the Commission also has authority. I think that you can't look at the statute and conclude from the statute that the SEC has the ultimate authority. I think you have to look at how the real world operates. In that framework I think both groups have authority. If Congress were to say, "We think the authority for setting financial accounting standards should be taken completely from the Commission and assigned completely to the Board," this is a decision that Congress could make, and I would not find it hostile to the way in which we operate. However I think Congress has generally indicated a desire for having different parties reviewing, rather than to concentrate authority, although there are some exceptions to that. It may be that they prefer the system as it works now to how it would work if the Board had total authority. There is also a question that if the Congress blessed the Board, whether or not the Board would indeed be in the private sector. Once Congress blessed it, the question then comes, "What happens next?" Once you have received the benediction, you may have certain obligations to the person who gave it to you. It may not be exactly what you want. There are problems that go that way, too.

Sterling. Sandy, you said that if you overruled the Board you might have a number of people trotting down to Washington and presenting their case to you again. Rumor has it that this is exactly what is happening now. They are trotting down to Congress and to the SEC every time they disagree with the Board. Many of these conflicts have been the result of management campaigns or political campaigns.

Burton. I think there is no question that there is a significant amount of this happening. It is happening a lot less than it would happen if the Commission routinely took what the Board said and said, "Now we are going to consider it, and we are going to go through the Administrative Procedures Act and publish it for comment, and then we are going to make an ultimate determination." That would multiply by a substantial factor the amount of lobbying that now exists. At the present time, most of this is informal, but it certainly is very real. Congress gets a lot of pressure, and I guess I get probably one or two letters a month from Capitol Hill on one particular subject or another. When something gets hot we get a lot more letters than that. At the present time it is fair to say that people are attempting to bring pressure. I believe right now the new Board has a certain amount of goodwill, which will no doubt be dissipated in less than forty years. I know that every effort is being made in the financial community to avoid pressure. You hear talks of various sorts saying, "Be very careful about running to the Congress." I am not sure how effective that exhortation will be. I am not sure how our exhortations to Congress will be heard, either, which generally are in the direction of "Do not use accounting as a tool of policy," if you will, rather than as a measurement system, because the long-run costs are very high. We weren't able to persuade Congress at the time of the investment credit. There are uncertainties. I think Steve is right in one respect: there are greater uncertainties today about the political process. It is clear that there cannot be just a quiet, chummy agreement between two parties in the process of setting accounting principles; but, on the other hand; I still believe that the coalition that does exist is an effective and a very powerful one.

Defliese. I think that I have been close enough to the scene over the past ten years or so that I recognize the type of partnership that Sandy refers to. It hasn't been, of course, a perfect partnership. No partnership is. There are all kinds of lapses of communication and understanding, which might make it appear to the rest of the world like an unreal partnership. We have our problems, but we work together fairly well. But there is one area where the partnership does break down, and I would hope that the Commission would give serious consideration to it: as has been pointed out before, most of our accounting principles are uncodified. There is a great vagueness in a number of major areas that could be resolved only on the basis of direct application. When this occurs and the Commission staff is involved, the partnership disappears. At that point there is frequently a confrontation, rather than a partnership. The Commission and its staff, in its own judgment, acts as prosecutor, judge, and jury.

This is where I think we need some better vehicle, a court. On occasion the chief accountant does call in other members of the profession to more or less pick brains in order to resolve an issue. But in the final analysis it is the Commission staff and the Commission that determine whether or not a certain accounting principle shall be formulated through the precedents. Unfortunately, the Commission frequently overrules its own precedents when it does this, and that makes for further consternation, particularly when a registrant has come to rely on a precedent. The frequent answer is, "We made a mistake, and we are not going to repeat it." This, therefore, calls for some rearrangement of the partnership whereby the profession can become more active in this area—call it a panel of consultants, call it an empaneling of a jury of experts—to assist in making this decision. This may result in a delegation of the Commission's authority, but I don't think it is any more of a delegation than the delegation to the FASB, recognizing it can always overrule if it wants to. I commend this idea to the Commission because it is a much larger area of the setting of accounting principles on a practical basis than the formalized opinions that we have in the public area.

Burton. I hear you. I am not sure I am listening, but I hear you. Of course the staff and the Commission have a review function which they undertake. It is a little uncertain because, in a sense, you start with the fact that the Commission, in theory, doesn't review. In other words, the Commission merely receives a filing and doesn't review it. The review process is one that has evolved over a period of forty years. The responsibility for review is one that is not statute oriented, but it is one that is accepted and recognized pretty well throughout the financial and the investor community. I am not sure of the extent to which the Commission would wish to either formalize its decision-making process (to the extent it does make decisions in this area) or to delegate it. I am just not sure.

If the profession were to establish a vehicle, such as has been suggested by Bob Sterling or like the court that Leonard Spacek advocated, whereby the facts of a particular case could be taken to an authoritative group other than the Commission staff, and receive an answer, I think it is not unlikely that the Commission staff would accept that answer. We have done this in the case of interpretations. There have been a number of particular situations where auditors have gone to the Institute for interpretations, and the Board has approved the interpretations, and we have accepted them. We have said, "All right, this is the wisdom of the Board." Now I understand that Marshall Armstrong has been asked on a couple of occasions, what, if anything, the FASB proposes to do along these lines. Do they propose to have any interpretation vehicle? Do they propose to deal with individual cases? In accounting so many cases are a matter of fitting a set of facts to principles. It is a question of what analogy you want to draw. How do you analogize the facts to an area where you have a principle? Marshall has indicated that he does not expect the FASB is going to have any group that does anything of this sort. If the profession were to develop one, we would certainly consider what they had to say in these areas. The extent to which we would make an ultimate delegation, I don't know.

Defliese. I appreciate that, but I think that there is a real practical problem here that needs to be dealt with. In an area that is completely unexplored there are no precedents. I can understand the regulatory feature if, for example, there is a clear principle that hasn't been followed;

obviously the disciplinary powers have to go into action. On the other hand, when you are dealing with an area in which there is absolutely no guidelines, then I think there is a need for a partnership to begin to function, one way or another.

Burton. Of course those are the areas in which individual practitioners have been whipsawed by clients, and where I would say that there are many people who feel that the Commission has not been sufficiently active in saying to auditors and their clients in particular situations, "That isn't a reasonable application." There are a lot of people who criticize the Commission for not doing enough in this respect. Again, to the extent that there can be some form of authoritative group or professionalized group established that can fulfill this function, I think that it would be useful.

Chapin. This is on a different subject, Sandy. Some years ago the SEC embarked on a program to strengthen the profession, improve its independence, improve its objectivity. It did that through various steps, the APA recording procedures being one, the use of the injunctive proceedings being another. I think that has had tremendous effects on the way that the profession conducts itself in examining financial statements these days. But the cases continue, the injunctions continue, *Equity Funding* poses a major threat to the continued confidence in the profession on the part of the public. I don't know whether I have a question or a comment, but I think that the SEC has to be concerned now, not as much as before with the independence of the profession, but with its state of health. I think that is a very serious concern—the state of confidence the public has in the work that we do and the financial statements that are presented to it. I hope that the Commission will think about that in its future actions and policies.

CHAPTER 8

The Marketing of Accounting Standards

CHARLES T. HORNGREN*

A prerequisite to the solution of a problem is the recognition of the existence of the problem. . . . Most of the literature that I read is in the nature of a fairy tale. . . . Specifically, the problem is that the accountant has been given a responsibility without concomitant authority. (Sterling, 1973: 63)

This article tries to expand and reinforce my previous description of a problem about the responsibility of the Accounting Principles Board in relation to the Board's place within an institutional structure. My hypothesis is that the setting of accounting standards is as much a product of political action as of flawless logic or empirical findings. Why? Because the setting of standards is a social decision. Standards place restrictions on behavior; therefore, they must be accepted by the affected parties. Acceptance may be forced or voluntary or some of both. In a democratic society, getting acceptance is an exceedingly complicated process that requires skillful marketing in a political arena.

The history of the APB provides evidence for the above perceptions. The focus of this paper is a description of a problem of accounting power. My conclusions do not include magic solutions, but they do include a plea to the Financial Accounting Standards Board to get equipped now for its marketing as well as its production responsibilities.

The terms *marketing, selling,* and *lobbying* are used occasionally in this article. These terms should not be narrowly interpreted as representing carnival hawking or shady dealings in smoke-filled rooms. Instead, they should be viewed in their broadest, most elevated light—the

---

*B.S., Marquette University; M.B.A., Harvard; Ph.D., University of Chicago. CPA, Wisconsin. Member, Accounting Principles Board. Edmund W. Littlefield Professor of Accounting, Stanford University. Author, *Cost Accounting: A Managerial Emphasis* (1972); *Accounting for Management Control: An Introduction* (1970); (with J. A. Leer), *CPA Problems and Approaches to Solutions* (1969). Contributor to professional periodicals.

art of getting packages of ideas accepted by all affected parties in a professional manner.

1. THE INSTITUTIONAL STRUCTURE THAT CONFRONTED THE APB

Decentralized Management

The APB is about to take its final breath. Its demise is largely attributable to institutional forces rather than to internal disintegration. Let us examine these forces to see what the FASB might learn so that its life can extend indefinitely (or at least forty years).

My previously published description of the institutional structure (Horngren, 1972: 37–41) is my framework for discussion. In sum, the institutional setup has been as shown in Exhibit 1. Although most accountants have claimed that the responsibility for the setting of standards has been kept within the private sector, this view is oversimplified and misleading.

EXHIBIT 1

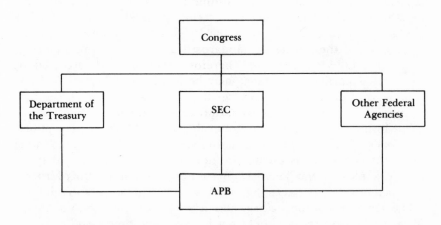

The (informal) organizational relationship is similar to that of decentralized management in industry. Exhibit 1 shows a single organization whose products are accounting standards. The key idea is a *decentralized* structure. A crude parallel can be drawn as you descend the chart. Congress has ultimate power, but with rare exceptions has delegated this power to the SEC (and other federal agencies). In turn, the SEC has delegated much of this power to the APB.

Decentralization is frequently defined as the relative freedom to make decisions. Top management adopts decentralization when it believes that lower management has more information and ability to make decisions that obtain the overall goals of the organization. In industry, the extent of decentralization varies from company to company. The heavier the decentralization, the greater the latitude of the lower-level managers to make a host of decisions, including acquisition of materials and equipment and sales of products and services. Decentralization lies along a continuum and is subject to recentralization, either selectively or totally, whenever high-level management so decides.

The implications of this informal decentralized organizational structure are far-reaching. Both the SEC and the APB are subjected to constraints exerted by superior management, Congress, and the entire organizational unit is subjected to the influence exerted by the customers, the parties affected by the standards (reporting companies, practitioners, and users of the reports).

The key to a successful enterprise is to generate a product that is *acceptable* to customers. The decentralized manager may develop what he perceives as a superior product, but his perceptions must overlap with those of his customers. If new standards are proposed that seem unacceptable, the customers must be persuaded otherwise. If the standards are sufficiently unappealing, the customer may complain to higher management (the SEC or Congress).

Of course, regarding particular standards, in the short run the customers have no alternative if the pinnacle of management (Congress) decides that lower management's product is desirable for society as a whole. But the product is complex, and top management may decide not to support innovation (because in an ultimate sense the customers in a collective, indirect way via their votes can replace top management itself).

Is the Description Accurate?

The foregoing description is not faultless, but I persist in defending its essential accuracy. Shortly after it was published, an APB member expressed his displeasure about my referring to the Board as lower management. The thrust of his objection was that the APB was not the obsequious lackey of the SEC. Of course, my article was not aimed at conveying the impression that the APB was the machine shop foreman in a factory run by a despotic plant manager. After all, the article stressed the *decentralized* nature of the structure. So I attributed his reaction to his failure to read with sufficient care.

But the January 1973 issue of the *Journal of Accountancy* reinforced the shortcomings of my May 1972 article. Apparently, the crucial idea of decentralization was overlooked by John Burton, who became Chief Accountant of the SEC during mid-1972. When he was asked whether he agreed with my top management-lower management description, Burton replied:

> No, I feel that, as Chairman Casey said, we are in partnership. . . . I do not believe that we are top management with veto power, although such power does legally exist. As a practical matter the strength of the private sector would dry up if Professor Horngren's article were a reflection of reality. No person of quality would want to serve on a principles board. (Burton, 1973: 26)

When asked whether Casey's "partnership" description of APB-SEC relations is correct, one practitioner reacted, "Well, in my firm there are partners and then there are partners!" The partnership description in its classic sense that implies an equal distribution of power may be handy public relations, but it is misleading. Moreover, does the assertion that "no person of quality would want to serve on a principles board" imply that no person of quality would want to be a junior partner in a public accounting firm or the head of a division in a decentralized organization? Do all persons of quality have to be managing partners and presidents?

Although my analogy of decentralized management may be imperfect, it is used here to stress the existence and interrelationships of forces that affect the setting of accounting standards. Alternatively, these forces may be likened to line-staff relationships, executive-legislative-judicial relationships, or partnership relationships. No matter what the analogy, power has been wielded by more than the APB alone. We need to study how the exercise of power affects the acceptability of accounting standards.

Working as Decentralized Management

The APB has been given great leeway to make many delicate decisions because it has been judged adequately objective and competent. However, the Board's freedom has definitely been constrained on several occasions. The scenario of the investment tax credit is well known, so it will not be repeated here. In that case, the APB and the SEC were united in their stand and they went down in flames together. The scenario of marketable securities is not well known, but it offers several lessons about how the APB contends with its environment.

The heart of the issue concerning marketable securities deals with when portfolio gains and losses should be recognized. There is a variety of views ranging from predominant present practice (whereby only realized gains and losses are included in income) to some version of spreading (whereby all gains and losses from changes in market prices are included in income but on some three-to-ten-year moving-average long-term yield basis) to a flow-through approach (whereby all gains and losses are included in income as the prices of marketable securities fluctuate from quarter to quarter).

Another set of issues concerns whether portfolio losses or gains belong in an income statement in the first place. Instead, some accountants believe that a two-statement approach is needed. If adopted, a separate statement of realized and unrealized gains would be used.

An even more fundamental issue is whether the controversy is much ado about nothing. That is, a growing body of academicians would maintain that if market values are disclosed in the balance sheet (as they are in the insurance industry), it makes no difference whether the related losses and gains are reported in the income statement as realized, on some spreading basis, or on a flow-through basis. Why? Because the essential data, market values, are already disclosed. Therefore, the aggregate investors are not fooled by how or when the related gains and losses affect reported income, if at all. (See Archibald, 1972: 22–30; Kaplan and Roll, 1972: 225–57; Beaver and Dukes, in press.)

The relative merits of the theoretical arguments are not germane here, but the history of the Board's deliberations is enlightening. An intensive study of this topic was begun in September 1968. Heavy interaction persisted between the APB and all interested parties, particularly representatives of the insurance industry, whose income statements would be dramatically affected by any new accounting standards. In May 1971 there was a two-day public hearing on the issues. (See Arthur Andersen, 1971.)

After about three years of spasmodic deliberations, the APB was ready to issue an exposure draft of an Opinion. The Board had narrowed its preferences to two methods using one income statement: either flow-through or spreading. In September 1971 the Board approved a draft favoring flow-through. The draft was to be "mini-exposed" to the SEC, the insurance industry, and others who had been actively involved. The intention of the Board was to have full public exposure of the Opinion after the October APB meeting.

The insurance companies were bitterly opposed to flow-through. They blitzkrieged Washington. The SEC, armed with its own preferences and buttressed by industry reactions, informed the APB that it could not support flow-through. At this point, flow-through was a dead duck because higher management (the SEC) had, in effect, overruled the APB.

At its October meeting, the APB again discussed the topic. Because flow-through was no longer an acceptable alternative, the Board changed its preferences to either spreading or a two-statement approach. The Board voted in favor of a two-statement approach, although strong voices were raised in support of spreading. In November, these alternatives were explored with the SEC and the insurance industry. At its December meeting, the Board was informed that the fire and casualty companies had also strongly objected to the spreading method. One potent spokesman for the SEC found some merit in the spreading method, but he informed the Board that the SEC would not *impose* it or any solution on an industry that was adamantly opposed to it. So spreading was dead.

The Board then discussed two alternatives: (1) some version of a two-statement method and (2) a modification of predominant current practice whereby all companies in all industries would show marketable securities at market value in the balance sheet, unrealized gains and losses in stockholders' equity, and only realized gains and losses in the income statement. However, the fire and casualty companies also vigorously opposed the two-statement method.

Note how the feasible alternatives changed in response to the likelihood of acceptability. The constraints became more binding as the months wore on:

September—flow-through or spreading

October—spreading or two-statement

December—two-statement or slight modification of status quo

Discussions of various versions of the December alternatives were renewed in early 1972. But the Board could not resolve the issues and the SEC was noncommittal on anything except "no flow-through." During the course of the discussions, the top managements of fifteen or twenty large insurance companies met together about the issue more than once and also with the SEC commissioners at least once.

An observer of a visit of Institute representatives to the SEC wrote to me that an SEC commissioner "asked the APB for a summary of the alternative methods together with the pros and cons of each. He also said that, once the SEC received this report, the SEC would tell the APB the parameters in which the APB could consider the subject. Presumably any method selected by the APB within these parameters would be acceptable to the SEC. . . . This event is perhaps the clearest demonstration of an SEC order to the APB that I can recall."

The marketable securities scenario was concluded by an APB Report to the SEC in March, 1972, that summarized the APB deliberations and the alternatives. However, the report offered no preferred solution.

Among the many inferences that can be made from this APB experience, three are notable here. First, this series of events is evidence that in relation to the SEC, the APB is not a "partner" but is a subordinate. Second, widespread industry hostility can constrict the feasible alternatives for setting standards. Third, the outlook for so-called fair value accounting is gloomy.

The failure of the APB to reach even an exposure draft stage for so obvious a candidate for fair value as marketable securities reinforces my pessimism about fair value as a goal over the next ten or twenty or more years. After all, if the fair value idea cannot be implemented for that category of assets, there is little practical hope for more radical schemes.

Obtaining Acceptance of Standards

How does a standards board attempt to market its product when it faces the constraints that are imposed directly by senior management and indirectly by customers? There are many general strategies, but consider the implications of three: (1) abdication, (2) confrontation, (3) incrementalism.

Complete abdication is an extreme alternative that is perceived as repugnant by most accountants. What would occur if accountants gave up their decentralized management status and assumed a submissive role to some governmental group similar to the Cost Accounting Standards Board? Who knows? Some (Sterling, 1973: 66; Moonitz, 1971: 344–45) have cited the possibility of enlightened governance that would be more clear-cut and less costly to the profession as a whole and to society in general. But most accountants evidently fear that unenlightened governance would result. They predict detailed, ponderous rules that would reduce the professional challenge of accounting, undermine the status of the profession, and fail to attract bright recruits to both practice and the universities.[1]

At the other extreme, the profession could take radical action to force confrontation on how accounting principles should be set. For example, suppose the Board voted to issue their Opinion on the investment tax credit that requires the deferral method, despite the recent Congressional legislation permitting latitude on accounting for the credit. Then, under the rules of the AICPA, public accounting firms would have to qualify their professional opinions for all clients using the flow-through method. Some idealists maintain that until accountants are ready to be that courageous, their independence will be tainted and their prestige will be limited. By being bold defenders of principle, accountants will force Congress and the Treasury to see the wisdom of letting the professionals set the accounting standards.

Most accountants probably favor a middle stance, which might be called incrementalism:

> Under the incremental approach, a policy-maker does not attempt to consider the whole range of hypothetical alternatives but limits his choice to a few that represent relatively small changes from the present state . . . because at most times "radically different" changes are not politically feasible. (Gerboth, 1972: 45) [2]

Despite existing constraints, these accountants believe that more progress can be made by some version of the current decentralized setup. To them, abdication is unthinkable. Similarly, confrontation is infeasible because of the high risk that any existing power will be recentralized. First, there is not enough unity within the profession itself to support bold moves. Second, outcries from industry will spur legislative action that will completely shut the private sector out from the throttles of power. Therefore, the profession should persist in pushing the constraints to see how binding they really are. Sometimes decentralized management will win a battle (for example, requiring the allocation of income taxes), but frequently it will lose. However, the most progress will be made when the Board judiciously uses its active role as a decentralized manager.

The informality of this decentralized setup and the uncertainty regarding acceptability often mean that constraints are unknown until some definite action occurs. On several occasions, the APB has attempted to discover the nature of the constraints by making early venturesome moves. The marketable securities scenario is an example; so is the full costing controversy in the petroleum industry. Another example is the board's early approach to the issue of business combinations. A preliminary draft of an Opinion was prepared that abolished pooling completely. (*Wall Street Journal*, Sept. 24, 1969: 10.) Its reception by industry and by many practitioners was unequivocally negative, and the SEC's attitude at best was neutral of likewise. So the Board retreated and was described by many critics as weak-willed. However, at least the Board tried to pinpoint the constraints by taking an activist stand with the hope that such would survive. Perhaps the APB could have avoided much criticism from practitioners and industry by being less brave from the start. At least the APB would not have appeared so vacillatory. But that posture would have engendered the criticism of excessive meekness from many parties. Of course, harsh words would be aimed at the Board from some important sources no matter what strategy it adopted.

2. PROBLEMS FACING THE FASB

My portrayal of behavioral patterns and authoritative structures for making accounting laws is a description, not a criticism. For example, within some limits I believe that industry and public accounting firms should have the freedom to state their case to governmental authorities. After all, as one SEC commissioner said: "Public officials must talk with people." Perhaps the present institutional structure is close to optimality. However, if the APB or FASB wants to win its points, it must contend with these imposing forces. More of us should see things as they are, not as we may wish them to be.

The euphoria surrounding the Financial Accounting Standards Board will be short-lived. The FASB will face intricate issues. Inherent complexity and great expectations are almost always conflicting terms. The same institutional and environmental problems that confronted the APB will still exist. Congress, the Treasury, the SEC, industry, and the public accounting profession are still there. If you picture the environment in a global sense, the APB has been replaced—but little else has changed.

Consider the comments of Leonard Savoie, who, as Executive Vice President of the AICPA, was directly involved in APB experiences:

> Can it be that the APB has been replaced not because of structural deficiencies but because of prevailing attitudes—attitudes within the public accounting profession and attitude of business?
>
> Is it possible that too many accountants and businessmen have been so determined to have their own way on matters of accounting principle that they preferred to bring down the structure rather than submit to an APB Opinion that impinged on their prerogatives?
>
> Although the APB's procedures for hearing all sides of controversial issues were substantially equivalent to the procedures recommended for the new FASB, is it possible that APB watchers have not been satisfied merely by communicating with APB?
>
> Let us look at some of the events of the last few years.
>
> In the case of certain proposed APB Opinions, opponents have issued press releases denouncing the APB, published briefs, circulated white papers, threatened to sue the APB, petitioned the SEC, asked the FPC for a ruling, sought Treasury Department intervention, asked Congress to put financial reporting flexibility into law.
>
> Will this happen to FASB?" (Savoie, 1972: 1)

How can the new structure better insure the general acceptability of FASB pronouncements? Many new provisions will help. Surely, the wider base of membership, the high-salaried full-time members, the independence of members from all other organizations, and the broad-based advisory council are features that should increase the likelihood of acceptability. On the other hand, the large accounting firms will no longer have a direct voice or vote. When the issues become torrid, will these firms be as inclined to accept the FASB pronouncements as well as they did the APB pronouncements?

Obviously, the pressures will not wither away. Gaining acceptance is a task of marketing or lobbying. The FASB is no more supreme in its stranglehold on power than the APB. The FASB needs strong voices in Washington. The tactics in 1971–1972 regarding the investment tax credit and marketable securities will indeed continue. (Leases got similar attention.) The sources of ultimate power such as Congress, the SEC, and Treasury will be buffeted by industry and practitioners. Therefore, some provision should be made at the outset for getting a stable of able spokesmen for FASB positions, individuals who will be listened to by commissioners, legislators, and cabinet members. Some of these individuals will be on the FASB, but some will not.

The FASB cannot depend solely on the impeccable logic of its Opinions to sway these ultimate sources of power. It must be equipped by the convincing credentials of its members and by their ability to sell their wares to the decision-makers in Washington. They must be articulate and persuasive as individuals and, in my view, they need professional help to represent their positions. The job, then, of the FASB is a twofold one of production and marketing: (1) to develop the best possible accounting standards, *and* (2) to see that such standards are accepted. The latter task is more formidable than the former. The ad hoc supplications that dotted the history of the APB are not enough.[3]

The new FASB structure has been created because its supporters perceive it as the best available means for setting accounting standards to benefit society as a whole. The lobbying effort probably should be a continuing one that stresses the principle of non-interference. The aim of such a strategy would be to convince Congress, the SEC and other powerful forces that the FASB is the premier group of experts on accounting standards. Furthermore, the reasoning would stress that, to benefit society at large, it is generally desirable to allow the experts to make the decisions without harassment. Lobbying may also have to be conducted on an issue-by-issue basis, but the long-run effort would be to persuade all affected parties that non-interference is the least costly way to benefit society as a whole.

The affected parties are not only the SEC and Congress. They include practicing accountants and financial executives. The FASB has been repeatedly cited as being the private sector's last chance for maintaining a direct role in setting accounting standards. The new Board should play this theme for all its worth. All interested parties should have an ample chance to voice their views as issues arise, but they should also be willing to accept the outcomes without devisive lament. These parties may maximize their immediate private good by undermining the work of the Board. Still, these short-run gains may come at the expense of society's collective good and may result in the eventual tearing down of the entire structure for setting standards. Therefore, in the long run, the affected parties may find it too costly to not accept the FASB decisions.

Of course, when specific issues reach a white heat, it is easy to ignore these long-run implications.[4] These issues are nearly always complicated: for example, each of two opposing views may be based on a plausible chain of reasoning.

3. CONCLUSION

This paper has described the marketing problems of the setting of accounting standards. The problems may be obvious, but they are not trivial. I have not raised these issues to voice a cynical or pessimistic view. On the contrary, I have focused upon them because I truly desire the successful implementation and operation of the new FASB. There is no visible alternative to keeping the function of setting accounting standards in private hands to the greatest extent possible. To be successful, we must recognize the political role of the new Board, the need to deal with pressures that will exist no matter what structure for setting standards is used—whether that structure be private, public, or some combination thereof.

In the 1960s and early 1970s researchers in accounting borrowed heavily from quantitative methods and the behavioral sciences. I hope that the 1970s see some concentration on the optimal methods for wielding accounting power in a democratic society. The literature of organizations, political action, social change, and social choice may be more closely related to the development of accounting standards than we have been willing to admit.[5] As Arrow (1963) states: "The notion of a 'democratic paralysis,' a failure to act due not to a desire for inaction but an inability to agree on the proper action, seems to me to deserve much further empirical, as well as theoretical, study."

More consideration might be given to the cost and value of information model and its implications for accounting standards, not only with respect to data-gathering costs, but also with respect to the costs of education of accountants, managers, and users regarding any suggested innovations. (See Feltham and Demski, 1970; and Demski, 1972.) In addition, what can we learn from social scientists about the theory and practice of policy making?[6]

In the tradition of articles by academicians, I end with a plea for more research. Given the FASB, are there better ways to obtain acceptability than accountants have used in the past? The political difficulties of setting accounting standards are not subordinate problems. How they are handled will affect the useful life of the FASB and, consequently, the useful life of the private sector's direct influence on accounting standards.

NOTES

1. For an example of such a prediction, see Burton (1969: 76–83).

2. Gerboth offers many references on the theory and practice of incrementalism.

3. For example, Steven S. Andreder (1972: 10) reports ". . . the Congressmen have taken an even more direct approach with the investment tax credit, despite efforts to head it off by the SEC and the Institute (which never got farther than a staff assistant to Rep. Wilbur Mills in presenting its case)."

4. See the letter by R. E. Pfenning (1972: 12–13). Pfenning, formerly chief financial officer of General Electric, criticizes the tactics of those who opposed the APB-proposed Opinion on the investment tax credit.

5. See Cartwright (1965); in particular, see his section on bases of power (28–39). Also see Cyert and March (1963: Chapter 6); Etzioni (1964: Chapter 8); Blau and Scott (1962: 59–86, 244–47); and Costello (1970: 161–68).

6. Charles A. Tritschler (1970) explores the problem of gaining acceptance of complex accounting innovations. Also see the references in Gerboth (1972).

REFERENCES

Andreder, Steven S. (1972) "Called to Account." *Barron's* (October 2).

Archibald, T. R. (1972) "Stock Market Reaction to Depreciation Switch Back." *Accounting Review* (January).

Arrow, Kenneth H. (1963) *Social Choice and Individual Values*, 2nd ed. New Haven, Connecticut: Yale University Press.

Arthur Andersen (1971) *APB Public Hearing on Accounting for Investments in Equity Securities Not Qualifying for the Equity Method, Cases in Public Practice.* Vol. 8. Chicago.

Beaver, William H. and Roland E. Dukes (in press) "Interperiod Tax Allocation and Depreciation Methods: Some Analytical and Empirical Results." *Accounting Review.*

Blau, Peter M. and W. Richard Scott (1962) *Formal Organizations.* San Francisco: Chandler.

Burton, John C. (ed.) (1969) *Corporate Financial Reporting: Conflicts and Challenges.* American Institute of Certified Public Accountants.

Burton, John C. (1973) interviewed in "Paper Shuffling and Economic Reality." *Journal of Accountancy* (January).

Cartwright, Dorwin (1965) "Influence, Leadership, and Control," pp. 1–48 in James G. March (ed.) *Handbook of Organizations.* Chicago: Rand McNally.

Costello, Timothy W. (1970) "Psychological Aspects: The Soft Side of Policy Formulation." *Policy Sciences* 1.

Cyert, Richard M. and James G. March (1963) *A Behavioral Theory of the Firm.* Englewood Cliffs, New Jersey: Prentice-Hall.

Demski, Joel S. (1972) "Choice Among Financial Accounting Alternatives." unpublished.

Etzioni, Amitai (1964) *Modern Organizations.* Englewood Cliffs, New Jersey: Prentice-Hall.

Feltham, Gerald A. and Joel S. Demski (1970) "The Use of Models in Information Evaluation." *Accounting Review* (October).

Gerboth, Dale L. (1972) "Muddling Through with the APB." *Journal of Accountancy* (May).

Horngren, Charles T. (1972) "Accounting Principles: Private or Public Sector?" *Journal of Accountancy* (May).

Kaplan, Robert and Richard Roll (1972) "Investor Evaluation of Accounting Information: Some Empirical Evidence." *Journal of Business* (April).

Moonitz, Maurice (1971) "The Accounting Principles Board Revisited." *New York Certified Public Accountant* (May).

Pfenning, R. E. (1972) letter in *Financial Executive* (June).

Savoie, Leonard M. (1972) Comments on David Solomon's "Financial Accounting Standards: Regulation or Self Regulation?" Stanford Business School (May).

Sterling, Robert R. (1973) "Accounting Power." *Journal of Accountancy* (January).

Tritschler, Charles A. (1970) "A Sociological Perspective on Accounting Innovation " *International Journal of Accounting* 5 (Spring): 39–67.

A Discussion of
Marketing Accounting Standards

Professor Horngren has presented a thoughtful statement concerning
the social and political environment that the FASB and our profession
must recognize, and the related implications for our profession to
maintain a viable role in establishing standards of financial accounting
and reporting. In my opinion, he is far more right than wrong in
the positions he espouses. This is, I am sure, because of his experiences
as an APB member, as an interested observer of the standard-setting
scene and as an intelligent and articulate academician.

Before we panic, however, and possibly reach the conclusion that
either our profession cannot have a lead position in the power structure
of establishing standards or that we should marshall an army of
"marketers" or "lobbyists," I would like for us to examine certain aspects
of Professor Horngren's paper and the environment he describes.

1. ORGANIZATION

Exhibit 1 of the paper presents an organization chart depicting the
institutional structure for establishing standards. This structure, as
depicted, omits certain key institutions, or power bases, and oversimpli-
fies the organizational relationships portrayed.

For example, Congress is shown in the top position on the chart,
thereby implying they have the top authority or power-position. Ignored
is the role of the office of the President. Both historically and currently
I believe and, in my opinion, Congress would agree, that the President
requires at least equal billing. Accepting this, this opens up, or recognizes,
a whole new avenue of impact on federal agencies which have had
relations with the APB, and prospectively that will have relations with
the FASB.

Further, there is no slot on the chart for the users of financial

*B.S. 1959, M.S. 1962, University of Kansas. CPA, Kansas, Illinois, et al. Managing
Partner, Chicago office, Arthur Young & Company.

statements. Granted this group is not as tightly institutionalized as the other groups shown; however, as Horngren notes in his paper, and as will be discussed later, this group is extremely important to the standard-setting process.

Concerning oversimplification, the organization chart portrays more clear-cut organizational relationships than actually exist, even if you accept the decentralized management concept that Horngren emphasized. To properly portray the inter-relationships requires adding more lines, since in actuality each of the organizational units has communication and persuasive interaction with each other unit. While this complicates the chart, the importance and impact of this interaction must be recognized.

Professor Horngren emphasizes the decentralized organization structure concept to support his argument that Congress and the SEC have ultimate authority over setting accounting standards, and degrades the partnership which many of us believe has in fact existed between the SEC and the sector of the private economy which sets standards. He supports his point concerning the ultimate authority of the SEC with certain examples, i.e., the investment credit and marketable securities issues.

In my opinion, he errs or at least states this position too strongly. While we grant that the SEC has the statutory authority to set accounting standards (for public companies only, we might note), we should not underestimate the tremendous influence the business and financial community has over the SEC in its utilization of that authority. Our financial community includes top financial executives and chief executive officers, with viewpoints to which the Administration and Congress are sensitive. Further, it includes commercial and investment bankers whose overall importance to the economy is well recognized by these parties. These factors have a very real tempering influence, directly or indirectly, on the SEC, thereby reducing the seemingly all-powerful statutory authority.

While I do not ignore the examples given in the paper to illustrate the perceived dominance of the SEC, neither do I believe these compel one to conclude that a partnership does not in actuality exist. As in marriage, each partner on occasion finds it necessary to prod or criticize the other. This does not mean the mutual respect and working relationship do not exist or are not sound.

While I disagree with certain aspects of the organizational or power structure as described by Professor Horngren, I do agree with his statements that "power has been wielded by more than the APB alone" and that "we need to study how the exercise of power affects the acceptability of accounting standards."

2. STANDARD SETTING STRATEGY

Professor Horngren poses a question in his paper concerning obtaining acceptance of standards by asking, "How does a standards board attempt to market its product when it faces the constraints that are imposed directly by senior management and indirectly by customers?" By senior management, I believe he is talking primarily about the SEC, and by customers is including issuers and users of financial statements, in addition to accounting practitioners.

There seems to be a basic premise throughout the article, and somewhat indicated by the phrasing of this question, that there are basic accounting truths that need only be found, or decided upon, by a standards board, with the major problem then being to "market their product," i.e., to gain acceptance of these truths or standards. This line of reasoning seems to consider (1) establishment of standards, and (2) obtaining acceptance of standards, as independent of each other. This I question.

Within a reasonable theoretical framework, it seems to me that worthwhile accounting standards are those that provide useful data to the *users* of financial statements, *not* to the originators or the accounting practitioner. If this be the case, then a major part of the process of setting standards is to obtain, in a meaningful way, participation of users in the standard-setting process.

Following this line of reasoning, we need not concern ourselves unduly with the three strategies of obtaining acceptance that Horngren discusses, namely (1) abdication, (2) confrontation, or (3) incrementalism. Rather, it seems that a participatory process by interested parties is the only appropriate strategy—incrementalism, if you will, but with a less negative tone.

To me this is the only viable process in the social/political environment in which we exist. We live in an environment—as children vs. parents, as professors vs. students, as partners in accounting firms, as top managers in industry—in which the decisions that are reached are not determined unilaterally. The views of each side must increasingly be listened to and given adequate consideration. Dictatorship is not a viable environment. Thus, if the process of interaction between interested parties in the setting of accounting standards—the sharing of power, if you will—leads to incrementalism in the establishment of accounting standards, so be it. One important result will be that decisions reached will be "our" decisions rather than "yours," and they should be respected for longer periods of time.

3. FASB

I do not minimize the task of the FASB—they do have a formidable job. And they have a significant marketing task. This marketing effort should include stressing the "principle of non-interference" to all interested parties, as discussed by Professor Horngren, in terms of their not trying to make an end-run around the standard-setting procedure, which includes the FASB as the focal point. Equally important is emphasis by the FASB on obtaining the participation of all segments of the financial community, of which the FASB is a joint effort, and productively interacting with the various governmental agencies and entities, who, to my knowledge, back the FASB. By having their participation, by sharing power with them, I believe the FASB has a high probability of retaining and consolidating its power and leadership role. Thus, I believe that through the FASB structure and envisioned approach, meaningful progress will be made in establishing financial accounting and reporting standards, and having them accepted by all interested parties.

There is no question, however, that as Horngren states, the FASB, and others interested in the standard-setting process, must understand the political and social environment in which they must operate. Significant effort by the FASB must be directed to continually monitoring this environment and refining, as necessary, the strategic policies and approaches to be used in gaining and retaining the participation and support of all entities interested in financial accounting and reporting.

Discussion

Horngren. I just have two brief comments. One, I don't think my paper said anything about basic truths. The job of developing a standard, whatever it might be, and the marketing of that standard are interchangeable, interdependent activities. Neither can be done in isolation. The search for basic truths may be a good place to start, but the trouble is that everybody's perception of truth differs. In regard to the criticism of the chart, I grant that it is an oversimplification and that the users—the practitioners, the general public, and the financial executives—certainly are threaded through the paper as being the parties who have to do the accepting of the standards. Even though they may not be on the chart, they certainly are very visible in almost every rule.

Revsine. This is directed to Professor Horngren. Given the kinds of power relationships that you were describing regarding industries that would be affected by accounting changes, does this imply that FASB pronouncements are likely to involve relatively innocuous kinds of accounting changes that would maintain the broadest possible latitude for management in terms of discretionary accounting income? In other words, do you think that as a consequence of these relationships we might anticipate only trivial kinds of changes from the FASB?

Horngren. It depends upon how skillful they are in developing standards that are acceptable and in marketing them. It was cited yesterday that the allocation of income tax was a major victory for a standard-setting group in the middle sixties in the face of widespread opposition from many industries. There was some conjecture as to how we put that one over. That certainly is a dramatic change and a reduction of the discretion. It depends upon how well they developed the standards in relation to the likelihood of acceptability. I do think that to come out with pre-expectations like those that accompanied the creation of the Accounting Principles Board (that we are going to set up a brand new framework and go on weekend retreats and come out with a brand new set of principles—onward and upward with replacement cost accounting) is fantasy. I think we ought to reduce our expectations. Why? Because we are in a democratic society. If we want to change this democratic society altogether, that is another issue.

Revsine. But surely the interested management groups are well aware of the potential impact that FASB pronouncements would have on their latitude. I am confused with regard to the marketing activities you are talking about. It seems to me that marketability implies a standard group should limit itself to innocuous, unimportant changes that are likely to meet with great acceptance at the inception. If that is the case, why bother?

Horngren. You can predict, by and large—and if I am too harsh it is because I have a general propensity for exaggeration—that financial executives in the aggregate will oppose almost anything that a standards group comes out with. If you want to generalize, that is a currently useful generalization. Therefore, the question is whether you can get support of the SEC and withstand the battering of the financial executives and other forces sufficiently to put it over. Leonard Savoie described the banking situation yesterday. That was an example of quite a dramatic change as far as the banking industry was concerned. It was put over despite their opposition.

Gerboth. I have some objection to the emphasis upon marketing of accounting ideas, accounting standards—the idea that we must direct our efforts toward getting acceptance of our decisions. I think that tends to emphasize the battle more than the objective. The objective is to obtain some financial standards that would be acceptable and useful for the business community, regardless of whether that means that everyone else accept our ideas—which is I think what you emphasized in the marketing analogy—or whether we gain cooperation, which may mean that we have to give up some of our pet points to someone else. I think the latter is a better way of looking at it.

Horngren. This is something that has disturbed me enormously about the criticism of the APB activity. What is going to be different about the FASB activity? I think the APB, in its operations, at least in the last five or six years that I have been closely acquainted with it, has engaged in a participatory process throughout. They have participated with the SEC *and* with interested parties from industry very actively. This new board is going to do the same thing. I don't see any change between the two.

Vanatta. I think that there is a bit of difference because the APB was not perceived by many people to have this full openness and the participatory process. That seems to me to be one of the hallmarks of the FASB. We are going into that new process or changed structure. This is why I was stressing the importance of continuing that and retaining it. If you like, the FASB is starting off with credibility, hopefully, and it is a problem of maintaining it.

Savoie. There is nothing about their participatory process that is much different from what the APB has been doing for years. They have been inviting comment, they have been exposing, they have been dealing with every conceivable interested group.

Defliese. Everyone who attended the oil and gas hearing we had would certainly recognize the full participation of all interested parties.

Vanatta. But that was a couple of years ago. The APB was established in 1959. I think it was in some of those early formative years that some of the impressions were created. Once you get that impression it is difficult to overcome it. When was the first public hearing of the APB?

Defliese. Seven years ago.

Dyckman. I would like to address a question, if I could, not to the speakers, but rather to some of the people in the profession who are here today and who occupy a rather significant position. Chuck has reported a couple of times about the importance that he put on the willingness of people to accept some of the pronouncements of the FASB on significant issues, regardless of the extent to which they find them compatible with their own reasoning, their own logic, and their own desires. I am sure he means that acceptance extends not only to the profession, but also to others who will have to work with them. We only have the profession here today. Do you people who are sitting here believe that that is likely to happen?

Kapnick. First of all, I think if we are going to address ourselves to that—and I hadn't intended to bring this in at this point—but I think you have to back off from what Chuck said for a moment and look at it in more of a philosophical approach. Anyway, I do. As far as the FASB is concerned, Arthur Andersen & Company will follow the rules as outlined by the FASB. We followed the rules of the APB, as did all major accounting firms. When you ask, will we back off from criticism, will we back off from analyzing the issues publicly, will we back off from—even though as Chuck said, we will never get fair value—promoting fair value? The answer is "no." We aren't going to back off.

I think that we have to recognize in the accounting profession that we have grown up, that we can have differences of opinion, and that we can articulate those differences of opinion. Accounting is never fixed and concrete. Ten years ago how many people were worried about leases? And yet today, all of us are concerned about leases. What is the right accounting? We are going to have to argue these out, and we are going to have to argue them out in public, but that does not mean a lack of support. I can't see, if the SEC has to overrule the FASB, that that is going to destroy the FASB. I think that if they insist on another rule these are the things that will happen. We have to go on from there.

Chapin. My views are not crystal clear on this point. It seems to me that the people who structured the FASB provided a vehicle for input of thought by setting up the advisory group. I also believe, although we may honestly believe that criticism is healthy (and it is to a point), we do have a new structure, and it is in delicate health, and it can be destroyed by excessive criticism or criticism that appears negative. I think that we should take a new look at the organization and try to find a better way to input knowledge into that organization, because I think we can destroy the FASB if we become too aggressive in presenting our own views of what accounting principles should be.

Linowes. I think that when we discuss marketing and accounting standards, we do an injustice to ourselves when we neglect to emphasize the broader aspect of what we are actually performing, and what we should be marketing; that is, the nature of the accounting service and the attest function. There is so much subjectivity that enters into our end product. I don't think we have gotten across sufficiently to the public the lack of precision in what we do. It is basic to our work. I think it is critical because we don't know who the recipients of our service may be next year. Harvey Kapnick made reference to the fact that from what happened five years ago, you could not predict what was going to happen today in a specific instance. We take too narrow an approach to our place in our economy when we just deal with one particular institution that happens to be created right now, whether it is an FASB or an APB. Our place in our economy is broad, and I think we do a disservice to ourselves and to society if we don't interpret, especially in a marketing seminar, this aspect of what we are all about.

Long. I have an observation for Tom, which is intended to broaden our perspective of this criticism issue. What about accounting professors, Tom? If you are to accept the proposition that it would be wrong to criticize, then if the FASB comes out and says, "Historical cost is the way," are accounting professors supposed to lay down their pens and quit talking about fair-value accounting or other concepts? I think there is a much broader aspect to the criticism issue than simply the public practitioners. The second observation I have is, that if we really think that criticism of the pronouncements of the FASB is going to deal the death blow, then we are dead, because pronouncements of the FASB will be criticized—they will be *strongly* criticized—and it will be these other forces that Chuck talks about in his paper who are quite likely to get very vocal about a lot of the issues that the FASB will report.

Mautz. I agree with a good deal of what we have heard from Chuck on the political nature of the process of setting standards. It really is a political process. I want to follow up on the point that Dale Gerboth made about the emphasis on marketing being unfortunate. I don't think I would send those people down to Washington to try to sell the decisions after they are made. I think I would send them out into the field to try to find out in advance what kind of decisions we ought to make.

I speak here with some experience. The Cost Accounting Standards Board is involved in the same sort of thing that the FASB will be involved in, on a much narrower scale, perhaps a much less difficult assignment, but one in which there is considerable interest all the same. We tried very hard at the very beginning to meet the kind of point that Chet Vanatta has made, that you establish a reputation for responsiveness, participation, and willingness to listen. You can do that with hearings of course, but we go well beyond that. Our people get out into the plants and into industry and find out how you people see this problem. Knowing that we are going to have a standard, say, on the allocation of G and A expenses to segments, how do you people see that problem? We are out talking to these folks, we send them questionnaires, we get discussion groups together, do everything we can, we go through a lengthy exposure process. We try to balance two things: our research is intended to determine first what theoretically should be—say we adopt a full-costing concept; then, second, how far we can realistically push it at this time. You have to decide what is theoretically best and then hope it is politically feasible. You try to get these two together. That is the reason for all the research, and that is why we have all those people working.

We get letters from Congress. Sandy, I think we may get more than you indicated you get. You should see my mail. Those letters don't tell us what to do. They are letters from a congressman or a senator which say, "I have received this kind of a complaint from one of my constituents. How do you suggest I answer it?" In effect, he is saying, "How would you answer it if you were in my position?" And we had darn well better be in a position to answer it before he gets the letter rather than after. The best answer we can give is to detail for him the very lengthy procedure that we have gone through with our staff before we came to our decision. I don't think there is any question that if we couldn't respond by saying, "We have given people every opportunity to express themselves, we have gone to them, we have invited their views, we have tried to get the issues exposed and resolved in such a way that there is acceptance," we would be in bad shape.

I know the term "general acceptance" is on the program this afternoon, and it may be a bad term where it is used, but the notion of general acceptance is absolutely vital to the establishment of principles. I have been using a phrase lately that comes very close to what Chuck was saying earlier, that in a democracy, there is no authority strong enough to establish a principle that is unacceptable. I think that holds for the CASB and the FASB. There are politically astute people who will get done what they want to get done. Unless you find a way to determine just how far you can go with acceptability, you aren't going to get very far. So I would take those people, and instead of acting dismayed, I would do a little marketing research first. I think it would be much more successful.

Defliese. I think it should be obvious to everyone that the demise of the APB is directly attributable to the carping of vicious critics and the vitriolic fashion with which this was developed within the profession. By that I mean both the academic as well as the practicing profession. It is one thing to produce an input, to contribute to the literature, to point to better ways, and another thing to tear down the edifice that is involved. This is largely the result of the fact that in many cases the ideas of people have not been accepted by the Board, and the criticism emerged almost before they were able to be implemented. This has to be dealt with in a more professional vein than it has been if the FASB is going to survive. If the same program develops, it will go down quickly. The press is quick to pick up controversy. If we go to the press with our views that the Board is not doing the job it should be doing, it will die within a few years.

I think we have to deal with it as professionals. I certainly have not agreed with everything the Board has published. Although I have dissented to only one opinion, there are many aspects of the other opinions that I have disagreed with and yet did not either dissent or qualify an assent because I subscribe to the incremental concept that was referred to earlier. Many people have not subscribed to that and have dissented purely on the basis that this does not go the whole way that needs to be gone in order to get the job done. We have to inch up on this and get the job done as easily as we possibly can with the least turmoil.

Chuck referred to the tax allocation opinion as being a dramatic success of the Board. As much as I would like to lay claim to that, I would say it is not true. The fact remains that at that point, tax allocation was almost universally accepted. All we were doing was codifying it and attempting to sift out some of the conflicting theories concerning it. Apart from one or two firms, this was something that was well accepted. Once it was put into effect, it did not cause a radical change, or have a radical effect, upon those who were involved. It demonstrates, however, how you can make progress through this incremental fashion and yet appear to be doing a tremendous job. We did the same thing with pension costs. Many people refer to that as being dramatic. Frankly, it didn't do half the job that it should have done. That was even recognized within the Opinion, since it says it is "transitional." I would hope that every opinion would be considered to be transitional. We are never going to get this job done completely. We have to do our homework in advance. We have to make sure that the Board is fully apprised of our viewpoints. We have to go about it professionally, make the input, but once the decision is made—and I am referring to both segments of the profession—we have to live with it before we start tearing it down. We must see what progress is being made before we criticize it.

Stettler. Perhaps what both Phil and Bob are saying is that this is partly a matter of timing, at any rate. One of the difficulties that the APB had was that it would take a tentative position, and then if they refused to give on that position, people felt that their views were never considered.

Defliese. I was referring in general to the exposure process, and here again there has been a constant criticism on the part of the press, naturally stimulated by a lot of people within the profession, that the Board backs down every time it changes a draft that it exposed. For what other purpose do we expose but to recognize the views of others and give cognizance to what needs to be done? If the FASB exposes a draft and then changes it radically afterwards, is the same criticism going to emerge and tear down the temple? Are we going to say, "They're backing down already?" We have to be more professional about it.

Holstrum. I have a question for Chuck Horngren. In your paper you have raised the idea of research that might be useful to the Financial Accounting Standards Board in understanding your marketing process. This is an intriguing idea, and I would be interested in hearing if you have some reasonably specific ideas as to what this kind of research might be and how it might help.

Horngren. You note that I had a very short passage on that giving some leads as to where to go. It is something that I would like to pursue. At this point I am describing a problem and saying, "We had better learn more about it." Accountants generally aren't very well educated or experienced in the political arena. Clearly, we are in the political arena, and maybe we ought to get educated. That is what I am saying, and I am just as uneducated as most of the rest of us in this connection. So I am saying, "Let's do something." But I don't know what to do. I don't know anything about it.

Miller. I didn't intend to raise a question. I am just confirming and reacting to something that Phil said. It has been my experience, or observation at least, that it would have been helpful if the Board, or the predecessor committee on Accounting Procedure, could have some-how differentiated between whether they were engaged in a confirming process in contrast to a leadership role. In the former, where a consensus already existed, that would be one type of activity where the incremen-talism is in different dimensions and the effective date has different consequences. I have always felt that if you are trying to take a leadership role, then the effective date ought to be pretty liberal, giving people time to adjust their budgets and their sights according to what the impact might be on earnings per share and on decisions, and things of this sort. I believe an awful lot of the static has come from the cases where you were involved in leadership, although maybe incremen-tal leadership, and you didn't take a more realistic, sympathetic view of the effective date. This is one thing I hope maybe the Standards Board might consider in its deliberations.

Burton. There are problems, of course, in effective dates, where the time horizon can become quite long. Say that you can bring out something in January and you don't want it to become effective before the following year end, you are talking two or three years in terms of when it is going to be reflected in financial statements. In today's environment, that is a long time.

Miller. When you are my age, three or four years isn't very long. I will gladly accept three years for an effective date and believe that many times the profession would be further ahead than if it said, "Now we have acted on it; we have to put it into effect right away." I just wish more attention were given to the effective date to permit people to adjust and accommodate. I believe management is entitled to ample time to adjust and modify its game plan to the new ground rules.

CHAPTER 9

Accounting Attitudes

LEONARD M. SAVOIE*

The accounting profession is a young, vigorous, growing profession, filled with great opportunities but beset with great inner turmoil. Throughout this century the profession has experienced rapid growth while at the same time it has harbored unresolved conflicts of the most basic nature—conflicts about the authorities and responsibilities of those practicing in the profession and conflicts about the determination of professional standards.

In seeking resolution of these conflicts, I suggest we examine the behavioral setting of the profession. As I am not a behavioral scientist, I express my views only as an accountant. I believe that prevailing attitudes of individuals and organizations often inhibit rather than foster attainment of their stated goals. In addition, actions are often inconsistent with professed attitudes, thus leading to an institutional setting different from that desired.

Broad Standards vs. Detailed Rules

Accountants often express a preference for professional standards of a broad general nature which permit the free exercise of professional judgment in a manner appropriate in the circumstances. Yet most actions, individually and collectively, lead to the development of increasingly detailed rules.

*B.S. 1946, University of Illinois. CPA, Illinois. Vice President and Controller, Clark Equipment Company, Buchanan, Michigan. Dickinson Fellow, Harvard Business School, 1962–63. Member, Professional Advisory Board, Department of Accountancy, University of Illinois. Contributor to business and accounting periodicals.

Accountants deplore the thought of financial accounting rules' attaining the volume and complexity of the Internal Revenue Code and Regulations, but rule-making bodies are moving rapidly in that direction. Accounting Principles Board Opinions are increasingly complex and detailed. They have been codified in a loose-leaf service and supplemented by lengthy interpretations. Statements on Auditing Procedure are also becoming thicker and more detailed; soon they will be codified. Securities and Exchange Commission Accounting Series Releases are being issued more frequently. The Cost Accounting Standards Board is writing detailed cost accounting rules.

In the light of expressed preferences for broad general standards, why are detailed rules proliferating? I believe actions of the profession and business demonstrate that broad standards are not enforceable whereas detailed rules are enforceable, and that accountants want the protection provided by detailed rules.

A good example of an unenforceable standard lies in Paragraph 33 of APB Opinion No. 9, issued in December 1966. In one sentence, the APB introduced the principle of "residual securities" for the purpose of computing earnings per share. Under this principle, an outstanding security deriving a major portion of its value from its common stock characteristics should be considered a "residual security" and not a "senior security" for purposes of computing earnings per share. This Opinion was issued at a time when imaginative new securities were being created, often for the main purpose of improving reported earnings per share. Attitudes of businessmen and professional accountants were not admirable in this case. Before the ink was dry on Opinion No. 9, a number of them gave virtuoso performances in avoiding residual securities, while still boosting earnings per share. This forced the APB into a reconsideration of earnings per share. In May 1969, APB Opinion No. 15 was issued, containing sixty-one pages of detailed rules on common stock equivalents and related matters on earnings per share, much of which replaced the one-sentence principle on residual securities in Opinion No. 9.

Detailed rules are made to plug loopholes inherent in broad general standards. In addition, detailed rules are sometimes thought to provide a safe haven for an accountant who follows them. In law suits against accountants, the defendant typically seeks to establish as a defense his adherence to professional standards.

The accounting profession has for years been trying to establish through professional pronouncements and court decisions that accountants should be held to the standards of the profession and not to some unknown lay standard of fairness developed after the fact. Each attempt to do so only serves to heighten the distinction between professional standards and fair presentation. In seeking a defense behind professional standards, the profession has broadened the possibility of being judged by unspecified lay standards of fairness.

Professor Sterling presents ample evidence that the responsibility of the accountant far outweighs his authority. He states that the ways to correct this imbalance are to increase the authority or decrease the responsibility. The accounting profession seems to oppose an increase in authority and favor a decrease in responsibility. Statements on Auditing Procedures often seem to be designed to reduce responsibility—to provide a rule which, if followed, will free the accountant of further responsibility. Much the same design appears to be built into Accounting Principles Board Opinions.

1. PUBLIC PROTECTION VS. MEMBER PROTECTION

The new code of professional ethics of the American Institute of Certified Public Accountants begins with this statement, "A distinguishing mark of a professional is his acceptance of responsibility to the public." Accountants often express the view that broad general ethical standards are needed rather than detailed rules and regulations. Yet the new code recognizes that only specific rules of conduct can be enforced. I believe that attitudes in the profession limit the effectiveness of the entire code and work toward substitution of detailed laws which are really enforceable.

Great stock is placed in the Institute's Code of Professional Ethics. CPAs point with pride to this Code and enforcement of it as evidence of high standards of professional conduct. The Code is a sound basis for professional practice. It is constantly being improved, a major revision having been adopted in January 1973. This ethics Code is probably as good as, or better than, that of most major professional organizations. But how effective is a code of ethics in providing public protection?

Most ethics codes are designed first to protect members from outsiders, second to protect members from each other and third to protect the public from unethical members. The AICPA Code of Professional Ethics is enforced quite effectively in matters dealing with protection of members. But disciplinary machinery works very slowly in matters affecting the public.

Enforcement of technical standards through the Code of Ethics is difficult in most circumstances and impossible in some circumstances. The most widely publicized cases of alleged violation of technical standards involve lawsuits against individual accountants and their accounting firms, usually one of the Big Eight firms. Damage claims in millions of dollars have become commonplace. In such a case the Institute's disciplinary procedures are ineffective. The defendants will not provide information to the Institute's Ethics Division as long as legal actions are pending, on the ground that release of information and possible Institute action on it may jeopardize their position in the lawsuit. The Institute cannot, or at least does not, take action until the defendant's last right of appeal in the courts has been exhausted, and this may be eight or ten years after the alleged violation of technical standards. Enforcement of the Code of Professional Ethics at this point is anticlimactic and trivial. The worst sanction under the code is expulsion from membership in the Institute, which is seldom imposed. When expulsion does occur, it usually is a mild discipline compared with that already meted out by the court.

Thus, in matters of major importance, laws and the courts provide the public with protection as to competence and technical standards of accountants. Self-regulation through the Code of Professional Ethics cannot do this.

This social and institutional setting makes the accounting profession appear defensive of its members and unmindful of public protection, quite the reverse of what the profession wants.

When an accountant is involved in a scandal, the public may view his performance in terms of carelessness, poor judgment, dereliction of duty or fraud. But the accounting profession seems to unite and associate itself with that performance, regardless of how tarnished it may appear to the public. The profession closes ranks and seeks to protect its wounded member instead of being indignant that a fellow member would so harm the reputation of the profession. It is no wonder that the public thinks the profession protects itself rather than the public.

One notable issue brought together a common concern for members of the accounting profession and for the public. In 1971 the SEC issued a rule calling for registered companies to notify it of a change in accountants and to file a letter for the public record stating whether the change involved a disagreement over accounting principles. This rule was aimed at stopping the practice of "shopping for accounting principles." It was designed to protect the public from inferior accounting principles and to protect accounting firms from unscrupulous competitors, although protection may come after the fact and merely serve to deter future actions of a similar nature.

To accomplish this, the accounting profession had to ask the SEC to make a rule, for the profession lacked authority to cope with the problem. That such a rule was sought is an indication of the intensity of competition in the accounting profession.

Changes in accountants reported under the rule raise questions about the attitudes of various accountants toward accounting principles. For each accountant displaced because he took a stand on accounting principles, there is a newly appointed accountant whose views on the same principles may not be revealed for some time. Until revealed, public suspicions may be aroused that the new accountant may be taking a more lenient position on accounting principles than his predecessor.

2. SETTING ACCOUNTING STANDARDS

The function of setting accounting principles, or accounting standards, to use the fashionable terms, presents an interesting area for the study of behavioral patterns. Let us start with the question which the Wheat Committee said overshadows all others, "Should the task remain the responsibility of the private sector or should it be taken over by a governmental body?" This is the one proposition for which, surprisingly, we have nearly unanimous agreement: Accounting standards should be set in the private sector; allowing this function to slip into the public sector would be detrimental to interests of the public, business and the accounting profession.

Alleged disadvantages of transferring the standard-setting function to the public sector are that government agencies would be more susceptible to political pressures than private bodies, government agencies would be inflexible and would lack responsiveness to the needs of investors, such a development would inevitably sap the vitality of the accounting profession, and a government agency's rules might not cover all organizations and therefore could involve coexistence of two or more sets of accounting standards.

In the past I, too, have embraced the foregoing conventional wisdom. For sentimental reasons I still prefer to see accounting standards set in the private sector, but I can no longer advocate this position with great conviction. My reasons are that standards are now being determined largely in the public sector and inevitably the function will be taken over completely by the public sector.

To support that statement, let me refer to recent Securities and Exchange Commission actions. In the last year, while the APB issued six Opinions and exposed four proposed Opinions, the SEC issued fifteen Accounting Series Releases of general applicability and exposed four proposed Releases. These Releases are sprinkled with references to APB Opinions, often in a way that modifies or extends the Opinion. One Release "encourages" the AICPA committee on Insurance Accounting and Auditing to define appropriate accounting for catastrophe reserves. Another release "urges" the new Financial Accounting Standards Board to place high on its agenda for consideration early in 1973 the subject of accounting for leases with lessors without independent economic substance.

Still another Release (ASR No. 138) dated January 12, 1973, calls for more detailed disclosure of extraordinary items than required by APB Opinion No. 9 and introduces for similar disclosure two new terms of art, "other material charges and credits to income of an unusual nature" and "material provisions for loss." This Release came shortly after the APB's December exposure of a proposed Opinion on Reporting the Effects of Extraordinary Events and Transactions, which would provide more definitive criteria for determining extraordinary items and would specify disclosure requirements for such items and for newly designated "unusual or nonrecurring items." The APB Opinion, when issued, surely will be anticlimactic and, unless it embraces the disclosures called for by the SEC, we will be faced with coexisting standards or more accurately—coexisting detailed rules.

A December 1972 proposed amendment to Regulation S-X calls for disclosure of reasons for and amounts of differences in income tax expense from an amount calculated by multiplying the U.S. corporate income tax rate by the income before tax.

Another December 1972 proposed amendment to Regulation S-X calling for disclosure of significant accounting policies would take a quantum leap from the base provided by APB Opinion No. 22 on the same subject. The APB Opinion was issued in April 1972 but I call it the best idea of 1932, for what was when George O. May was advocating it as appropriate for that stage of development of financial reporting. Now the SEC proposal would require disclosure, where significant, of an estimate of the dollar impact on net income of use of the principle followed as compared to alternative acceptable principles:

1. When the company uses more than one accounting principle in reporting similar kinds of transactions; or
2. When the company has changed its accounting principles in the past two years, or
3. When the principle used is not the prevailing principle used by companies in the same industry.

As examples of such situations, the SEC gives FIFO and LIFO inventory valuation methods, straight line and accelerated depreciation, and full cost accounting and individual property cost accounting in the petroleum industry. As these disclosures often are either difficult or impossible to make, the proposal may or may not be adopted in this form.

There are other recent SEC proposals, but those I have cited reveal where the power and direction lie for setting accounting standards.

Furthermore the SEC has been accelerating its pace in use of this power, both to issue its own rules and to goad the APB into action. Its rules are now being issued by the chief financial analyst, who occupies a newly created position, as well as by the chief accountant. Although the SEC is limiting its own rules to matters of disclosure, the proposal on alternative acceptable principles, if adopted, may have the practical effect of eliminating some accounting methods.

SEC spokesmen frequently state that they do not want to set accounting standards, that they want the accounting profession to do the job. For example, former SEC Chairman William Casey said recently:

> The accounting profession has undertaken a renewed effort to develop uniform accounting standards. The Commission, believing that accounting standards should be set in the private sector, intends to fully support the profession in achieving it.

Their actions, however, are not consistent with their stated objectives. Many of us have known that from the beginning the APB could not take a position without getting SEC approval. On the other hand, the SEC can and often does issue a release without consulting the APB. Communication between the APB and the SEC can be a one-way street.

Now all of us may read in the daily newspapers a blow-by-blow description of what the APB wants and their likelihood of getting it past the SEC. For example, progress on the highly controversial audit guide on land development companies was reported in the press almost daily. The APB held out for and got SEC acquiescence for accrual accounting over the SEC's preference for installment accounting. But this should not be taken as an indication that the APB has the power of self-determination. It may be one small concession to preserve, in the view of some observers, the cherished notion that accounting standards are set in the private sector.

The SEC has shown a keen sense of strategy in other ways. After extolling the virtues of profit forecasts for many months, the SEC stated it would issue a Release "permitting" profit forecasts to be included in prospectuses. It does not require them. Permissiveness is easier to accept than absolute requirement. Few can protest if left with a free choice. Yet I wonder how free the choice will be if underwriters insist on exercising that free choice, as I predict they will. In these conditions profit forecasts would become a virtual requirement in prospectuses, but unhappy managements and accountants would find it hard to criticize the SEC rule, which is only permissive.

The SEC occupies a dominant position in determining accounting standards and the APB a subordinate one. With the transition under way from the APB to the new Financial Accounting Standards Board, we should examine the organizational relationships that can be expected under the new structure. In my view, the only change is a direct substitution of the FASB for the APB. The FASB will have the identical relationship with the SEC that the APB now has. That is, the SEC will be dominant and the FASB will be subordinate.

The securities laws give the SEC the authority to make rules and regulations regarding accounting and financial statements. The APB has no such legislative authority. The FASB has no such legislative authority. The Wheat Committee considered but rejected the proposal that a board be established by law as an official self-regulatory agency.

Therefore, we can expect the SEC to continue to use the private sector body, soon to be the FASB, for doing the research and detailed rule-making within parameters set by the SEC. This is a convenient arrangement for the SEC. It permits the SEC to function with a small accounting staff while enjoying the extensive expert services of the private sector Board. This arrangement also diverts almost all criticism and some pressures to the Board. The SEC has good reason to want to continue this arrangement. But there is no assurance that circumstances will always permit this arrangement or that future commissioners will be pleased with it.

With the accounting profession and business united in the desire to have accounting standards set in the private sector, why has this function moved more and more into the public sector? I believe this has resulted from behavioral patterns that are inconsistent with the stated goal.

In business there seems to be a craving for simpler days when there were fewer rules and regulations—days before a huge federal bureaucracy regulated virtually every phase of business. Yet where problems arise which affect the public interest, regulation often is the only answer. Business has had a rather consistent record of opposing most new regulatory incursions. But we have learned to live with them and for the most part would find it difficult to live without them. The surprising thing is that accounting regulation has been so slow in coming.

When the APB was formed, first efforts were directed at broad postulates and principles of accounting. Many people refused to accept the APB as a rule-making body. Also, many people, including some who were most dedicated to a private sector body, refused to accept the authority of the new APB's Opinions. Although attitudes shifted during the APB's stormy existence, the failure of business and the accounting profession to accept the authority of APB rules and regulations is the main reason its function has moved further into the public sector. A continuation of this attitude will assure the FASB an even stormier and shorter existence.

In a field where there are no eternal verities, differences of opinion will abound. In accounting, there has been no bashfulness in expressing opinions which differ from those of the profession's rule-makers.

The APB has been unable to solve controversial issues. On any such issue, a decision is bound to displease some. On an occasional issue, any decision is bound to displease all. By their actions and attitudes, businessmen and professional accountants seem to be saying, "We want accounting rules to be set in the private sector only if we agree with the rules."

3. UNRESOLVED ISSUES

A review of some recent rule-making attempts reveals this pattern all too clearly. The APB was making good progress and gaining in stature and public respect in 1969 when it began to consider the subject of business combinations. This was a highly controversial and emotion-charged issue. After taking an initial unequivocal position based on principle, which would have ruled out pooling-of-interests accounting, the APB was hit by intense pressures to back away from that position. As the months went by and pressures mounted, the APB backed down step by step to a weak position under which poolings remain alive and well and living in the United States today. Industry and the accounting profession joined in fighting the APB. Some groups wrote to key congressional committees suggesting this subject should more appropriately be left to the legislative and regulatory functions of the federal government. Others threatened to sue the APB if the Opinion was issued.

Some of the APB's opponents were not satisfied with defeating the APB on business combinations. They precipitated meetings which resulted in formation of the Wheat Committee early in 1971. In so doing, their determination to bring down the structure rather than submit to a professional pronouncement was apparent.

Further examples of extra-professional efforts to thwart the APB emerged in 1971. The most widely publicized effort related to the investment credit. I will not describe the episode in detail, but I do wish to stress its significance. Here was a display of raw power that should forever be a lesson to those who wish to set rules without having authority to do so. Businessmen and professional accounts went directly to Congressmen with the story that the APB was trying to remove an economic incentive granted by Congress. No amount of accounting logic about matching costs and revenues could overcome this economic argument and legislative challenge. SEC support of the APB was not enough to make a difference, nor was it enough to attract blame for the debacle. The APB seemed to get all of the blame.

Attitudes displayed here plainly indicate that some businessmen and professional accountants wanted to destroy the APB if that was necessary to have their way on the investment credit. If the same people were removed from the emotional issue of the investment credit, most of them would probably be strong supporters of standard-setting in the private sector. Strangely, one accountant filed a statement with the House Ways and Means Committee asking Congress to specify in the law the accounting for the investment credit, and a few weeks later his partner was trying to convince Congress to leave accounting out of the law.

In 1971 the APB was studying accounting for investments in marketable common stocks. Board opinion was moving toward carrying securities at market value with changes in market value included in income currently. This would have a great effect on companies with a substantial portfolio of common stocks, such as fire and casualty insurance companies. Chief executives of insurance companies held meetings with each other, with an APB committee and finally with the SEC in an effort to head off an APB Opinion. They succeeded well in this effort with the result being that the SEC directed the APB into a narrow band of acceptable solutions, which did not include carrying securities at market value. The APB dropped the project.

In 1971 the APB was also considering full cost accounting vs. successful effort cost accounting in the oil industry. The APB expressed a tentative preference for successful effort accounting. On the other hand, the Federal Power Commission had already issued a regulation, in accordance with a petition from an accounting firm, requiring full cost accounting by natural gas pipeline companies. The industry was divided and opposing positions were drawn up. Once again industry, together with accounting firms, took the issue before the SEC and forced an impasse, thus assuring the status quo for some time to come.

Along about the same time, the subject of accounting for leases was being considered. The APB had not formed a position and in fact had barely begun discussions of the subject. Nevertheless, knowledge of these discussions caused certain leasing companies to begin lobbying in Congress to head off any possibility of an APB Opinion which would require capitalization of leases. Dozens of letters from Congressmen, together with form letters from "a constituent," reached the APB. This campaign was quite successful, for the APB tabled the matter of leases. But the lobbying continued after that, and I believe leasing company lobbyists are ready to begin battle again any minute like the Minutemen of old.

These issues remain critical. The new FASB will have to give early attention to accounting for leases, marketable securities and oil exploration costs. In addition, I believe that someone will force the subject of business combinations onto the agenda again. To deal effectively with these issues, the FASB will need to develop an effective way to conduct relations with Congress. Perhaps the two remaining positions on the FASB, which seem to be so difficult to fill, should be granted to skilled lobbyists rather than skilled accountants.

4. CONCLUSION

What hope then have we for resolution of the many conflicts in the sociological and institutional structure of the accounting profession? Will prevailing attitudes change? I doubt it. At least attitudes will change, not swiftly, but perhaps gradually.

Does this mean that turmoil within the accounting profession will continue indefinitely? Probably some dissension will always occur in an institutional structure in a democratic society. This is not all bad. After all, the profession has grown in size, importance and respect throughout the last few stormy decades. I believe it will continue to grow in prosperity and in stature, though growth will be not quite as much as might be obtained if attitudes could be changed.

Accounting Attitudes: A Critique

THOMAS J. BURNS*

Mr. Savoie reports on two sets of accounting attitudes, those of professional accountants (and their clients) and those of the SEC. Regarding the first set of attitudes, those of accountants, he emphasizes two contradictory attitudes:

Attitude No. 1. Detailed rules are favored over broad standards since the former are more enforceable and provide more protection for accountants than the latter. The essence of this attitude is that many accountants favor decreased responsibility for themselves and oppose increased authority for themselves.[1]

Attitude No. 2. Accounting rules should be set in the private sector. This would seem to suggest more responsibility and more authority for accountants. But the actions of many accountants suggest that this attitude is acceptable only to the extent that they agree with the rules. If they and their clients don't agree with the rules, they appeal to the public sector.

Regarding the second set of attitudes, those of the SEC towards the AICPA, the SEC regards the AICPA as its research subsidiary and, within the parameters established by the SEC, as a detailed-rule-making subordinate body. These attitudes towards the AICPA provide the SEC with extensive, expert, and free services, while diverting almost all criticisms and some pressures to the AICPA. In short, the SEC expects the AICPA to undertake considerable responsibility for setting and enforcing public accounting standards, while it retains all of its legal authority for doing so.

In regard to the SEC's attitudes about the AICPA, and Mr. Savoie's and many other accountants' views about the SEC attitudes, I am reminded of the story that Walter Lippman tells about a very important Englishman, possibly the Prime Minister.

*B.B.A. 1950, University of Wisconsin; M.B.A. 1957, University of Michigan; Ph.D. 1963, University of Minnesota. CPA, Wisconsin, Illinois. Visiting Professor of Accounting, University of California, Berkeley; Professor of Accounting, Ohio State University. Author, *Behavioral Experiments in Accounting* (1972); (with H. S. Hendrickson) *The Accounting Primer* (1972) and *The Accounting Sampler* (1972). Contributor to accounting periodicals.

Several years ago, after dinner and, presumably, during the cigars and the brandy, this Englishman told him that England had had the Empire, and then she had had the Commonwealth, and now she had to have the Common Market, because she had to run something. So Walter Lippman said, "Why do you have to run something?" The Englishman said, "Because we have the power to do that—not the power but the intellect and the knowledge. We know how to run things; we ought to run things." "Well," Walter Lippman said, "you tell that to the French." (Lippman, 1973: 20)

If the powerful French are comparable to the SEC and the powerless English are comparable to the AICPA, then Savoie's prediction that the SEC will regard the FASB in exactly the same way as it did the APB is probably an accurate one. But what Savoie did not say is that probably the SEC regarded predecessor of the APB, the Committee on Accounting Procedure (which functioned for twenty-one years from 1938 to 1959), and the two still earlier committees which set standards (the first from 1933, the year the SEC got its start, until 1936, and the second from 1936 to 1938) very similarly to the APB. (See the *Journal of Accountancy*, 1959: 70–71.)

Similar to the relationship between the SEC and the APB, the relationship of the SEC with the Committee on Accounting Procedure (hereafter referred to as the CAP) was not always a harmonious one. Indeed, disagreements over the Bulletins of the CAP and the Releases of the SEC were sometimes open and carried on in public. This was so, despite the remarkable advantage that the AICPA enjoyed in its relationship with the SEC during much of that period; namely, that its Director of Research (from 1944–1961) was former SEC Chief Accountant, Carman G. Blough, and that William W. Werntz, another CPA active in the AICPA standard-setting activity of that era, was also a former SEC Chief Accountant.

The amount of public discord between the SEC and the AICPA that erupted periodically in the 1940s and the 1950s is rather remarkable, too, when one remembers that, in those decades, accounting standard-setting activity was largely a private activity, not yet considered public policy and not yet subject to the sustained criticism of a free press and the pressures of a pluralistic society, which have floodlit such activity in the last decade.

Yet in this relatively tranquil period for accounting, an accounting historian reports the following public disagreements between the SEC and the AICPA:

> In at least one instance, a subject for a proposed . . . bulletin was withdrawn in the face of SEC opposition. On a few occasions, the committee seems

to have been discouraged by the SEC from issuing bulletins. In at least four situations (Accounting Series Releases 50, 53, 70, and 76), an SEC . . . Release has departed from an institute pronouncement already in effect. Once, the SEC Chief Accountant made public a letter expressing disagreement with a recently issued . . . bulletin. In a historic confrontation, the SEC sought to incorporate several of its accounting principles as well as a few accounting principles not contained in prior releases, into its rulebook on financial disclosures, Regulation S-X. As a part of this action, the SEC also proposed to issue a rule asserting its preferred solution to a controversy on which the SEC and the [CAP] . . . had been unable to reconcile their divergent views for many years. (Zeff, 1972: 152–53)

To elaborate, in the early 1940s a proposed bulletin (comparable to an APB Opinion) was withdrawn when the SEC opposed it. The subject was the treatment of premiums on the redemption of preferred stock. In 1943 the SEC issued its Release No. 45 on this subject.

Another disagreement between the SEC and the CAP was over income tax allocation. The CAP issued Bulletin No. 23, favoring income tax allocation, in December of 1944; and after considerable controversy, in 1945 the SEC issued Release No. 53, in which it objected, less strongly than was expected, to only a portion of Bulletin No. 23. Two months later, the CAP authorized a statement regarding the application of Release No. 53 for companies filing reports with the SEC.

In 1945 the CAP issued Bulletin No. 24, which discouraged the writeoff of intangibles against capital surplus. Later the same year, the SEC issued Release No. 50, which prohibited this writeoff. Eight years later, in 1953, the CAP adopted the SEC's position in Bulletin No. 43.

In 1947 the CAP issued Bulletin No. 32, favoring the current-operating-performance concept of the income statement; this was contrary to the SEC's preference for the all-inclusive concept. The SEC's Chief Accountant wrote a letter to the AICPA's Director of Research, stating that the SEC would take exception to current-operating-performance income statements. At the request of the SEC, this letter was published in the *Journal of Accountancy* in 1948. Later in 1948 the CAP issued Bulletin No. 35, which recommended that extraordinary items excluded from the income statement should be disclosed in the surplus statement and presented as a combined income and surplus statement. Not withstanding this partial capitulation by the CAP, the SEC continued to press for the all-inclusive income statement and in 1949 proposed that a general amendment to Regulation S-X be issued requiring that all income statements filed with the SEC be of the all-inclusive variety. This controversy was temporarily resolved by a compromise solution in which a net income would be shown before the addition or subtraction of the "special items." Years later in 1966, the CAP's successor, the

APB, finally endorsed the SEC's preference for the all-inclusive concept in its Opinion No. 9.

In the same proposed amendment to S-X, the SEC incorporated several accounting principles not previously considered, together with the contents of several Releases. Only after both the AICPA and the American Accounting Association, at their annual meetings in 1950, passed resolutions opposing this proposal did the SEC relent sufficiently to propose a compromise. It agreed not to include material on accounting principles in its rulebook, provided that the CAP would codify its Bulletins.

In 1948 the CAP declared in Bulletin No. 37 that stock option compensation should be measured when the right becomes the grantee's property. In 1953 CAP revised the Bulletin when it decided to change the measurement date to the date when the option is granted to a specific individual. Later the same year, due to the lack of unanimity among accountants about the appropriate measurement date, the SEC called only for footnote disclosure.

In 1950 the CAP passed unanimously a proposed Bulletin which dealt with the general upward restatement of assets under quasi-reorganization procedures; the SEC asked CAP to postpone publishing the Bulletin, and the CAP complied. Early in 1951 the SEC informed the CAP that they would not accept financial statements reflecting the kind of write-ups authorized in the proposed Bulletin. Consequently the CAP did not issue the Bulletin.

This brief historical excursion has attempted to show that, even when one allows for the changed environment in which accounting standards are now established in the public sector, perhaps the SEC's attitude toward the APB was not so much different from its attitude toward the CAP.

Regarding the other set of attitudes that Savoie analyzes, the attitudes of accountants, it will be remembered by most of us here that a chief criticism of the CAP in the 1950s was that it favored detailed rules over broad standards and that the demise of the CAP was hastened by accountants who challenged its rules in the public sector.

Savoie [Sec. 2] reports that the SEC expects the AICPA to do the research for the setting of accounting standards. If this expectation is correct, and I do not challenge it, the SEC must have been disappointed in the past. During the lifetime of the CAP at least two notable crises occurred over the lack of adequate research activity. The first of these happened in the early forties and was alleviated by the hiring (in 1944) of Carman G. Blough, who immediately quickened the pace of research activity (Zeff, 1972: 145). The second crisis over the lack of sufficient research activity was a fatal one; it brought about the death of the

CAP and the subsequent birth of the APB.

The APB was founded in the expectation that greater attention would be given to the research activity of the AICPA. The APB was to consider subject areas after its researchers had publicly disseminated the results of their research on these subjects. As the Wheat Study Group and others have observed, research activity, in any formal and public sense, was lacking in the last years of the APB, about which Savoie writes.

Of the Opinions Nos. 13 through 27, issued by the APB from 1968 through 1972, only Nos. 16, 17, 19, and 27, or slightly more than one-third, can be linked in even a casual way with prior research studies. Of the twelve research studies published by the APB through 1972, seven were assigned to researchers in 1960. These were basic postulates, broad principles, business combinations, income taxes, leases, pensions and funds. In 1961 two other published research studies, on price-level and foreign operations, were commissioned. In summary, 75 percent of the research studies published by the APB through 1972 were started in these two early years of the APB. Only the Grady Inventory, goodwill, and extractive studies were subsequently started and completed, more than a decade later. For the five years of 1967 through 1972, the APB did not authorize any new studies. As Zeff (1972: 224) observed:

> Whatever the reasons, the contribution that formal research studies were to make to the board's process of developing opinions, as contemplated by the Special Committee on Research program in 1958, seems to have been largely absent in recent years. In this respect, the [APB] . . . [has been] working in very much the manner of its predecessor, the [CAP] . . ..

The basis for standard-setting is research; thus, unless the FASB fulfills its research function adequately (and by adequately, I mean that it achieves the performance criteria for the function as previously defined), then the FASB, like the CAP and APB before it, will be regarded as only a political mechanism.

I do not disagree with the main aspects of the attitudes Savoie has written about. But I do not quite agree that the SEC has the interest in setting accounting standards that he claims. If the SEC does have this inclination, how do you explain that the SEC does not challenge the accounting standards set by the regulatory agencies for regulated industries?

In summary, first I have tried to supply a little historical perspective to suggest that these SEC attitudes existed prior to the APB, and over essentially the entire history of SEC-AICPA relationships. Second, I propose that the failure of the APB research function, along with the earlier failure of the CAP research function, has been a major factor in "an ongoing arc of development" of these attitudes for accountants, their firms and their clients, and the SEC.[2]

NOTES

1. Savoie does not make it clear to me whether he is referring to individual CPAs, who, for themselves, favor decreased responsibility and decreased authority, and, for the AICPA, favor increased responsibility and increased authority; or whether he means that CPAs favor decreased responsibility and authority for the AICPA, themselves, and their firms, or some other combination altogether.

2. Savoie speaks of the SEC's strategy of permitting profit forecasts, and he predicts underwriters will require companies to furnish them. But isn't this the same strategy so successfully employed by the APB with fund-flow statements? First, the APB recommended (but did not require) in Opinion No. 3 that fund-flow statements be published; and only after most companies found it necessary to publish them (due to the urging of the New York Stock Exchange and the Financial Analysts Federation among others) did the APB make such statements mandatory in Opinion No. 19.

REFERENCES

Journal of Accountancy (1959) "History of the Accounting Procedure Committee—From the Final Report." Official Releases (November).

Lippman, Walter (1973) "Walter Lippman: An Interview with Ronald Steel." *New Republic* (April 14).

Zeff, Stephen A. (1972) *Forging Accounting Principles in Five Countries: A History and an Analysis of Trends.* Arthur Andersen & Co. Lecture Series, Champaign, Illinois: Stipes.

Discussion

Savoie. I was much impressed by the review of prior history. I had forgotten almost all those things that were going on. I don't think I said that this was a particularly new phenomenon—the behavioral patterns—but I think that that does provide additional light on the subject. I certainly agree with you that things have always been more or less that way. With regard to the Institute's research, no new research has been undertaken lately because it has taken ten years or so for every project to be finished. It *has* failed. I don't know what people expect of accounting research but I certainly have my fingers crossed for the new Financial Accounting Standards Board research program. There seem to be no standards for conducting research. I don't know what it takes to have research that is acceptable.

Buckley. I can link my remarks here to Chuck's comments. He posed the question, what should the FASB do differently, what has it learned from the APB? I think one lesson is that perhaps a research project for a policy-making body ought to aim at the impactive nature of the legislation. In the final analysis, the issue does not hinge on some strange accounting theory, but rather on who is going to get rich or who is going to get poor as a result of that particular legislation. It seems to me that policy makers have to attempt to measure that impact before they issue the legislation. Research that aims at discovering that impact I think would be valuable research.

Savoie. Perhaps that should be coordinated with the market research that Bob Mautz has been suggesting.

Buckley. The other point where we have sensed a failure in the CAP and APB—and I hope this can be corrected with the FASB—is in a sort of global attitude, which in a sense can be preventive in nature but which will bring the public's attention to emerging trends and developments long before they reach a crisis point. I am not pointing to any particular company or industry, but rather advocating the issuing of a simple statement that a new practice is developing which requires caution and attention while it is being studied. Most of our accounting legislation has looked at very nitpicky things and has ignored the holistic problems of accounting practices, which in many cases cut across industries and across countries. I don't know how that is going to be incorporated within the FASB.

Carmichael. I think part of the failure of the research function could

334

be attributed to a misplaced hope for a comprehensive, basic, underlying theory—a lack of recognition that accounting is an applied field and the implications of that. I don't think that in auditing we have had any difficulty recognizing that it is an applied field, and we have had more success. In the auditing research effort there has been a close interrelationship between research and pronouncement development— the research has been useful—in the pronouncement development activity. I think that in our continuing accounting research effort at the AICPA we recognize that. We have no thought that we are going to develop a comprehensive theory of accounting. We are definitely viewing accounting as an applied discipline, as well as viewing auditing as an applied discipline. I think the same is true at the FASB. The research effort will be aimed very much at specific problems, be very much problem oriented, very much more concerned with developing the alternatives and support for those alternatives, rather than arriving at a grand conclusion. In our research activities at the Institute we intend to pursue that same plan. We don't want to place stress on the overall conclusion reached by the researcher. It is more important for the researcher to develop information to be viewed as input for the policy maker. So the researcher's final conclusion is not nearly as important as the inputs to that conclusion and the way that he has used them. I think the FASB intends to do that. One significant change that I think will lead to some improvement is that they are going to issue a discussion memorandum sixty days before they have an exposure draft taking a position, so that the discussion memorandum will indicate what the alternatives are and what the support is for those various alternatives without giving any indication of what position the Board is going to take. The pot shots and the criticisms at that point can be leveled at a particular alternative that a group or a company or a firm disagrees with. It would be apparent after that is done and after the Board releases an exposure draft that they will have considered those criticisms and viewpoints. I think it will be much more difficult to criticize the position finally taken in the exposure draft since it will be clear that they have considered the criticism.

Savoie. I would like to say I think you are right in that respect, but my experience has been that the APB has considered every opposite view. However, when the APB took a position that didn't agree with the views of the opponents, the opponents said, "You didn't consider my position." I think people are going to take that attitude regardless of what procedure you follow.

Carmichael. Perhaps, but I think it will be more difficult. We have run into the same thing in auditing. When the Auditing Committee issues an exposure draft, we get a lot of letters and comments that have been clearly considered and hashed out before, and it must seem like the letters aren't read and are totally ignored. They probably *are* ignored because as soon as the Committee sees the point being made, they know that they have considered all those points. The letters seldom raise new points. But in the activities of the APB and the present activities of the Auditing Committee those things are quite submerged. The writers are not aware that those points have been considered, and the natural reaction is to think that the letters are being ignored. I think the FASB's process will make it much more difficult for people to have that impression.

Sterling. Not if a man's own ox is being gored. If his ox is being gored he is still going to think that his point hasn't been seriously considered because it wasn't implemented.

Carmichael. Having had the opportunity both to present written comments and oral comments in the public hearing, he will find it more apparent that his position hasn't been implemented because he has failed to justify it.

Savoie. That is what the APB has been doing. They have been getting written comments; they have been holding hearings. Lots of luck, is all I say.

Carmichael. The hearings are recent. I originally shared your doubts (that I have heard other people express also), but as the establishment of the FASB has developed, I have been more encouraged. Overall, the position that they are starting from, which the APB was working up toward, of definitely operating in the open, in public, in a goldfish bowl, has a lot of merit and will hold more potential for success.

Long. All of this sounds good—the idea of research, the notification, the sixty days' exposure—but I wonder if perhaps the thing that we ought to do is to suggest the FASB explore the possibility of issuing opinions that *do* go all the way with the setting the time line for accomplishment of that major step. Break it down incrementally, so that by such a period of time we will do this, and then a year later or two years later, something else. I wonder if by taking that kind of approach you wouldn't assure yourself that you capitalize on the incremental step, but at the same time set up an orderly way to accomplish the total objective over a time frame in which business can maneuver. They would know what is going to happen and then they could make those decisions that they need to make on a prospective basis.

Arnold. I have a question concerning the establishment of specific rules for the sake of protection. Weren't you saying that there would be more legal protection if you had more specific rules? It seems that in some of the court cases that we talked about yesterday the court is saying, "Forget these specific rules. Look more at what the reasonable man would do. What he would think, what he would report." Do you see any conflict?

Savoie. I don't think that that is what the court cases are saying. In the principal case, if you are getting back to *Continental Vending* again, there was no specific rule that would apply and therefore the accountants had nothing to fall back on for protection. It was the absence of rules that permitted the court to determine that they should follow standards of fairness that would obviously be independent of the professional standards because the professional standards were inadequate.

Fiflis. In fact, the court said that if there were a specific rule there may have been a different case.

Bentz. I would like to go back to John's point. It seems to me that even if you send out exposure drafts or comment letters, you are still dependent on the rhetoric of the people involved—those whose ox is being gored—and you are still somewhat at a loss to know the extent to which their oxen are being gored. That is what John was saying: that unless you really know the impact of the decision on earnings, then the basis of choice *appears* to be political, whether it is or not. If a person can't document a position, or cite research to document the position that the effect will be significant, then there is clearly a basis for ignoring his comments. The feeling is now that everybody has an equal voice in the decision. People are coming in individually with their own perspectives, without the research and without the data. Therefore, there is no empirical basis to show why he took such a position. I think that is John's point—not so much that you aren't getting inputs; you get the inputs. But how do you evaluate them?

Willingham. I have two brief comments that relate to what Chuck said. It seems that if by marketing he meant market research prior to issuance, maybe the FASB is in for a worse time than the APB. In other words, why expose yourself twice to all the criticism? Why not do market research and simply put out a statement and stick with it? I am not sure, but it struck me as Tom went through the history that the Committee on Accounting Procedure put out statements entitled "Accounting Research Bulletin" which involved no research. Then we overhauled the system, established the APB and explicitly set out to do research which would be the basis for something that could very well be called "Accounting Research Bulletins." But these bulletins were renamed "Opinions," which implied no research since one can give an opinion without any basis. I am wondering how the Institute decided to name these things. By the way, this is still going on—the statements on auditing procedure have been renamed, and they still deal largely with procedure, although I won't deny there are some standards included. Maybe that is a minor marketing point. How did those names come about?

Savoie. I don't know how they came about, but I don't think they mean a darn thing. What they are are just plain detailed rules, no matter what you call them. I don't think the marketing of them is that significant in regard to terminology.

Sterling. I want to go back to what John Buckley calls impactive research and follow up on it. It might be interesting data, John, to know the effect of an Opinion on earnings per share or total assets, but what do you do with it? Take the extreme case of the computer leasing company that has recently made the news. We all know that if that company had written off its goodwill, they would have shown a deficit instead of a rather large amount of retained earnings. It doesn't take much research to determine that. You just write off the goodwill against the retained earnings, and you find out that you have a deficit. But where does that lead you? What does that tell you about whether or not you *ought* to write off that goodwill? You know beforehand that the management of that company is going to resist an Opinion that would require them to write off that goodwill and show a deficit. So what do the data tell you? To put the question another way, how would you go about marketing that kind of a product? When you know that an Opinion is going to gore a man's ox and he knows that it is going to be gored, how are you going to convince him to accept the Opinion?

Buckley. Bob, it is a very good thing that Statement No. 3 was of a recommendatory nature rather than obligatory because the result of price level adjusted statements would shift resources from capital intensive industries to commercial and retail organizations *en masse*. That point, incidentally, doesn't appear anywhere in the rhetoric surrounding Statement No. 3, or in the Research Study No. 6 (which supposedly should have looked at this issue). Unless accounting policy makers can anticipate the results of what will happen in relation to their policies, they have no business making policy. Unless we can examine the fact that a policy such as price level adjusted statements is going to cause a massive shift in the flow of funds in the economy and then make the judgment as to whether that shift is desirable or not, we shouldn't come out with statements at all. Having anticipated the results of shifts in the economic resources, it seems to me that the question then becomes a policy one. In this case capital intensive industries ought to be a better break, and this need ought to be taken care of simultaneously if the policy is to be implemented.

Moonitz. If they are making a lower rate of return than is being reported now, why shouldn't there be a shift?

Buckley. They need more of a policy break, a tax break.

Moonitz. Why?

Buckley. Because we need capital-intensive industries. We need steel mills and factories.

Linowes. I am a little concerned here because we seem to be stressing specific rules. It is being urged here, and it is being expected of the FASB. I think we might be well advised if we looked to some of the professions that are also not as precisely scientific as the accounting profession for some guidance. I am thinking primarily in terms of something like the law, where they apply the prudent man rule. In medicine, when they talk about a person who is in "good health," they are not worried if he has slightly elevated blood pressure or flat feet. They don't give you a complete rundown of all his ailments as long as the entire person, the entire unit, is satisfactory. I think if we come to expect specific rules to resolve all of our problems, this can never be, and we will be in for letdown. Whereas, if we make the requirement that these statements be presented fairly, and we so charge our practitioners through appropriate disciplinary procedures, perhaps we will have a mechanism that we can live with, without the increasingly strong likelihood of government interference in our profession.

Defliese. I think I have to support both Len and John in this approach. The attempts made at research by the Institute failed principally because they did not apply the results of the research to live cases—to the real world. Had that been done, the problems in the research would have been obvious, and perhaps there would have been less divergence between the recommendation of the research and the ultimate APB Opinion. In many cases the APB members themselves conducted their own research in order to provide for their own guidance. I have seen the reaction already of the academicians and theorists who say, "Damn the torpedoes, we're not concerned about the results here; the important thing is principle." This gets back to the marketing question that Chuck raises. That is that you are not going to be able to market your efforts unless you can convince people that what you are doing is going to produce a reasonable result. Basic to that is a rather detailed specification of what you are attempting to do. The APB went through this and found out the hard way that unless you have specific rules, this just isn't going to work. It is the nature of the business community, and the profession who are applying it, to feel themselves free to apply a general rule as they see fit. Consequently, general standards just don't work. The best demonstration of that was Opinion 9 on earnings per share. As soon as that came out it was supposed to clean up the earnings per share question rather quickly, and of course it created a morass that required about two years of study, public hearings and the like, before we came out with 15—probably the most detailed Opinion we have ever written. Yet you find very little controversy concerning earnings per share today, at least in practice. Sure, there are still some theoretical hang-ups involved, but by and large it has worked, and it is working only because it was carefully drafted. The idea of a common stock equivalent or residual security had to be developed. In the process the members of the Board did their own research. We had tab runs of all kinds of common stock equivalents that we generated ourselves in order to arrive at that magic 66 2/3 percent that everybody points at and says, "My God, how did they find that one?" We found it only by experimentation on something we came up with which we thought was going to be a reasonable result. It worked, but it is not supportable by any great principle. The important thing is, let us get something that is going to work. If the FASB does its research properly, gets some real empirical research into its research studies and demonstrates to the public the effects that it would create, it will then be able to do the marketing job which is essential.

Ross. It appears to me that there is a basic problem in research that is even more urgent than those obviously important areas that we have been discussing: that is, research into the area of how you do get effective consultation. This seems to me in a democracy a tremendous problem. There are millions of statement users. Even if you go by associations of users there are so many manufacturing groups, so many professional groups, and so on, that you have a vast group of people. If you want to get any of them into the act at all, obviously you must have some kind of an exposure draft for them to discuss. As everybody knows, to prepare a reasonable draft takes a tremendous amount of work and preparation. By the time you have the exposure draft it is almost too late for a general discussion of principles all over again. I think that one research effort might be directed to what techniques you can use to get research consultation, for example who gets consulted at what stages, how much consulting you hope to do, and at least you might be able to produce some clearer ideas on the limitations of consultation. Everybody thinks consultation is a good thing, but how to do it is a difficult question.

Holstrum. I agree with both John and Phil regarding the importance of the impact of opinions upon the economy and reported companies and shifts of capital markets and so forth. The thing that really concerns me is that some of the research may lead to the type of wholesale statement that I felt John was making. We can do research by looking at capital intensive industries and labor intensive industries, and we can say if we used price level adjustments, then we would change the numbers and decrease income to a greater extent with capital intensive industries than we do with labor intensive industries. I think this has been done. There have been some studies by Jones in the past that show that this is the case, but you really can't come up with a statement on the basis of that kind of research, that therefore there would be a shift away from capital intensive industries into labor intensive industries. That is the thing that I really fear. If you change the score and lower the number for a particular industry, does it mean that the capital market only has this amount of information? That is to say, is it fixed on the accounting number? If it goes down, therefore there will be a shift away from those lower earnings numbers to something else. The thing that I fear most about that kind of research is that it is going to be much too narrow in its interpretation of how the economy reacts and how markets react. It will lead, therefore, to an incorrect analysis of what the real impact is. So when you talk about research on the impact I don't want it to be limited to the type of thing that seemed to be implied in your statement, John, and in yours, Phil, that you would look and see whether the numbers were going to be higher or lower and therefore come up with some deduction about the impact upon society.

Defliese. I didn't mean to imply that we would back into a result. The important thing is to know where your pronouncement is going to lead you and know what the result is before you attempt to use it. I don't think that that has been done with many of the proposals that are being made.

PART IV
VIEWS FROM PRACTICE

CHAPTER 10

The Economic Case Against Capitalization of Leases—A New Look at Facility Accounting

PHILIP L. DEFLIESE*

As the APB commends its spirit to the FASB, one cannot help but ponder over the depth and scope of unfinished business transmitted in this changing of the guard—an agenda much larger than that which existed at the APB's inception. So large is the backlog that the new full-time group, with enlarged research and administrative staff, has had to set priorities in forming an initial agenda.

The report of the Study Group on Objectives of Financial Statements has not yet been issued. The delay of that report has, no doubt, influenced the choices made by the FASB for its opening agenda.[1] It is still not certain whether the Study Group will recommend that fair values and price level changes should impact financial reporting. Until the reception accorded any recommendations along those lines is clear, it was thought wise to defer consideration of the accounting for market changes of equity securities, oil exploration costs, goodwill[2] and other intangibles, business combinations, and a host of others. It appears that many of the questions given priority can be resolved, or their consideration at least gotten underway, before this issue is settled.

It seems altogether appropriate that for the immediate future we should expect the retention of historical cost accounting (with possibly a requirement for some supplementary data based on price levels or fair values to provide perspective) as the framework within which to resolve some of the more pressing issues currently facing the accounting profession. Certainly, the effort to reduce alternatives in many areas, or to establish appropriate criteria for the use of alternatives, can,

*B.B.A. 1938, M.S. 1940, City College of New York. CPA. Managing Partner, Coopers & Lybrand. Chairman, Accounting Principles Board. Member of Council, AICPA. Author (with N. J. Lenhart), *Montgomery's Auditing* (1957).

with limitations, proceed nevertheless. Once this is done the stage should be set for the big debate that must be undertaken before such a far-reaching change as the adoption of fair value can be implemented. This paper is predicated upon this assumption, and upon two others: first, that within this historical cost framework accounting can be made to approximate more closely (but not completely) to the underlying economic facts; second, that until more fundamental changes in accounting theory are made, the pervasive principles that are summarized as the "matching" of costs and revenues will dominate income determination concepts (APB Statement No. 4, 1970: Para. 147).

There are four major issues that can be debated in this environment, and possibly resolved for the most part. They are:

1. *Capitalization of leases.* This issue has been a burning one since 1964 and before. In the view of many, APB Opinion No. 5, "Reporting of Leases in Financial Statements of Lessees" (1964), fell far short of the mark when it required the capitalization of only those finance—type leases under which an ownership equity was being built up. APB Opinion No. 7, "Reporting of Leases in Financial Statements of Lessors" (1966) promised a reconciliation of the conflicting views on this subject; the promise is still unfulfilled. In the meantime, major facility leases of the "off-balance sheet financing" type have proliferated, and the arguments rage.

2. *Discounting of Deferred Taxes.* Even before the APB adopted comprehensive tax allocation (APB Opinion No. 11, 1967), it outlawed the discounting of deferred taxes (APB Opinion No. 10, 1966: Para. 6) on the assumption that prior consideration should be given to the broader subject of discounting as it related to all items in financial statements. Since that time this issue keeps cropping up despite the fact that the Board ultimately deemed deferred taxes a deferred credit account and not a liability account and continued the ban on discounting (APB Opinion No. 11, 1967: Paras 35, 36). Many feel that the issue of whether deferred tax accounts are deferred credits, liabilities, or valuation accounts (net of tax concept) should be reopened, as well as the discounting issue.

3. *Depreciation.* The equal acceptability for financial accounting purposes of accelerated methods and the straight-line method of depreciation—and the SEC ban on use of sinking-fund depreciation[3]—hardly makes for comparability. Accountants generally do not question use of the straight-line method even though other companies in the same industry may use accelerated methods. Not all companies attempt to relate circumstances to the judgement decision in selecting a method. This problem is further complicated by substantial variations, within some industries, in the estimated useful lives of major facilities.

4. *Capitalization of Interest.* The acceptance by regulatory agencies in the public utility field of the capitalization of an allowance for interest on plant construction in progress has a substantial theoretical and practical basis. This practice has spread among other industries and is generally accepted in practice and the AICPA has formally accepted it for the retail land sales industry (AICPA, 1973). Questions arise as to the appropriateness of capitalizing interest on all long-term holdings of inventory,

such as stocks of tobacco and liquor, and facilities, such as equipment, timber, oil, and mineral deposits. The cost of money has received increased recognition in accounting thought so that a thorough review of this basic question is now clearly in order. (See APB Opinion No. 21, 1971.)

Accountants have a propensity toward segmenting their problems, particularly in the theoretical area; this is, no doubt, a carryover from their transaction-oriented heritage. Probably few would acknowledge the fact that the four foregoing issues are so interrelated that their resolution cannot be separately achieved. However, this is precisely the case. And although the solution may require the adoption of some revolutionary concepts—and some restructuring of financial statement presentation—it can nevertheless be carried out within the framework of historical cost. (Obviously, the adoption of fair value accounting would require some further modifications, but none very startling). Before we can proceed with that resolution we must consider these four issues in greater depth.

1. CAPITALIZATION OF LEASES

"Off-balance sheet" financing has been growing rapidly since World War II; prior to that time the term was rarely used. Initially, the thrust was to minimize debt on the balance sheet, thereby retaining a debt-equity ratio which would facilitate future borrowing, or to achieve the same result within existing debenture restrictions. With the widening of lease commitment disclosure requirements and the growth in creditor and investor sophistication, this motive has lost much of its significance. Today most off-balance sheet financing is designed to level the cost of the facility over its useful life to avoid reflecting the impact of the combination of straight-line depreciation and higher interest in the earlier years (on a large, gradually declining debt). The theory is that if (all other things being equal), a facility's ability to generate revenues in its earlier years is no greater than its ability in later years, the levelling would make possible a better matching of costs and revenue. To put it another way, without levelling the result would be skewed. The recognition of interest as a holding cost is widely prevalent in today's atmosphere of heavy debt financing.

Proponents of capitalization of leases by lessees argue that such levelling overstates income in the early years because of the omission of the heavier charges—which result when interest and depreciation are substituted for level rental payments. There are, of course, legal differences between lease and debt commitments, but these usually only become effective on bankruptcy. Many believe the legal distinction is enough to require different accounting; others feel legal form should be ignored. Substantively and economically there is no difference between a full pay-out[4] lease and ownership with 100 percent (or nearly 100 percent) debt. Consequently, it seems reasonable that their accounting should produce the same results. But the real question is, which result is more appropriate?

By tradition, interest is treated as a period cost despite the inroads made in this concept by the practice of capitalizing it during construction periods. The notion of delaying the expensing of interest, once the related facility is operative, would ordinarily shock most accountants. But aren't the lessees on the right economic track when they seek to level the holding cost of a facility that provides the same service year after year? Consequently, the better approach is to capitalize the aggregate interest cost with other costs of the facility and to allocate this total holding cost over the facility's useful life on a level basis (or in proportion to the estimated range of revenues). The cost of equity money invested in a facility should receive the same treatment. This will be discussed later.

2. DEPRECIATION

The differences between "book" and "tax" depreciation are well known today. Tax depreciation is no longer dependent upon accounting rationale as it was in the earlier days of the Internal Revenue Code. The federal government has recognized the role the Code plays in stimulating and fine-tuning the economy of the country. Accelerated methods are offered, extremely short lives can be elected, minimal salvage can be assumed, and investment credits are granted—all for the purpose of facilitating a quick recovery of invested capital, thereby encouraging reinvestment and quicker replacement; reliance upon recapture rules minimizes abuses. The congruence of book and tax depreciation is a theory of the past; their divergence is more than an open secret—it is a policy. Consequently, in any discussion of financial accounting, tax depreciation must be ignored—except as it relates to the question of deferred taxes, which will be discussed later.

But what about book depreciation? Little progress has been made in finding ways to allocate realistically a facility's loss in value to the periods benefited. Thinking on the subject is fettered still by tax overtones and conservatism—salvage values have been kept down and estimated lives have been arbitrarily set. Thus companies under tight regulation, such as public utilities and railroads, are commonly required to spread costs over long periods without adequate regard for the obsolescence that might reasonably be anticipated or without any consideration of a sensible, economic replacement policy, whereas non-regulated companies frequently follow the reverse policy. A typical victim of the straight-line depreciation requirement is the commercial real estate investment company which must report losses in the early (high interest) years despite full occupancy and a property that is appreciating instead of depreciating. Commercial properties that are properly maintained and periodically renovated can usually be resold many years after purchase at prices approximating their cost or higher if inflation and other causes of appreciation are considered. Present depreciation methods usually ignore these factors. And the accruing of maintenance and renovation costs (to spread these costs properly over productive life) is not general practice.

Current practices in depreciation accounting fail in many cases to produce results that adequately reflect economic realities. This is nowhere better demonstrated than in the area of allocating maintenance and expiration costs (loss of value based on historical cost) over useful life (as determined by realistic replacement policy). Here, new approaches must be developed, industry by industry, in order to achieve a proper matching of costs and revenues. All this amounts to a virtual overhaul of accounting depreciation practices, an undertaking that can only be carried out if certain long-standing attitudes and prejudices are disregarded. Consideration might even be given to replacing the term "depreciation," since the concept has outgrown the narrow denotation.

3. DISCOUNTING OF DEFERRED TAXES

As previously indicated, accounting theorists divide into three camps on the subject of deferred taxes (excepting, of course, those who would ignore some or all tax effects because of a flow-through, roll-over, or selectivity theory—a diminishing lot). Those who espouse the liability theory reason that one must assume profitability (without which a company cannot long survive); consequently, the tax benefit must eventually be paid back, perhaps even at a higher rate. Recognizing the factor of cost of money in accounting, they make the greatest case for discounting such a long-term liability. (See APB Opinion No. 21, 1971.)

Those who refute the liability theory point out that no liability exists until future profits are earned, hence, discounting is improper; they insist that the deferred tax is only an advance recognition of the tax benefit of depreciation which must be deferred and matched with future book depreciation that receives no tax benefit, in order to achieve proper matching. Still others view deferred taxes in the same light as any other tax benefit—a sharing of the cost of every expenditure with the government. And if the government thus elects to return capital quicker, a lesser investment exists in the meantime—hence, they advocate the net-of-tax, or valuation account concept. When the net-of-tax people agree (few have spoken lately) to allocate the unrecovered investment on a rational (preferably, level) basis, they achieve a result very similar to those who advocate discounting.

Each of these theories has merit, and there are those who believe in all three. Similar mysteries exist in theology and must be resolved by faith. About the only point on which all deferred-tax people agree is that there should be a proper matching of cost and revenue. But what is cost in this case?

Today discounted cash flow has become the yardstick of comparison of all values; recognition of an interest factor is inherent in the exercise. (Accounting has already recognized this with long-term receivables and payables that may not carry an appropriate interest rate. (See APB Opinion No. 21, 1971.)

A business that invests in a tangible, productive facility has a cost at risk equal at all times to the net unrecovered cash invested (net of tax benefits realized and the portions previously recovered through depreciation charges to operation) plus the costs (maintenance and renovation) necessary to maintain the facility until its estimated salvage is realized. Assuming revenues from the facility are level, it is reasonable to suggest that the aggregate costs should also be spread on a level basis. To ignore this relationship is to ignore economic realities.

4. CAPITALIZATION OF INTEREST

This brings us to the last link in the chain—interest. The cost of money—whether equity or borrowed—invested in a facility is a basic element of cost of holding or operating that facility.[5] This is not a new idea. The arguments for interest as a cost, rather than as an element of profit, were summarized almost fifty years ago.[6] From an economic standpoint there is no justification for reflecting differing costs for purchased facilities and rented facilities (or for facilities purchased with equity money or borrowed money) because the same costs are incurred. The problem lies with the traditional income statement and net income concepts. True net income should first recognize a cost equivalent to interest on capital investment.

Accordingly, interest, whether imputed or real, on unrecovered investment should be added to the cost of a facility[7] to determine its overall cost to be spread among the accounting periods benefited.

There are alternative views with respect to the question of capitalizing interest on equity capital. They are:

1. Interest on equity capital should not be capitalized—only debt interest should be capitalized and applied to those facilities for which the debt was created. This is simple and direct, but it is also arbitrary and unrealistic. A facility financed out of equity money is no different from one financed out of debt; the selection is arbitrary.
2. To overcome the objections to (1), a proportionate approach could be used, i.e., apply interest to all facilities in proportion to the debt/equity ratio.

While method (2) eliminates arbitrariness and is, therefore, preferable, it provides nevertheless only a partial recognition of the cost of holding a facility. Consequently, an interest charge (net of tax) for equity funds as well as debt funds should be applied to all assets during their holding period. To the extent such charges exceed interest actually paid the credit will appear separately in the income statement as a non-operating return on investment, and operations will receive their appropriate charge as the holding costs (which include the interest factor) are expensed or amortized.

5. THE INTERRELATIONSHIP

By now the interrelationship of the four foregoing problems should be apparent:

The cost of holding a facility[8] should consist of:

1. All construction and acquisition costs, *plus*
2. All costs of major maintenance and renovation during the holding period to point of disposition (new of income tax benefit, *less*
3. All recoveries of total investment in the form of tax benefits of depreciation (including accelerated depreciation) and investment credits, *plus*
4. Interest (real or imputed)—net of income tax benefits—on the resultant unrecovered net investment over the holding period.

Once this aggregate cost is determined, it should be allocated (less the expected residual or salvage) as a loss in value over the realistically estimated holding period on a basis proportionate to revenues. In the absence of evidence requiring a different approach, the allocation would be level over the years held. The holding period should give due consideration to obsolescence and the expected replacement policy of the company.

Essential to this view is the concept that depreciation, as accountants use the term, should be considered a means by which a company recovers its net unrecovered investment (as defined above) through operations. Put another way, the cost incurred by the loss in the value of the net investment in the facility must be charged to operations over the period of use in a rational manner, with some attempt to match such cost with projected revenue, which thereby recovers the cost of the investment over its holding period. (When revenues differ from projections, the gain or loss is operational in character and not attributable to the facility.) Since interest on the unrecovered investment—giving due regard to the tax recoveries—is an element of cost, it, too, must be spread in the same manner.

The manner in which this newly-defined depreciation is allocated to the periods of use is a matter that requires the exercise of logic and judgment. The arguments for accelerated methods or sinking-fund methods are no better (in the ordinary case) than for straight-line, especially if matching is the more pervasive motivation. All these methods rest on arbitrary premises. The fact that interest (whether from debt or equity) is included as a cost should not alter this view. Similarly, the fact that unamortized interest resides in the balance sheet amount of the unrecovered investment in the facility should not be disturbing (as long as that balance is not in excess of net realizable value on a going-concern basis)[9] if it can be agreed that interest is a holding cost.

This approach solves many of the problems concerning capitalizing of interest and discounting of deferred taxes because interest on unrecovered investment is included in the computation, the actual tax benefits are considered a recovery of investment as received and thus reduce the interest on unrecovered investment, and the balance is allocated on a level basis (in essence a form of discounting has taken place). It also puts depreciation on a realistic basis (recognition of loss of value in the wider financial sense rather than through wear and tear) and better matches this cost with revenues.

It also makes academic the issue of capitalizing leases (disregarding for the moment the issue of disclosure) because, except for the element of major maintenance and renovation—a cost the lessee usually bears—most financing lease terms approximate the same results. Consequently, if finance-type leases were capitalized, and the suggested accounting followed, the results would be about the same. In structuring a lease, most financing lessors use essentially the same model, making certain that their yield on unrecovered investment (giving due consideration to investment credits and tax depreciation recovery) is a constant predetermined percentage. What this really amounts to is leasing accounting today produces a result more in accordance with the economic facts than does ownership accounting, despite our feeble attempts at allocating income taxes and despite the token capitalization of interest during construction. Is it any wonder that many companies would rather lease today than buy? A skewed accounting result usually provides ample reason to avoid a detrimental business decision.

6. THE CONTRARY ARGUMENTS

Arguments against this approach are both conceptual and practical.

Interest

Perhaps the greatest resistance will arise in connection with the interest factor:

1. Capitalization of interest, or deferment of interest to other periods, will be opposed on the ground that it is a period cost and a financing cost—traditionally accrued and expensed on the basis of the debt balance during the period. To the recipient, interest income must always relate to the unrecovered investment, although opinions vary as to what constitutes unrecovered investment at any given time. But why is interest cost different from any other cost for which there are continuing benefits? The same accountants who might object to deferral would probably have no hesitation in deferring appropriate start-up costs and productive R & D, and expensing them on a basis designed to match costs and revenues.

2. The imputation of a return on invested capital for inclusion in accounting costs (and capitalizing a portion of it) is a revolutionary idea for most traditional-minded accountants. This approach goes to the heart of the concept of net income. Under present accounting it is assumed that net income includes a return equivalent to interest on invested capital, and no attempt is made at determining that portion which is attributable to those elements of profitability apart from a basic return for the use of capital. This concept will require a breakdown of income into its two elements—capital and entrepreneurial: that is, one portion representing the interest which should be earned on invested capital, and another representing the excess due to the entrepreneur's operational efficiency— the return on equity compensating for the risks assumed beyond that of a creditor. Such a presentation will be more revealing, but it should not be opposed for this reason. The effect on public utility accounting could be revolutionary. Regulatory agencies do not presently allow interest as a cost (except that portion capitalized on construction in progress). Instead they allow a return on utility investment base, giving some consideration to the proportion of capital that is borrowed in setting an allowable return.[10]

3. One stumbling block to the implementation of this concept is the determi-

nation of the rate of interest to be capitalized. With debt created specifically to acquire a facility the answer seems obvious. On equity capital, the answer is not so easy. Good arguments can be made for both the current rate of return being earned on invested capital and the current debt rate obtainable. If income is to be segmented, as previously discussed, rate of return on equity would also require some assumptions. Obtaining the current debt rate would also have its problems. Also, there is the further question: should the rates change as interest rates fluctuate? All these questions are in the nature of minor conceptual and implementary details that can be ironed out later—they do not go to the heart of the concept. For the present this paper will assume that the debt rate existing at the time of the investment is the appropriate one to use for all imputations and that it should remain constant throughout the holding period. This essentially approximates the facts available when a buy vs. lease decision is made, especially if the money for the purchase is borrowed.

Discounting Deferred Taxes

Those who feel that deferred taxes should be discounted at all times will probably not object to this approach on that account; the differences are minor. Some discounters, and some who feel that no discounting should take place (deferred credit people), will take issue with the following assumptions:

1. The cash flows from accelerated tax depreciation are assured. This assumes sufficient profitability annually throughout the holding period to utilize the tax deductions thus provided. Accountants have a reluctance to anticipate tax benefits based on future profits.
2. The cash flows in excess of debt repayment requirements can earn the same rate of interest.
3. The same tax rate will prevail throughout the holding period.

While these assumptions are admittedly a bit more far-out than those an accountant adopts when he predicates his traditional results on a going-concern basis, they are nevertheless as reasonable as most assumptions made in estimating useful life and salvage value in setting a depreciation policy. When facts change, accounting estimates change. Thus, whenever the facts of the model change, a recomputation is required and the unamortized balance is spread over the remaining period, as in any other depreciation recomputation. And there is always net realizable value as the ultimate safeguard.[11]

Depreciation

Some of the oldest theories in accounting concern depreciation. Arguments for and against the various methods are well known and need not be repeated here; similarly, the evolution of the various acceptable tax methods is not relevant—their stimulative origins have been referred to.

Financial accounting presently permits the recording of depreciation under any of several methods without much regard to circumstances. It would appear that the simplest cure would be to establish criteria for their use rather than advocate straight-line, or levelling, as has been proposed. There are, in fact, few situations (within a historical cost framework) that, when analyzed carefully, will be found to justify methods other than straight-line. Accelerated methods have been recommended in situations involving a high risk of obsolescence (principally as a means of implementing a conservative approach). Unless there is good reason to expect revenues to diminish over time, the better approach is to shorten the estimated useful life. The counterbalancing of high maintenance in the later years is generally more of a myth than a reality. Except in those cases where excessive use will speed replacement (trucks, dies), the unit-of-production method carries the matching of costs and revenues too far (the holding cost of an idle machine can't be ignored).

The sinking-fund and similar interest methods[12] rely on a replacement reserve or fund build-up theory for support and have few adherents today. They were frequently recommended years ago for investment real estate property as a means of offsetting higher interest on debt in the earlier years and thus achieving a form of level costing. Such results are laudatory but are difficult to support without close consideration of the interest on unrecovered investment concept developed here. Except for the inclusion of tax effects, the proposal made in this paper has a remarkable kinship to the sinking-fund concept.

7. ILLUSTRATIVE SCHEDULES

To illustrate the similarity of ownership and lease accounting espoused by this paper, two schedules are attached. They are over-simplified in order to demonstrate the principle more clearly.

Schedule I assumes purchase of a facility for $1,000,000 entirely using money borrowed at 10 percent interest. Schedule II assumes lease of the same facility from a financing lessor who borrows the entire amount at 10 percent interest. (An equivalent result is obtained if equity money is used and a return of 10 percent [before taxes] is required on his unrecovered investment.) As a further simplification, no use of equity money is assumed and all net cash flows, including the net charge to operations for holding costs (or rentals) are considered

SCHEDULE I

AMORTIZATION OF INVESTMENT IN PURCHASED FACILITY

Year	Unrecovered Net Investment @ Beginning of Year	Add Interest On Net Investment (After Tax)*	Depreciation For Tax Purposes	Tax Benefit of Depreciation	DEDUCT Investment Tax Credit	DEDUCT Sale of Residual (Net of Tax)	Annual Allocation of Net Holding Cost (Net of Tax)	Unrecovered Net Investment @ End of Year
0	$1,000,000							$930,000
1	930,000	$ 46,500	$285,714	$142,857	$70,000			790,574
2	790,574	39,529	204,082	102,041			$ 43,069	684,993
3	684,993	34,250	170,068	85,034			43,069	591,140
4	591,140	29,557	136,054	68,027			43,069	509,601
5	509,601	25,480	102,041	51,021			43,069	440,991
6	440,991	22,050	52,041	26,020			43,069	393,952
7	393,952	19,698	0	0			43,069	370,581
8	370,581	18,529	0	0			43,069	346,041
9	346,041	17,302	0	0			43,069	320,274
10	320,274	16,014	0	0			43,069	293,219
11	293,219	14,661	0	0			43,069	264,811
12	264,811	13,241	0	0			43,069	234,983
13	234,983	11,749	0	0			43,069	203,663
14	203,663	10,183	0	0			43,069	170,777
15	170,777	8,539	0	0			43,069	136,247
16	136,247	6,812	0	0		$100,000	43,059	0
TOTAL		$334,094	$950,000	$475,000	$70,000	$100,000	$689,094	

*Equivalent to after-tax cost of interest on debt, which is capitalized rather than charged to income.

Net Investment	$1,000,000
Add: Interest (net of tax benefit)	334,094
Less: Tax Benefit of Depreciation	(475,000)
Investment Tax Credit	(70,000)
Sale of Residual (net of tax)	(100,000)
Net cost of holding the facility	$ 689,094
Annual allocation of net holding cost (16 years)	$ 43,069

Assumptions:

(1) Purchase price $1,000,000, with money borrowed at 10% interest payable at year end.

(2) Tax rate is 50% throughout the period with 7% investment credit obtainable at time of investment (year 0). Annual net taxable income (before depreciation) is equal to or greater than depreciation allowable for taxes.

(3) Estimated useful life 16 years, with a residual of $150,000 ($100,000 net of tax recapture) at end of year 16. Productivity and revenues are level throughout this period.

(4) Tax depreciation: 7 years; ADR, double declining balance for the first two years and sum-of-the-years-digits for remaining life; salvage $50,000.

(5) All net cash flows, including annual net holding cost, are assumed available at year end and applied as reduction of debt.

SCHEDULE II

AMORTIZATION OF LESSOR'S LOAN TO PURCHASE LEASED FACILITY

Year	(1) Required Annual Rental	(2) Interest On Unamortized Loan Balance (Before Taxes)	(3) Tax Depreciation	(4) Tax Gain (Loss) $1 - (2 + 3)$	(5) Tax Benefits (Expenses)	(6) Operating Cash Flow $(1 - 2)$	(7) Net Cash Flow (After Taxes) (Reduces Loan Balance) $(5 + 6)$	(8) Unamortized Loan Balance
0								$930,000
1	$ 86,137	$ 93,000	$285,714	$(292,577)	$146,289	$ (6,863)	$139,426	790,574
2	86,137	79,057	204,082	(197,002)	98,501	7,080	105,581	684,993
3	86,137	68,500	170,068	(152,431)	76,216	17,637	93,853	591,140
4	86,137	59,114	136,054	(109,031)	54,516	27,023	81,539	509,601
5	86,137	50,960	102,041	(66,864)	33,433	35,177	68,610	440,991
6	86,137	44,099	52,041	(10,003)	5,001	42,038	47,039	393,952
7	86,137	39,395	0	46,742	(23,371)	46,742	23,371	370,581
8	86,137	37,058	0	49,079	(24,539)	49,079	24,540	346,041
9	86,137	34,604	0	51,533	(25,766)	51,533	25,767	320,274
10	86,137	32,027	0	54,110	(27,055)	54,110	27,055	293,219
11	86,137	29,322	0	56,815	(28,407)	56,815	28,408	264,811

12	86,137	26,481	0	59,656	(29,828)	59,656	29,828	234,983
13	86,137	23,498	0	62,639	(31,319)	62,639	31,320	203,663
14	86,137	20,366	0	65,771	(32,885)	65,771	32,886	170,777
15	86,137	17,078	0	69,059	(34,529)	69,059	34,530	136,247
16	86,117	13,625	0	72,492	(36,245)	72,492	36,247	100,000
	$1,378,172	$668,184	$950,000	$(240,012)	$120,012	$709,988	$830,000	

Loan Balance @ End of Year 16	$100,000
Less: Sale of Residual (Net of Tax)	100,000
Net Loan Balance	$-0-

Assumptions: Same as Schedule 1, except that lessor borrows $930,000 ($1,000,000 less $70,000 investment credit) at 10% interest payable at year end.

reduction of the debt (or investment) after payment of interest to date. Major maintenance and renovation are assumed to be zero.

Schedule I produces an annual depreciation charge of $43,069 (net of 50 percent income tax) over a sixteen-year productive life. Depending on how the income statement is ultimately restructured, this charge can be shown as a gross charge of $86,137, before taxes, or as a net charge of $43,069. Schedule II produces an annual rental payment of $86,137, before taxes, over the same period, which results in a net charge to income of $43,069 (the net cash cost to the company). In each case the only net charge to income (after consideration of all interest and tax effects) is a constant $43,069. Not only are the accounting results the same, but they reflect the economic realities of the circumstances.

8. CONCLUSION

Unless there are compelling reasons to spread all holding costs on a basis other than evenly over the holding period, level costing of all such costs (including interest on unrecovered investment) is the appropriate accounting for facilities. Except for the element of major maintenance and renovation (which should be appropriately spread in any event) such accounting closely approximates the charges under finance-type leasing, as demonstrated by the models provided herein for illustration. Thus, from an economic standpoint, lease accounting provides a better form of accounting than is presently permitted for ownership accounting. Disregarding for the present the question of disclosure, it would seem inadvisable to require the capitalization of finance-type leases by lessees until such time as the areas of interest capitalization, discounting of deferred taxes, and depreciation, and their interrelationships are thoroughly reviewed and redefined.

NOTES

1. The FASB's initial technical agenda comprises the following:
Accounting for foreign currency translation.
Accruing for future losses (such as catastrophe reserves of casualty insurance companies, losses on foreign operations, and self-insurance).
Reporting by diversified companies.
Accounting for leases by lessees and lessors.
Accounting for certain costs (such as research and development, start-up and relocation).
Criteria for determining materiality.
Broad qualitative standards for financial reporting.

2. For a discussion of the problems on goodwill, see Defliese (1973: 20f).

3. The SEC, on an informal basis, will not accept sinking-fund depreciation. It is acceptable in other countries.

4. A "full pay-out" lease is one in which the terms assure the lessor of a recovery of his investment plus a reasonable return for the use of money subject only to the usual credit risks and realizability of the residual.

5. The same is applicable to all assets and unamortized deferred charges. This paper ignores this aspect for simplicity only and deals only with tangible operating facilities.

6. See Clinton H. Scovell (1924). Mr. Scovell was co-founder of the firm Scovell, Wellington & Co., Accountants and Engineers, subsequently merged with Coopers & Lybrand.

7. See footnote 5.

8. See footnote 5.

9. Facilities that are operating profitably, and are expected to continue to do so for their anticipated useful life, are usually not given a net realizable value test.

10. The greater impact of this paper on public utility accounting would be the elimination of flow-through to income of the tax benefits of the excess of accelerated depreciation over straight-line depreciation in many jurisdictions.

11. See footnote 9.

12. See footnote 4.

REFERENCES

American Institute of Certified Public Accountants (1973) *Accounting for Retail Land Sales*. New York.

Defliese, Philip L. (1973) *The Objectives of Financial Accounting*. New York: Coopers & Lybrand.

Scovell, Clinton H. (1924) *Interest as a Cost*. New York: Ronald Press.

Commentary on
The Economic Case Against Capitalization of Leases

ROSS M. SKINNER*

When I first saw the title to Mr. Defliese's paper I wondered how it could be fitted in to the main theme of this conference, which is the Socio-Economic Environment of Accounting. After some thought, I finally concluded that we could find a link if we talked about the capitalization of leases of premises occupied by public accounting firms. Certainly office premises literally form the environment of a public accounting firm. The lease is undeniably part of the firm's economics. To bring in the "socio" angle is more difficult—but perhaps we could talk about the stress caused by landlord-tenant relations in modern society. (This is not as far-fetched as you might think. When my own firm's largest office moved into a new building about four years ago officials of the landlord are said to have offered to recompense the senior partner negotiating the lease if he would not act for other tenants.)

You may think I speak in jest, but in fact I am going to say something about leases on public accountants' premises because I have a case history which has some relevance to some of the problems Phil was talking about. The case history in question is that of my own firm. Up until a little over four years ago the principal office of our firm was housed in its own building in downtown Toronto. This unusual situation for a public accounting firm developed probably as much as anything by happenstance. The original part of the building in question was built as a bank in 1845. The firm became a tenant in the building sometime before the first World War. In the 1920s the then senior partners bought the whole building. In the middle 1950s a major expansion of building space became urgent and the senior partners sold it to the firm as a whole, feeling that such an important aspect of the firm's operations should be owned by the partnership at large. Throughout the whole of the period subsequent to the

*B.Com. 1944, University of Toronto; C.A. 1949, F.C.A. 1962, Institute of Chartered Accountants of Ontario. Partner and National Director for Accounting Standards, Clarkson, Gordon & Co. Chartered Accountants. Author (with R. J. Anderson) *Analytical Auditing* (1966); *Accounting Principles—A Canadian Viewpoint* (1972).

depression, it was from time to time necessary to throw out wings or add stories to the existing building, until by 1965 the building as a whole served as the centre of operation for some five hundred professional and other staff members. At that time space needs again became pressing and after some abortive attempts to develop a new plan for the property as a whole, it was decided to sell out and lease space in a new bank tower then being built.

Several accounting problems are illustrated by this history:

1. The property was sold at a substantial profit owing entirely to rapidly rising land prices in downtown Toronto between 1956 and 1966. How should these profits be divided? They accrued over the entire period, but in the absence of fair value accounting, no recognition to increasing value was given in the accounts until sale. Unless a retroactive distribution of profit were made, arguable some partners who retired or died before the sale were inequitably treated vis-à-vis others who continued or new partners who were admitted in the period.
2. The property was bought by the bank that leased premises to us. There is no question but that the bank's principal purpose in buying our property was to obtain a substantial tenant for its new building. In fact, if I remember correctly, the two deals were contingent one upon the other. Here was a sale and lease-back with a twist. The premises leased back were not the same property, but otherwise there were strong similarities to the normal sale and lease back. Should we have deferred the profit to be amoritzed over the period of the lease?
3. Now that we are in the new premises we find we seem to have much the same problems as when we owned our own building. We still need more space from time to time (and rights to acquire the same at periodic intervals are built into our lease), we are always moving things around, we have a good deal of maintenance work (though of course not as much as when we owned our own building), and so on.

The moral of this is that leasing in economic terms is a substitute for ownership of assets if those assets are held for use and not for the purpose of speculation. Formerly we owned the building to meet certain needs. Today we lease space to fill the same needs. Moreover we have taken on a long-term obligation to pay rent which, short of bankruptcy, is about as permanent as if we had become indebted. There are only two differences to my mind:

a. We do not have a stake in a permanent asset such as land.
b. The twenty-year term of the lease is shorter than that of a new building (although it could be just as long as that of an older building which conceivably might have been bought).

I must say I don't see that these differences are substantial in terms of the economics of the situation. In other words, not only do I think the "material equity" test of APB Opinion No. 5 was ill conceived, in my opinion the ownership equivalence test under the financing lease provisions of APB Opinion No. 7 is too limited. In my view *any* lease is a substitute for ownership. A twenty-year lease is rather like buying a twenty-year life asset, a ten-year lease is like buying a ten-year life asset and so on.

In a discussion of lease capitalization I was expounding this theme one day not long after our move, and one of my partners asked me if I would be willing to see the lease on our firm's premises capitalized, and distributable profits charged with the resulting accounting depreciation and interest. My reply (which unfortunately I didn't think of until one-half hour after the discussion) was of course yes—provided depreciation was calculated on the annuity or sinking fund basis. Which finally brings me around to the theme of Phil Defliese's paper.

Mr. Defliese has told us that we are probably going to stick with historical cost accounting for the immediate future, that the matching principle will continue as the dominant influence in income accounting for the time being, and that the matching approach can be improved to approximate economic reality more closely. I agree with this short-term prognosis if for no other reason than that one of the strongest forces in the world is inertia.

In the midst of the familiar and comfortable surroundings of the matching principle, Defliese offers us a radical proposal for improvement of the whole process—namely, that interest (including imputed interest on equity funds) should be added to the cost of investment in all assets so long as such cost remains unrecovered, or perhaps we might better say unmatched against revenue. He sees several advantages to this:

1. The cost matched against revenue will better represent the sacrifice actually made in acquiring and holding the asset.
2. In the income account we will charge operating income with an all-inclusive cost for assets consumed, including cost of capital, so that we will see whether we are really ahead of the game to be in business; and we will show separately the income we derive or should derive from our capital investment. In Defliese's words we will break down reported income into two elements, income on capital and entrepreneurial income.
3. We will solve several current accounting anomalies.
   a. The fact that we do not really have a rational basis for acceptance of the various alternative depreciation patterns that we do accept in practice.
   b. The fact that we get a different charge against operating income if we lease an asset rather than buy it, and furthermore the charge is heavier (in the initial years at least) if we own the asset than if we leased it, whereas, if anything, we would expect the converse to be true.
   c. The fact that we carry a cost in the accounts for an asset that has been constructed or developed by ourself which is different from the cost we would show if we bought the identical asset from an outside party, on terms that represent an equivalent economic sacrifice.

d. The differing theories as to the nature of deferred taxes and the problems in conveying the substance of many transactions such as leveraged leases, real estate income recognition, etc., unless a discount factor is used to reflect the timing of tax obligations.

I have called Defliese's proposal radical and so it is if one judges by the magnitude of the change it would bring about in accounting practice or the opposition he rightly says it will arouse. But the basic idea does have a long and respectable lineage. Defliese has mentioned the 1924 book by Scovell. (In passing, I think it significant that the firm Scovell, Wellington was a firm of accountants and *engineers*.) I remember also in my university days studying a work entitled *Risk, Uncertainty and Profit,* by the economist F. H. Knight (1921), in which, if my memory serves, Knight drew a basic distinction between interest in the sense of the basic wages or return on capital, and profit, being the excess of return earned over the basic wages of capital and forming the reward for entrepreneurial risk taking. This corresponds very closely, if not exactly, to the income breakdown Defliese suggests between interest on capital and operating income. One might also mention that Defliese's concept is consistent with the concepts of actuarial science and with the works of many managerial economists.

Further, as Defliese says, there are marked similarities between his ideas and those that have historically been used to support the annuity form of depreciation or its first cousin, sinking fund depreciation. The contribution Defliese has made, so far as the accounting world is concerned, is his extension of the basic concept of adding interest to assets held to all assets, not just those subject to depreciation accounting.

In the main, I wholeheartedly agree with Defliese's proposition as a theory. It seems to me its ramifications need exploration in a much longer study and only the highlights can be touched upon in a short paper or in comments such as mine. In the time available, I shall make some random observations on some aspects that I would like to see considered more fully.

1. I am not clear about the proposal to credit the benefit from tax depreciation against the unrecovered net investment. Would this be so credited as it was realized or would the presumed present value of the tax deduction feature be set up as a separate asset to be amortized against income on the basis of original expectations? If the former interpretation is the right one the effect will be that the tax expense line in the income statement will be inflated beyond the actual tax outlay while the depreciation line will be correspondingly reduced. It may be that this is not what is intended, but I would like to see the problem worked out and illustrated to form a better opinion. I am not sure also that the interest factor would not be just as well dealt with under the discounted liability theory of deferred tax, or by applying a discount factor to the deferred tax balance even when it is not regarded as a liability.

I used to think that the deferral approach precluded the possibility of discounting. I have recently changed my opinion on this by using the reasoning that the deferral theory objective is solely to arrive at a correct measure of the expense that should be charged against current year's income. However, where the dollar outlay corresponding to the expense is deferred over a period of some years into the future it seems to me it must be discounted to arrive at a correct measurement of the expense to be recognized currently, even though the future obligation is not an actual liability as of the current date. It seems to me that there is an analogy here to recognition of expense under a pension plan. No one would dream of putting up an undiscounted figure as a current expense. Perhaps more generally what I am saying is that one argument for specific recognition of interest in accounting is that it is necessary to recognize the time value of money in order to achieve a rational matching of expense and revenue.

In another medium (Skinner, 1972: 390–92), I have suggested that one might solve the problem of interest in relation to tax expense by providing accelerated depreciation on a portion of an asset's cost if that asset qualifies for accelerated tax allowances. The portion of the asset cost to be so depreciated would be equivalent to the present value of future tax allowances. This is somewhat similar to the proposition put forward by Defliese, but I cannot tell without a more detailed exposition whether the two ideas are essentially the same.

2. I am not entirely clear what Defliese has in mind with respect to depreciation patterns under his proposal. He says, variously:

> The manner in which this newly defined depreciation is allocated to the periods of use is a matter that requires the exercise of logic and judgment. The arguments for accelerated methods or sinking fund methods are not better (in the ordinary case) than for straight-line, especially if matching is the more pervasive motivation. All these methods rest on arbitrary premises. [Sec. 5]

> . . . There are in fact a few situations (within a historical cost framework) that, when analyzed carefully, will be found to justify methods other than straight-line. Accelerated methods have been recommended in situations involving a high risk of obsolescence (principally as a means of implementing a conservative approach). Unless there is good reason to expect revenues to diminish over time, the better approach is to shorten the estimated useful life. [Sec. 6]

> Unless there are compelling reasons to spread all holding costs on a basis other than evenly over the holding period, level costing of all such costs (including interest on unrecovered investment) is the appropriate accounting for facilities. [Sec. 8]

> Assuming revenues from the facility are level, it is reasonable to suggest that the aggregate cost should also be spread on a level basis. [Sec. 3]

> Once this aggregate cost is determined, it should be allocated (less the expected residual or salvage) as a loss in value over the realistically estimated holding period on a basis proportionate to revenues. [Sec. 5]

In this last quotation (which appeared in the earlier part of his paper) Defliese has set out what I regard to be the guiding principle; namely, that costs as he defines them must be spread over the holding period *on a basis proportionate to projected revenues.* It is not the manner of allocation of depreciation to periods of use which requires judgment, it is the pattern of expected revenues that requires judgment, and this was not clear to me on reading the paper. When we look at it this way we see that a straight-line pattern of writeoff is only justified when we have a straight-line pattern of revenues (or perhaps I should say net cash inflows) from the asset use. Defliese suggests that this is the normal expectation. I would have thought that this is not true but rather that the patterns vary rather widely depending on the type of asset. I would expect that if we had complete knowledge we would find quite a number of assets where the net revenue inflow would rise for a short period (say for the first 10 percent of the asset's life) then would be level for the next half to two-thirds of its life and then would decline fairly steadily for the remainder of the service period.

It seems to me, however, that the question of net revenue patterns is almost wholly a matter of opinion in our present state of knowledge. I do not know of any convincing evidence that tells us what pattern is to be expected with respect to capital assets generally or even with respect to particular types of capital assets. (Where second-hand markets exist, one might deduce such patterns merely by the action of the market, if we assume that buyers act rationally and determine the prices they are willing to pay more or less on a discounted cash flow basis.)

The difficulty in ascertaining revenue patterns except by deduction from market information is evidenced even more conclusively when we consider that we buy the vast majority of fixed assets individually but that they only produce revenue in combination with other assets. Consider, for example, the furnishings in the president's office. What contribution these assets, as such, make to revenue seems to me a pure guess. Here we come up against a gaping hole in the matching theory which goes some distance to explain why general practice has accepted for so long the various contradictory methods of depreciation complained about in Defliese's paper. To point this out is not to criticize Defliese's theory as such, which he specifically states is within the context of the matching principle, but rather to emphasize the gulf that can exist between good theory and good practice.

3. Defliese identifies the problem of determining what rate of interest should be capitalized and I agree that this problem is a conceptual stumbling block. On pragmatic grounds I think I could accept the suggestion that "the debt rate existing at the time of the investment is the appropriate one to use for all imputations" but I imagine other considerations will need to be dealt with.

4. Defliese advocates that the credit for interest capitalized on equity funds should appear in the income statement. This, of course, is what happens with respect to "interest" capitalized during construction by public utilities. It is, however, contrary to the long standing accounting tradition that you don't earn money by building assets, you earn it by operating them. Defliese's answer to this, no doubt, will be that he envisages a clear distinction between the operating section of his income section and what I will call, for want of a better term, the "return on capital" section. I think his

answer is entirely justified within the confines of his theory but, if implemented, it would require a fairly radical change in the way people read and analyze financial statements. Personally, I think such a change is desirable, but I am not optimistic that it will be achieved without quite a struggle.

5. Defliese concludes that adoption of his theory makes academic the issue of capitalizing leases. I would agree that it makes this issue much less important, but I think it is arguable that it does not eliminate it entirely. In the first place, the balance sheet still has some uses and if a lease obligation is really very similar to debt, there are reasonably sound arguments for making it look like debt in the balance sheet. My view is reinforced by a second theory of mine to the effect that, when we think about leases to be capitalized, we should not just think about leases which are, in essence, equivalent to installment purchases of property. I would contend that all leases are substitutes for ownership of property for a certain period of time, and it is relatively unimportant whether or not a given lease covers the use of a property over the entire period of its life.

Finally, I would conclude with two brief comments on practical problems in implementation of Defliese's theory.

First, the theory rests rather more heavily upon forecasts of the future than does present practice, although I would agree that the difference is one of degree and not of kind. To mention only two points, it will be necessary to forecast (1) future maintenance and repair costs on physical assets and (2) future holding periods for all assets, in order to establish the base amount to be amortized against income from use or consumption of the asset. To illustrate the latter problem, consider the prepayments which pipeline companies are now making to gas exploration companies that are to be repaid out of future deliveries of gas. Under the Defliese theory, interest will be included as part of the cost of these prepaid assets. Thus, for the purpose of striking an amortization rate on such asset at the time that gas deliveries commence, it will be necessary to estimate at what rate and over how long a period such deliveries will take place. Somehow if the theory is implemented we are going to have to persuade accountants to accept the necessity for an increase in the judgmental element of accounting and this of course has implications for problems of comparability, auditing, etc.

Secondly, Defliese's theory is, in general, less conservative than present accounting practice. Consequently, the application of a net realizable value test becomes relatively more important. Defliese suggests that we do not now customarily apply such a test to facilities that are operating profitably. I think it would have been better to say that so long as a facility appears, under present accounting practice, to be operating profitably there is a pretty good probability that it has a net realizable value in excess of its carrying value. This proposition will be less certain under the accounting methods proposed. Moreover, and a good deal more seriously, there will be a large number of cases where a realizable value test is, as a practical matter, impossible. I would think this would be true, for example, for all manner of deferred costs, costs accumulated by companies in the development stage, many long-term investments and so on. This problem relates back to my earlier remarks on the probable resistance to proposals for recognizing income on acquisition of assets as well as from operation of assets. If, as in the case of a development stage company, little by way of operations is carried on it may seem strange to have an income account. Yet the development stage company is only an extreme example of the problem that will be encountered by all companies that include development as part of their ongoing operations. Again, it would seem that if the proposed method is implemented a higher degree of sophistication on the part of readers of financial statements will be required that we have seen evidence of to date.

In summary, Defliese has made a proposal that has strong conceptual appeal. I look forward to a detailed exposition of its merits and discussion of its potential problems.

REFERENCES

Knight, Frank H. (1921) *Risk, Uncertainty and Profit.* Reprint (1965) New York: Harper & Row, Harper Torchbooks.
Skinner, Ross M. (1972) *Accounting Principles—A Canadian Viewpoint.* Toronto: Canadian Institute of Chartered Accountants.

Discussion

Cramer. Does your approach include the possibility of negative depreciation, as it should? I note that you make the initial schedule of allocation on the basis of some expected revenue function by years.

Defliese. No. I would like to clarify the point. I said "projected revenues," but in this context I assumed that revenues would be level. In other words, I recognized the practical aspect of Ross's comments that there is a potential level revenue from a facility. You buy a lathe and obviously it is impossible for you to determine what the specific revenues on a year-by-year basis will be for that lathe. So the practical alternative is to level the depreciation. I would say that this would be the approach except where it would be clearly demonstrated that there was a basis for relating the cost to the revenues on other than a level basis.

Cramer. So you are speaking of the same old notion of the "cost package," but it seems to me that you have a fluctuating rate of return on that same asset every year.

Defliese. I am not attempting to determine the rate of return. The rate of return fluctuates by virtue of the income statement that is restructured to show the operating section and the return on capital section. Now the return on capital section will not fluctuate. The operating section will.

Cramer. Are you saying that you are going to add this interest cost to assets and then amortize this total cost package in relation to some revenue function?

Defliese. On a level basis, unless it could be demonstrated that there is a better revenue basis for it than leveling.

Cramer. It seems to me you are confusing two rates.

Defliese. I am attempting to determine the holding cost of the facility over its life. The holding cost of the facility consists of the monies expended for it, less the tax recoveries, plus the interest on the unrecovered portion, giving recognition to the incidence of the tax recoveries and then leveling the aggregate cost that results on the basis that this is my overall economic loss that has to be allocated to the periods benefited.

Cramer. You confuse me because once you get those figures which you are going to call the "cost" of facilities, if you are dealing at the

370

level of opportunity costs, you still have imputations to make on the imputations that you have already made. This would be required for every period.

Defliese. I don't follow your "imputations on imputations."

Cramer. On unrecovered cost of including previously "imputed interest," since basically you are commingling non-homogeneous sets of data.

Defliese. What is wrong with that?

Cramer. It is illogical.

Defliese. What is illogical about taking all your costs and putting them in a basket?

Cramer. My point at this moment is that once you have derived this figure—you call it cost of the facilities—each period, if this is your cost and if you are going to impute some additional interest back into this year, you will then be imputing interest on. . . .

Defliese. On interest. It is compounding, there is no question about that. Why shouldn't it be compounded?

Skinner. May I interject here? I think you are saying either you add interest year by year as you go along under the traditional sort of annuity pattern, or else you calculate the whole interest load over the period, capitalizing it right at the beginning. I would assume that if you did that, then you would have a credit somewhere, which would be a deferred credit that you would have to bleed into your income account year by year.

Defliese. That is a different mechanism, but it would produce the same result.

Skinner. That's right. but under either of those you wouldn't be adding interest to interest.

Cramer. My last comment is that it seems to me that what we should do is to consider the *overall subject matter of accounting for executory contracts* before we attack this particular problem. I think that this was the mistake of the APB when it first started working on the subject of leases. What we need is a generalized model to incorporate all executory contracts, for which a lease is just one form. I will write you a letter on the subject.

Skinner. May I just make one comment on that? I am not sure a lease *is* an executory contract, because the landlord has delivered the premises to the tenant. I don't know what your law is down here, but up in Canada the tenant can kick him off the premises.

Cramer. This is what makes it an executory contract.

Skinner. I may not understand your term. I thought an executory contract meant a contract which was unperformed or partially unperformed by both parties. So I would say under a lease contract the landlord has performed when he delivers the premises. That is the distinction I would draw.

Cramer. I look at the quiet enjoyment aspect of it.

Vance. This is not a criticism or a question, but a comment. It underscores the point that Ross made just before he sat down and that is that all people have the habit of thinking a title is an individual thing—you either have it or you don't have it, you are a lessor or you are an owner. This is the mistake. I think if you examine it you will find that the title is a very divisible thing. You can have all sorts of pieces and parts of it. For example, if you buy an automobile and you sign a conditional sales contract, the contract will say that the seller reserves all rights, title, interest in and to this vehicle, and all the buyer has is the right to drive it. As long as the buyer makes the payments the seller won't do anything about it. The buyer doesn't really have very much of a title. What he has is the security interest, which is a little piece of the title, and it says the seller can take it back if the payments aren't made. The seller has virtually all the incidence of title. If you think in those terms, you will reach the conclusion that I think Ross expressed; that is, if you have a series of lease payments for a period of time you don't worry about residual interests or equity interests or ownership interests. It is a right you have that you can value. So forget about who owns it. Various people will own various parts of it.

Pichler. Phil's paper raised an interesting prospect with respect to opportunity costing. If one buys a piece of property for a million dollars and sells it ten years later for two million, economists would want to see opportunity costs included instead of showing a profit of one million. Perhaps an opportunity loss was actually incurred in the transaction. Of course to attain absolute values of opportunity costs in real rates of return one would have to know what all the opportunities were. That approaches an infinite set. I myself would be satisfied, and I think most practicing economists would be, if you accountants would consider the market. A number of people choose a number of different alternatives, each of which produces a relative rate of return. If the statements reflected the *relative* wisdom of their decisions, I would be much more satisfied than I am presently. Even if financial statements would not reflect the absolute resource rate of return, it would be a long step forward if they would enable one to rank order the wisdom of the decisions.

Defliese. I recognized the practical problem that exists in that and said that obviously this is a measurement problem (a loaded phrase) and if we go anywhere in this direction we will have to agree on some premise. The premise I am suggesting for the moment (and it is purely a suggestion) is that we use the current borrowing rate. I think that is usually the choice that exists with respect to a company that is facing a buy-or-lease decision.

CHAPTER 11

Let's Abandon "Generally Accepted"

HARVEY KAPNICK*

Today investors conclude that certain financial statements are of higher quality
than the economic facts warrant. "Generally Accepted" Accounting Principles
cannot be defined and imply an unwarranted stamp of approval.

Today we find the accounting profession under the heaviest attack
in its history, with Congress, regulatory agencies, the investment community, the general public, and even corporate management seriously
questioning its ability to fulfill its responsibilities. It is clear that the
profession must take bold steps toward improving its public credibility.

Recently the profession did take action with the establishment of
the new Financial Accounting Standards Board, and this step has been
applauded by all sectors of the financial community. The profession
did establish a committee to consider the objectives of financial statements, but the results of that committee's work remain uncertain.
Unfortunately, having taken these steps, the profession may want to
rest on its laurels, but this approach can only lead to disaster. These
actions were to catch up on what should have been done in the decade
of the 60s. Now, in the decade of the 70s, we must move aggressively
forward as never before to change many of the outmoded concepts
that are strangling the profession and confusing the public.

One important step that we should take now is to abandon the use
of the term "generally accepted" in all references to accounting principles. This step would significantly improve the public's understanding
of our role in reporting on financial statements, since this so-called
stamp of approval, even though at one point it may have beeen useful,
may well be the most important underlying issue in the deteriorating

*B.S. 1947, Honorary D.S.B.A. 1971, Cleary College, University of Michigan Graduate
School of Business 1947–48. CPA. Chairman, Arthur Andersen & Co. Contributor to
accounting periodicals.

confidence in the accounting profession.

Now, while investor confidence has not been completely lost and with the FASB in a position to begin operations, we are on the brink of a new era in the development of accounting principles. We might ask ourselves whether the term "generally accepted" is fact or fiction. Many act as though it is a fact and hide behind "generally accepted" as a basis for approving less acceptable accounting principles under the guise that those principles meet the "generally accepted" test. All too often, when public companies change auditors over a dispute, it really is not the accounting principle per se that is at question; rather, it is the judgment applied by the auditor in the application of the accounting principle. Unfortunately, often the question gets down to the point where the accounting is accepted only because it meets the dubious test of being "generally accepted." This is unfortunate, since the real test is not the general acceptance of the accounting principle, but the fair presentation of the financial data resulting from the application of the principle. If there ever was any question as to the real test, we need only to look at recent court decisions where we have been told that financial statements are not necessarily to be viewed on the basis of generally accepted principles, but, rather, on whether they have been fairly presented.

It is this basic question that gives rise today to the increased questioning of the accounting profession. No longer can we fall back on "generally accepted" when for forty years the profession has been unable to define that term. The concept of "generally accepted" has only misled readers of financial statements into believing they were of a higher quality than may be the case.

1. "GENERALLY ACCEPTED" HAS NEVER BEEN UNDERSTOOD

A generation ago these troublesome words, "generally accepted," received from the accounting profession the equivalent of a Good Housekeeping Seal of Approval. They have appeared in millions of audit reports and so frequently in the literature and in discussions among accountants, investors, professors, students, and businessmen that the abbreviation GAAP soon may be found in dictionaries, along with SOS, OK and PDQ. Such frequent usage usually would imply understandability. But in this case, such a conclusion certainly would be erroneous. Furthermore, whatever communication was accomplished in the past by the term certainly does not exist today. The term has grown in obscurity with the passage of time.

In fairness to these words, some may believe that they do connote quality. Certainly they "read well" in audit reports. They give the auditors' report a degree of class—a certain respectability. But this is the crux of the problem. They imply something that is not the case, and now that the public realizes this, the accounting profession has its back to the wall. We must provide a different basis on which to base our opinions—one that is meaningful and understandable to both the profession and the public.

Until the early 1930s, auditors reported on fair presentation without making any reference to accounting principles. Possibly to provide a standard against which to judge financial statements, the words "accepted accounting principles" began to appéar in audit reports. Soon the word "generally" was added. If the term "generally accepted" was adopted as a real standard, it has not worked. If the concept was adopted because of some hope that it would somehow generate progress by reducing the number of alternative practices, it hasn't done that either. All things considered, the test of general acceptance has hindered progress as much as helped it.

From the beginning, the term has raised questions such as: "Acceptance by whom?" and "How much acceptance constitutes 'general' acceptance?" Another popular question has been, "If financial statements should be prepared in accordance with accounting principles that are generally accepted, how can a company ever use a new, and presumably better, principle?" More pointedly, the question is, how is innovation possible if general acceptance is an effective standard? I can assure you that these questions are not completely hypothetical, and that is why I say the term has hindered progress in the accounting profession.

If the words are read without searching for a special meaning, they imply that authority comes from usage. Underlying this approach was a belief that usage implied the existence of a process of selection that led to a broadly based supporting consensus. There was a presumption that for a consensus to arise in favor of a particular principle or method, it must have met a kind of "market-place" test. Those preparing and attesting to financial statements were thought to have weighed the alternatives and selected the one most appropriate for the circumstances. It was an environment where, supposedly, the sound principle would receive an endorsement and the unsound a rejection.

This kind of reasoning supported the approach used to give an authoritative status to the Accounting Research Bulletins of the 1940s and 1950s. Each ARB stated that "the authority of the bulletins rests upon the general acceptability of opinions so reached." In other words, if the bulletins were followed, that is, accepted, they became authoritative. In the early years, even the Accounting Principles Board carried on with this approach.

This plan reflected a philosophy that a broad consensus should be given time to emerge before any enforcement is undertaken. If one had faith in the selection process that accompanied the financial reporting activity, it would be unwise to try to force the adoption of any particular principle or method before a consensus emerged because of the chance that the inferior would be enforced rather than the superior. The hope was that good would triumph over evil in the long run.

Waiting for a consensus may have been a prudent philosophy for another reason. An attempt to enforce prematurely would risk exposing the minimal dimensions of the power base then held by the accounting profession.

The Securities and Exchange Commission in 1938 gave its strong endorsement to the notion that usage generates authority. In effect, its ASR No. 4 reinforced the traditional view that general acceptance generated substantial authoritative support.

Although usage is a force or factor that deserves consideration, accountants have come to question whether widespread acceptance and the interaction supposedly associated with achieving a consensus will lead to the rejection of the unsound. The record certainly demonstrates that the approach which relies on general acceptance, plus consensus has permitted the continuing existence of many alternatives. If this condition is undesirable or defenseless, then general acceptance as a standard must be judged a failure.

There is also the concern that general acceptance has fostered a process of adverse selection. This concern assumes that not all equally acceptable alternatives are of equal quality. It also recognizes that the tendency of statement-users to evaluate companies by comparing their financial statements leads to a kind of protective reaction that exerts a downward pressure rather than an upward pressure in the adoption of accounting policies. A policy that makes a company's financial statements compare less favorably is handicapped. Thus, in some cases, Gresham's Law has come into play and, rather than good surviving over evil, bad alternatives have driven out the good alternatives.

2. THE PURPOSE SERVED BY "GENERALLY ACCEPTED" HAS PASSED

Even if the doubts just raised about the merits of the words "generally accepted" for the auditors' report can be overcome and even if that usage is conceded to have been a respectable, defensible criterion for the profession to adopt in the 1930s, it does not follow that these concessions justify retention of these words today.

The accounting profession no longer operates under 1930-type conditions. In those days, there was less regimentation of professional practice, less specification of accounting principles by authoritative institutions and fewer detailed, prescribed rules. Also, many of the major problems we face today either did not exist at all or were much less significant. Independent accountants necessarily relied more on their individual professional judgment than on the collective judgment as stated by pronouncements of professional groups. A kind of environment prevailed where it was perhaps reasonable to believe that the practices adopted by others were the result of decisions reached after careful consideration had been given to the accounting issues involved and that the accounting issues had dominated the considerations weighed.

Under such conditions, usage had some appeal as a sensible guideline. It certainly was a standard, even with its limitations, relied on by the independent accountant. There were no ARBs, no Accounting Series Releases, and no SAPs to turn to. Authority in accounting principles had not become institutionalized. The sociological structure of the accounting profession was, in a sense, primitive in form.

3. TODAY'S ENVIRONMENT DOES NOT SUPPORT "GENERALLY ACCEPTED"

In contrast, consider today's environment. Today, FASB, APB, SEC, and Rule 203 of the Code of Professional Ethics[1] outrank general acceptance. They are more likely to provide the reasons why an accounting principle has been adopted. Today, it is specific acceptance by some authoritative institution that counts rather than general acceptance.

Thus, justification today is for the use of an accounting principle attributed to rulings, decrees, releases, pronouncements and rules of ethical conduct, rather than to the general acceptance of the principle. Of course, rules haven't yet reached the stage where they cover the entire universe of accounting and reporting matters; but they are gaining ground at an alarming rate.

As noted earlier, those who believed in the merits of waiting for a consensus to emerge as support for general acceptance looked upon the process of achieving a consensus as a way to accumulate and evaluate the sum total of real-world experience in dealing with accounting and reporting problems. It was something like acting on collective judgment accumulated both within and beyond the profession.

Under today's conditions, in areas where rules are displacing the "common law," such collective experience can have an influence only to the extent that the rule-makers are willing to seek such input through public hearings and reactions to exposure drafts. Experience gained from usage may still be a factor today, but a portion of it is evaluated through different channels. If those charged with setting financial reporting standards discover and rely on the consensus, the resulting standards, or rules, may be no better or no worse in qualitative terms than those standards produced by general acceptance. They may be only more specific and probably less responsive to changing conditions.

Not only has the force formerly derived from a consensus been subdued and redirected, so to speak, but the attitude that held that enforcement should not precede a consensus has changed. This change was signaled with heated debate at that history-making meeting of the Council of the American Institute in 1964. It was decided there that an independent accountant must view an APB Opinion as automatically satisfying the generally accepted test, but it did not rule out other principles and practices from also meeting that test.

When the membership of the AICPA voted in 1972 in favor of Rule 203 of the Code of Professional Ethics, it took another step away from reliance on general acceptance as conceived in the 1930s, when those words were introduced to the auditor's report. There is an indication that the SEC's views about the value of relying on a consensus is also changing.

4. "GENERALLY ACCEPTED" IS BUT ONE OF MANY CRITERIA TODAY

Today, the independent auditor must look to a variety of sources for his standards: (1) practices in industry which remain a source, but this source is no better, and is probably less reliable as a guideline, than it was when general acceptance was the predominant standard; (2) pronouncements by professional bodies, whose opinions have been granted authoritative status by voluntary action; (3) rulings of governmental agencies, whose decisions have the support of law; and (4) policies, of individual accounting firms, developed generally to cover those matters not adequately prescribed by other sources.

As the above listing suggests, the number of sources that must be considered when searching for standards has expanded. Even more expansion can be expected. For example, the new Cost Accounting Standards Board, whose standards have the force and effect of law in the area of government contracts, may prove to be a force that will have a considerable influence on financial reporting.

The growth in the number of sources that have acquired some authoritative status has introduced considerable confusion into financial reporting. For instance, what ranking should be given to the several standard-setting sources? The accountant surely must consider the force of a position taken by the SEC. In case of conflicting authority, is he, or should he be, compelled to rely on that standard above all others? What are his options if he believes the SEC to be "dead wrong"? The accountant certainly is aware of the growing stature of opinions supported by the American Institute and equally aware of the added burden he is forced to assume if he should lack confidence about whether such opinions provide an acceptable standard in some special circumstances.

Sometimes he will be impressed by the merits of an industry practice; but in other situations, no amount of documentation showing that a particular practice has been used by other companies (and apparently with the approval of other independent accountants) will convince the accountant of the wisdom of relying on that kind of evidence for his standard. But given reference to general acceptance in the short-form report, where is the balance between the accountant's fairness to his client (who may feel justified in conforming accounting policies with those widely used in the same industry and who may feel that a different accountant would not object to the practice being questioned) and the accountant's commitment to that elusive notion of fair presentation also referred to in the opinion portion of the short-form report? Throughout all of this searching for, evaluation of, and choosing between standards run the common threads of contention and vagueness.

The independent accountant's dilemma over "generally accepted" is clearly demonstrated in the recent controversies over the "front ending" of income by companies granting certain types of franchises and companies in the real estate field. At one point in time, it would have been difficult to dispute that "front ending" was a generally accepted practice in these areas. As a result, when an independent accountant took the position that this method produced unfair results, he often was replaced by one who would agree to the accounting method by relying on its general acceptance.

We have confused methods with principles and general acceptance of methods with a fair presentation from the application of a principle. The independent accountant who holds out for the latter—and correct—test loses out to the one who takes advantage of the existing confusion over the term "generally accepted." The ultimate result of all this can only be further uncertainty over the role of the independent accountant and an increase in the growing credibility problem of the profession.

5. NOW IS THE TIME TO ABANDON
"GENERALLY ACCEPTED"

The fact is that, at present, the independent auditor is relying on several sources for his standards and the standards followed have varying authoritative stature whose ranking is unclear. Furthermore, the relevance of some of the standards in financial reporting is far from settled. If the independent accountant isn't facing a dilemma, he is at least in a predicament. The accountant is using an unstable mixture of standards whose proportions can vary from engagement to engagement. Some of these standards, and an expanding number of them, he feels compelled to use. Others he adopts by choice because he considers them to be appropriate under the circumstances. His freedom of choice seems to be contracting, which further complicates the problem. All of this leads up to the question, Is he relying on "general acceptance" for his standards?

In view of the growing complexity and vagueness which surrounds the standards matter, it is time to drop "generally accepted" from the standard short-form report. These words can no longer be reconciled with today's and tomorrow's conditions. They no longer communicate. If they were ever a good choice of words, they no longer are. Their retention would require those relying on the auditor's report to perceive that auditors have changed and are continuing to modify the ordinary meaning of these words and attributing a different and specialized meaning to them. This imposes a condition hardly conducive to creating confidence in the role of the accounting profession.

6. WE MUST ESTABLISH THE
OBJECTIVES OF FINANCIAL STATEMENTS

It will be difficult, if not impossible, to determine relevant standards for the accounting profession to use in reporting on financial statements until we determine the objective of those financial statements.

To illustrate, in Germany the accountant's standard is to determine that the financial statements comply with German law. For his standards, the German auditor looks to the law. The law provides the basis for comparison. Usage that conflicts with that prescribed by law would have no status as a standard. A standard well established in some other country might have no standing in Germany because it would lack relevance for that objective. In Germany the objective of the financial statements is specific. Agreement with a law is a concept easily understood, although it obviously may have some weaknesses insofar as a fair presentation of the facts is concerned.

In contrast, consider the accountant's standard in the United Kingdom. There the auditor is required by law to determine whether the financial statements "give a true and fair view of the state of affairs of the company as at the end of its financial year and of the profit and loss of the company for the year then ended." The determination of the valuation methods and other accounting and reporting practices that will lead to the presentation of a "true and fair view" generally is left to the company and its auditors. However, the Board of Trade has wide powers concerning reporting practices. Also, the professional accounting organizations in the United Kingdom have had a substantial influence on accounting and reporting practices. Their releases are recognized as an authoritative source of what the best accounting practices are, but the releases are not binding on the members.

In the United States, according to the wording of the short-form report and the opinion expressed in a recent court case, the audit objective is to confirm that the financial statements "present fairly." Whether the CPA is irrevocably bound to this standard is an interesting question, because fair presentation is a nebulous, vague concept that to date has proven difficult to describe and specify. When the standard is so unclear, so vague and so complex, the relevance of some financial reporting practices can be difficult to establish. Which accounting methods will produce a fair presentation? Is one presentation "fairer" than another? Will cash-basis accounting result in a fair presentation? Will a "generally accepted" method result in a fair presentation? For that matter, will the application of an APB Opinion, say APB No. 17, which requires the arbitrary amortization of goodwill, result in a fair presentation?

This problem is only compounded when we think of today's multi-national companies. How should the financial statements of a U.S. company owned by a German corporation be presented? What about the French subsidiary of an American company? In these and countless other situations, what constitutes a "fair presentation?" If the concept is "general acceptance," then general acceptance by whom—the French or the Americans?

To point out the differences that exist in this area among the various industrial countries of the world today, I have attached an appendix showing the form of auditors' report used in thirteen countries other than the United States. It is interesting to note that with the exception of Argentina, Brazil, Canada, Japan and Mexico—all of which have been heavily influenced by U.S. practices—no other country follows the concept of "general acceptance" in reporting on financial statements. In this era of widespread international operations, it is difficult to see how much of the industrial world can rely on financial reports prepared on the basis of generally accepted accounting practices when such practices vary significantly by country.

7. TODAY'S FINANCIAL REPORTING
PRACTICES MAY NOT GIVE A FAIR PRESENTATION

Fair presentation also has another problem. Accountants are saddled with financial reporting concepts that place great reliance on historical cost, realization, and matching. These concepts have not resulted in a meaningful portrayal of the impact of inflation. They do not isolate the consequences of technological change. Attempts to apply conventional accrual accounting to some of the "newer" industries have resulted in much dissatisfaction. Consider the case of real estate companies, or energy companies, or natural resource companies. Are their financial statements, based on historical cost, realization and matching, presenting fairly—with sufficient frequency?

Conventional accrual accounting emerged from simple times—before there was much in the way of research and development, before income taxes, before the threat of obsolescence was of much concern, before poolings of interest, before leveraged leases, and before accounting was a topic worthy of a colloquium at the University of Kansas. Times have changed. Yet we continue to rely on cost, realization, and matching to produce a fair presentation.

Some of the uncertainty about what constitutes a fair presentation could be eliminated if there were agreement about the objectives of financial statements. If these objectives were established, they could provide some guidelines that might help define the boundaries of fair presentation. Adoption of a reporting standard that obviously conflicted with the objectives of financial statements would lessen the prospects for a fair presentation. The relevance of an industry practice or the merits of an APB or FASB Opinion could be tested by comparison with the objectives of financial statements.

By accepting a responsibility to express an opinion about fair presentation, the independent accountant also is subjected to a requirement that can be fulfilled only if he has the freedom to exercise his professional judgment over the full range of accounting and reporting matters. But does he have that freedom? In an environment where so much authoritative status has been given to professional society pronouncements and SEC approvals, reliance on alternatives that lack APB, FASB, or SEC favor but whose adoption is necessary to achieve a fair presentation will be viewed by statement-users with greater and greater suspicion. Encroachment on the professional accountant's option to depart from the "rules" already has set in—and it is likely to expand. Fair presentation is not a concept that is compatible with financial reporting via detailed rules which restrict the ability to use professional judgment.

Until agreement on the objectives of financial statements is obtained and until the question of the independent accountant's right to override a specified rule has been more fully explored and resolved, I favor dropping "presents fairly" from the auditors' report. The elusiveness of the concept at present makes those words misleading.

This proposal should not be interpreted as favoring a reduction in the role of the independent accountant. I hope we will want to continue to assume a truly substantive role to the public, not one requiring less responsibility and less professional judgment. However, until the concept of fair presentation is more precisely described and standards are established on that basis, it seems compatible with simple honesty to put those words on the shelf until we can live up to them.

8. THE ACCOUNTING PROFESSION MUST FULFILL ITS PUBLIC RESPONSIBILITIES

To begin to draw together my beliefs, given the environment I have described as existing today and the direction in which things are moving in the profession, it is my firm conviction that a substantive objective of reporting on financial statements, as is implied by the concept of fair presentation, will never be attained by the creation of and reliance on a detailed set of rules. Unless the confusion that presently surrounds the entire area of reporting standards is significantly reduced, there is likely to remain a credibility gap between what the public believes the auditor has accomplished by his assurance that a fair presentation has been achieved and what indeed has been accomplished by his work. The public's expectations about "certified" statements prepared on a "generally accepted" basis in too many instances exceed reality. Something must be done to narrow the gap.

If the accounting profession continues to drift along with rule-making, whether by the FASB or various governmental agencies, and accepts compliance with such rules as satisfying its standards, it will sooner or later have to settle for a smaller, less significant role out of simple fairness to the public and revise its audit report to conform the wording to the reality of what is being achieved by its audit. Such a revised wording would have to acknowledge the extent to which the financial statements had been prepared in compliance with specified rules and identify the authoritative institutions that have done the specifying.

Thus, the gap will have been narrowed, but by a movement in the direction of a lesser role goal. This is a move in the wrong direction and is not responsive to the public need.

I am not willing to accept a lesser role for the independent accountant, in spite of a generation of frustration with standard-setting. So I believe we must urge the following:

1. The profession should acknowledge that the words "generally accepted" no longer communicate and they should be abandoned if for no other reason than to remove the impression they seem to create. The more accurate terminology at present would be "accounting principles appropriate in the circumstances."

2. For the present, and until the objectives of financial statements are announced and agreed upon as representing economic reality, the profession should discontinue the reference to "present fairly" in the auditors' report and merely say "present."

3. The Financial Accounting Standards Board should stick to standards and refuse to engage in rule-making.

4. The profession should resist any further expansion of governmental control over accounting and reporting via rule-making.

5. The profession should not support any activity that will encroach on the independent accountant's right to exercise his professional judgment or excuse him from the necessity of exercising professional judgment.

In essence, the above reflects my confidence that a reduction in the vagueness and confusion that clouds the whole reporting-standards area is an achievable goal. It has not been a case of unwillingness by the profession to devote time and talent to the problem area. Perhaps if the profession added a new ingredient—greater collective independence—some solid progress would emerge. Independence of thought and action can do a great deal to make the accounting profession function as the courts and the public believe it is now functioning though it too often isn't.

APPENDIX

AUDITOR'S REPORTS
IN THIRTEEN COUNTRIES OTHER THAN
THE UNITED STATES

Argentina

We have examined the balance sheet of XYZ of Buenos Aires S.A. (an Argentine company) as of December 31, 19--, the statement of profit and loss for the year ended on that date, and the supplementary schedules (Exhibits A, B, and C). Our examination was made in accordance with generally accepted auditing standards, and accordingly included such tests of the accounting records and such other auditing procedures as we considered necessary in the circumstances.

In our opinion, the accompanying balance sheet and statement of profit and loss present fairly the financial position of XYZ of Buenos Aires S.A. as of December 31, 19--, and the results of its operations for the year then ended, and the supplementary schedules present fairly the information contained therein, in conformity with generally accepted accounting principles applied on a basis consistent with that of the preceding year. Also, in our opinion, the accounting records have been maintained in accordance with the requirements of the law and these financial statements and supplementary schedules conform with the provisions of Decree No. 9795 of 1954.

Australia

We have audited the balance sheet of X Limited at 30th June 197-, and the related statement of profit and loss for the year then ended. Our audit included such tests of the accounting records and such other auditing procedures as we considered necessary in the circumstances. In our opinion,

(a) The accompanying accounts give a true and fair view of the state of affairs of X Limited at 30th June, 197- and of the profit (loss) for the year then ended.

(b) The accompanying accounts are properly drawn up in accordance with the provisions of the Companies Act 1961 of Victoria and so as to give a true and fair view of the matters required by section 162 of that Act to be dealt with in the accounts.

(c) The accounting records and other records and the registers required by the Companies Act 1961 of Victoria to be kept by the company have been properly kept in accordance with the provisions of that Act.

Brazil

We have examined the balance sheet of XYZ Brasileira S.A. (a Brazilian corporation) as of December 31, 19--, the related statements of profit and loss, changes in shareholders' investment and source and application of funds for the year then ended, and the accompanying notes which are an integral part of these financial statements. Our examination was made in accordance with generally accepted auditing standards, and accordingly included such tests of the accounting records and such other auditing procedures as we considered necessary in the circumstances.

In our opinion, the accompanying financial statements present fairly the financial position of XYZ Brasileira S.A. as of December 31, 19--, and the results of its operations and the source and application of funds for the year then ended, in conformity with generally accepted accounting principles applied on a basis consistent with that of the preceding year.

Canada

We have examined the balance sheet of _____ as at _____, 19____ and the statements of income, retained earnings and source and application of funds for the year then ended. Our examination included a general review of the accounting procedures and such tests of accounting records and other supporting evidence as we considered necessary in the circumstances.

In our opinion, these financial statements present fairly the financial position of the company as at _____, 19____, and the results of its operations and the source and application of its funds for the year then ended, in accordance with generally accepted accounting principles applied on a basis consistent with that of the preceding year.

France

We present our report relating to our appointment as statutory auditors by your general meeting of . . .. In connection with this appointment, we have carried out all the work recommended by the rule of diligence and have examined, in particular, the accompanying balance sheet of your company as of December 31, 19--, and the related general operating and profit and loss accounts for the fiscal year ended on that date and investigated the methods by which the inventory of the various assets and liabilities existing at December 31, 19--, has been drawn up. As permitted by Article 229 of the Law of July 24, 1966, we employed an expert, Mr. . . . of Cabinet _____, to assist us in all of our work.

Our examination, which was made in accordance with generally accepted auditing standards, included such auditing procedures as we considered necessary in the circumstances.

In our opinion, the inventory and the accompanying balance sheet, general operating account, and profit and loss account which have been presented to you, are regular and fair in their presentation of the company's financial position as of . . . and the results for the year then ended.

Further, we have checked to the accounts of the company the information concerning the financial position and accounts of the company for 19-- and prior years presented in the annual report of the Board of Directors. It shoud be understood that it is not our intention or responsibility to judge the evaluations expressed by the Board concerning the past or future progress of the company's affairs.

Germany

Form used to report on stock corporation (AG)

According to our audit, made in conformity with our professional duties, the accounting, the annual financial statements and the report of the board of management comply with German law and the company's articles of association.

Form used to report on limited liability company (GmbH)

As instructed, we have examined the financial statements of ABC GmbH (a subsidiary of . . .) as of December 31, 19-- in the scope prescribed by the Corporation Act. Our audit work at the company's premises was completed (date).

The management has furnished us willingly with all requested explanations. Analyses of the accounts shown in the financial statements have been recorded in our working papers. As instructed, we have omitted further details and explanations of these accounts from this report.

Based on the results of our examination, we express an opinion on the financial statements of ABC GmbH (place of company's registration) at December 31, 19-- (Exhibits I and II) as follows:

> According to our audit, made in conformity with our professional duties, the accounting and the annual financial statements comply with German law and the company's articles of agreement.

Japan

We have examined, in accordance with item 2 of article 193 of the SEC regulations, the balance sheet of XYZ KABUSHIKI KAISHA as of December 31, 19--, the related combined statements of income and retained earnings, the statement of appropriation of surplus and the supplementary schedules for the year then ended. Our examination was made in accordance with generally accepted auditing standards, and accordingly included such auditing procedures as we considered necessary in the circumstances.

Based on our examination, we agree that the Company's accounting principles and practices currently applied are in conformity with generally accepted accounting principles, that the principles are applied on a consistent basis with the previous year, and that the presentation of the financial statements is in compliance with the regulations dictated by the Ministry of Finance.

In our opinion, the above mentioned financial statements present fairly the financial position of XYZ Kabushiki Kaisha as of December 31, 19--, and the results of its operations for the year then ended.

We do not have an economic or financial interest in the Company.

Mexico

First two paragraphs same as U.S. form

Third paragraph as follows:

On the basis of the examination described above, and in compliance with Article 57 of the Federal Commercial Revenues Tax Law, we report that during the year the Company has filed the tax returns required by such law.

Norway

We have examined the balance sheet of XYZ Inc. as of December 31, 19-- and the statement of income for the year then ended.

Our examination was made in accordance with generally accepted auditing standards and in accordance with the Corporations Act of July 6, 1957 and the rules issued by the Ministry of Commerce on December 8, 1964. In this connection, we have made tests and analyses of the transactions of the company and such other auditing procedures as we considered necessary in the circumstances to be able to render an opinion on the financial position and results of operations of the company.

The annual financial statements, together with the related comments in the annual report of the board of directors, in our opinion, present fairly the financial position of XYZ Inc. as of December 31, 19-- and the results of its operations for the year then ended, in agreement with careful and prudent business practice. In our opinion, the company's accounts have been maintained and closed in accordance with the requirements for proper accounting on a basis consistent with that of the preceding year.

We do not know of any other matters which, in our opinion, would be of significance in the evaluation of the presented financial statements and we are therefore able to recommend that the financial statements be approved.

South Africa

We have examined the balance sheet of ABC Limited (a South African company and wholly owned subsidiary of XYZ Corporation) at December 31, 19--, and the related statements of income (loss) and retained earnings (deficit) and changes in financial position for the year then ended. Our examination was made in accordance with generally accepted auditing standards, and we have examined the securities, books, accounts and vouchers of the Company to the extent that we considered necessary for the purpose of our examination and have obtained all the information and explanations that we considered necessary.

In our opinion, the accompanying financial statements give a true and fair view of the state of the Company's affairs at December 31, 19--, and of the results of its operations and changes in its financial position for the year then ended, and comply with the requirements of the Companies Act, 1926, as amended. Also, in our opinion, the Company has kept proper books of account with which its financial statements are in agreement.

Sweden

In our capacity as appointed auditors to XYZ, AB we hereby submit the following report for the year 19--.

We have examined the annual report of XYZ, AB submitted by the Board of Directors and the Managing Director, the minutes of meetings and other pertinent documents regarding the Corporation's administration and financial affairs, and have carried out such other audit steps as we considered necessary in the circumstances.

In our opinion, the signed balance sheet and statement of income present fairly the financial position of XYZ, AB as of December 31, 19-- and results of its operations for the year then ended in conformity with appropriate accounting principles applied on a basis consistent with that of the preceding year. Since our examination has not caused us to object to these financial statements or the Directors Report, we recommend that the balance sheet referred to above be approved.

Nothing came to our attention during our examination that caused us to object to the accounting documents we inspected, the corporation's accounting, the inventory of its assets or other matters concerning the administration of its operations. Accordingly, we recommend that the Board of Directors and the Managing Director be discharged from further responsibility for the period covered by the Annual Report.

In our opinion, the distribution of available surplus proposed by the Board of Directors and the Managing Director conforms with the legal requirements for the allocation to reserves and does not conflict with sound business practice considering the company's financial position and the results of its operations. Accordingly, we recommend that available surplus be distributed as proposed.

Switzerland

We have examined the balance sheet of XYZ AG (a Swiss corporation) as of December 31, 19--, and the related statement of income and retained earnings for the year then ended. Our examination included such tests of the accounting records and such other auditing procedures as we considered necessary in the circumstances to enable us to form the opinions expressed below.

In our opinion, the accompanying financial statements present fairly the financial position of XYZ AG as of December 31, 19--, and the results of its operations for the year then ended, on a basis consistent with that of the preceding year.

As statutory auditors, in our opinion (1) the accompanying financial statements are in agreement with the books of account, (2) the books of account were maintained in an orderly manner and (3) the accompanying financial statements and the proposal of the Board of Directors regarding the distribution of unappropriated retained earnings (Note . . .) are in conformity with the applicable provisions of the law and the Company's bylaws. Therefore, we recommend you approve the accompanying financial statements.

United Kingdom

We have examined the balance sheet of X Limited at December 31, 19--, and the related profit and loss account for the year ended on that date.

In our opinion, the accompanying accounts give a true and fair view of the state of affairs of the Company at December 31, 19--, and of the profit for the year ended on that date, and comply with the Companies Acts 1948 and 1967.

NOTES

1. Rule 203 holds that a member shall not express an opinion that financial statements are presented in conformity with generally accepted accounting principles if such statements contain any departure from an accounting principle promulgated by the Financial Accounting Standards Board, except in unusual circumstances which would result in financial statements that would otherwise be misleading. In such a case, a heavy burden of disclosure and justification is placed on the CPA.

The Concept: A Commentary

DONALD H. CHAPIN *

Mr. Kapnick has presented a paper which on its face and for most of its pages deals with the semantics of the independent auditor's report. It is only at the end that his more important proposals are revealed. I disagree with much of what he says throughout the paper, but my chief concern is with the suggestions at the tail end of his paper—suggestions to the effect that the profession give up the rule-making process that has been binding on the members of the profession and put greater emphasis on standards and individual professional judgment. These suggestions are made without also developing how we would actually operate if these things were to come to pass. With this gap, I do not understand how we can achieve uniformity and consistency of treatment in financial statements when circumstances are similar. It would appear that Kapnick's proposals would lead to less uniformity and consistency, which would, in turn, tend to dissipate the public's confidence in our profession, increase the legal jeopardy which we now face and lead to more government rule-making.

My comments, which follow, deal with a number of the points which I believe are controversial in the whole of Kapnick's paper, but my chief concern will show from time to time as I discuss his paper.

He says, and I agree, that the accounting profession is under the heaviest attack in its history; I do not agree, however, with his basic view of why this is so. In my opinion, the "generally accepted" concept of accounting principles is not, as he says, the most important underlying issue causing deteriorating confidence in the accounting profession. I believe that failure to find the facts and a less than full disclosure of the facts—basically auditing problems—are more important than any of the problems relating to accounting principles. The public expects the independent CPA to be a competent and objective "Mr. Clean," and the publicity accompanying the cases which allege fraud, the auditing negligence cases, and the uncontested SEC injunctions against CPA

*B.A. 1950, Williams College; M.B.A. 1951, University of Pennsylvania. CPA, Pennsylvania. Partner, Director of Auditing, and Director of Practice Development, Arthur Young & Company. Member, AICPA Ad Hoc Committee on Scope of Practice.

firms because of poor auditing performance have all undermined confidence. The biggest blow to the profession has just been struck. Equity Funding has shaken confidence in the efficacy of audits; no matter what is eventually decided about the auditing problems involved in Equity Funding, confidence in the profession has been weakened significantly. Our confidence problems are, more importantly, auditing quality control problems than they are accounting principles problems.

I do not say that we should not be concerned with accounting principles. We should be and we are. But whether you subscribe to Kapnick's view of the most important problem or mine, let's not emphasize the wording of our report too much in trying to deal with confidence and accounting principles. I accept the notion that the general public regards our report as the equivalent of the Good Housekeeping Seal of Approval. But, for the most part, this is not because of the words we use. Rather, it is because historically we have not objected when corporate presidents and financial people have fostered the notion that our letter was the seal of approval. We have felt flattered when that notion was advanced, and have prospered because of it. Now that the notion is well established and we are guardians of the public interest, let's not try to change our position with the public, as Kapnick suggests we try to do. Our concern with our report should not be to try to change the public's expectations of the profession. Our concern with our report should be primarily to see that it copes with the present legal environment and, if possible, comes closer than it now does to really expressing the public's expectations. I shall have more to say about this later.

I see little point in Kapnick's attack on the phrase "generally accepted." I can more easily read the words "generally accepted" as encompassing both accounting principles and rules set by authoritative bodies and developed in usage than I can as only encompassing usage. I translate "generally accepted" as "professionally accepted" and I think others may also. With this view of the words, I take exception to his statement that the words "generally accepted" have grown in obscurity with the passage of time. As we see usage increasingly replaced by ASRs, APBs and the like, we must conclude that generally accepted accounting principles have more definition rather than less. The authoritative bodies who set accounting principles and rules have been hard at work narrowing accounting alternatives, and we are making progress. What we do when we use the words "generally accepted accounting principles" is describe the language used in stating financial statements. That language is becoming better understood as we give its words and idioms more and narrower definition through the pronouncements of authoritative bodies.

The related but more important question that Kapnick raises is: What should we do about continuing accounting alternatives? Should we have more rules or something else? His attack on accounting rules within his paper seems to be based on the fact that conflicts in the various rules set by different authorities—industry practices and the like—make such rules hard to apply, and his attack is also based on the position that there is an essential conflict between "fair presentation" and the alternatives available under generally accepted accounting principles. He would apparently solve this problem by doing away with rules and, in their stead, establishing more fundamental standards and restoring more individual professional judgment. The idea that we ought to have standards is appealing, but it is hardly new. To date, we haven't been able to do anything with the idea and do not now have before us a comprehensive proposition for accounting standards which we might consider. It would be nice if the Objectives Study Group headed by Mr. Trueblood would define the objectives of financial statements with sufficient clarity to point the way to all the standards we need, so that we can get rid of our accounting cookbook of principles and rules. But I believe that the Trueblood effort will not be fully successful if measured by that standard. We will probably always need a cookbook.

Our accounting cookbook is not so bad as some of its critics assert. The fact that our detailed accounting principles and rules do not solve all the problems of how to use our accounting language, or that they occasionally create conflicts because they come from various authoritative sources, should not cause us to throw up our hands. It requires more professional capacity than ever before to master and know how to use our increasingly complex and definitive accounting language and to deal with occasional conflicts in authorities, but professionals should not be disturbed by that requirement. Furthermore, harmonizing generally accepted accounting principles and the concept of fair presentation is not the problem it once was. The new ethics Rule 203 and its interpretation makes it clear what to do when the accounting principles are set by the APB or FASB. *Continental Vending* establishes the fairness concept for disclosure questions, and it is conceivable that another court could make fairness overriding even when there are authoritative accounting principles established. But I believe the FASB is not likely to promulgate an accounting principle that a judge or jury will decide is unfair. Practitioners, also, are getting the message about the importance of fairness, and their collective backbones are being stiffened by the legal cases and various actions of the SEC. I think responsible practitioners are applying this concept. When accounting alternatives exist, it may take good judgement and frequently requires courage to determine what is fair, but I think we are unlikely to be

that far off the mark if we address our accounting problems with competence, objectivity and care.

The practical solution to our problem is to make our accounting cookbook more complete. I find it alarming that Kapnick finds "alarming" the fact that accounting rules "are gaining ground," because the alternative, in my view, is less uniformity and consistency in accounting and an end to real progress in improving accounting principles. Most of the areas of accounting principle where we have had trouble and criticism have been those which the accounting authorities have not dealt with or have dealt with incompletely. Having a complete rule book won't stop progress either. As economic conditions change and as our ability to make economic measurements improves, we should have change for the better in our rules. It is my observation and belief that the members of the APB have been concerned with a fair presentation of economic reality as they have gradually narrowed accounting alternatives, and they have been willing to change basic accounting concepts as well as principles and rules to meet this objective. The new FASB will hardly be less motivated in this direction.

Unless and until we have the accounting standards which will point the way clearly to all professionals, and I doubt that we shall ever have this utopian situation, we will need detailed principles and rules to:

1. Achieve change and improvement in accounting.
2. Obtain uniformity of accounting presentations when circumstances are similar and eliminate alternatives not justified by the circumstances.
3. Apply the collective judgment of accountants rather than the more fallible judgment of individuals or firms in creating financial statements.

I believe Kapnick's concern about the words "presents fairly" is somewhat misdirected. The historical cost, realization, and matching concepts still produce a reasonably fair presentation in most cases. I believe that when these concepts prove to be unfair because our accounting language ceases to portray an understandable and useful view of economic reality, we shall adopt other concepts. The fact that we have retained these concepts in large measure—although not without some bending and some exceptions to meet new developments—is attributable to their utility in producing usable financial statements which are objective and verifiable. This does not mean that I don't believe that we will see in the future some additional inroads on these concepts, with gradual implementation of fair value accounting concepts. Accounting leaders and authorities will modify the old concepts or adopt new ones as it becomes necessary to portray an understandable and useful view of economic reality in financial statements. Uncertainty about what constitutes a fair presentation does exist, but I don't believe it has really held back progress that much.

In my view, our biggest problem with the words "presents fairly" is whether the courts will accept reasonable limitations on the application of the concept of fairness. There are two aspects of this problem. The first, which I have touched on before, is: Will the courts agree that accounting principles established by authorities normally do result in a fair presentation? Nothing they have said thus far affirms they will not accept established authority, although I would agree that there is uncertainty here. I believe that the courts will eventually affirm that the presumption is that accounting principles and rules established by authorities do present fairly and that the burden is on those who think otherwise to show that there were unusual circumstances, such as new legislation or a new form of business transaction, which were not contemplated by the accounting authorities who established the principle. This is essentially the concept incorporated in the new ethics rule just adopted by the profession. If we in the profession believe that this concept will be affirmed, what we need to do is to get to work and establish principles or rules in areas where usage is presently controlling.

The second aspect of the problem is: Will the courts agree that "presents fairly," insofar as this concept requires full disclosure, only encompasses historical economic information of the type traditionally given in or with present financial statements? If the full disclosure concept is broadened to require judgments about (say) the quality of the management of the business, then I believe we in the profession are in trouble. I think we might be able to cope with a broadening of the concept to require, for example, reporting on the quality of business controls then in effect but, of course, we would have to know about such requirements in advance and gear up to deal with them. This aspect of the "presents fairly" problem worries me more than the first. But both concerns lead me to agree that we ought to change the way we express the fairness concept in accountants' reports.

Should our report wording problems be resolved the way Kapnick suggests? I think not. His suggestion that we use the words "accounting principles appropriate in the circumstances" removes the suggestion which I find in the words "generally accepted" that there is a substantial body of authority and usage governing the accounting principles applied. In my view, his words are a clear step backward and they open the door to more accounting alternatives. Also, in my view, his proposal to use the word "present" by itself rather than "presents fairly" is too big a step backward. Trying to put aside the fairness concept, even for the time being, will produce a reaction among the public, who will think that we are backing away from our responsibilities, and this will not be accepted.

Having rejected Kapnick's suggestion, I offer this for your consideration. I suggest that the second or "opinion" paragraph of the standard short-form accountants' report should be amended to read as follows: "In our opinion, the above mentioned financial statements have been prepared fairly using generally accepted accounting principles." This language attempts to use the word fairly in the context of the financial statements rather than the results-of-operations and financial position and thereby to reduce the possibility that someone will think that we are covering other information which has a bearing on financial position or results of operations but is not directly related to the financial statements. Changing the positioning of the word fairly does two things. It accepts the fairness concept as overriding but also, to those outside the profession it suggests more strongly than does our present language that fairness is to be construed in terms of generally accepted accounting principles.

As long as we are changing words, I would not object to replacing the word "generally" in "generally accepted" by the word "professionally." This language may communicate the source of our accounting principles a little better.

Since there are international differences in accounting principles, we do have a problem about whose principles are being used. In this respect, I cannot help agreeing with Kapnick. But I believe that reports which circulate in U.S. capital markets and are used by U.S. stockholders and lenders should be prepared based on U.S. accounting principles, or should have a section which converts the essential information in the foreign statements to a U.S. basis as supplementary information. In the latter event, the auditor's report should indicate the country whose principles were used in preparing the primary statements. If that sounds too parochial for multi-national companies, so be it. The U.S. investor and lender need to be protected from lack of uniformity of accounting presentations when circumstances are similar. We must do everything in our power to move closer to a situation in which results of different companies can be compared and investor-creditor decisions facilitated.

In conclusion, let me touch on the big question which has been referred to from time to time throughout these sessions: Will we be successful in establishing better professionally accepted accounting principles? In my view, this depends to some degree on whether the Trueblood committee or some other group can decide on the objectives of financial statements, but it mainly depends on whether the FASB can make the standards, principles, and rules that they write *stick*. This, in turn, depends upon the quality of the people handling these tasks and upon the support given to their conclusions by the preparers, users, and attestors of financial statements and by public authorities.

The Trueblood and FASB people have been appointed and we can only hope they are up to the task. Will what they say get support? Kapnick says that the FASB should stick to standards and *refuse to engage in rule-making,* and I believe there must be some rule-making. Kapnick says that the profession *should not support any activity* that will encroach on the independent accountant's right to exercise his professional judgment, and I believe that rule-making should and will so encroach on individual or firm judgment. If rule-making continues, and I think it will be with us forever, I hope that all members of the profession will support FASB rules. This means more than just complying with them. If important members of the profession fail to support the rules, we will destroy the FASB and end hope of achieving uniformity and consistency of treatment through voluntary action. The direct result of this will be that legal attacks will find us unduly vulnerable, because it will be easy to find accountants who will testify that they would have reached a different conclusion about the appropriate accounting presentation. Also, and more importantly, our status as a profession in the minds of the public, as well as the government and other public authorities who have power over our future, will suffer. The end of this process will be increased government rule-making, the very thing that Mr. Kapnick says he opposes.

Discussion

Kapnick. I understood Don to say in the early part of his presentation that he thought that the seal of approval which the short-form certificate has come to mean to the American people should be retained. This is an impressive argument and one that many people use, even though some of us do not accept it. It seems to me that your entire structure of that proposal is defeated with your latest proposal of changing the words. Are we now down to how we change the words, and in agreement on the other issues? When you come to saying that you would prefer this word instead of the other, that is negotiation, that is discussion. I am wondering what your position is.

Chapin. I think you misunderstood me, Harvey. My proposed wording is addressed primarily to deal with the legal problems involved in the cases which come increasingly to the fore, but also incidentally to affirm rather than deny that we speak to the fairness of the financial statements. I think that the words that I used do that better than the words we use now. I think the words aren't really anything more than the affirmation of the position that we impart a seal of approval.

Kapnick. You are for a change in wording?

Chapin. To strengthen that position.

Kapnick. Well I think mine strengthens it better, so now we are both for a change in wording and the argument is over which words.

Carmichael. I just wanted to bring to your attention something that you might not know about that illustrates the extent to which auditors use the phrase "present fairly" as a term of art. Consider the report of a multi-national company. For instance, if there were a U.S. parent and a U.K. subsidiary, and U.S. auditors were asked to report on that for the U.S. parent in consolidated statements filed here, they would use U.S. standards. If, in addition, they were asked to report on the U.K. subsidiary to U.K. owners following U.K. standards, current practice would result in a report something like this: the auditors would say that the statements for that subsidiary which would be prepared in conformity with U.S. standards, "presented fairly in conformity with GAAP." They would then refer to additional supplemental information describing the differences and adjustments to the statements and would say when those adjustments were made the statements presented a "true and fair view"—the U.K. language. That is current practice. In discussions of that with the accountants that we talked to, they see

401

no problem of a reader interpreting those words literally—to say that one set of statements "presents fairly," but if you make these adjustments then it is "true and fair." So they definitely are viewed as terms of art. We have a couple of related projects dealing with the meaning of "present fairly," and the auditing committee is working on "purport to present," which is the last matter that Don dealt with. Now we say the report refers to what the statements purport to present: financial position and results of operations. That is a problem that hasn't received a great deal of attention. "Present fairly" has, and our study has to come to essentially the same conclusion that Don did, and that is that we have to first decide what our responsibility should be—to come to a clear statement of responsibility—before we begin to work with the words and switch them around.

Linowes. I got the impression that Don was in opposition to Harvey both at the beginning and end of his comments, but then in the middle when he suggested a change in the opinion paragraphs stressing the fairness concept, he was in agreement. I would like to inject another aspect which underlies the problem we are wrestling with. That is the artificial and arbitrary cutting off of a fiscal year at a specific time. It seems to me that perhaps we might give some thought to dealing with a moving average for our operating statements, perhaps a three-year or five-year moving average. That would make it possible to side-step the very difficult, arbitrary decisions which arise when we cut off at the end of a twelve-month period.

Kapnick. That problem is even more complicated. Consider some of the things Phil Defliese was saying earlier on some of the leasing situations, where he tried to bring some of these terribly difficult and complex problems down into a monthly financial reporting and then say that it was fairly presented in accordance with something.

Defliese. I hear you, Doug, but as a practical matter, we have been telling the American public that we have been able to determine earnings per share on a quarterly basis for years. To now try to tell them that we have been kidding them for twenty years just won't work. We all know they are estimates, and I think all we can hope to accomplish is to emphasize the fact that they are estimates, that they have to accept them as such.

Long. The thought that struck me is that there is no general disagreement among those of us here about understanding these terms of art. I don't think that is the issue. I think the issue is, what do they mean to somebody else? I think Len Savoie illustrated it beautifully with his story about the corporate director, who I am sure is much more astute than the reasonable man or the prudent investor, and yet these terms mean nothing to him. So I think you have to focus on who you are trying to reach. I think the English situation substantiates that, Doug. How could you reach any other conclusion reading what they said there? Here it is this way, which presents fairly, but that is not true and fair. I think, too, the general presumption of for whom you are rendering that opinion in England is somewhat different in this country, if not legalistically, certainly by tradition and the fact that you don't have the widespread public ownership of stock over there that you do here. So I think you cannot forget the user. Do those terms of art have any meaning to him?

Defliese. I would like to ask Doug whether he and his group that were researching the origin of this recognized that at one time it was "fairly presents," and before that it was "correctly presents," and that the objective of going from "correctly presents" to "fairly presents" was to avoid the concept of "correctness," which couldn't ever be achieved. We have gotten off on a tangent, I think. Shouldn't we try to get back to what we are trying to say?

Carmichael. We could identify what it was intended to mean and then try to choose words that would better express what we originally intended to mean. Unfortunately it is not that simple because we now have many suggestions for expansion of the function, and many meanings that have been attached that the profession may or may not have asked for but which nevertheless attached. The first step will have to be a clearer expression of the responsibility that we should have. Whenever you talk about it you eventually get around to the point, as Don did in his talk, of choosing words that express what he thinks the responsibility should be, and then people begin to quarrel with the words, and that is why it is taking the auditing committee so long to advise the short form report. It is really troublesome when they agree on the words but they know they disagree on the responsibility.

Kapnick. I had always been told that the words "generally accepted" were created by George O. May in connection with the 1933 fiasco on the study of the New York Stock Exchange. If you go back and read him, and Mr. May is pretty articulate on these things, he says that really we should be reporting on the accounting principles and standards *used by the company.* He doesn't talk about "generally accepted." How that has been transformed later to sort of putting on the seal of approval is interesting. Even at that point of time it wasn't considered that "generally accepted" was good terminology.

Dyckman. I listened to Don talking about the auditor becoming looked upon as the guardian of the public interest and to Bob Long's comments about who is supposed to be involved in the understanding of these words. I would like to address a question to the lawyers that we have with us. Will merely changing the wording of the form have any kind of legal implications?

Fiflis. My reaction to the discussion is the same as Leonard Spacek's reaction to Statement No. 4. A few years ago he gave a speech in which he made the statement that it was all "words, words, words," intimating that it meant nothing. This is because, in this context, these words are code words. We have been talking about what form of words to use to convey a meaning when we haven't agreed upon the meaning.

Kapnick. Would you define GAAP then, as a lawyer?

Fiflis. No. I mean to say that in my estimation, the discussion about meanings of these words is nonsensical because what people have said here today is that we don't know what the accountant's responsibility is, we haven't agreed on what that responsibility is, and yet we are trying to communicate to the public what that unagreed-upon responsibility is through changing the form of words.

Kapnick. Let me take you one step further on that because I am very appreciative of that line of reasoning. I don't care what words you use, but if you get the "generally accepted" out and if you state the principles that are used in *this* financial statement, it seems to me that you have told the reader exactly what he can look to to evaluate that statement. So you see that you can take all the suppositions that you make and say, since we can't agree on GAAP we will put that aside for the time being and hopefully some day the FASB may get a codification of all these things that they are supposedly dreaming about for the future. But today is the problem, and legally if we are reporting to the public something we know we can't define, isn't it better to change our wording now to say "in accordance with the principles that the controller selected"?

Savoie. I appreciate what has been said. I think regardless of what term of art we would use, the public regards this as a Good Housekeeping Seal of Approval. I suspect that if we continued to practice the profession in the same way but used a different term of art, they would continue to regard it at such. I don't know how that would affect any legal liability, but I must say I was terribly encouraged when I heard Harvey say he wasn't worried about law suits.

Chapin. Wouldn't you say that if we were to change our words to "principles appropriate to the circumstances" and dropped the word "fairly" out of our report that the public would think that we were trying to back off from the position as their protector and the giver of the Good Housekeeping Seal of Approval?

Defliese. As I said before, to say that any balance sheet presented a financial position fairly without the modifier "in accordance with

GAAP" would be a lie, because we know it doesn't. In the abstract, no balance sheet ever fairly presents financial position. I think we have to recognize that.

Sterling. Perhaps we should change the balance sheet instead of changing the wording of the certificate.

Vanatta. If you eliminate GAAP in the wording, how do you measure—what is your measurement for fairness?

Kapnick. I have taken that out, too, because I would say that the financial statements are prepared and are presented on the basis of the principles outlined in the footnotes which are appropriate in the circumstances—they are correctly applied. I am not saying they are fairly presented.

Burton. What does appropriate mean if it doesn't mean fair?

Kapnick. Appropriate in the circumstances. That means that each principle can be taken as appropriate within the crucial circumstances that exist and on which you are making a decision. You are not saying they are accepted.

Burton. Aren't you saying they are fair? You are offering a judgment that the accounting principles are appropriate in the circumstances. That in effect is a judgment as to fairness.

Kapnick. We are saying that it is a fair selection. Take sinking fund depreciation which Phil used earlier. I don't think you could say sinking fund depreciation in this country is appropriate in the circumstance because it is not an acceptable method or rule.

Vanatta. It sounds to me like you are saying that they were compiled accurately based upon these principles without saying whether they are appropriate, fair, or anything.

Kapnick. Do you think that most of these financial statements today *fairly* present financial position?

Liggio. My problem here is that there is some basis of comparison between companies at the present time. There is some uniformity that is present in the existing use of GAAP. To the extent that we adopt what I interpret Mr. Kapnick's suggestion—no overall system, but instead what is appropriate in the circumstances—we may be asking for more trouble in a legal liability sense. Then the people who are using the financial statements may have three or four companies which are using three or four different sets of accounting principles, each of which is appropriate in the circumstances for that particular company, or so they believe, and there is no basis for the investor or the user of the financial statements to make any comparison between the companies. I would rather stay with GAAP from a legal liability standpoint. Where Mr. Kapnick or anybody else believes that a fair presentation requires something else, he should deviate in that circumstance and use as the basis for deviation the new code of ethics requirement which says that if we don't feel that the statements are an accurate and fair presentation, then we have to deviate from generally accepted accounting principles.

Kapnick. I don't see how you can come to any conclusion that today there is comparison between various sets of statements. One uses LIFO, another uses something else, one uses accelerated depreciation, another one doesn't use accelerated depreciation. So I think that if an investor is looking at these as being comparable, he is out of his mind.

Burton. Harvey, how about "the most appropriate under the circumstances"?

Kapnick. No, I think that is a very interesting comment. How could Kapnick sign "most appropriate in the circumstance" when you as the SEC require me to amortize goodwill? As an individual public accountant I can accept the amortization of goodwill because the APB said this is the way it is going to be and the SEC has allowed it to be. But if you say to me that Arthur Andersen must express it as most appropriate in the circumstance, then there is no way that I can sign that Opinion.

Burton. You could have a little exception paragraph which says, "with the exception . . ."

Kapnick. Then you won't accept it.

Simmons. I wanted to ask a question about the study that you mentioned. I am curious about the scope. I am also curious to know if you are making any attempt to find out if the investor is misled by the phrase "generally accepted accounting principles." Finally, since we are concerned about terminology, I would like to know if you are studying investor needs or investor wants.

Kapnick. Investor needs, essentially. This is in progress with some outside professors at the moment. We intend to expand the study to see what we can do. For years we have felt the place to begin was with what it is that an investor needs to make an informed decision. We felt that if we were going to continue to press on that point that we should at least have done the research ourselves to see if we can come up with something on that basis. I am very encouraged by it.

Simmons. You are investigating his decision model, then. You are not just simply taking what he says he wants.

Kapnick. No. In the end we hope that that will lead into what we have concluded to be the objectives of financial statements and run into what will we conclude should be the appropriate accounting standards or principles.

Defliese. That is going to lead you into forecasting because what he wants is an indication of where his stock is going to be next year.

Kapnick. We will show him how to evaluate that, but we won't show him how to get there.

Buckley. First of all, I think the avoidance of legal liability is no basis for professional motivation. In fact it is a hygiene factor. Second, seeing we have two attorneys here, I would like to try to settle an issue that has been raised many times, i.e., whether or not more rules will lead to greater security in these matters. The question I would like to pose is this: it seems to me that where professional judgment is the basis for action that a lay jury would be an inappropriate forum for deciding that issue, and hence, only one's professional peers should be entitled to pass judgment on professional action. This leads me to believe that very specific rules to not avoid liability, but rather enhance it and make it easier to prosecute the accountant.

Liggio. I think that you have to divide the question into two parts, because if you try to group your auditing liability and your accounting liability in the same breath, you are never going to come out with the same answer. If you are talking about auditing, I think the only forum that you really can be judged by is that of your peers. The layman can judge that to the extent that when you have more rules and more guidelines you are going to have greater protection from liability. To the extent that it is a question of accounting treatment, then this may be something that the public can form a judgment about, and you may not have as much protection by more guidelines. Then we have something that is in between. Is disclosure an accounting treatment, or is it an auditing treatment? In SAP 33 disclosure is considered as a standard of auditing, but a lot of people I think would look at disclosure as a standard of accounting. I don't know if you set down definitive guidelines for disclosure requirements whether that would help you or not help you. I tend to think that it would be more of a help, but it is not going to be an absolute defense.

Buckley. What other professional group is going this route of codifying its rules? How do you judge the liability of a doctor, an attorney, or any other professional person?

Liggio. If you are a doctor, they are codified by practice, in a sense.

Buckley. You are looking at whether in those circumstances he exercised his professional judgment in a case-by-case method.

Liggio. To use an example used yesterday with the doctor's situation, there may be a standard procedure for requiring a counting of sponges after an operation, and if you didn't comply with that standard procedure, it is not a question of the exercise of judgment.

Buckley. It is not a stated procedure, but rather a state-of-the-art procedure.

Fiflis. The procedure is apparently for doctors to delegate to nurses the duty of counting the sponges. It is an "accounting" problem. Nevertheless, although that is a standard procedure, the courts have no difficulty imposing liability on doctors for following that standard procedure, because they say it ought not to be the standard procedure. Therefore doctors' standards don't cover that question.

CHAPTER 12

Social Structure of the Accounting Profession

DAVID F. LINOWES *

To discuss meaningfully the social structure of the accounting profession, we must first examine the milieu in which the profession exists—that is, the environment of which it is a part. Let us then take a look at society; more specifically, at the make-up of society—its organizations.

Organizations as a phenomenon are all about us, yet very little serious effort has been applied towards a study of them. Particular institutions doing specific jobs have been analyzed and examined, and their own basic organizational structures studied and recast, but "organization" as an institution itself to my knowledge has never been examined.

Social structures have been largely taken for granted and therefore have been subjected to the same neglect as air and water. Recently society has awakened to the need for effective action to stop the polluting of these latter vital resources from destroying our nation's health; but we have not yet become sufficiently aroused to demand the kind of action that will result in a better understanding of many of our institutions, to stop them from imprisoning our minds and destroying our nation's creativity.

Although organizations are not an invention of the twentieth century, because of the overwhelming increase in population and general complexity of society, organizations have become the most important phenomenon of our time. It is through organization that man and resources are brought together in order to accomplish an objective—

*B.S. 1941, University of Illinois. CPA. Partner, Laventhol Krekstein Horwath & Horwath. Chairman, Trial Board, American Institute of Certified Public Accountants. Chairman, National Council, U.S. People for the United Nations. Chairman of the Board of Directors, Mickelberry Corporation. Director, Chris-Craft Industries, Inc., the Horn & Hardart Company, Piper Aircraft Corporation, and World Magazine, Inc. Author, *Managing Growth Through Acquisition* (1968); and *Strategies for Survival* (1973). Contributor to accounting periodicals and other publications.

whether that objective be the manufacture of an automobile, the education of a child, the fighting of a war, or the practice of a profession.

To place my observations in perspective, we should recognize that social structures are as old as man. Prehistoric nomadic tribes were among the early social organizations. When man stopped roaming the land in search of food and settled down to begin cultivating crops, forms of community organizations had to be invented. The family itself was the first social structure, with all members of the family giving obeisance to the father or, as in some cases, the mother. As the head, he or she delegated chores, set up procedures and meted out punishments for infractions of the rules. In Biblical times, social structures were studied, and the subject of much discourse. In Chapter 18 of Exodus considerable space is devoted to the advice given to Moses by his father-in-law, Jethro, on how to organize his people for effective management.

Social organization is the process or method which brings together resources, whether they be labor, land, and capital, or manpower and clients, in such a way and in such quantities as to make them produce desired results. In its effective form it is the setting of an objective; analyzing that goal into simpler component elements; establishing authority and responsibility for each of these elements; and coordinating all of the facets.

Philosophers tell us that man, as a human being, does not change, that human nature is relatively constant. And even a casual reading of the ancient dialogues of Plato support man's relative sameness. This is not true of social structures.

Groupings of men exist to accomplish defined purposes and are drastically affected by numbers of people, kinds of equipment which technology has furnished, and the general expectant comfort level of man in his particular environment. The sheer weight of numbers or scale of activity can change an organization from its original nature without conscious effort on anyone's part.

In primitive times, society centered around the individual: the hunter, the warrior, the medicine man, the father-to-son teacher of a trade. Organizations of those days supported the individual. Even as recently as the early twentieth century, the rugged individualist held center stage. Men such as Henry Ford, Andrew Carnegie, and John D. Rockefeller built massive industrial and philanthropic organizations, each institution an extension of the man himself. In accounting we had such men as Arthur Andersen, Elijah Watts Sells, Colonel Montgomery, and Arthur Young, among others.

By mid-twentieth century, however, the organization seized center stage. Individuals now support the institution. The Ford Motor

Company, Ford Foundation, Exxon, Rockefeller Foundation, Haskins & Sells, Price Waterhouse and Co., all are living organisms in their own right. Executives come and go, but the social structure continues, each with its own personality and character.

This shift of emphasis to the institution has been brought about by two basic factors: the large population and the advanced state of science and technology. To educate tens of thousands of students at a time requires large universities; to provide facilities for millions of people in one place requires large cities; to build moon rockets requires many, many skilled specialists and immense supplies of materials; to build even one jet airliner requires the services of hundreds of trained technicians and scientists. And, to audit one multi-national corporation requires hundreds of personnel. Today, all activity, education, government, research, production, requires massive aggregations of people and things.

Because of the immensity and complexity of organizations, the job of directing splintered segments of them also has outgrown the capacity of individuals acting alone. Even with the aid of the computer to help identify options for management decisions, increasingly senior executives are joining together collectively to wrestle with different aspects of the same decision. A few organizations are trying out a multi-headed chief executive officer—two or more men to handle separate parts of the same job.

Large organizations are common in every phase of society. The University of Illinois runs operations costing $200 million a year; so does the state of New Hampshire; so does Hershey Chocolate Company and so do several accounting firms. Each of these institutions is concerned with personnel and material. Each represents control over massive quantities of resources and large numbers of people to get a job done. Each institution has great power to be exercised. The medium is the social structure.

A social organization comes into being to accomplish a purpose; soon it finds itself expanding its horizons, taking on other functions. After a few years of existence, the organization is a complex web of intertwined relationships with overlapping responsibilities and authority. If no action is taken to keep the administrative processes sharp and meaningful, the organization grows barnacles. These growths cling persistently to each unit of activity, retarding and restricting essential movements, especially with inter-related functions.

In time the superfluous appendages grow their own crustaceous exteriors, which join together creating a hard wall of involved procedures fencing in progress or change, or even cooperation within one firm. When this occurs, decay is on its way. Too many levels of intricate procedures frustrate and discourage the creative minds.

The rigid social structure is a determined personality of its own, constructed on the many protective dimensions set up at each administrative level. Much of the sluggishness in society today, including some areas of our own profession, is the result of overlapping internal organizations, many of which have hardened outgrowths. Because organizations are the means by which all society functions, an understanding of this underlying phenomenon is essential in order to begin to do something about many of society's ills as well as to help re-stimulate creativity.

The social organization itself is not always the root of all the evil; it is often the *love* of the organization which underlies many of our problems. The organization is a living phenomenon whose life, habits, and personality are entirely separate and distinct from the individuals composing it. People will frequently develop an attachment to the institution itself, an attachment of affection, and the relationship will go through the same vicissitudes as any experience of devotion, namely love and hate.

Bigness makes it possible to throw immense resources and expert specialists into an effort, but it spawns duplications, overlappings, conflicts. People at one end of an institution do not know what their colleagues in different parts of the organization are doing, even when they are performing the same general function. The federal government is especially susceptible to this weakness. For example, health programs for the country are administered by the Public Health Service, the Social and Rehabilitation Service, the Social Security Administration, the Food and Drug Administration, the Administration on Aging, and the Office of Education. Not only are their operations not coordinated, but until quite recently the budget of the Department of Health, Education and Welfare did not show in one place the total cost of the country's health services.

When the scope or size of the task for which an organization was created becomes greater because of an expanded volume of activity, the organization enlarges by increasing its facilities—both human and material. As long as this expansion is within reasonable bounds so that the weight of numbers does not force a breakdown of administrative control, the institution continues functioning effectively.

However, when organizations subtly and imperceptively change their original functions, or become larger in order to take on functions for which they were not designed, such as when a university establishes and operates an industrial enterprise or an accounting firm takes on a computer service center, or even certain dimensions of management advisory services, tax planning, or research, and the basic structures remain unchanged, then we may be heading for trouble.

The structures of many older institutions were created for objectives and functions which may not be as relevant today. Yet, because tradition, habit, or even age tend to be misconstrued for need and expertise, organizations may function outside of their areas of present-day competence or even requirements and become square pegs frozen into round holes. Frozen tradition is the infrastructure of slowed progress and decay.

It is the rare organization which is master of its own destiny, largely because most organizations neglect to exercise the opportunities which are at their disposal. Organizations which make no determined effort to dominate their environment themselves become dominated by it. This has happened to a number of the older and larger local and national accounting firms.

The computerization of society is speeding up change. Institutions which were created and developed during slower-paced times cannot keep pace with the newer speeds. They are breaking down. Foremost among the casualties are social structures as we have known them in the nineteenth century and early twentieth century.

Today's despotism in our society is one of institution versus man. The constraints we feel come from duly enacted laws, traditions, company procedures, firm policies, and that large body of usage, social custom. More lasting harm to organization effectiveness is done in the name of "This is the way it has always been done around here," than is commonly recognized.

Young people perceive this condition in society, and even in our profession, and do not like it. They refuse to accept oppression by the established institution. Their minds are still free and unharnessed for the race towards the "success" goddess. Our over-thirty generation should appreciate that such idealism continues to exist and thrive in our society, and applaud that this searching for high perfection has found voice through teenage activism and peaceful protest. Would that some of this search for perfection would permeate many of our sluggish institutions.

Oppression by an organization has its roots in the principle which states that whatever is best for the entire body, be it a nation, a company, an accounting firm, or an educational institution, is also best for the individual in the long run. Applying this principle to our institutions need not be faulted. What should concern us is the procedure whereby an organization determines what is best for itself. When the institution is sluggish and frightened, people become little more than automatons following rigid paths. Under these circumstances, what we really have are decisions and policies based on a composite of precedents which evolved out of some forgotten historical past.

People are inclined to comply with what they *think* are the general desires of a group; and, of course, those who make up a group are a part of a society or a firm.

People by their nature want to go along with the group, want to conform. This is the way they act in society, and this is the way they act within a particular professional association. They do not want to involve themselves in anything which may disrupt their comfortable nine-to-five environment. When organizational or professional lethargy reaches the point where waste and inefficiency are readily apparent, some people will turn their eyes to avoid the unpleasant sight.

All disciplines seem to be burdened with some degree of status-quoism in their social structures, including our own, which is the fastest growing established profession in the nation.

Within the accounting profession there is a plethora of social structures. From the viewpoint of the practitioner, the structure ranges from the individual running his own one-man office to large international firms with hundreds of partners and thousand of employees. What is the optimum size for an accounting firm? Obviously, often the individual practitioner is too small a practice unit to effectively serve a broad spectrum of clients. Some say the large, widespread national and international firm structure is too all-encompassing. Nevertheless, all dimensions continue to exist side by side, without any effort being made by anyone to analyze and evaluate this potpourri of specialized organizations. Obviously, some extensive study of accounting firm structures is called for.

From the viewpoint of our professional societies, there are the American Institute of CPAs, the American Accounting Association, the National Association of Accountants, the Federal Government Accountants Association, the National Society of Public Accountants, state societies in each of the states, and regional accounting organizations such as the Middle-Atlantic States Accounting Conference, not to mention the American Management Association, the Society for the Advancement of Management, the Financial Executives Institute, organizations of computer men, and many other organizations which bring together people who are dedicating their professional lives to carrying out functions, most of which fall within today's definition of accounting practice. Are all of these organizations necessary? Are there areas in which these organizations overlap and are there areas in which these organizations miss vital subjects and functions because certain subjects and functions tend to fall between the slats separating each of the organizations?

Each of these organizations spends millions of dollars in administration and in servicing its members. In addition, each makes tremendous demands upon the time of its membership to perform services for the good of the profession. At no time, however, has any person or any group of people attempted to evaluate the work being performed by these various organizations, weighed this work against the cost in funds and manpower, and in a scholarly and scientific fashion attempted to make a determination whether the profession is mis-organized through this multiple-organization structure and whether a major realignment is appropriate. As John W. Gardner has pointed out,

> The most important thing the accounting profession should be thinking about on the fundamental level is the trend toward ever-larger and more intricately organized groupings; the extremely elaborate, still inadequately described, interlocking of American society.

To intelligently deal with this problem, I recommend that a research program of major proportions be undertaken, such a research program to address itself to the organization of accounting firms and the way the accounting profession itself is organized. This research project, I estimate, would take three years to complete at a cost of about $400,000 a year, or $1,200,000.

Financing could be shared by societies themselves and be supplemented by voluntary contributions from accounting firms. I feel confident that this investment would repay itself many times over within the decade in improved effectiveness of accounting practice, better functioning of professional organizations and increased service to society. Continuing delay in undertaking such a program permits the continuance of the proliferation of accounting societies with their overlappings, and lends encouragement to the present helter-skelter composition of accounting practitioners.

A Commentary On
Social Structure of the Accounting Profession

DALE L. GERBOTH *

Difficult as it is to disagree with Mr. Linowes' paper, it is harder still to find something in it that I could comment on productively. Not that Linowes dealt with an unimportant topic; to the contrary, he discussed what I consider to be among the more important concerns of accounting: its institutional structure. But Linowes' discussion left out the critical element—the suggestion of a way to organize accounting's institutional structure and its theory into one system. What I am driving at is the need for a perspective that views accounting theory and its events, personalities, and organizations as an interrelated whole and attempts to understand the way accounting in that more inclusive sense functions.

We already have enough descriptions of accounting institutions. They may be at the bland level of run-of-the-mill high school civics textbooks, but they at least identify the institutions that make up the accounting profession and its environment and describe their nominal relationships. We also have at least enough treatises on accounting theory. Moreover, Carey (1969, 1970), Zeff (1972), and others have given us comprehensive histories of accounting, both theory and organization. What we need is a system to organize accounting's institutional structure and its theory in a way that reveals their interrelatedness, for only by learning how its institutions and its theory affect each other can we hope to explain and, more importantly, influence the direction of accounting.

1. A LESSON FROM LORD KEYNES

The sterility of treating institutions apart from theory was illustrated by the plight of economists during the Great Depression. The standard economics textbooks of the day recognized two separate interests. One

*B.S. 1959, University of Kansas. CPA. Project Manager in the Technical Research Division, American Institute of Certified Public Accountants. Contributor to accounting periodicals.

416

was the history and description of banks, trade unions, securities markets, and the whole institutional paraphernalia presented simply as an inventory unorganized by theory. The other was the classic economics theory of general equilibrium under perfect competition. But neither interest had anything to do with the other. According to the classic theory, the market balanced automatically. Institutions were merely the passive instruments of market forces; any active contribution they made on their own was treated as a special problem of no theoretical relevance. As a result of that split perspective, when crisis struck and economic institutions were obviously malfunctioning, economists had neither the theory to explain what was happening nor a practical strategy for intervening. It took the genius of Keynes to suggest both. Although in form Keynes did no more than revise an unrealistic theory, his real contribution was more profound—he changed economists' perspective from one of theory divorced from institutions to one in which institutional activity had theoretical significance.

Before we unduly exalt economics, we should acknowledge that it is not an exact science and probably never will be. Economies respond to human intervention in part only, and the leading economists still disagree about the relative merits of particular intervention strategies. But this much economists did learn from the trauma of the 1930s: there is no autonomous realm of economic theory; rather, economics is a system that organizes real-world events, personalities, and organizations. Thus even though economists may disagree about particular features of the system, it has real-world references, and the disagreements are, in principle at least, subject to empirical test.

But accounting has not yet progressed that far. Its present state resembles nothing so much as the state of economics forty years ago when economists wrestled with their general equilibrium model in a vain effort to make it explain a nation with one-third of its work force unemployed. That accounting too faces a crisis of sorts is a cliché. The professions's future status depends on its ability to reconcile a growing disparity between what accounting offers and what society expects of it. But we lack a strategy for intervening to narrow that gap. Instead we argue, for example, the relative merits of various accounting measurements, naively believing that those arguments touch upon matters of substance. But considered apart from the real-world events, personalities, and organizations that make up the accounting system, those arguments will contribute little to an understanding even of accounting theory, much less suggest effective strategies for accounting action.

Several reasons explain why theory and institutions are regarded as separate. Prominent among them must be the separation of economic concerns, in the broad sense that includes accounting, from political concerns, including the activities of accounting institutions. Although we accept that separation as natural, it arose from a particular coincidence of events and philosophies that one observer has termed a freak of history (Polanyi, 1944). But regardless of its background, the separation of economics and politics is a form of intellectual schizophrenia with all the lost contact with reality that the term implies. Economically relevant actions are not restricted to economic activity in the narrow sense, and accountants have been slower than economists to recognize that.

Related to that reason but with roots of its own is the acknowledged difficulty of dealing with the human concerns that are intrinsic to institutional study. We are skilled in coping with matters that have no human ingredient, as in the physical sciences. And we are fairly good at problems involving human considerations to a limited degree, as in manned space expeditions. But we perform poorly at tasks requiring the understanding and—even more—the changing of social phenomena.

Not only are human problems exceedingly tough, but in some cases we are motivated *not* to solve them by entrenched interests—often our own. An investigation of social phenomena, particularly when the object of the investigation is to explain and control those phenomena, may reveal power relationships we would rather keep hidden. Worse still, we may find that somebody's power, perhaps—God forbid—our own, should be curtailed. Little wonder we would rather argue the relative merits of different accounting measurements. It's safer!

2. ACCOUNTING SUPERMEN

Obviously, to understand accounting in the broad sense that I have urged would require a person of many talents. He must be knowledgeable not only in accounting, but also in economics, psychology, philosophy, sociology, and political science, at least. And knowledgeable not just at the level of mere familiarity, but at a level of competence that would enable him to develop theory in those fields, for their existing bodies of theory are in many cases poorly developed and largely irrelevant to accounting. In short, I am describing an academic superman. But supermen do not exist, and when one is born, he just might not choose a career in accounting. Thus our problem is this: Can we come close enough to instilling knowledge that is broad enough in enough accountants to make the effort worthwhile? Or will we merely ruin a good discipline—accounting in its present form—by trying the impossible?

The answers to those questions are not clear, but this much can be said with reasonable assurance: The sheer complexity of modern society places an increasingly smaller value on narrowness of focus. The late President Johnson found that out the hard way when he became so deeply involved in such details of the Vietnam War as how high the bombers flew and the size of the bombs they carried that he lost sight of the war's wider context. While accountants have shown no indication of making the same mistake, the risk is there. For accounting in its pure form may be viewed as occupying a narrow crack between economics and the behavioral sciences. Perhaps its only uniquely accounting contribution was to thrust double-entry expression between its two neighboring fields. Whatever other knowledge it has added has been out of one or the other of those fields. And we must continue to expand our skills outside accounting until it becomes apparent that we have reached practical limits. He who knows only his field doesn't know even that.

In particular, we should recognize that accounting theory cannot be dealt with successfully apart from accounting's institutional structure. Attempts to do so are equivalent to treating ideas apart from the social environment and personalities that developed them; when that is done, much that is important to understanding simply drops out of the picture. If we want to understand how accounting got where it is today, and if we want to influence where it goes tomorrow, we must understand all of accounting.

REFERENCES

Carey, John L. (1969) *The Rise of the Accounting Profession From Technical to Professional, 1896–1936.* New York: American Institute of Certified Public Accountants.

Carey, John L. (1970) *The Rise of the Accounting Profession to Responsibility and Authority, 1937–1969.* New York: American Institute of Certified Public Accountants.

Polanyi, Karl (1944) *The Great Transformation.* New York: Rinehart.

Zeff, Stephen A. (1972) *Forging Accounting Principles in Five Countries: A History and Analysis of Trends.* Champaign, Illinois: Stipes.

Discussion

Linowes. It is obvious that Dale hasn't disagreed with anything I have said, so I completely agree with him. Frankly, I would like to obtain some focus on the practice unit in a critique of my observations, so I would certainly welcome comments from those here in that direction.

Johns. I agree with some of your observations, but not necessarily the crux of the direction of your conclusions. I do not spend that much time looking at these things as some of the people involved in the management of a firm do, but it seems to me that it is true that a firm, like a person, has certain capabilities and certain limitations. It is true that a firm, like a nation, imposes constraints upon the individual, as well as opportunities. But it seems to me that a better description of the relationship might be more what Sandy Burton was describing as a partnership or coalition, in the best sense of the word, than it is of one imposing some thing on the other. By the same token, the firm is limited with me and my peers as to our abilities and limitations. The firm as a unit and how the firm can advance is nothing but the sum total of what we do. I think rather than looking to a study of optimum size of a firm or what the average firm is, it is more akin to looking to an individual and what an individual's health is. While what you propose is useful, I am more concerned with the organization to which I am related—how strong is it, how responsive are we to change, are our priorities the right priorities—and looking at that which we are able to do in the short run in making a change. You can't make radical changes. Our organization can't. I don't think any organization can. So we look to that which is progressive, and progressive in the short run. I also try to understand my contemporaries, and I also try to remember that no one really stands still—that what we think of as progressive may be an impression from five years ago. I see it more as a partnership with potentialities and limitations on both sides. It is important to ask the questions you are asking but to ask them with the reference, what can I do in relation to what I am doing myself, what can the organization do?

Linowes. Again we are in agreement. I am merely suggesting that there has never been a project to examine the structure and methods of supervision of the practice of accounting. I am suggesting that we begin to direct some of our efforts there.

Johns. I guess my only difference with you would be that I think it is more individualistic in that what is perfect for one is not necessarily the same for another. There can well exist differences in style and differences in emphasis. Not everyone has to be the most aggressive. It is natural that institutions, as well as individuals, assume greater and lesser roles of leadership. I do agree with you, though, that a model to compare with might be useful.

Linowes. I am not trying to anticipate what a research project would come out with. It may very well come out with the exact conclusions you are now stating. I am merely suggesting that we get on with it and recognize that some good can come of this study, even if its conclusion is to continue doing exactly as we are doing.

Kapnick. I think several points were excellent. I would like to touch on just a few of them from a practitioner's standpoint. First, the professors might be interested in why we, and I in particular, are so adamant against these rules. I think today we are building and training a completely different young man than you and I were when we were trained. Back in the days when I was trained it was, "professional judgment, is it right or wrong?" Today the boys gather around to see whether or not this is in accordance with a rule. Your whole social outlook is changing. I think that that is something that people need to recognize as one of the results of this rule making that we are all talking about.

Going over to the other side of what you were talking about, it might be interesting to some of you to know something I mentioned to one of the top men at the SEC—not Sandy Burton, is that one of the principal questions within the profession today has to be the control over one's practice. He was stunned that the problem would be recognized and that I would bring it up. I don't know whether it can be studied. I don't know if you can get the firms to agree to it, because some of the most sensitive questions have to be answered. The Equity Funding situation raises several very interesting questions which you would have to approach in such a study: Can you merge firms? Is there a relationship between the sizes of fees? Can you assign people whom the client requests? If the client says, "I want Kapnick on a job," can you put Kapnick on the job if you are the management of a firm? There are several of these very unusual questions which I think are raised by Equity Funding over and beyond the financial fiasco. So when you get into that, I would ask, How do you control a firm? I am not so sure the size has much to do with it. How do you control a firm in its context of public responsibility? It takes in scope of service; it takes in local partnerships. How do you administratively structure yourself? Do you have two partners or one partner on a job? There are so many variances between the firms: as Gordon says, each of us has our own personality. I would be all for such a study, but I am not so sure that the profession has the ability to undertake it today.

Linowes. I certainly think it is something worth trying. I have a suspicion, in view of the fact that our professional practice units are getting to be increasingly on the defensive—and I think as time goes on they will be more so—they would be pleased to begin giving up a little of their secrecy in order to benefit by collective action. It happened to industry in the fiasco of the 1930's when the SEC came into being. Suddenly business was willing to expose a lot of what it thought were important inner secrets. Personally, I think a lot of this secrecy is poppycock. I think we do ourselves harm by keeping things too close to our chests.

Holstrum. I agree with both you, Dave, and with Dale on the need for research on the institutional structures. I take exception to some of the thrust of your remarks, Dale. I am concerned that some people who are doing institutional research, or research for institutions, tend to define research in terms of the need of the particular institution for which they are employed. Their research gets a little narrow. I guess the one statement you made that I don't think should be allowed to go without challenge was this: you said we already have enough treatises on accounting theory, implying that we have enough research in this area now, let's go on in another area. If you look at the example you gave, we would really still be, in a sense, muddling through with classical economics had it not been for Keynes. Keynes basically presented a theory, and so it was this allowance of the research, the thrust for a new theory which would put everything together and explain it, which was very desirable. I think that the need for research into the institutional structures is very great. I just wouldn't want to give the implication that research should be limited here and that we therefore have gone far enough in explicating accounting theory.

Gerboth. I think I would tend to agree with you. I was trying to promote a switch in emphasis obviously, because I do think we have not paid enough attention to accounting in the broader sense as I have described it. Certainly I would not be one to discourage research either in theory by itself, which you say (and quite rightly so) might well lead into an understanding of accounting in the sense that I have described it. Nor would I want to discourage research into the individual practice unit, again with allowances for the limitations of any analogy; this might be somewhat comparable to the macro-/micro-economics difference. Certainly one does not necessarily come at the expense of the other. Both need research. I do think, however, that for too long we in the accounting profession have looked upon theory and institutions as separate topics, never considering the possibility that they are linked in some very direct ways, and that there are interrelationships existing between the two that need to be studied and must be studied if we are going to understand how we can move the profession.

Dyckman. There are two points I would like to make. One, when we go about a study of the nature that you have suggested I would urge us not to ignore what has been done in the behavioral sciences, as we academic researchers are often apt to do. I asked Paul Montagna if he would leave me with some references to behavioral studies that have looked at organizations' structure. I have four such references he left me that I will pass on to you and anybody else that might have been motivated by Dave's interesting suggestion.

One of the areas where I think accountants in general have been unsuccessful, and where other professions may not have experienced so much lack of success, is the interplay between the academicians and the practitioners on research and the implementation of that research, and then more research and more implementation. This interaction can be of benefit to both parties. I don't think that we are presently structured to allow for this interaction. I don't mean here at this conference, which is somewhat unusual, but rather in general. We need research between practitioners and academics that I think would help those of us who are in academic work have more relevance to what is going on in practice. I have my own ideas about how some things along that line might happen, but we sure have not been successful in those dimensions. I wish in the next four years that we would make some strides in this direction and that might speak also to the problems that Dale was referring to. I understand his emphasis. I think it is an important one. I can even agree with Gary and still think that Dale's emphasis is an important one.

Linowes. I appreciate your reference to behavioral scientists. It is quite likely that such a study would be headed by a behavioral scientist. Inviting in members of other disciplines is precisely the route we took when the AICPA got ready a number of years ago to undertake a research study which was eventually called the Beamer Committee Report. We sought out the Carnegie Foundation to participate financially, not because we wanted their money, but because we wanted their guidance. The American Institute didn't especially need financial help, but their guidance was what we wanted. The Carnegie Foundation said they would participate, provided the head of that project was not an accountant. So we hired Rob Roy, from Johns Hopkins, and we got a magnificent study. We know this interdisciplinary approach is very beneficial for us. I could very easily picture a behavioral scientist conducting the kind of study into our firms about which I speak.

Sterling. I fully agree with you about the gulf between practitioner and academic in accounting. One of the purposes for this Colloquium is to try to reduce that gulf.

Carmichael. I would be remiss not to point out that the focus on practice units only came across in the oral discussion. There wasn't anything in the paper to indicate what type of organizations or institutions you had in mind. I was worried that you might be complaining that the Institute dues were too high. But the focus on practice units that did come across in the oral discussion I think is appropriate. We are looking for somebody to do a study on how you run a firm, which relates to quality control and the subordinate question, how you run an audit. We don't have a budget as big as the one you mentioned, however.

Linowes. I made this same suggestion at the floor of Council several days ago. Later I was approached by one of the AICPA staff who said, "I'm glad you made that statement; we sorely need it." He said, however, the American Institute doesn't feel ready to undertake it. That is one of the reasons why I suggest in my paper that this is something the American Institute could spearhead with the financial contributions of many of the larger firms. It is a pittance compared to the cost of administering a firm of any size.

Carmichael. It is very much tied up with our present dispute with the SEC on quality control.

Kapnick. I would like to ask one other question: How can the profession react? I think that is the key question that has to be asked. We talked about accounting principles today, we talked about all the very important things for each of us in earning our livelihood, but we haven't addressed ourselves to how the profession can react. What is the profession? Too often we think the AICPA is the profession. The AICPA isn't the profession. That really needs to be part of the study, too—How do you get these things settled? I know if Dave decides what he is going to do in his firm, and I decide what I am going to do in our firm, we have a means of doing it, but as a profession we don't have the means to implement the findings.

Gerboth. That is a part of what I was addressing my comments to. How can you get action from the profession as a whole? Both Dave and I have proposed research into how we can act at two levels. One, at the level of a firm, how we can change whatever we might find to be wrong at that level. Two, how we can begin to get a handle on the profession as a whole in terms of directing it toward the advancement of its interest.

Kapnick. We have done some thinking about that. How can we

undertake research, as a professsional accounting group, looking at ourselves? For example, I would be violently opposed to mergers between two firms, and yet if another firm came in and looked at me, they would say, "You don't believe in mergers but that is not important." It seems to me that until you can attack the top problem, you can't attack the sub-problem. Doug realizes I am very much opposed to the program where the American Institute is going to come in and look at Arthur Andersen any time they want. But to have an ad hoc group come in, all you are doing is proliferating standards the same way that the accounting principles have been proliferated. They are going to have an ad hoc committee who is going to criticize me with no authority. No way, no way. You must attack these questions first: How do you control the profession? What is the profession?

Gerboth. Which was essentially my point, so I can't disagree with you.

Bentz. That sounds like something other than a research-type question or a research-type project.

Kapnick. It is a different point, but the problem is the same. That is a disciplinary issue which the American Institute is looking at right now in connection with the SEC.

Bentz. The role of a researcher coming into your organization is much the same as your role going into a client. You have to establish the bases (1) that he would be there for a specific purpose, and (2) that he would carry out his activities in a professional manner.

Kapnick. And objectively. That is the reason why I say, in regard to one firm reviewing another firm as to whether or not the policies are right or wrong, the basis from which they start may not be objective. I didn't realize, Dave, that we had the Carnegie Foundation in that long range study, but this is the objectivity that could be brought to bear.

Linowes. They are the ones who insisted on a non-accountant or they wouldn't participate.